China's Employment

Ministry of Human Resources and Social Security
of the People's Republic of China

China Labour & Social Security Publishing House

Working Committee

Director Zhang Jinan

Deputy Directors You Jun, Li Zhong, Zhang Xiaojian

Members Zhang Yali, Liu Yanbin, Wang Zhe, Mo Rong, Zhang Ying, Zhang Lixin, Gui Zhen, Wang Keliang, Hao Bin, Zhai Yanli, Liu Kang, Fan Yong, Zhang Bin, Huang Weilai

Authors Li Yanping, Yun Donglai, Yang Yi, Liu Peng, Zhuan Sunjing, Liu Mingyuan, Chen Rui, Guo Rongrong, Wang Qi, Chen Yin, Su Ying

Translator Deng Baoshan

Reviewer Liu Genghua

Preface

Employment is pivotal to people's well-being. In its 2001 "Global Employment Agenda", the International Labour Organisation proposed that employment had become the core of people's life, not only because people depended on employment for their survival, but also because employment was a means for people to integrate into society, realise their own values and bring hope to future generations. Therefore, employment has become a key factor in social and political stability. China has a large population, and people's well-being has become the primary issue. Employment is related to the survival and development of workers and the vital interests of hundreds of millions of workers and their families. It is both an economic and social foundation and an important condition for guaranteeing and improving people's livelihood; it is also an important symbol of building a well-off society in an all-round way to meet people's aspirations for a better life. Therefore, promoting employment has become a top priority to ensure and improve people's livelihood. In the 70 years since the founding of the People's Republic of China, the Communist Party of China and the Chinese government have always attached great importance to employment, made every effort to promote employment and reduce unemployment, and made great efforts to achieve continuous growth in total employment, adjustment and optimisation of employment structure, gradual improvement of employment quality and better reflection of employment equity. It has promoted the steady growth of people's income and a significant reduction in the number of poor people, and has made remarkable achievements. In 2017, international authorities conducted a comprehensive assessment of a number of development indicators around the world and ranked China's employment performance as the first in the world.

China's employment has experienced many major challenges in its development. From the rapid resolution of the problem of millions of unemployed people left over from old China in the 1950s to the timely handling of the problem of tens of millions of educated urban youth working in the countryside returning from the countryside to the city for employment in the 1970s, to the proper resolution of the re-employment problem of 30 million laid-off workers at the turn of the century, to the response to the impact of sudden natural disasters and the international financial crisis on employment in the 21st century. In response to the different pressures faced in different periods, the Chinese government has timely adopted corresponding policies and measures, so that the employment contradiction has been properly resolved and the employment situation has remained basically stable, and thus to ensure sustained economic development as well as social and political stability.

After the reform and opening up in the 1980s, a series of reforms have been made in China's employment system. Gradually the system has been changed from the management system of "Centralised Employment Allocation" under the past planned economic system to the current employment system of market mechanism-oriented. The unified and standardised human resources market has been fostered and established. At the same time, the system of laws and regulations has been gradually improved, and the employment policy and service system have been continuously improved to ensure the sustained and healthy development of employment. Since the beginning of the 21st century in particular, the Chinese government has adhered to the development strategy of giving high priority to employment, formulated and implemented a proactive employment policy, thereby promoting new development in employment and entrepreneurship in the new era.

In the course of the 70 years of development of the People's Republic of China, especially the 40 years of reform and opening-up, the Chinese government has learnt from the successful practices of other countries, explored the law of doing a good job in employment and accumulated a lot of valuable experience. It is on the basis of the experience that, in recent years, the Communist Party of China and the Chinese government have clearly stated that they will adhere to the strategy of giving high priority to employment and a proactive employment policy, and that fuller and higher quality employment will be the mission and goal of the new era. To this end, a series of strategic arrangements have been made and more comprehensive and systematic policy measures have been put in place to promote employment and entrepreneurship. This not only reflects the new requirements put forward by the Chinese government for employment in order to improve people's livelihood and build a well-off society in an all-round way. Employment cause will continue to forge ahead along the road of socialism with Chinese characteristics.

China's Employment systematically introduces the reform and development process as well as the basic situation of employment since the founding of the People's Republic of China 70 years ago, expounds several challenges and historic achievements in China's employment, comprehensively summarises the experience gained by the Chinese government in practice, and looks forward to the future development of China's employment. This book provides readers at home and abroad with a window to deeply understand China's employment, and also provides important reference materials for relevant professionals at home and abroad to study the evolution of China's employment system, policy framework and work system. We hope that this book can show the world from one side the unremitting efforts of the Chinese government in adhering to the people-centred development path, and let readers see the progress of the Chinese people in realising a happier and better life.

December, 2019

Contents

Chapter 1
Employment Profile in China

1. Basic Employment Situation in China

1.1 Overview

Employment is pivotal to people's well-being. China has a large population and abundant labour resources (Table 1.1). It has always been a major task for the Chinese government to solve the employment problem for workers by expanding employment and reducing unemployment. Ever since the founding of the People's Republic of China in 1949, the Chinese government has always attached great importance to employment, given high priority to employment in economic and social development, made great efforts to maintain the long-term stability of employment situation, and played a significant and positive role in stabilising the overall economic and social situation and improving people's livelihood. Especially since the introduction of reform and opening to the outside world in 1978, along with the reform of economic system, the reform of labour and employment system has been continuously deepened. Such reform has changed the centralised labour allocation pattern under the planned economic system, which was featured by limited access of jobs, the invariable employment form and job market lacking of vitality. Various measures have been taken to create jobs and expand employment for workers, while vigorously developing the economy. After decades of hard work, the employment management system has been formed, which could basically meet the need of the socialist market economy. Market mechanism has gradually shown its

Table 1.1 Population Size and Composition

(Unit: 10 thousand, %)

Year	Total population	Population over 16 years	Active economic population	By gender				By urban and rural			
				Male		Female		Urban		Rural	
				Population	Ratio	Population	Ratio	Population	Ratio	Population	Ratio
1952	57,482	—	—	29,833	51.9	27,649	48.1	7,163	12.5	50,319	87.5
1957	64,653	—	—	33,469	51.8	31,184	48.2	9,949	15.4	54,704	84.6
1962	67,295	—	—	34,517	51.3	32,778	48.7	11,659	17.3	55,636	82.7
1965	72,538	—	—	37,128	51.2	35,410	48.8	13,045	18.0	59,493	82.0
1970	82,992	—	—	42,686	51.4	40,306	48.6	14,424	17.4	68,568	82.6
1975	92,420	—	—	47,564	51.5	44,856	48.5	16,030	17.3	76,390	82.7
1978	96,259	—	40,682	49,567	51.5	46,692	48.5	17,245	17.9	79,014	82.1
1980	98,705	—	42,903	50,785	51.5	47,920	48.6	19,140	19.4	79,565	80.6
1985	105,851	—	50,112	54,725	51.7	51,126	48.3	25,094	23.7	80,757	76.3
1990	114,333	—	65,323	58,904	51.5	55,429	48.5	30,195	26.4	84,138	73.6
1995	121,121	—	68,855	61,808	51.0	59,313	49.0	35,174	29.0	85,947	71.0
2000	126,743	—	73,992	65,437	51.6	61,306	48.4	45,906	36.2	80,837	63.8
2002	128,453	—	74,492	66,115	51.5	62,338	48.5	50,212	39.1	78,241	60.9
2003	129,227	—	74,911	66,556	51.5	62,671	48.5	52,376	40.5	76,851	59.5
2005	130,756	—	76,120	67,375	51.5	63,381	48.5	56,212	43.0	74,544	57.0

Continued

Year	Total population	Population over 16 years	Active economic population	By gender				By urban and rural			
				Male		Female		Urban		Rural	
				Population	Ratio	Population	Ratio	Population	Ratio	Population	Ratio
2010	134,091	—	78,388	68,748	51.3	65,343	48.7	66,978	49.9	67,113	50.1
2011	134,735	110,932	78,579	69,068	51.3	65,667	48.7	69,079	51.3	65,656	48.7
2012	135,404	111,586	78,894	69,395	51.3	66,009	48.7	71,182	52.6	64,222	47.4
2013	136,072	112,197	79,300	69,728	51.2	66,344	48.8	73,111	53.7	62,961	46.3
2014	136,782	112,825	79,690	70,079	51.2	66,703	48.8	74,916	54.8	61,866	45.2
2015	137,462	113,296	80,091	70,414	51.2	67,048	48.8	77,116	56.1	60,346	43.9
2016	138,271	113,833	80,694	70,815	51.2	67,456	48.8	79,298	57.3	58,973	42.7
2017	139,008	114,289	80,686	71,137	51.2	67,871	48.8	81,347	58.5	57,661	41.5
2018	139,538	114,678	80,567	71,351	51.1	68,187	48.9	83,137	59.6	56,401	40.4
2019	140,005	115,028	—	71,527	51.1	68,478	48.9	84,843	60.6	55,162	39.4

Source: *Statistical Yearbook of China* and the website of the National Bureau of Statistics.

basic effects on labour allocation and evidently broadened employment channels for urban and rural workers. It has facilitated a continuous growth of gross employment rate and optimisation of employment structure. In this process, in accordance with *Constitution of the People's Republic of China* (hereinafter referred to as the Constitution) and *Labour Law of the People's Republic of China* (hereinafter referred to as *Labour Law*), *Law of the People's Republic of China on Promotion of Employment* (hereinafter referred to as *Employment Promotion Law*) and other laws and regulations, apart from ensuring the employment rights of workers, various policies and measures have been taken to actively promote employment, to continuously meet the employment needs of workers. As a result, the quality of employment has been significantly improved. Especially in the past decade, under the leadership of the Communist Party of China (CPC) Central Committee, with Comrade Xi Jinping being its core, the strategy of giving top priority to employment and the more proactive employment policy have been fully implemented. The reform of employment and entrepreneurship mechanism has been deepened. The employment-oriented social climate has been increasingly strengthened by all parts of the country. A positive interaction between economic development and employment expansion has been realised. More high-quality employment opportunities have been created in the course of promoting high-quality economic development, which has played an important supporting role in ensuring the sustainable and healthy development of the economy and the society.

1.2 Expansion of Employment Scale and Optimisation of Employment Structure

1.2.1 Increasing Expansion of Employment Scale

In the past 70 years since the founding of People's Republic of China, the total employment increased 3.3 times, from 180 million in 1949 to 780 million in 2019. In this period, urban employment increased 27.9 times, while now reaching 440 million in total.

(1) From 1949 to 1957, China achieved rapid employment growth. When the People's Republic of China was founded (in October 1949, the same as below), 180.82 million people were employed across the country, 15.33 million of whom were in urban areas, with a large number of urban labour forces being unemployed. Apart from taking various measures to control unemployment, governments at all levels actively developed the economy and took great efforts to expand employment. In 1952, the number of urban workers rose rapidly to 24.86 million. During the years of China's first Five-year Plan (1953-1957) for national economic and social development, China started a large-scale economic construction, which effectively led to the rapid expansion of employment. By 1957, the number of employed persons in the country reached 237.71 million, with an increase of 56.89 million over 1949, and an average annual increase of 3.5%. Urban employment grew even faster and reached 32.05 million in 1957, more than doubled compared to that in 1949, with an average annual increase of 9.7%.

However, from 1958, China's economic construction encountered a setback, with big fluctuations and a slow increase in employment scale. In 1961 and 1962, the number of employed persons decreased by 8 million yearly. In 1978, the total employment reached 401.52 million, 95.14 million of whom lived in urban areas, with an average annual increase of 2.1% and 3.0% respectively over the past 20 years.

(2) Since the implementation of China's reform and opening-up policy, urban employment has been rising relatively quickly. Since December 1978 (same as below) when China's reform and opening-up policy was implemented, CPC and the government

Chinese government attaches great importance to employment and provides jobs for job seekers every year through various channels such as job fairs. (Photo taken by Xinhua News Agency reporter Shengjian Zhao.)

have stuck to the people-centred philosophy, taken numerous ways to create new jobs and achieved simultaneous increase in economic development and employment expansion. In 2019, China's employment reached 774.71 million, 442.47 million of whom were employed in urban areas, with an increase of 3.7 times over 1978 and an average annual increase of 3.9%. Especially since the 18th National Congress of the CPC (in November 2012, same as below), in the context of the new normal of economic development, due to the State's vigorous implementation of giving high priority to employment strategy and proactive employment policy, together with the entrepreneurship-driven employment promotion measures, China's total urban employment increased by more than 71.45 million people, with an average annual increase of over 10 million people.

1.2.2 Continuous Optimisation of Employment Structure

In the past 70 years since the founding of the People's Republic of China, the continuous optimisation of employment structure between rural and urban areas, and that of different industries and corporate ownerships has achieved sustainable employment growth.

(1) Urban employment rose over years and accounted for half of total employment. In 1949, employed persons in urban areas accounted for only 8.5% of the country's total employment, with most working people in rural areas. After the founding of the People's Republic of China, the gradual recovery of national economy, especially the acceleration of industrialisation process, attracted a large number of rural labour forces to work in urban areas. In 1978, urban employment reached 95.14 million, accounting for 23.7% of the country's total employed population. Over the past 30 years, the proportion of urban employment increased by 15.2 percentage points with an average increase of 0.5 percentage points per year.

China's reform and opening-up policy greatly liberated and developed productivity and unleashed the vitality of the labour market. Urban employment increased rapidly. In 2014, urban employment surpassed that of rural areas for the first time, reaching 50.9%. In 2019, the total number of urban workers reached 442.47 million, accounting for 57.1% of the country's employment. It represented an increase of 33.4 percentage points over that at the beginning of China's reform and opening-up policy, with an average annual increase of 0.8 percentage points.

(2) The employment in the secondary and tertiary industry grew steadily. At the beginning of the founding of the People's Republic of China, most of the workers were in agriculture industry, because of the weak industrial foundation and the lagging service industry. In 1952, the proportion of employed persons in the primary industry was 83.5%, and that in the secondary and tertiary industry was 7.4% and 9.1% respectively. As a relatively full spectrum in modern industrial foundation started to form, employment in the secondary and tertiary industry increased rapidly. In 1978, employment in the primary industry decreased to 70.5% of the total employment, while the proportion in the secondary and tertiary industry increased to 17.3% and 12.2% respectively.

After China's reform and opening-up policy, the secondary and tertiary industry absorbed more employment year by year. In 1997, employment of the secondary and tertiary industry exceeded that of the primary industry. In 2011, employment in the secondary and tertiary industry accounted for 29.5% and 35.7% of total employment respectively. The tertiary industry exceeded the primary industry for the first time, ranking the first among three industries in terms of employment absorption. Since 2014, the number of employed workers in the primary industry has been the least and the ratio decreased year by year. In 2018, the number of employed workers in three industries in China reached 202.58 million (26.1%), 213.9 million (27.6%) and 359.38 million (46.3%) respectively (Figure 1.1). To date, modern industrial model led by a flourishing service industry has been formed gradually, which resulted in a more optimised employment structure. From 2013 to 2018, the share of employment in the service sector increased by an average of 1.7 percentage points per year, about 1.0% faster than that from 1978 to 2012.

(3) Non-public economy turned to be the major channel for urban employment. When the People's Republic of China was founded, the individual and private economy accounted for a large proportion of the national economy, and self-employed workers made up 47.2% of the urban employment. After 1956, the public-owned economy changed into the main pillar of the national economy, while the individual and private economy shrunk totally. In 1978, urban employment was 95.14 million, with only 150,000 self-employed people, and the rest concentrated in the state-owned and collective units.

Since China's reform and opening-up policy, the number of people employed in by non-public economy increased rapidly. In 2018, the proportion of urban non-public economy employment increased from 0.2% in 1978 to 83.6%, 139.52 million of whom were in urban private enterprises and 104.4 million were self-employed (Table 1.2), accounting for 32.1% and 24.0% of urban employment respectively.

Figure 1.1 Employment Composition by Industry at the End of the Calendar Year Since 2006

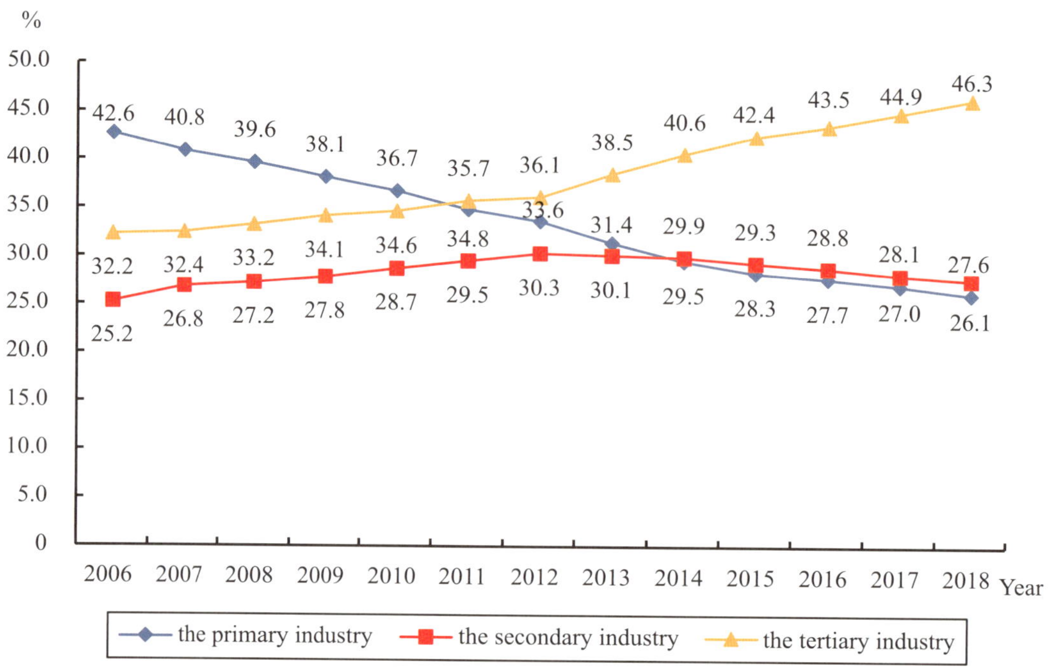

Source: *Statistical Yearbook of China* and the website of the National Bureau of Statistics.

1.3 Improvement of Employment Quality and Manifestation of Employment Equity

1.3.1 Evident Improvement of Employment Quality

In the past 70 years since the founding of the People's Republic of China, especially since the introduction of reform and opening-up policy, with the increase of total employment and the optimisation of employment structure, more and more attention has been paid to employment quality. Since the 18th National Congress of the CPC, more emphasis has been placed on promoting high-quality employment. Driven by economic development and policy measures, employment quality has been improved significantly.

(1) The quality of the employed people has been improved greatly. When the People's Republic of China was founded, due to the poor quality of education, workers were generally illiterate and semiliterate, and very few received tertiary education.

Table1.2 Basic Employment Situation

(Unit: 10 thousand)

Year	Total employment	Employment by industry			Employment in urban and rural areas		Employment in non-private units by type of business registration								Employment in private enterprises and self-employed with business registration			
		Primary industry	Secondary industry	Tertiary industry	Urban employment	Rural employment	State-owned	Urban collective unit	Joint-stock cooperative	Joint operation	Limited liability company	Limited company	Hong Kong, Macao and Taiwan business investment enterprise	Foreign investment enterprise	Urban private enterprise	Urban self-employed	Rural private enterprise	Rural self-employed
1952	20,729	17,317	1,531	1,881	2,486	18,243	—	—	—	—	—	—	—	—	—	883	—	—
1957	23,771	19,309	2,142	2,320	3,205	20,566	—	—	—	—	—	—	—	—	—	104	—	—
1958	26,600	15,490	7,076	4,034	5,300	21,300	—	—	—	—	—	—	—	—	—	106	—	—
1962	25,910	21,276	2,059	2,575	4,537	21,373	—	—	—	—	—	—	—	—	—	216	—	—
1965	28,670	23,396	2,408	2,866	5,136	23,534	—	—	—	—	—	—	—	—	—	171	—	—
1970	34,432	27,811	3,518	3,103	6,312	28,120	—	—	—	—	—	—	—	—	—	96	—	—
1975	38,168	29,456	5,152	3,560	8,222	29,946	6,426	1,772	—	—	—	—	—	—	—	24	—	—
1980	42,361	29,122	7,707	5,532	10,525	31,836	8,019	2,425	—	—	—	—	—	—	—	81	—	—
1985	49,873	31,130	10,384	8,359	12,808	37,065	8,990	3,324	—	—	—	—	—	—	—	450	—	—
1990	64,749	38,914	13,856	11,979	17,041	47,708	10,346	3,549	—	—	—	—	—	—	57	614	113	1,491
1995	68,065	35,530	15,655	16,880	19,040	49,025	11,261	3,147	—	—	—	—	—	—	485	1,560	471	3,054

Continued

Year	Total employment	Employment by industry			Employment in urban and rural areas		Employment in non-private units by type of business registration								Employment in private enterprises and self-employed with business registration			
		Primary industry	Secondary industry	Tertiary industry	Urban employment	Rural employment	State-owned	Urban collective unit	Joint-stock cooperative	Joint operation	Limited liability company	Limited company	Hong Kong, Macao and Taiwan business investment enterprise	Foreign investment enterprise	Urban private enterprise	Urban self-employed	Rural private enterprise	Rural self-employed
2000	72,085	36,043	16,219	19,823	23,151	48,934	8,102	1,499	155	42	687	457	310	332	1,268	2,136	1,139	2,934
2005	74,647	33,442	17,766	23,439	28,389	46,258	6,488	810	188	45	1,750	699	557	688	3,458	2,778	2,366	2,123
2010	76,105	27,931	21,842	26,332	34,687	41,418	6,516	597	156	36	2,613	1,024	770	1,053	6,071	4,467	3,347	2,540
2011	76,420	26,594	22,544	27,282	35,914	40,506	6,704	603	149	37	3,269	1,183	932	1,217	6,912	5,227	3,442	2,718
2012	76,704	25,773	23,241	27,690	37,102	39,602	6,839	590	149	39	3,787	1,243	969	1,246	7,557	5,643	3,739	2,986
2013	76,977	24,171	23,170	29,636	38,240	38,737	6,365	566	108	25	6,069	1,721	1,397	1,566	8,242	6,142	4,279	3,193
2014	77,253	22,790	23,099	31,364	39,310	37,943	6,312	537	103	22	6,315	1,751	1,393	1,562	9,857	7,009	4,533	3,575
2015	77,451	21,919	22,693	32,839	40,410	37,041	6,208	481	92	20	6,389	1,798	1,344	1,446	11,180	7,800	5,215	3,882
2016	77,603	21,496	22,350	33,757	41,428	36,175	6,170	453	86	18	6,381	1,824	1,305	1,361	12,083	8,627	5,914	4,235
2017	77,640	20,944	21,824	34,872	42,462	35,178	6,064	406	77	13	6,367	1,846	1,290	1,291	13,327	9,348	6,554	4,878
2018	77,586	20,258	21,390	35,938	43,419	34,167	5,740	347	66	12	6,555	1,875	1,153	1,212	13,952	10,440	7,424	5,597

Source: The website of the National Bureau of Statistics.

Through the development of formal school education as well as "literacy classes", night schools and other informal education, the cultural competence of workers was rapidly improved.

After the initiation of reform and opening up, the development of education has facilitated a remarkable improvement of the nation, and the market-oriented employment mechanism has been gradually developed. Workers paid more attention to the improvement of their own competence in order to enhance their competitiveness in the labour market. According to preliminary estimates, the proportion of employed persons with college or tertiary education rose from 0.9% in 1982 to 20.1% in 2018, that with high school education increased from 10.5% to 18.0%, that with middle school education increased from 26.0% to 43.2%, while that with primary school education and below decreased from 62.6% to 18.7%.

Vocational training in China covers various training programmes, such as pre-employment training, on-the-job training, job-transfer training and entrepreneurship training. Moreover, labour reserve system has been implemented, with various training programmes for skills development available. Vocational skill appraisal system and vocational certification system have been developed and improved. Technical schools are comprehensive vocational training bases whose key role is training skilled workers, while organising all kinds of short-and long-term training programmes. In 2017, students enrolled reached 3.38 million and the trainees for short-and long-term training reached 4.56 million. Enterprises and various training institutes train more than 15 million people each year. In 2015, there were 165 million skilled workers nationwide, 27.3% of whom (i.e. 45.01 million) were highly skilled.

(2) Wage income grew rapidly. Before the initiation of reform and opening up, the national average wages grew slowly. From 1952 to 1978, the average annual wages of all employees increased from 445 *yuan* to 615 *yuan*, with an increase of 38.2%. After allowing for inflation, the real increase was only 10.3%.

After the initiation of reform and opening up, urban workers' average wage increased rapidly as the economic development stepped up to new levels one after another, together with a series of policies and measures such as the minimum wage standard issued by the government. In 2018, the average annual wage of the people employed in urban units nationwide reached 82,413 *yuan* (Table 1.3), 134 times of that in 1978, with an average annual growth rate of 13.0 percent. After allowing for price factors, the actual increase was 18.3 times and the average annual real growth rate was 7.7 percent.

Table 1.3 Average Annual Wages and Indices of Employed People in Urban Units by the Type of Business Registration

Year	Average annual wage/*yuan*				Index (100 in the previous year)			
	Total	State-owned unit	Urban collective unit	Other units	Total	State-owned unit	Urban collective unit	Other units
1981	772	812	642	—	101.3	101.1	103.0	—
1982	798	836	671	—	103.4	103.0	104.5	—
1983	826	865	698	—	103.5	103.5	104.0	—
1986	1,329	1,414	1,092	1,629	115.8	116.6	112.9	113.4
1987	1,459	1,546	1,207	1,879	109.8	109.3	110.5	115.3
1988	1,747	1,853	1,426	2,382	119.7	119.9	118.1	126.8
1989	1,935	2,055	1,557	2,707	110.8	110.9	109.2	113.6
1991	2,340	2,477	1,866	3,468	109.3	108.5	111.0	116.1
1992	2,711	2,878	2,109	3,966	115.9	116.2	113.0	114.4
1993	3,371	3,532	2,592	4,966	124.3	122.7	122.9	125.2
1994	4,538	4,797	3,245	6,302	134.6	135.8	125.2	126.9
1996	5,980	6,207	4,312	8,521	111.8	111.8	109.6	110.3
1997	6,444	6,679	4,516	9,092	107.8	107.6	104.7	106.7
1998	7,446	7,579	5,314	9,241	115.5	113.5	117.7	101.6
1999	8,319	8,443	5,758	10,142	111.7	111.4	108.4	109.8
2001	10,834	11,045	6,851	12,437	116.1	117.0	109.8	110.7
2002	12,373	12,701	7,636	13,486	114.2	115.0	111.5	108.4
2003	13,969	14,358	8,627	14,843	112.9	113.0	113.0	110.1
2004	15,920	16,445	9,723	16,519	114.0	114.5	112.7	111.3
2006	20,856	21,706	12,866	21,004	114.6	114.4	115.1	114.4
2007	24,721	26,100	15,444	24,271	118.5	120.2	120.0	115.6
2008	28,898	30,287	18,103	28,552	116.9	116.0	117.2	117.6
2009	32,244	34,130	20,607	31,350	111.6	112.7	113.8	109.8

Continued

Year	Average annual wage/*yuan*				Index (100 in the previous year)			
	Total	State-owned unit	Urban collective unit	Other units	Total	State-owned unit	Urban collective unit	Other units
2016	67,569	72,538	50,527	65,531	108.9	111.1	108.4	107.6
2017	74,318	81,114	55,243	71,304	110.0	111.8	109.3	108.8
2018	82,413	89,474	60,664	79,453	110.9	110.3	109.8	111.4

Source: *Statistical Yearbook of China* and the website of the National Bureau of Statistics.

Note: Other units refer to joint-stock cooperative units, joint venture units, limited liability companies, Hong Kong, Macao and Taiwan businessmen investment units, and foreign investment units.

(3) Employment stability has been improved constantly. China's reform and opening-up policy abolished the lifelong job and established labour contract system which facilitated the mobility of workers and inspired their creativity as well. In response to some employer's problems on labour contract compliance, the State constantly improved relevant laws and regulations, strengthened labour law enforcement, standardised the signing of labour contract. While maintaining the vitality of the labour market, employment stability was improved continuously. According to the statistics of the Ministry of Human Resources and Social Security (MOHRSS), over 90 percent of enterprises nationwide signed labour contracts, and the collective contracts in validity period and reviewed by MOHRSS totalled 1.75 million, which covered 155 million employees nationwide. In the meantime, a tripartite negotiation mechanism among governments, trade unions and enterprises/employers in line with China's national conditions has been established to communicate and negotiate major issues related to labour relations. Moreover, the labour dispute mediation and arbitration system has been established to settle labour disputes in accordance with the law.

(4) Social security has been strengthened continuously. In the last 70 years since the founding of the People's Republic of China, China's labour and social security system experienced an impressive progress, starting over from scratch, extending from urban to rural areas, from enterprise workers to urban and rural residents, and from incomplete to relatively complete system. A relatively sound labour and social security system has been established, which has realised the transformation from unit welfare to social insurance featured as social pooling and solidarity. In 2019, the number of people participating in basic old-age insurance nationwide increased from 57.1 million in 1989 to 967.48 million, that of people participating in basic medical insurance increased from 2.9 million in 1993 to 1,354.36 million, that of people participating in unemployment insurance increased from 74.43 million in 1992 to 205.43 million, that of people participating in work-related injury insurance increased from 11.04 million in 1993 to 254.74 million, and that of people participating in maternity insurance increased from 5.57 million in 1993 to 214.32 million. At the same time, the Chinese government has continuously improved and fully implemented national standards on occupational safety and health to ensure workers' safety and health.

(5) More balance has been established between work and life. When the People's Republic of China was founded in 1949, China practised the single-day off weekend, with yearly legal holiday being 59 days in total. After China's reform and opening-up policy, to better ensure workers' holiday rights, the two-day weekend system was finally implemented after many revisions, with yearly legal holidays and paid vacations being up to 120 days. In recent years, the State has issued a series of laws and regulations to clearly stipulate the system of working hours and overtime payment. As enterprises adopted more standardised employment practices, overtime employment was alleviated and workers' workload was effectively reduced. By the end of 2018, the average working time of employees in enterprises nationwide was 46 hours per week.

1.3.2 Better Manifestation of Employment Equity

(1) Chinese law stipulates that in seeking jobs, workers shall not be subject to discrimination because of their ethnic backgrounds, races, gender, religious beliefs, etc. Employing units are strictly prohibited by law from recruiting minors under the age of 16. Illegal use of child labour, recruiting child labour and introducing jobs for child labour will be strictly investigated and severely punished. By intensifying law enforcement and supervision, Chinese government urges enterprises to earnestly implement the provisions on equal employment and corrects various discriminatory acts in labour market, as well as supports and encourages workers to use the law to protect their labour and employment rights and interests.

(2) Women's labour participation rate increases. Chinese laws have specific provisions on the protection of women's employment rights. The State protects women's entitlement of equal labour rights with men, eliminates gender discrimination in employment, applies equal pay for men and women for equal work, and exercises special labour protection for female workers during menstruation, pregnancy, confinement, nursing period and some other special workplace cases. Women's employment fields are constantly expanding and the number of female workers is constantly increasing as well. The number of women workers in urban and rural areas in China increased from 291 million in 1990 to 338 million in 2017, accounting for 43.5% of the total employed persons. In the same period, the number of women employed in urban units increased from 58.61 million to 65.45 million (Table 1.4), accounting for 37.1% of the total employees in urban units. In 2018, the proportion of female workers in China continued to increase, accounting for 43.7% of the total employed persons. In recent years, China's female labour force participation rate remains around 70%, ranking on the top over the world.

Table 1.4 The Number of Employed Women in Urban Units by Type of Business Registration in Year-end

(Unit: 10 thousand)

Year	Employed women
2011	5,228
2012	5,459
2013	6,338
2014	6,546
2015	6,527
2016	6,218
2017	6,545

Source: *Statistical Yearbook of China* and the website of the National Bureau of Statistics.

(3) Employment migration and mobility of rural workers come into being. In the industrialisation, reform and opening-up process in China, the migration of rural labour force and the development of urbanisation are important symbolic events. Chinese government has adopted the policy of fair treatment, rational guidance, better management and good service for rural workers entering the cities, vigorously strengthened employment services and skills training, protected their legitimate rights and interests, and helped them to solve the problems relating to employment, social security, housing, children's education and public services when they migrating into urban areas. From 2008 to 2018, the number of rural workers transferred from agriculture industry increased from 225 million to 288 million, inclusive of the number of rural migrant workers moving to urban areas increasing from 140 million to 173 million.

(4) Employment aid is provided for the people who have difficulty in finding

jobs. Chinese laws request governments at all levels to establish and improve employment aid system, which specifies the target groups of employment aid, major measures and employment support policies. Various effective measures have been taken to give priority support and special assistance to the people with employment difficulties. The range of public welfare posts is expanded to ensure that at least one member is employed in each urban family that needs employment. From 2010 to 2019, more than 1.6 million people with employment difficulties were employed each year. For the rural poor households, precise poverty alleviation through employment has been advocated. Governments at local level provide them with opportunities of accessing skills development so that they can be employed. By the end of 2018, 9.88 million poor labourers were helped to have transferred employment.

Chinese law stipulates that the State guarantees the disabled the right of work, makes overall employment plan and creates conditions for their employment. The employment policy implemented for them follows the principle of combining concentrated employment and scattered employment. Favourable policy and supportive measures have

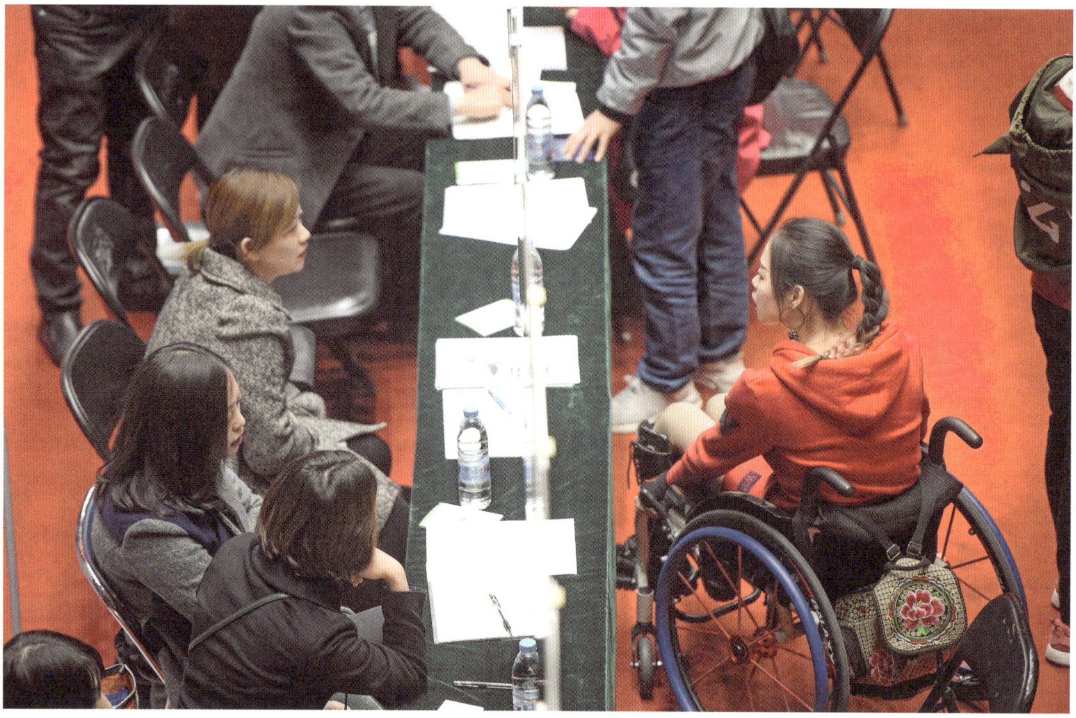

Special job fairs on employment aid for the disabled are organised to help them seeking jobs. (Photo taken by Xinhua News Agency reporter Kaihua Feng.)

been adapted to promote their employment with multiple channels, tiers and forms. In the meantime, the government and social organisations positively provided them with employment services, including free occupational guidance, job recommendation and vocational training. By 2018, the number of vocational skills training delivered to the disabled reached 2 million person-times. China's total number of employment for the disabled amounted to 9.48 million, with employment rate of 56%.

2. Employment Policy and Employment System

2.1 The Leap from Centralised Employment Allocation to Labour Market Mechanism

In the planned economy period, the employment management system was developed in China featured as "centralised employment allocation", under which the State centralised all the employment positions and assigned them to urban workers, while enterprises' recruitment was regulated by a unified job quota system. This implied that labour market in real sense almost did not exist, as employment channels were getting narrower, enterprises lost vitality in recruitment and workers had little autonomy in job-seeking. After the initiation of reform and opening up, from early 1980s, the national "three-ways combined" employment guideline was introduced to widen employment channels. Under the guideline, the government made an overall employment plan and delivered relevant guidance, and labour departments at each level recommended job opportunities while workers took initiatives in seeking jobs or getting self-employed on the voluntary basis. In the mid-1980s, four reforms concerning labour system were implemented to change the fixed employment system at enterprises level. In early 1990s, the concept of labour market was officially proposed and the labour market started to develop. In late 1990s, the new era's employment guideline was enacted and implemented, under which employment was chosen by labour force independently, regulated by the market and promoted by the government. This indicated that a market-oriented employment mechanism was gradually established and improved. Labour market grew rapidly because of the fast development of urban and rural private economy, foreign-invested enterprises as well as the gradual expansion of state-owned enterprises' autonomy in employing people. After decades of cultivation and development, the labour market gradually became mature, and the decisive role of market mechanism in allocating human resources was strengthened. Firstly, employment channel was diversified. More and more workers were employed by private enterprises, foreign-invested enterprises, business start-ups and various new forms of employment. A large number of rural labourers transferred from agriculture industry to work in urban areas. Secondly, employment form was diversified. Many new forms of employment didn't have to follow the strict restriction on time and location. Part-time job, freelancing, flexible employment and so on started to emerge gradually. Thirdly, the attitudes toward employment were more market-oriented. Workers were willing to move either for a position or for higher income. This broke down the boundaries between urban and rural areas, regions, industries and corporate ownerships. New employment philosophy, such as self-determined job choice, entrepreneurship and lifelong learning, became more and more popular.

2.2 Employment Laws and Regulations Gradually Improved

China enacted and implemented a series of complementary laws and regulations, confirming the status of market-oriented employment system. *Labour Law* came into force in 1995, which clarifies the legal status of the various subjects of labour relations, stipulates in legal form that all types of enterprises shall practise the system of labour contracts for all employees, and guarantees the right of enterprises to employ workers on their own and the right of individuals to choose their own jobs. *Labour Law* has laid a solid legal foundation for the construction of the labour market. In 2008, *Employment Promotion Law* was implemented, clarifying the prominent position of employment in economic and social development, and institutionalising the national employment promotion policies. The decisive role of the market in employment is clearly defined to promote that the employing units employ workers independently and the workers choose jobs on their own, and to guide the rational flow of workers. The law clarifies the government's responsibility to promote employment, mainly through policy guidance and services delivery to create a good environment for promoting workers' employment, and help the disadvantaged groups to be employed. The law also clarifies that the institutional system on public employment service shall be established for all workers, and the lifelong training system and policy for workers shall be formulated. The implementation of *Labour Contract Law of the People's Republic of China* (hereinafter referred to as *Labour Contract Law*) in 2008 has improved the employment contract system and clarified the rights and obligations of both parties involved by the contract, which is conducive to the construction and development of harmonious and stable labour relations.

After the promulgation of *Employment Promotion Law*, relevant laws and regulations have been formulated and put into effect. Meanwhile, the enactment of a series of ministerial regulations has further improved the law and regulation system on employment promotion.

2.3 Employment Policy and Service System Continuously Perfected

In 2002, Chinese government started to establish the basic framework on proactive employment policy system, which mainly included economic policies conducive to employment growth, policies to encourage workers' entrepreneurship and flexible employment, policies to encourage enterprises to absorb more workers, policies to assist the people having difficulty in finding jobs, policies to strengthen public employment services, policies to strengthen vocational skills training, policies to increase investment in employment funds, policies to regulate and control unemployment, and policies to facilitate the linkage between social security and employment promotion. These policies

The government provides free vocational trainings to re-employed workers. (photo taken by Xinhua News Agency reporter Zidong Liang.)

were institutionalised in 2008 through the legal form of *Employment Promotion Law*. In response to the international financial crisis, a more proactive employment policy was formed from 2008 to 2009. Since the 18th National Congress of the CPC in 2012, more emphasis has been placed on the close integration of entrepreneurship and employment as well as on supporting the development of new employment forms. More segmented and well-targeted guidance and policies were delivered to various labour groups according to their characteristics.

In short, with the development and changes of employment situation in China and the need of business development, in the course of solving the outstanding problems at different stages, the proactive employment policy was gradually developed into a relatively complete policy system with wide coverage, strong support and rich contents. As it is constantly enriched, improved and upgraded through innovation, the policy box has guided and facilitated the national employment and business start-up undertaking to make new progress step by step.

In order to ensure and improve people's livelihood, Chinese government implements the strategy of giving high priority to employment, and provides workers with policy support and all-round services for their employment and entrepreneurship. (Photo taken by Xinhua News Agency reporter Jiaguo Wang.)

In this process, China has gradually established a five-level public employment service network distributed in provinces, cities, counties, neighbourhoods (towns) and communities (villages), which basically formed an all-round multi-functional public employment service system covering both urban and rural areas throughout the whole service process. More efforts have been made in accelerating the construction of information system on employment services and that of service delivery system at neighbourhood and community level. Strongly promote one-stop service and package service for both employing units and job seekers, including services such as employment information, vocational guidance, job recommendation, skills training, entrepreneurship guidance and agency service. Public employment services for workers are free of charge and subsidised by the government. In recent years, more than 40 million workers have registered for job seeking each year, and more than 16 million people have received vocational guidance services.

3. Major Measures to Promote Employment and the Revelation of Chinese Practice

Over the past 70 years, the Communist Party of China (CPC) and Chinese government have always regarded employment as the top priority in governing the country. In response to different employment pressures faced in different periods, CPC and the government have promptly adopted corresponding employment policies and measures, and constantly reformed the employment system and mechanism, so that the employment contradiction has been properly resolved, and a basically stable employment situation has been maintained for a long time.

3.1 Major Initiatives and Achievements in Addressing Unemployment Challenge

3.1.1 Quickly Solving the Employment Problems Left over by Old China

In 1949 when the People's Republic of China was founded, because of historical problems, the number of unemployed people amounted to 4.742 million in urban areas, with an unemployment rate of 23.6 percent. CPC and the government took a number of measures to stabilise employment situation, and resettled the previously unemployed by adopting measures such as "work relief" and "self-relief by engaging in production". Moreover, a combination of various employment forms, such as recruited employment, introduced employment and self-employment were used to expand employment. By 1952, urban unemployment decreased to 3.766 million and unemployment rate declined to 13.2%. Thanks to the successful implementation of the first Five-year Plan, employment situation was further improved. Urban unemployment rate further declined to 5.9% in 1957.

3.1.2 Timely Dealing with the Employment Problem for the Educated Youth Returning to Cities

From 1962 to the end of 1979, a total of 17.76 million urban young people moved to rural areas for work. In 1979, "the Movement of Educated Urban Youth Working in the Countryside or Mountain Areas" was ended. Millions of such urban educated youth swarmed back to the cities within one year. In 1979, the total number of people waiting-for-jobs in urban areas accumulated to 15 million, the number of registered urban unemployed persons reached 5.68 million, and the registered urban unemployment rate was 5.4 %. In 1980, the Central Committee of CPC put forward the afore-mentioned "three-ways combined" employment guideline, and implemented a series of policies and measures. Moreover, the government started to reform employment management system. As a result, new policies quickly relieved employment inconsistency in urban areas at that time. In 1983, registered urban unemployment rate declined to 3.2%. The urban unemployment problem, including that of the educated youth returning to cities, was basically addressed in most areas in the country. In 1984, registered unemployment rate further reduced to 1.9%.

3.1.3 Properly Resolving the Re-employment Problem for Laid-off Workers

In 1998, the economic restructuring in China and the Asian financial crisis triggered a large number of enterprise closures and bankruptcies, and a large number of enterprise workers were laid-off or unemployed. From 1998 to 2002, the number of laid-off workers from state-owned enterprises (SOEs) accumulated to 20.23 million. Adding those laid-offs before 1998, it totalled 27.15 million. While ensuring the basic livelihood of laid-off workers, CPC and the government made a series of favourable policies to encourage and support workers to start up their own businesses and enterprises to absorb re-employed workers, including tax and fee reductions and exemption, social security subsidies, micro-secured loans [①], training subsidies and employment services. These policies promoted the re-employment of the laid-offs and unemployed persons. From 1998 to 2005, 19.75 million laid-off workers from SOEs were re-employed. By the end of 2005, the number of laid-off workers in SOEs dropped from a peak of more than 6.5 million to 610 thousand. The impact on urban employment caused by the concentrated laid-off workers in enterprises is basically eliminated.

3.1.4 Responding to the Impact of Natural Disaster Outburst and the International Financial Crisis on Employment

In May 2008, Sichuan experienced severe earthquakes, a large number of workers in the disaster area lost their jobs. The central government implemented special employment aid policies to the disaster-stricken areas, such as developing public welfare posts, absorbing employment by means of reconstruction projects, increasing supports to business start-ups, and mobilising other parts of the country to carry out "Peer Employment Aid". These policies did ensure a basically stable employment situation in the disaster areas.

At the end of 2008, as the international financial crisis spread, China's economy was also severely impacted, and employment faced severe challenges: the number of new jobs in urban areas declined sharply, the closure and production suspension of enterprises led to a great loss of jobs, migrant workers returned to their hometowns, and college graduates experienced difficulties in finding jobs. In response, while maintaining economic growth, the central government made a decisive decision to formulate and implement a more proactive employment policy. A set of integrated policies and measures for stabilising and expanding employment has been formed by increasing employment through economic development, helping enterprises to stabilise employment, encouraging business start-ups through policy support, making overall employment plans for key groups, reinforcing training to improve employment, and strengthening services to promote employment. The policy package made China's economy and employment being the first to get out of the impact of the international financial crisis. One year after the implementation of a more proactive employment policy, the number of new urban jobs nationwide rose from 380

[①] On 21 April 2015, the State Council executive meeting changed the micro-secured loans to business start-up secured loans.

thousand per month in December 2008 to 1 million per month in December 2009, and the year-end urban registered unemployment rate declined to 4.3% in 2009 (Table 1.5), approximately returning to its pre-financial crisis level.

3.1.5 Actively Responding to the New Employment Situation in the Context of Slowing-down Economic Growth

Since the 18th CPC National Congress, in the face of enormous pressure of the total employment number and the prominent employment structural contradiction, as well as the economic growth shifting from high-speed to medium-high-speed, the central government positively nurtured and expanded new momentum. China has been vigorously developing the service industry, improving the business environment, encouraging entrepreneurship and innovation, and supporting the development of private enterprises and small and micro enterprises, which ensures a sustainable and stable employment situation. From 2013 to 2018, key employment groups, such as college graduates, veterans, rural workers and people with difficulties, had their employment secured. New forms of employment and opportunities constantly emerged, with new jobs created each year being around 13 million in urban areas. The national surveyed urban unemployment rate remained stable at a low level of around 5.0%, while the registered urban unemployment rate being around 4.0%.

Table 1.5 The Year-end Registered Urban Unemployed and Registered Urban Unemployment Rate

(Unit: 10 thousand, %)

Year	Registered urban unemployed	Registered urban unemployment rate
1978	530.0	5.3
1980	541.5	4.9
1981	439.5	3.8
1982	379.4	3.2
1983	271.4	2.3
1984	235.7	1.9
1985	238.5	1.8
1990	383.2	2.5

Continued

Year	Registered urban unemployed	Registered urban unemployment rate
1995	519.6	2.9
2000	595.0	3.1
2005	839.0	4.2
2006	847.0	4.1
2007	830.0	4.0
2008	886.0	4.2
2009	921.0	4.3
2010	908.0	4.1
2011	922.0	4.1
2012	917.0	4.1
2013	926.0	4.1
2014	952.0	4.1
2015	966.0	4.1
2016	982.0	4.0
2017	972.0	3.9
2018	974.0	3.8
2019	945.0	3.6

Source: *Statistical Yearbook of China* and the website of the National Bureau of Statistics.

3.2 Revelation of Chinese Practice on Employment

In the reform and development process, China has been searching for a unique path for the employment undertaking. China not only made an outstanding achievement, but also learnt valuable experience in this field, which provided inspiration and examples for the future work.

3.2.1 Adhere to the People-centred Philosophy in Promoting Employment and Firmly Upholding the Governing Philosophy of Employment Being Pivotal to People's Livelihood

Sticking to the people-centred philosophy is the concrete demonstration of the Chinese government in exercising the state power for the people. Employment relates to the vital interests of millions of people. For workers, it is the foundation of their livelihood, and it is the most direct and most concerned realistic major issue. Thus, it is the top priority in safeguarding and improving people's livelihood. For the country, it can produce an enormous impact on national economy and the whole society, whether employment issue is resolved or not, as it has a vital bearing to the stability and healthy development of the country. Therefore, employment promotion is the national strategy of stabilising a country.

Looking back the 40 years of reform and opening-up process, it is clearly seen that, after the Cultural Revolution, the stability of the Chinese society is attributable to the solution of unemployment problem for the educated youth returning to cities by all efforts, which has ensured that CPC and Chinese government kept sole intention in seeking development. At the turn of the century, China faced both internal pressure from reform and adjustment and external pressure from financial turmoil, it was the prompt settlement of laid-off workers and implementation of a series of effective measures to promote re-employment that ensured the victory of reform at the critical stage. Entering the new century, a more proactive employment policy was implemented to provide timely employment aid in helping the disaster-affected residents to obtain employment in case of major disaster and to respond to the financial crisis shock positively. These policies and measures have laid the foundation for ensuring economic growth, people's livelihood and social stability. To sum up the past experience, the most fundamental one is to adhere firmly to the people-centred philosophy, and the philosophy of employment being pivotal to people's livelihood while employment promotion being vital to the national stability. Also, China takes these principles and philosophies as the fundamental guidelines for employment undertaking, and implements them throughout the practice.

3.2.2 Insisting on Market-oriented Employment Reform, Clarifying and Strengthening the Government's Responsibility on Employment Promotion

Market-oriented employment reform is the fundamental driving force for the development of independent employment pattern. After China's reform and opening up, organised employment and self-employment were driven by reforming the employment system of "centralised labour allocation" and the expansion of employment channels. Enterprises employment was vitalised by reforming fixed-term employment practice and introducing labour contract system. Public employment services were strengthened. A two-way selection mechanism between workers and employers as well as the tendency of workers seeking jobs on their own initiatives were developed. The integration of employment in rural and urban areas as well as employment equity were promoted by breaking down the segmentation between urban and rural areas and providing rural migrant workers with policy support and employment services. Step by step, the market-oriented employment mechanism was developed, which mobilised workers' enthusiasm in choosing jobs on their own. In the process of deepening the reform, a more integrated, standardised and flexible human resources market was established, which could play a basic role in regulating the market. This not only promoted the rational flow and optimal allocation of human resources, but also facilitated the full development and effective utilisation of human resources.

It is an important guarantee to solve the employment problem by constantly reinforcing the government's responsibility in employment promotion and giving full play to the functions of the government. CPC and the Chinese government regarded employment as the basis of people's well-being and an important strategy for economic and social development. Especially when the market mechanism was incomplete and the workers' initiative was inadequate, the government had to share more responsibilities in nurturing market mechanism, standardising market behaviour, remedying market deficiencies and assisting the disadvantaged groups in getting employment. By implementing employment expansion strategy and enforcing proactive employment policy, increasing fiscal investment and improving public service, positive progress on employment and re-employment has been achieved with effective protection of workers' employment rights and interests. Moreover, the government shall play a leading role in facilitating business start-up, such as formulating relevant laws and regulations to protect and support workers' start-up activities and encouraging workers to establish production-related service schemes or to start up their own businesses so as to create more jobs for more people. More business development services have also been provided to entrepreneurs to pave their way for business start-up and to reduce their future worries. In short, these all drilled down to the combination of reinforcing government responsibility and better playing of workers' employment initiatives.

3.2.3 Sticking to Employment and Facilitating the Positive Interaction between Economic Development and Employment Expansion

Entering the 21st century, while studying and researching the experience from the international community, especially from the developed countries, China constantly updated and refined its own development concept by correcting the tendency of only focusing on economic development and GDP indicators. The government took ensuring and improving people's livelihood as an important direction of economic and social development, and setting employment promotion and full employment as a priority goal of national economic and social development. These changes reflected a different understanding of the relationship between employment and economic development, full compliance with objective laws and the development of strategic thinking. Entering a new era, the people-centred development philosophy has been further put forward at the 19th CPC National Congress (held in October 2017) that injected fresh power into the implementation of giving high priority to employment strategy, and made a rational choice on the sustainable socioeconomic development.

It is a fundamental way to solve the employment problem by correctly handling the relationship between employment expansion and socioeconomic development, by well integrating employment expansion and economic development and facilitating its common development. The situation of China with abundant human resources, also determines that employment expansion strategy must be implemented for a long time. The employment strategies, objectives and tasks must be made scientifically in line with the objective laws on socioeconomic development and must be based on reality. By constantly refining proactive employment policy, increasing funds input and improving public resource services, the process of sustainable and healthy economic development should also be a process of sustainable employment expansion. In the overall layout, factor input, goal setting and specific arrangement concerning economic development, employment expansion should be regarded as an important component. By doing so, more employment opportunities could be created while achieving rapid economic development.

3.2.4 Promoting an Integrated Employment Development between Urban and Rural Areas Based on China's Actual Conditions

Based on China's reality, we determine employment objectives, guidelines and formulating policies, by which we make decisions to solve the problem of urban and rural employment. China is a developing country with a large population and abundant labour resources. Such realistic conditions need to be sufficiently considered in solving employment problems. In the long run, the main employment conflict is the contradiction among workers' demand of full employment, oversized aggregate number of labour forces, and workers' competence not matching the job requirement. At the present stage, the employment problem in China seems to be more complex, unlike the developed countries, other developing countries and countries in transition, which mainly face a single problem, such as structural unemployment, huge aggregate number of workers, or transitional unemployment. China, however, is facing a co-exiting contradiction between total supply and demand of labour force, the structural contradiction of employment, the increasing urban employment pressure and the acceleration of surplus rural workers migrating into cities, and the contradiction between the employment of new entrants to labour market and the re-employment of the unemployed. Therefore, the task of employment in China would be a long-term one, hard and arduous. After the People's Republic of China was founded in 1949, the idea of "eliminating unemployment" and the practice of moving urban workers to the rural areas in large numbers did exist for some time. All in all, such profound lessons resulted from making decisions in a vacuum which was incompliance with objective laws.

3.2.5 Keeping Pace with the Times in Determining Employment Principles and Policies, Strengthening the Implementation Capacity and Striving for Practical Results

Looking back at the employment reform and development course in China, we have always adhered to the principle of keeping pace with the times in determining the employment strategy, policies and target tasks for each period according to the development and changes of the employment situation and tasks, especially when the economic situation fluctuated and employment was confronted with new major problems, for example, from the solution to the major employment problem for a large number of laid-off and unemployed persons in the process of restructuring state-owned enterprises, to the overall employment promotion for various categories of workers, and to the combination of employment promotion and encouraging entrepreneurship. In terms of employment strategy, it started from "sticking to employment expansion strategy" to "putting employment expansion in a more prominent position in socioeconomic development", to "sticking to implementing the strategy of giving high priority to employment". Regarding the employment guidelines, they started from "insisting on market-oriented employment mechanism and, at the same time, reinforcing government liability in implementing positive employment policies," to "employment chosen by workers independently, regulated by the market and promoted by the government", then to "implementing more proactive employment policy and combining business start-up with employment, so as to create job opportunities by innovation and entrepreneurship". To sum up, these changes are attributed to firstly advancing with the times. Policies were extended, refined, improved with thorough persistence in openness and tolerance as situation changed. International experience was referred and learnt. Local creativity in conjunction with local reality was encouraged. Secondly, be positive and take initiatives. At each policy-making stage, every policy component, such as the starting point, the objective and the positive implication of the policy, would be fully considered in order to motivate both enterprise and workers' initiatives. Thirdly, make comprehensive administration and effective enforcement. For policy enactment, it requires not only general principles, but also to emphasise its operability. In terms of policy implementation, not only the standpoint of the central and local governments should be considered, we should also go down to the grass roots. Apart from taking temporary solutions to current problems, long term measures should be proposed that could address the problems permanently from the institutional perspective. Strategic research and policy reserve should be available so as to lay a good foundation for the enactment of new employment policies at crucial moments.

Since the founding of the People's Republic of China in 1949, the Communist Party of China and the Chinese government united in leading the Chinese people to achieve a series of glorious accomplishment in employment area. The employment management system has undergone tremendous changes. The labour market has been increasingly improved. The number of employees has increased significantly, and the employment situation has remained stable for a long-time. However, currently and for a period to come, great hurdle and problems remain there in China in its economic and social development journey. How to properly deal with employment remains a long-term, complex and uphill task. To this end, we must adhere to the guiding ideology of socialism with distinctive Chinese features for a new era, while thoroughly implementing the important principles and policies on employment and a series of arrangements made by the Central Committee of CPC and the State Council. We will strive for fuller and higher quality employment by sticking to the market-oriented employment reform, sticking to the government's responsibility on employment promotion, sticking to principle of achieving a positive interaction between economic development and employment expansion, sticking to the overall employment development planning in urban and rural areas, and keeping firm confidence and endeavouring in a pragmatic way.

Chapter 2
Giving High Priority to Employment: From Strategy to Policy

1. Initiation and Development of Giving High Priority to Employment

1.1 Initiation of Giving High Priority to Employment

Giving high priority to employment was initiated in the 1990s, and has gradually reached a consensus in international community. The Declaration adopted at the World Summit for Social Development (Copenhagen, 1995) pledged to promote the goal of full employment as a basic priority of economic and social policies, and suggested that all countries should promote patterns of economic growth that maximise employment creation. At that time, the premier of the State Council of P. R. China signed the Declaration on behalf of the Chinese government together with the other heads of States or governments participating in the summit. In 2001, International Labour Organisation (ILO) put forward in *Global Employment Agenda* that governments should place full, productive and freely-chosen employment at the centre of economic and social policies. In *ILO Centenary Declaration for the Future of Work 2019*, ILO pledged to take an important role in promoting policy coherence in pursuit of its human-centred approach to the future of work, recognising the strong, complex and crucial links between social, trade, financial, economic and environmental policies. The Chinese government participated in the discussions on the above ILO documents, and not only agreed with these ideas, but also put them into practice.

From the end of the 20th century to the beginning of the 21st century, the reform in China was at a critical stage. The Asian financial crisis not only severely hit the national economy, but also put China in an extremely difficult employment situation: the new entrants in urban labour market reached its peak, while the problem of laid-off workers in state-owned enterprises was prominent and the flow of surplus rural labour force quickened, forming a three-in-one overlying difficult situation. The contradiction between supply and demand of labour force was intense, and the structural unemployment problem was very prominent. Employment turned to be the most concerned problem affecting reform, development and social stability. At this critical moment, the Chinese government made a timely and significant decision to vigorously promote employment and re-employment. In 2002, the CPC Central Committee and the State Council jointly convened the National Re-employment Conference, the highest-level meeting on re-employment, to make arrangements for better employment and re-employment, proclaiming that "employment is pivotal to people's well-being and a strategic policy to stabilise the country". The national strategy on expanding employment was also proposed. The proactive employment policy was formulated and implemented accordingly, thus starting a new era for the employment in China. Afterwards, as employment situation was changing, especially when economic situation changed and employment faced big challenges, the Chinese government always insisted on the principle of starting from the realities, and determined employment strategy, policies, goals and tasks for every phase. It guided China to advance with the times and to develop healthily in the right direction in terms of employment.

1.2 Giving High Priority to Employment: Development from Strategy to Policy

1.2.1 Employment Strategy Constantly Upgrading and the Employment Priority Becoming Clearer

The Chinese government has attached great importance to employment and has continuously stressed the important position and prominent role of employment in light of economic and social development. In *the 10th Five-year Plan for National Economic and Social Development* (2001-2005), it was proposed to regard employment expansion as an important goal of economic and social development, and to implement economic and social policies conducive to employment expansion. In *the 11th Five-year Plan for*

National Economic and Social Development (2006-2010), it was clearly specified to put employment expansion at a more prominent position in economic and social development and to implement the proactive employment policy. In *the 12th Five-year Plan for National Economic and Social Development* (2011-2015), arrangements and requirements were made on the implementation of giving high priority to employment strategy and proactive employment policy, and it proclaimed to take employment promotion as a priority for economic and social development and to improve the mechanism to combine self-selection of jobs by labourers, employment regulation by market and employment promotion by government. In *the 13th Five-year Plan for National Economic and Social Development* (2016-2020), it was further specified to ensure relatively full and high quality employment, and to give greater prominence to the realisation of full employment and set this as a priority goal for economic and social development. From 2018 to 2019 when national employment was facing a new situation and tasks, especially the complex and ever-changing international environment and various unfavourable factors, new requirements on placing pro-employment policy at the macro-policy level and making

"Giving high priority to employment" has been listed as the guideline of *the 12th Five-year Employment Plan*. It is of great strategic significance to regard employment as the priority goal for economic and social development. (Photo taken by *Journal of China Employment* reporter.)

them fully operational were made so as to ensure people's well-being and steady economic growth while stressing stable employment. Placing pro-employment policy alongside the fiscal and monetary policies at the macro-policy level, it was a significant decision made by the Central Committee of CPC and the State Council from the overall situation and strategic perspective which formally transformed giving high priority to employment from a goal to a policy so as to realise the organic unity of employment policy goal and policy tools.

1.2.2 Employment Guideline Keeping Pace with the Times and the Employment Task Gradually Expanding

In 1980 when reforming employment system and promoting employment, the Chinese government put forward the employment guideline, which was under the overall national plan and guidance, to implement a combined policy with job placement by labour departments, voluntary job-matching and self-employment. This guideline opened up a variety of channels for better solving the accumulated unemployment problem for the educated youth returning to cities and for the newly arising workforce in urban areas. After the year 2000, in the process of deepening reform and promoting employment, it was further specified to adhere to the reform of a market-oriented employment mechanism, to strengthen the responsibility of the government, and to implement proactive employment policy. At the same time, implementing the guideline of employment chosen by workers independently, regulated by the market and promoted by the government. The revised guideline did not only realise the reform of market employment, promoting the re-employment of laid-off workers from enterprises, but also promoted the overall planned employment in urban and rural areas and facilitated a significant progress in urban employment promotion and the transfer of rural workers to other jobs. In 2015, in the context of promoting mass entrepreneurship and innovation and expanding employment, the government further clarified the guideline of employment chosen by workers independently, regulated by the market, promoted by the government and entrepreneurship encouraged by the government. While stabilising and expanding employment, the government encouraged and supported more business start-ups by all categories of workers so as to create more jobs. This shows that China has adjusted and adopted different employment guidelines in light of different time and different employment situation, so as to promote the employment undertaking to make progress one after another.

1.3 Giving High Priority to Employment Being of Great Significance and Playing a Positive Role in Ensuring and Improving People's Well-being and Promoting Economic Development

1.3.1 Employment Being of Top Priority to Ensure and Improve People's Well-being

In the past 70 years since its founding, the People's Republic of China has come to realise that employment is of top priority to ensure and improve people's well-being. Since the beginning of the 21st century, the Chinese government has made it clear that ensuring and improving people's well-being should be regarded as the starting point and objective of national development. In China, the specific areas in ensuring people's well-being can be generally summarised at three layers. The first layer is to ensure the basic needs of the people, including employment, wage income and social security. The second layer is to meet the development needs of the people, including education, medical care and housing. The third is to ensure the safety needs of the people, including the safety of life and production, ecological protection and public security. Moreover, the spiritual and cultural needs of the people should be also satisfied. Among the key items of people's livelihood, employment is related to people's survival and development. It is vital to the immediate interests of millions of workers and their families. It is not only the economic and social basis and important condition for ensuring and improving the people's well-being, but also an important indicator for fully achieving a well-off society in an all-round way and satisfying people's hope for good life. Therefore, it is called "the foundation of people's well-being" and "the greatest livelihood of the people".

History has proved that from the reform of state-owned enterprises at the turn of the century to the response to the international financial crisis in 2008, from the tide of migrant workers in the 1990s to urbanisation in the 21st century, it is the determination of the Chinese government and the great efforts made by the government that has opened up more employment channels and created employment opportunities for 30 million laid-off workers, millions of university graduates and migrant workers. It is the government that has relieved working people of unemployment worries and ensured their jobs and livelihood security. It has not only enabled the country to ride out the difficulties of reform and development, but also laid a solid foundation for the improvement of people's well-being, the increase of workers' income and the accumulation of social wealth. Taking the situation since 2001 as an example, the number of urban employees increased from 241.23 million to 346.87 million in 2010 and to 434.19 million in 2018, with an increase of 80% in 17 years. The average annual salary of employed workers in urban units rose from 10,870 *yuan* to 37,147 *yuan* in 2010, and then to 84,744 *yuan* in 2018, with an increase of 6.8 times over the same period. The GDP per capita increased from 8,717 *yuan* to 30,808 *yuan* in 2010, and to 64,644 *yuan* in 2018, 6.4-fold increase over the same period. All these fully illustrated the extremely important role of employment in guaranteeing and improving people's well-being.

In the past decade or so, the facts on employment aid and poverty alleviation also proved that a large number of urban people who had difficulty in finding jobs and the poor rural labourers could hardly survive if they just relied on government relief. Only by obtaining employment and re-employment and relying on their own hard work to obtain income, they could make themselves and their families out of difficulties. In 2018, for example, the number of people in difficult groups in urban areas who got jobs through employment aid reached 1.81 million, and the number of people in rural areas who were lifted out of poverty through employment aid reached 3.88 million. It showed the important role played by employment in helping poverty alleviation.

1.3.2 Employment Having a Supporting and Safeguarding Effect on Economic Development

Reviewing the course of the past 70 years since the founding of the People's Republic of China, especially the 40 years of reform and opening up, we can see the objective existence and ever-changing interaction between economic development and employment growth. In general, economic development can drive employment growth, and promoting employment growth also has an important positive impact on maintaining the healthy development of the economy. The two sides shall complement each other, but if not properly handled, it may possibly bring about negative impacts.

Since China's reform and opening-up policy, the economy and employment have shown a sustained trend of growth. In the past 40 years since 1978, the average annual growth rate of GDP was 9.5%, and the average annual growth rate of urban employment was 3.9%. On the one hand, China maintained high-speed economic growth, and the number of employed people kept increasing. On the other hand, the increase of the employed population and the increase of labour input also promoted the sustained growth of the economy. The interaction between development and employment growth in tertiary industry, in particular, was even more obvious. Compared to 1978, in 2018 tertiary industry output increased 51 times, and the share of GDP increased from 24.6% to 52.2%, with an increase of 27.6 percentage points. Over the same period, workers in tertiary industry increased from 48.9 million (1978) to 359.38 million (2018), with an increase of 6.3 times, and their share of total employment rose by 34.1 percentage points from 12.2% to 46.3%.

Learning from the lessons of some other countries, which can be described as "high growth but low employment" and/or "economic recovery without employment", China has also carried out research and analysis on the mismatch problems between domestic economic development and employment growth in some periods and some regions, and has taken measures to solve them. First, we changed the tendency of using GDP as the main index to measure economic and social development so as to prevent economic growth and social development from being lopsided or even deviating from the direction of improving people's well-being. The central government requested local governments at all levels to focus on the improvement of people's well-being from governing philosophy and practical work perspectives, and to implement the strategy of giving high priority to employment as the starting point and objectives in developing economy. Second, we changed the irrational pattern of industrial structure, enterprise scale and economic type in economic development so as to prevent the separation of economic growth from employment which led to high economic growth but less employment. A new positive and interactive pattern between economic development and employment growth was formulated to optimise economic layout, making it more conducive to employment promotion and expansion. Third, aiming at the problem of the shortage of talents needed by modern manufacturing industry, service industry, especially emerging industries, high-tech industries and skilled occupations, we changed the structure of human resources to adapt to economic upgrading and transformation. To accelerate the build-up of knowledgeable, skilled and innovative workforce, great efforts were made to facilitate the full development and efficient utilisation of human resources through promoting the optional re-grouping and rational allocation among human resources factor and the factors such as capital, technology and land, so as to better motivate workers' enthusiasm, initiative, innovation and entrepreneurship. Forth, in tandem with high-quality economic development, we promoted fuller and higher quality employment in order to maintain the synchronous growth of national economy and residents' income, the synchronous increase of labour productivity and labour remuneration, and to realise the healthy development of national economy and the continuous improvement of people's well-being at the same time.

1.3.3 The Implementation of Giving High Priority to Employment Strategy Relying on Both the Overall Requirements of the Strategy and Concrete Policy Measures

At present and in the coming period, the pressure on total employment will not decrease, and the structural contradictions will be more prominent in China. It is common for enterprises to have difficulty in recruitment due to the shortage of technical workers and skilled workers. The gap between the employment concept and ability of the working group with employment difficulty leads to the increasing difficulty of being employed. Workers' high turnover leads to increasing employment instability. In particular, the rapid development of new technology brings about the crowding-out effect on employment due to workers replaced by industrial robots. New economy and new business models contradict with the traditional forms of employment. Many enterprises, in particular the small and micro enterprises undergoing operational difficulties, are facing the pressure of industrial transformation and the reduced production capacity. As a result, their ability in expanding employment will decline. Impacted by these contradictions and uncertainties, economic growth has been dragged down, and the lagging effect on employment begins to appear. There is an increasing trend for structural unemployment, cyclical unemployment, and frictional unemployment. In response, the Chinese government is designing and implementing a set of policies and measures to promote employment for different regions, key industries, various enterprises and working groups. Moreover, the efforts have been made to prevent mass layoffs and unemployment, and to maintain sustained and stable employment growth by further strengthening macro-regulation so as to ensure the smooth running of the economy and by using relevant policies to adjust market imbalance.

At the same time, in the process of achieving fuller and higher quality employment, the Chinese government has also taken effective measures to improveboth practical work and policy system so as to meet the diverse demands of the vast number of workers on job opportunities, career development, reasonable wage growth, competence improvement, occupational safety, employment stability and social insurance benefits. Efforts have been made to solve the problems relating to labour relation, social security and employment stability for the workers in new business forms and the flexible workers, and to further increase the flexibility of the labour market, while enhancing the capacity of public employment services and strengthening the training and education programmes for workers.

2. The Connotation of Giving High Priority to Employment Strategy and Policy

2.1 Basic Requirements

(1) Continue commitment to people-centred philosophy. The implementation of pro-employment policies must be based on furthering the concept of people-centred philosophy of development, assuming power for the people, safeguarding and improving people's well-being as the fundamental task. In order to make employment the first item to meet the criteria in the process of realising the well-off society, the principle should be adhered that employment stability and employment promotion are regarded as the basis for the welfare of the people. Starting from solving the most immediate and realistic interests of the people, full efforts should be taken to achieve fuller and higher quality employment.

(2) Insist on a positive interaction between employment and the high-quality growth of the economy. Employment stability and promotion remained the prioritised goal for national economic and social development. In the process of properly handling economic growth and high-quality development, dealing with the transformation of old driving forces and the cultivation of new engines, as well as the upgrading of traditional industries and the development of emerging industries, policy orientation should well mastered so that the policy outcomes could better serve employment promotion. If necessary, efficiency, effectiveness and structural transformation should to some degree give way to expanding employment and reducing unemployment. Capital gains should give way to the benefits of labour factors in some extend, and thus to realise the organic combination and mutual benefit between employment promotion and economic growth.

(3) Adhere to the coordination and link up employment policy with socioeconomic policy. While advancing with times and enriching to improve employment and entrepreneurship policies, we should also increase the weight to employment policies at the macroeconomic regulation level, and strengthen coordination among macro-policies such as fiscal, monetary and industrial policies. We should coordinate employment and entrepreneurship policies with relevant economic and social policies, so as to develop a well-coordinated and integrated operational mechanism, and to create a new employment promotion pattern featured as a holistic approach, joint efforts and mutual benefits.

2.2 Main Orientation

(1) Give high priority to employment in the overall layout of economic and social development. Full employment was put at the top of the list of the four macro-control objectives. Efforts were made to achieve the organic unification of strategy making, industrial planning, investment policies, project implementation and employment expansion. When drawing up and implementing socioeconomic development plans and major programmes, priority was given to employment objectives and its core indicators. When adjusting economic structure and optimising industrial distribution, more consideration was given to its ability in job creation and employability improvement. Before planning regional development and implementing major construction projects, exclusive evaluation on employment was listed as precondition and major evidence in making decisions. Human resources development and utilisation were also considered as the major content in decision-making.

(2) Realise a positive interaction between facilitating economic growth and employment expansion. New employment growth points were constantly developed from the new economic growth engines. From the perspectives of industrial structure, economic types, enterprise scale and employment forms, a development model, which was conducive to the mutual complement and positive interaction between continuous employment expansion and sustainable economic growth, was formed by paying attentions to support industries and trades with a large employment capacity and high-quality jobs, to develop private enterprises that offer more jobs, to help small, medium and micro enterprises with low costs but a large number of jobs, and to promote flexible employment and new forms of employment.

(3) Make efforts to reduce the impact of economic restructure on employment. In the process of promoting economic restructuring, accelerating industrial upgrading and the transformation of production capacity from the old to the new, these efforts were made, such as mastering the intensity, rhythm and social tolerance concerning the above-mentioned issues, and making relevant arrangements in advance for the protection of workers' rights and interests and for the re-employment of the unemployed. In short, it aimed to reduce the impact on employment and to ensure the overall stability of labour transfer and adjustment. When dealing with adverse factors at home and abroad, which might have a greater impact on the employment of key regions, key industries and enterprises, special policies such as assisting enterprises to stabilise their employment and relieving burden for them by reducing taxes and fees, were used as counter-cyclical adjustment tools to help enterprises out of temporary difficulties and control unemployment at its source.

(4) Enable the proactive employment policy to play its role in macro regulation and control. On the basis of increasing employment demand, we should actively promote entrepreneurship-driven employment. The policies on supporting the development of new employment forms, which was in parallel with the new economy, were formulated so as to create more jobs, at same time, to promote economic growth. On the basis of improving labour supply, vigorously organising vocational training programmes to improve workers' competence, so as to provide support for high-quality economic growth while alleviating the structural employment tensions. On the basis of adjusting and matching labour supply and demand, strengthening public employment services in an all-round way, employment assistance should be used to ensure the basic line of employment for the disadvantaged groups. On the basis of responding to big fluctuations and big shocks, implementing special policies to assist enterprises to stabilise their employment so as to help both enterprises and workers out of difficulties.

Consultation services were provided on employment policy and rights protection for job seekers. (Photo taken by Xinhua News Agency reporter Wenkui Zhang.)

(5) Formulate and implement comprehensive socioeconomic policies conducive to employment promotion. Employment promotion was regarded as the basic objective and core content in formulating, implementing and adjusting the integrated socioeconomic policies. Any financial input, industrial adjustment, project layout and corporate development conducive to employment expansion were encouraged by improving the coordination among different polices, such as employment promotion policies, fiscal and taxation policies, monetary and investment policies, industry adjustment policies, education and training policies, income distribution policies and so on.

In different periods of economic development, in accordance with the need to achieve the objectives of the employment task, the supportive policies such as financial funds, tax reduction and exemption, business start-up credit, interest rate reduction and lower bank reserves, etc were timely introduced to increase the vitality and momentum for market and enterprise, and to boost new growth point of employment. Relevant departments and employment authorities worked together. On the one hand, the pro-employment policy was fully implemented through measures such as lowering the threshold, simplifying procedures and providing convenient services. On the other hand, policies and practices that might hurt and obstruct employment should be corrected in time.

3. Important Measures to Implement Pro-employment Policies

3.1 Major Policies

(1) Place emphasis on realising employment first target. First, we should implement macro adjustment and control that regarded employment as the minimum limit. We took fuller and higher quality employment as the priority goal of economic and social development, putting employment stability as the minimum limit of a reasonable range of economic performance, and the employment indicator as the decision-making basis for macro adjustment and control. Taking into account the adjustment of demographic structure, changes in economic operation and the needs of employment situation as a whole, we scientifically set employment targets and tasks, and incorporated them into the national socioeconomic development plan and annual plan. Focusing on the need to achieve the employment goal, we implemented fiscal and monetary policies conducive to expanding employment, and effectively used counter-cyclical adjustment tools and strengthened pre-adjustment and fine-tuning. Second, the employment statistics monitoring mechanism was improved. We established an employment information monitoring system, improved the quality control mechanism for statistical monitoring, strengthened the comparison and analysis of employment data with macroeconomic and market data, and enhanced the ability to analyse and judge the employment situation. Third, an employment impact assessment mechanism was established. When formulating important policies on reform and development, as well as industrial restructuring and social management, the impact of policy implementation on job creation, employment and entrepreneurship environment, employment quality and fair employment became an important component of the risk assessment report. Priority will be given to these projects with strong job creation abilities. In the course of implementing major policies, and carrying out key projects and special rectification, in case of any closure and/or transfer of enterprises, the placement of workers would be well arranged simultaneously. Fourth, an anti-employment risk mechanism was established. In case of severe employment situation and increasing large-scale unemployment risk, we supported enterprises to lighten their burden and secure their jobs by increasing tax and fee reduction, expanding the scope of unemployment insurance fund expenditure, relaxing labour relations regulation, suspending the adjustment of minimum wage standard, extending the entitlement period of employment and entrepreneurship policies, and so on.

(2) Give priority to macro-policy support. First, industrial policies gave higher priority to employment. It's necessary to build a modern economic system more conducive to employment expansion, and to continuously improve business environment as well as to support the integration of primary, secondary and tertiary industries in rural areas, and to support the transformation and upgrading of traditional manufacturing industries as well as the innovation and development of modern service industries. It's also necessary to support the development of small and micro enterprises and private enterprises so as to create an upgraded version of "Mass Entrepreneurship and Innovation", and to guide a coordinated promotion among labour-intensive, technology-intensive and capital-intensive industries. Following the principle of inclusiveness and prudence, we expanded the room for flexible employment and new forms of employment by guiding the development of gig economy, street vendor economy and night-time economy. Second, the effective allocation of human resources was promoted simultaneously by regional policies. We speeded up the establishment of a new mechanism for coordinated regional development, and broke through local protection and regional segmentation, so as to vigorously and orderly advance industrial gradient transfer and at the same time to guide the orderly migration of labour force. A two-way flow of workers between urban and rural areas and equal employment were promoted by improving the quality of urbanisation and accelerating the reform of household registration system. Third, strengthen the interlinkage of polices involving people's livelihood and employment. To facilitate the free movement of workers of all kinds, efforts were made in accelerating the development of national pooling for old-age insurance and facilitating the portability of social insurance benefits by deepening the reform of social security system. The income distribution system was optimised by following the principle of more pay for more work and increasing the proportion of labour remuneration in the initial distribution of income so as to develop a fair and efficient income distribution system that could stimulate employment vitality. Efforts were also made in rationally determining the unemployment benefit, minimum living allowance and social assistance standard so as to increase employment willingness and the stability for the unemployed and those having difficulties in finding jobs.

(3) Focus on stimulating the vitality of business start-up and new forms of flexible employment. First, strength the support for entrepreneurship-driven employment policies. Start-up business is an important way to bring workers' initiatives into play so as to achieve employment, with multiplier effect of employment promotion. To this end, the State provided more supports, such as funds input, credit and financing, tax and fee reduction and exemptions, space arrangement, business start-up training, advisory and guidance services to promote of entrepreneurship, so as to create more job opportunities by encouraging workers to start up their own business with their own funds and run by themselves. Second, adopt a more relaxed and secured policy. Workers were encouraged and supported to find more job opportunities and better payment opportunities in new forms of employment and/or flexible employment.

(4) Give priority to the development of human resources. First, optimise and adjust education structure. Initiatives should be taken in meeting the national strategy and market demand and establishing an interactive mechanism among employment and enrolment planning, personnel training, funding allocation, institute setting and faculty and speciality readjustment, so as to optimise the structure of tertiary education adapting to economic and social development. Vocational education system was improved through deepening the integration of production and education as well as the cooperation between schools and enterprises, and promoting the enrolment expansion of higher vocational colleges. We also vigorously developed technician education and implemented the quality improvement project on technician education. Second, improve the lifelong vocational training system. We vigorously promoted vocational skills upgrading action programme, comprehensively implemented the new apprenticeship system in enterprises, and implemented special training programmes for enterprise employees and key employment groups. We expanded the scale of skilled workers training programmes, implemented high-skilled workers training projects, and strengthened the establishment of high-skilled workers training bases and skill master studios. Third, strengthen the building-up of basic training capacity. We increased central budget to support the expansion of public training bases. Efforts were made in fostering a group of enterprises which would integrate their production into vocational skills education. The training of trainers and the development of training materials were also strengthened. We implemented the new occupation development plan and the training plan for workers in urgent need, and promoted the application of "Internet Plus" training model.

(5) Give priority to key employment groups. First, implement and improve the employment and entrepreneurship policy system for key groups. Focusing on key groups with high unemployment rate and great difficulty in employment, i.e. college graduates, migrant workers and veterans, we continued to improve and implement the employment and entrepreneurship policies that supported enterprises to absorb employment, encouraged workers to start up their own businesses, and strengthened the guarantee arrangements for the hard-to-place people. Second, promote the employment of college graduates and other youth groups. We thoroughly implemented the employment and entrepreneurship promotion plan and the grass roots growth plan for college graduates. The graduates were guided to actively link their employment expectation with the national development strategy as well as industrial development direction, and to obtain employment in strategic and emerging industries, small- and medium-sized enterprises and grass roots communities. The service platform was established to provide accurate employment services, including vocational guidance, practical experience, and training and internship. Specific programmes, such as youth internship programme and the youth employment start programme, were also available to the unemployed youth. Third, do a good job in transferring rural labour force. An employment policy system adapting to the context of rural revitalisation was established, guiding rural labour force to move out for employment in an orderly manner, to obtain employment in the nearest place, and to return home to start up their businesses. We improved the long-term poverty alleviation mechanism by means of employment, and solved the problem of relative poverty by improving the level of organised services and consolidating four employment channels, such as employment provided by poverty alleviation workshops, entrepreneurship-driven employment, organised migration and public welfare jobs.

3.2 Safeguards

(1) Ensure the prioritised implementation of employment responsibilities. First, strengthen the organisation and leadership on employment. To consolidate the joint efforts and team work on employment, we gave full play to the role of the Employment Leadership Group of the State Council in facilitating all departments to perform their duties and responsibilities, and gave full play to the initiatives of various non-government organisations. We established and improved a multi-ministrial coordination mechanism for the implementation of pro-employment policies, clarified the objectives, tasks and responsibilities, and assigned the responsibilities for the organisations involved at each level. Taking the whole country into account, we established a coordinated response mechanism for major risks across administration levels, departments and regions. Second, strengthen the performance assessment on employment. The accomplishment of employment targets and the implementation of employment plan and activities were integrated into the high-quality development and comprehensive performance assessment mechanism as well as the performance appraisal system for the government at all levels. Units and individuals that made remarkable achievements in employment and entrepreneurship work were motivated. In contrast, those who failed to perform their duties, or even worse, having resulted in adverse social effects, should be criticised or punished. Third, put more funds in employment. We continued to increase the funds input in employment subsidy at all levels, and to make good use of unemployment insurance funds and special subsidy funds, ensuring the funds input for the implementation of employment policies and the funds for personnel engaged in this work. We strengthened the supervision on funds management, and optimised the expenditure structure, so as to improve the efficiency of funds use.

(2) Vigorously strengthen employment services, protect rights and interests and assist the people in hardship. First, build up a comprehensive public employment service system. In order to provide workers and enterprises with free public employment services such as policy advice, job recommendation and employment guidance, we improved the network of service agencies covering urban and rural areas as well as the unified national employment and unemployment registration system, and promoted the equalisation and standardisation on service delivery. We promoted intelligent services by accelerating the application of big data and cloud service technology, establishing a unified national public employment and entrepreneurship service information platform, and improving the job information collection and distribution system. The service process was simplified and optimised in hope of delivering comprehensive and convenient service at "one door, one counter, one network and one time". Second, accelerate the development of human resources services. Focusing on cultivating key backbone enterprises, we implemented the action plan for the development of human resources services. We strengthened the overall planning and policy support for the human resources service industrial park, and promoted the specialised and complementary development pattern between the public and private employment service delivery agencies. Third, strengthen the protection of workers' rights and interests. We improved the labour relation coordination mechanism, comprehensively implemented the labour contract system, improved the tripartite mechanism for labour relation coordination, and accelerated the development of labour disputes mediation and arbitration system. We strengthened the supervision of the human resources market, cracked down on illegal acts that infringed workers' rights and interests, such as employment discrimination and illegal job recommendation, so as to create a fair and good employment environment. Fourth, make the employment bottom line always available for the people in difficulties. We improved the employment assistance system and gave priority support and special assistance to people in difficulties. For those having difficulties in obtaining employment through the market channels, the government provided them with public welfare jobs to dynamically ensure no zero-employment families existed. Unemployment insurance, temporary living allowances, social assistance and other security policies were implemented for eligible persons.

Chapter 3
Proactive Employment Policy

1. Initiation of the Proactive Employment Policy

1.1 Background of the Proactive Employment Policy

From1949 when the People's Republic of China was founded to early 1990s, China had formulated and implemented some key policies and targeted measures to solve the unemployment problem in different periods, but no systematic and sustained employment policy had been formed. Since 1990s, Chinese government has made great efforts to solve the re-employment problem for laid-off workers, exploring the methods to establish a market-oriented employment mechanism. Through continuous and accumulated efforts, innovation and improvement from the practices, a proactive employment policy system with Chinese characteristics has been gradually formed.

(1) In the process of solving the problem of laid-off workers and unemployment, the re-employment work was put on the agenda. In the late 1990s, with the further deepening of the reform of state-owned enterprises (SOEs), which took main responsibility in job placement in the era of planned economy, the redundancy within SOEs became a more and more obvious problem. Additionally, under the shock of the Asian financial crisis and the impact of global economic restructuring, SOEs experienced large-scale business losses, and many workers in SOEs were laid off or unemployed. In June 1998, the Central Committee of CPC and the State Council made a timely decision to take the assurance of the basic living standards for the laid-off workers in

SOEs as the primary task. The government also positively promoted the interlinking of three protection floors, i.e., basic living allowance for laid-off workers, unemployment benefit, and minimum subsistence allowance for urban residents. SOEs were required to establish re-employment service centres to keep the laid-offs in the centres with basic living allowance available until they got re-employed. Being a transitional measure in the context of incomplete labour market system and deficient social security system, it did guarantee the basic living of the laid-off workers. However, in the second half of 2001, the number of unemployed workers increased sharply due to a large number of laid-off workers leaving the re-employment service centres. Various problems accumulated in a long time emerged one after another. Re-employment of the laid-offs turned to be an urgent and outstanding problem. Aiming at this, the central government of China decided that, on the basis of effectively guaranteeing the basic livelihood of the laid-off workers, efforts must be made to promote their re-employment, and regard this as an important measure related to the overall situation of reform, development and stability as well as the internal requirement of improving social insurance system.

(2) In the face of various contradictions in one period, the most important one should be solved first. With the changing of demographic structure and the adjustment of rural policies in China, the number of newly arising workforce in cities and towns increased by nearly 10 million each year, reaching the peak during the 10th Five-year Plan period. In addition to the laid-off and unemployed workers accumulated in the past years, every year about 22 million to 23 million urban workers needed employment in urban areas. However, only 7 million to 8 million new jobs could be created each year. The annual gap between labour supply and demand was 14 million to 15 million. Moreover, 150 million rural labour surpluses urgently needed to be transferred to new jobs. In short, a complex

Make every effort to do a good job in re-employment for the laid-off and unemployed people. (Photo taken by Xinhua News Agency reporter Peng Wang.)

situation emerged, when the re-employment of laid-off workers, youth employment and rural labour transfer intertwined at the same time. In this situation, the Central Committee of CPC and the State Council made it clear that the employment and re-employment problem must be solved by taking into consideration the long-term overall situation and making overall plans. More importantly, the focus of work should be clarified as to solve the main contradiction in some time by concentrating limited financial and human resources. For this purpose, it further clarified that during this period, the focus was to address the re-employment problem for the laid-off and unemployed workers.

(3) In the reform of promoting market employment, employment policy should take the lead. In 1998, the Chinese government issued *the Notice on Practically Doing a Good Job on Basic Living Security and Re-employment for the Laid-off Workers in State-owned Enterprises*. It set out the goal of trying to initially establish a social security system and an employment mechanism adapted to the requirements of socialist market economy in about five years. At the same time, it also emphasised the content of market employment reform, which was to establish and improve the market employment mechanism and implement the national employment guideline, namely, under the guidance of national policies, employment chosen by workers independently, regulated by the market and promoted by the government. In the process of nurturing and regulating the market and promoting employment, the government needed to establish and implement a complete policy system and service-delivery system, including formulating policies to promote employment and control unemployment, establishing public employment service system, and providing special assistance to the disadvantaged groups, and at the same time, gradually developing a better social security system.

1.2 Basis for Formulating the Proactive Employment Policy

(1) Favourable conditions were created by the sound economic development situation in China. After 2002, China's economy entered a high-speed growth stage. The rapid economic development was conducive to the adjustment and improvement of industrial structure, industrial layout and economic organisational form. It provided a broad space for solving the employment problem in China, and also created material conditions to support employment from fiscal, taxation and financial aspects.

(2) Solid foundation was laid with the exploration and practices of all regions and relevant departments. In the previous practices of implementing "re-employment project" and basic living allowance for the laid-off workers from SOEs, the active exploration in promoting re-employment conducted by all regions and relevant departments in accordance with the unified deployment and requirements of the central government, formed a practical foundation. For example, income tax deductions and exemptions boosted the development of service sector and increased employment. Favourable tax and micro credit encouraged the laid-off and unemployed workers to be self-employed and start up their own businesses. Wage subsidies to the people with employment difficulties helped them to be re-employed. At the same time, relavent experience was also extracted from the successful practices in strengthening employment services and re-employment training.

(3) Important references were provided by the useful experience of the developed countries. Specific studies made by the Ministry of Labour and Social Security revealed that many countries took employment promotion as an important part of their policy programmes. They gave much attention to policy instruments such as taxation, financing, credit, trade and human capital investment on promoting employment, mitigating unemployment pressure and ironing out the fluctuation of unemployment rate in the economic cycle. These international practices were worth learning, such as encouraging and supporting the development of small- and medium-sized enterprises (SMEs), supporting the unemployed to start up their own businesses, providing subsidies to job seekers as well as post allowance, and encouraging enterprises to recruit people with difficulty in finding jobs. On the basis of the national conditions in China, the useful experience learnt from other countries had broadened the relevant policy-makers, minds in formulating the proactive employment policy.

1.3 Main Direction of Formulating the Proactive Employment Policy

(1) Promote the positive interaction between economic development and employment expansion, and expand employment channels. China actively explored economic development mode conducive to employment expansion, and promoted the increase of total employment. By optimising the industrial structure, we developed new employment channels by accelerating the development of service industry, individual businesses in non-public economy and small and SMEs. First, great efforts were made to develop tertiary industry and community services. Second, in order to absorb more laid-off and unemployed people, China encouraged the development of multi-ownership economy so as to actively develop market-demanding labour-intensive enterprises and SMEs. Third, labour migration cooperation and labour migration services were facilitated between labour exporting and receiving areas. Fourth, large-and medium-sized SOEs were supported to separate their subsidiary businesses from the main business and reform the ownership of subsidiary businesses, so that the laid-off workers could be allocated to the subsidiary business. Fifth, more laid-off and unemployed workers were encouraged to start up their own businesses or to be flexibly employed.

(2) Encourage workers to find jobs or start up businesses on their own. To solve the problem for the laid-off and unemployed workers, a better way was to carry out more active, quicker and better employment promotion, instead of simply and passively relying on unemployment benefit and living allowance. One of the important elements was to encourage and support workers to start up their own businesses and promote employment through entrepreneurship. The policies should be improved by supporting entrepreneurship and self-employment, including solving financing problems through micro-secured loans and financial discount, reducing operation burden through tax reduction and exemption, enhancing the capacity of entrepreneurs by providing subsidised entrepreneurship training, and supporting them in the business premises.

(3) Strengthen vocational training and employment services. First, training was regarded as an important basis and effective means to promote employment and re-employment. The vocational training system for all workers was established and improved to organise multi-level and multi-form skills training. Order-based training and designation-based training were conducted to increase the practicality and effectiveness of training. Entrepreneurship services, including entrepreneurship training, business start-up guidance, business idea assessment and follow-up services, were provided to support entrepreneurs. Second, the employment services system was established and improved covering both rural and urban areas. The "one stop" service and the "all-in-one" service were provided to job seekers and employers with services such as providing employment information, vocational guidance, job recommendation, training programmes, entrepreneurship guidance and agency services on human resources and social security affairs, etc. Efforts were made in accelerating the construction of the employment services information system and the street community service system. The re-employment training and employment services for workers were free of charge and subsidised by the government.

2. Development Phase of the Proactive Employment Policy

There are four phases for the development of China's proactive employment policy as of its initiation in 2001 (Table 3.1).

2.1 Phase I: Responding to Economic Adjustment, Creating and Expanding Proactive Employment Policy (2002-2007)

At the end of the 20th century, Asian financial crisis broke out, which had a severe impact on China's economy. At the same time, China's employment was facing a severe situation as the reform moved to a critical stage. The Central Committee of CPC and the State Council, basing on a careful review of the previous experience in implementing the "re-employment project" and the "two guarantees programme", made significant decisions and plans to vigorously promote employment and re-employment. The National Conference on Re-employment was held in September 2002. An important policy was issued in the same month to further improve the re-employment for the laid-off and unemployed workers. Its basic guiding ideology included: promoting employment and creating more jobs by economic development, improving market mechanism and persisting in the basic role of market orientation, and strengthening government responsibility and giving full and effective play to the role of the government in promoting employment and re-employment. The document consisted of 5 pillar policies: ① macroeconomic policies to improve the ability of economic growth in stimulating employment; ② supporting policies to promote the re-employment of the laid-off and unemployed workers; ③ labour market policies to promote a better matching of market supply and demand through strengthening employment services and vocational training; ④ unemployment control policies to regulate the streamline of enterprises, guiding large enterprises in resettling redundant employees, and reducing the unemployment pressure on society; and ⑤ social security policies to ensure the basic livelihood of the laid-off and unemployed workers, especially the difficult groups. In order to promote the implementation of the policies, the Ministry of Labour and Social Security and other 11 ministries and organisations jointly formulated and issued 8 inter-linked supporting and operational documents. At the same time, at the national and local level, the inter-department joint conference system for employment, the target responsibility

Table 3.1 Formulation and Development of China's Proactive Employment Policy

Phase / Contents	Formulation and expansion phase (2002-2007)	Crisis response phase (2008-2011)	Upgrading and innovation phase (2012-2017)	Incorporate into macro-control phase (2018 to present)
Strategic tasks	Taking the promotion of re-employment and expanding urban and rural employment as an important objective	Giving high priority to stabilising and expanding employment and implementing the strategy of expanding employment	Making the promotion of employment and entrepreneurship as a priority goal of socioeconomic development, the stability and expansion of employment as the minimum limit of the interval regulation; implementing pro-employment strategy; striving to achieve better quality employment	Placing pro-employment policies at the macro-policy level and making them fully operational; and creating better quality jobs and achieving fuller employment
Objectives	Responding to the structural adjustment, solving the problem of re-employment and starting to coordinate employment in urban and rural areas	Responding to natural disasters and international financial crisis; stabilising and expanding employment	Responding to the transformation and upgrading of industrial structure; combining entrepreneurship with employment; promoting entrepreneurship and innovation-driven employment	Coping with the downward pressure of economic development, the changing factors at home and abroad, and the impact of trade conflict and promoting steady growth by stabilising employment

Continued

Phase / Contents	Formulation and expansion phase (2002-2007)	Crisis response phase (2008-2011)	Upgrading and innovation phase (2012-2017)	Incorporate into macro-control phase (2018 to present)
Target groups and contents	Focusing on re-employment of the laid-off and unemployed workers in SOEs, transferring employment of the surplus rural labour force and employment of the new members of the urban labour force	Starting to assist enterprises to stabilise their posts with the focus of stabilising the employment of enterprise workers; strengthening the job-creation for college graduates, re-employment of the unemployed, employment of rural migrant workers, and placement of veterans	Encouraging and supporting entrepreneurship-driven employment in all areas; promoting employment of the key groups in a well-coordinated way; and providing more employment assistance to those in difficulty	Expanding assistance to enterprises so as to stabilise their posts and maintain stable employment; encouraging and supporting entrepreneurship and new forms of flexible employment; organising large-scale training programmes for corporate workers, key groups and poor workers; providing assistance to help the unemployed and disadvantaged groups to be employed
Landmark policies	*Notice on Furthering the Re-employment for the Laid-off and Unemployed Persons* *Notice on Further Strengthening Employment and Re-employment* (No. 36, 2005, the State Council) *Law of the People's Republic of China on Promotion of Employment* (No. 70, Order of the President of the People's Republic of China, 2007)	*Notice on Doing Well in Employment under the Current Economic Situation* (No. 4, 2009, the State Council) *The Outline of the 12th Five-year Plan for National Economic and Social Development*	*Notice on Distributing Employment Promotion Plan* (2011-2015) (No. 6, 2012, the State Council) *Opinions on Doing Well in Employment and Business Start-up under the New Situation* (No. 23, 2015, the State Council) *Opinions on Furthering the Employment and Business Start-up in the Current and Future Period* (No. 28, 2017, the State Council)	*Some Opinions on Doing Well in Promoting Employment at Present and for Some Time to Come* (No. 39, 2018, the State Council) *Notice on Distributing the Action Plan for Vocational Skills Upgrading (2019-2021)* (No. 24, 2019, the General Office of the State Council)

system in employment, and the supervision and inspection mechanism on employment issues were established and came into effect. The employment service delivery system was established, improved and extended to the street community.

By the end of 2005, after three years of implementation of the above-mentioned policies, most problems relating to the laid-off workers in SOEs had been solved, but new problems emerged in the new employment situation, such as the stability of the re-employed, the laid-off workers from collective enterprises, the increasingly prominent employment problem of the rural migrant workers and the employment of young people. In November 2005, the State Council continued, expanded, adjusted and enriched the above policies, which enhanced the relevance and effectiveness of the policies. It is clarified in the revised policies that focusing on solving the re-employment problems for the laid-off and unemployed workers resulted from the transitional system, the government would strive to do a good job in the employment of the new members of the urban labour forces as well as the transfer employment of the surplus rural labour forces, to improve step by step the coordination of the employment in urban and rural areas and to improve the labourers' competence, exploring the establishment of a long-term employment promotion mechanism under the Chinese socialist market economy.

In August 2007, adopted at the 29th Meeting of the Standing Committee of the 10th National People's Congress, *Law of the People's Republic of China on Promotion of Employment* (hereinafter referred to as *Employment Promotion Law*) was promulgated and went into effect in 2008. *Employment Promotion Law* established 5 employment systems: ① employment responsibility system shared by the government, ② public employment service and employment aid system, ③ human resources market management system, ④ vocational skills development system, and ⑤ unemployment insurance and prevention system. At the same time, it determined 10 employment promotion policies as follows: ① industrial policy to promote employment, ② fiscal policy to promote employment, ③ taxation policy to promote employment, ④ financial policy to promote employment, ⑤ urban and rural overall employment promotion policy, ⑥ regional overall employment promotion policy, ⑦ overall employment promotion policy for specific groups, ⑧ labour and social insurance policy to promote flexible employment, ⑨ employment aid policy, and ⑩ unemployment insurance policy to promote employment. *Employment Promotion Law* took employment expansion as an important goal of social and economic development, clarified the priority of employment in social and economic development, defined the important responsibilities of the government in promoting employment, and legalised the effective proactive employment policy and made it work in the long term.

2.2 Phase II: Responding to Crisis, and Developing the More Proactive Employment Policy (2008-2011)

In 2008, China experienced the Wenchuan severe earthquake. Meanwhile, as the international financial crisis spread, China's economy was also severely impacted, and employment faced severe challenges. The number of new jobs in urban areas declined sharply. The closure and production suspension of enterprises led to severe job losses. Millions of rural migrant workers lost their jobs and returned to their hometown, and millions of college students faced difficulties in finding jobs after graduation. In the face of the crisis, while maintaining economic growth, the central government made a decisive decision to implement the more proactive employment policy. It mainly included: ① promoting employment through economic development, ② helping enterprises to stabilise employment, ③ starting up business to create jobs, ④ implementing special vocational training programmes, ⑤ launching a series of public employment service activities, and ⑥ taking special measures to promote employment for key groups such as college graduates, rural migrant workers and people with employment difficulties. At the same time, the central government further increased its financial input in employment. In this period, the measures, such as the 4 trillion *yuan* investment to ensure growth and promote employment, the "five deferring, four reducing and three subsidies" ① for enterprises in difficulty to stabilise employment, and promoting entrepreneurship to create jobs, played a crucial role in maintaining employment stability and eliminating the adverse impact of the emergency events on employment.

In 2011, *the Outline of the 12th Five-year Plan for National Economic and Social Development* made important arrangements for the implementation of giving high priority to employment strategy and the proactive employment policy. It incorporated a series of important measures that developed in dealing with the major challenges and crisis into the national policy and thus formed the more proactive employment policy system.

① It allowed enterprises in difficulty to defer their contribution to the five social insurance programmes, including basic old-age insurance, unemployment insurance, basic medical insurance, work injury insurance and maternity insurance within a certain period of time. The four social insurance contribution rates for basic medical insurance, unemployment insurance, work injury insurance and maternity insurance for urban workers were reduced at different stages. The unemployment insurance fund was used to pay social insurance subsidies or post subsidies to enterprises in difficulty, using Special Fund for Employment to support enterprises in difficulty to carry out on-the-job training for employees.

2.3 Phase III: Responding to Transformation, and Upgrading and Innovating the Proactive Employment Policy (2012-2017)

Notice on Distributing Employment Promotion Plan (2011-2015) issued by the State Council was an important basis for the government to fulfil its duty on employment promotion. *Employment Promotion Plan (2011-2015)* regarded employment promotion as the priority goal of economic and social development by taking the economic and social development during the 12th Five-year Plan period as the main line and closely combining it with the needs of ensuring and improving people's well-being. It requested that the more proactive employment policy and entrepreneurship-encouraging policies should be implemented to continuously develop more employment channels, so that the process of economic restructuring and accelerating the transformation of economic development mode could become a process of constantly improving the ability to boost employment. It also requested that attention should be paid to improve the quality of employment while expanding the scale of employment. In July 2012, the State Council held a national commendation conference on employment and entrepreneurship. It stressed that promoting employment was the top priority in ensuring and improving people's well-being. It was necessary to further enhance the understanding of the extreme importance of employment and put employment promotion and entrepreneurship in the priority position of various work. In November, the report of the 18th National Congress of the CPC clearly proposed to promote the realisation of higher quality employment. In order to promote entrepreneurship-driven employment and to enhance employment stability, the State Council successively issued a series of policies and measures to support the development of SMEs, to support the employment and entrepreneurship of young groups, in particular college graduates and disadvantaged groups, to improve the public employment and entrepreneurship service system in urban and rural areas; to build a lifelong vocational training system for workers; and to enhance the function of unemployment insurance system in both unemployment prevention and employment promotion.

As China's economic development entered the new normal, employment was facing new challenges. Efforts are needed to nurture mass entrepreneurship and innovation engines, to implement the more proactive employment policy, and to combine entrepreneurship with employment to promote employment through entrepreneurship and innovation, and to create new momentum for socioeconomic development. In April 2015, the State Council issued guidance on further improving employment and entrepreneurship under new circumstances. The first was to continue to implement the pro-employment strategy and the proactive employment policy with a wider range of coverage. The second was to actively promote entrepreneurship-driven employment policy with more specific measures. The third was to promote the employment of key groups as a whole, with further expanded and flexible supporting policies available in promoting the employment of college graduates, helping the people with difficulties or the disabled and veterans to be employed, and transferring rural labour force. The fourth was to strengthen employment services, business start-up services and vocational training and business start-up training, with more innovative measures and enriched contents. The fifth was to enhance organisational leadership and funds input, making the requirements clearer and guarantee measures more effective. In 2016, the State Council issued documents successively to require the resettlement of the laid-off workers in the process of resolving excess manufacturing capacity in the steel and coal industries. In April 2017, the State Council issued guiding opinions on doing well in employment and business start-up at present and for some time to come, with main ideas as follows. First, adhere to the implementation of pro-employment strategy. Second, support the development of new employment forms.

Hold technical competitions to encourage college students to innovate and start up their own businesses. (Photo taken by Xinhua News Agency reporter Shiyao Yang.)

Third, promote entrepreneurship-driven employment. Fourth, focus on employment and entrepreneurship of key social groups. Fifth, strengthen education and training as well as employment and entrepreneurship services.

Compared with the previous phase, the proactive employment policy at this phase had a wider range of target groups, which covered all types of urban and rural workers, i.e. the beneficiary coverage of the policy was expanded. At the same time, the State Council also issued a number of documents to promote mass entrepreneurship and innovation, which formed a new round of policy integration and innovation with distinctive features of combining encouraging entrepreneurship and promoting employment. The function of the policies was shifted from increasing the employment for all kinds of workers to a combination of employment promotion and entrepreneurship encouragement. These polices were featured by more positive orientation, more detailed measures, stronger operability, more valuable policy contents and even better implementation effect.

2.4 Phase IV: Responding to the Changing Economic Situation at Home and Abroad and the Impact of Various Complex Factors, and Incorporating Proactive Employment Policy into the National Macro-policy (from 2018 to Date)

As socialism with Chinese characteristics entered a new era, the major social contradictions in China have changed. In the field of employment, it appeared to be the contradiction between the growing demand for fuller and higher quality employment and the unbalanced and inadequate employment development pattern. At the same time, under the influence of new unstable and uncertain factors, such as the increasing economic downward pressure, the heavy task of economic transformation, uncertain domestic and foreign economic variables, and Sino-US trade friction, structural unemployment, cyclical unemployment and frictional unemployment started to co-exist and intertwine with each other, even showing a tendency of getting worse. In July 2018, the central government proposed to ensure stability on six fronts (i.e. employment, the financial sector, foreign trade, foreign investment, domestic investment and expectations). It took ensuring the stability of employment as top priority of all to achieve steady growth. In December, the State Council issued a document titled *Some Opinions on Doing Well in Promoting Employment at Present and for Some Time to Come*. It put forward clear requirements on how to comprehensively implement the decision and arrangements made by the central government so as to stabilise employment. It consisted of fifteen measures covering five aspects. The five aspects included supporting the stable development of enterprises, encouraging and supporting employment and business start-ups, actively conducting training programmes, timely providing assistance to the laid-off and unemployed persons, and fulfilling the responsibilities of all stakeholders involved.

In March 2019, report on the work of the government delivered by Premier Li Keqing at the 13th National People's Congress clearly proposed that the pro-employment policies should be fully implemented. For the first time, the pro-employment policies were put at the macro-policy level in order to raise the awareness of all departments and stakeholders to the policy orientation in supporting employment. It was an important new decision on employment and macro-control for the central government to develop giving high priority to employment from strategy to policies and to macro-policy level. In May 2019, the State Council's Leading Group on Employment was set up to replace the Inter-ministerial Joint Committee that had been in place since 2003. The committee was headed by a vice premier of the State Council in order to provide organisational guarantee for employment promotion at high level. In the same month, the General Office of the State Council published *Vocational Skills Upgrading Action Plan (2019-2021)*, which promoted vocational skills training on a large scale as a national initiative. The plan explicitly stated that more than 50 million people should be trained with various types of subsidised vocational skills over three years, so as to promote stable employment and to actively prevent unemployment. These important arrangements were made for putting employment in a strategic context and raising it up to the macro-control level. It was a positive response to the changing factors at home and abroad and to the impact of Sino-US trade frictions. It was also an important measure to ensure and improve people's well-being and to promote high-quality economic development.

3. Key Contents of the Proactive Employment Policy

Since 2002, the proactive employment policy with Chinese characteristics has officially stepped onto the historical stage of employment. With the development and changes of China's employment and the need of regular work, the proactive employment policy has been constantly adjusted and improved in the process of solving the outstanding problems at different stages. A relatively comprehensive employment policy system has been gradually formed which covers a wide range of areas, offers strong support and consists of rich project contents (Table 3.2).

Table 3.2 Framework for the Proactive Employment Policy System

Policy highlights	Policy contents
1. Economic policies conducive to employment growth	(1) Macroeconomic policies to promote employment growth (2) Developing the service sector to expand employment (3) Developing non-public economy (4) Promoting cross-regional collaboration of sending and receiving migrant workers
2. Policies to encourage workers to start up their own businesses and to have flexible employment	(1) Taxation reduction and exemption policies (2) Administrative fee reduction policy (3) Micro-secured loans policy (4) Premise arrangement policy (5) Encouraging flexible employment
3. Policies to encourage enterprises to absorb workers and create jobs	(1) Tax incentives policy (2) Social insurance subsidies policy (3) Micro-secured loans policy
4. The assistance policy for people with employment difficulties	(1) Social insurance subsidies and post subsidies to public welfare job (2) Social insurance subsidies to enterprises (3) Social insurance subsidies to flexible employment
5. Policies to support the large- and medium-sized SOEs to separate main business from the subsidiary business and reform the ownership of subsidiary business	(1) Taxation reduction and exemption policies (2) Decreasing registered capital
6. Policies to strengthen public employment services delivery	(1) Consultation on employment policies and regulations (2) Publishing information on supply and demand of jobs, guiding lines for wages of different posts in the market, and vocational training (3) Vocational guidance and job recommendation (4) Employment aid to people having difficulty in finding jobs (5) Registration of employment and unemployment, etc (6) Other public services on employment

Continued

Policy highlights	Policy contents
7. Policies to reinforce vocational skills training	(1) Providing the unemployed persons and the entitled rural migrant workers with vocational training subsidies to attend vocational training (2) Providing people having difficulty in obtaining employment and the rural labourers seeking employment in cities with a one-time subsidy if they obtain the vocational certificate at the first vocational skill appraisal (only required in specific types of work)
8. Policies to increase funds input on employment	(1) Special employment funds arranged by people's governments at county level and above (2) 7 provinces and cities in East China carrying out pilot projects to appropriately expand the scope of unemployment insurance fund expenditure (3) The central government giving subsidies to local governments through special transfer payments
9. Policies for unemployment control and governance	(1) Establishing the early warning mechanism of unemployment, improving unemployment monitoring system, and taking adjustment and control measures (2) Steadily pushing forward the restructuring, closing down and bankruptcy of SOEs (3) Regulating the staff reduction behaviour of enterprises (4) Guiding the owners and managers of enterprises to raise their awareness of social responsibility
10. The interactive policy between social security and employment promotion	(1) Determining the reasonable unemployment benefits and minimum living allowances standard for urban residents (2) Promoting the formation of incentive and restraint mechanism of employment promotion (3) Expanding the coverage of social insurance

3.1 Basic Content of the Proactive Employment Policy

(1) Economic policies conducive to employment growth are made. Expanding employment through economic development is the fundamental solution to employment problem. The government continued to solve the problem of employment in the course of development and strove to achieve a positive interaction between promoting economic growth and expanding employment. For this purpose, it is stipulated in the policy: ① we should coordinate macroeconomic policies, deepen economic system reform, intensify structural adjustment, maintain necessary growth rate of national economy, and expand employment. We should strengthen the coordination of industrial, fiscal, financial and other policies with employment policies. When formulating economic and social policies involving the overall national situation and determining the construction of major projects, we should consider employment expansion as an important factor, and constantly create new employment growth points while focusing on improving competitiveness and creating new economic growth points. ② We should optimise the industrial structure. In terms of industrial types, we should pay attention to the development of labour-intensive industries, vigorously develop the tertiary industry, continue to expand the traditional service industry, and actively develop the emerging service industry, especially the community service industry. ③ We should focus on economic form and enterprise type. In terms of economic type, we should pay attention to the development of non-public ownership economy; in terms of enterprise scale, we should pay attention to supporting SMEs. We should gradually clear up the restrictions and barriers on the development of non-public economy, increase the protection of private enterprises and personal property, strengthen the service on enterprise operation and credit, increase fiscal, taxation and financial supports, and improve the development environment for non-public economy. ④ We should expand international and domestic labour market. Facing the international and domestic markets, we should encourage cross-regional labour cooperation and organise transfer employment in domestic market, and for international market, we should implement "going out" strategy and strive to expand international labour market.

(2) Policies are made to encourage labourers to start up their own businesses and to have flexible employment. Entrepreneurship is an important form for labourers to obtain market employment by starting their own production or service projects, starting up their businesses or engaging in self-employment. Through entrepreneurship, labourers can obtain employment themselves and also make more job opportunities for other people at the same time. In order to encourage and support more labourers to be self-employed, start up their own businesses and get flexible employment. The policies stipulate that: ① tax deductions and exemption shall be granted. For the laid-off and unemployed persons engaging in individual business-related projects, sales tax, urban maintenance and construction tax, educational surtax and individual income tax shall be deducted in sequence in fixed amount within 3 years. ② Administrative fee reduction and exemption shall be granted. For the registered unemployed engaging in individual business, administrative fees such as management, registration and license fees should be exempted within 3 years. ③ Micro-secured loans shall be provided. Eligible candidates, who are self-employed, start up their own businesses or partnership business and participate in voluntarily organised employment, with guarantee provided by credit guarantee agencies, can apply for micro-secured loans for the insufficient amount of their own fund. For the laid-off and unemployed persons who are engaged in partnership business or organised for employment, the amount of loans can be appropriately increased according to the number of such persons. For those engaging in low-profit projects, the central financial department should discount interest in full amount according to actual facts. ④ Premise arrangement shall be made. Governments at all levels and their departments concerned, such as land, planning and urban management departments, should make overall arrangements for the production and business sites needed. Incubators can be established within the scope of urban construction land as determined in the general plan for land use, or in the originally approved economic and technological development zones, industrial parks, high-tech parks, university science parks. Effective training and guidance services and policy support for a certain period should be available to the small enterprises entering the incubators. ⑤ Business start-up training and guidance service shall be provided. In light of the changing labour market and industrial structure, great efforts should be made to enhance vocational education and re-employment training. Public employment service system should be established and improved. Free re-employment training and free job recommendation should be organised. Social forces, especially private training institutes with their own characteristics, should be encouraged and supported to conduct vocational skills training. Entrepreneurial training and services, such as business start-up guidance, business idea development, micro-secured loans and follow-up services, should be available for the urban and rural workers, who are ready to start up their own businesses. ⑥ Flexible employment shall be encouraged. Flexible and diverse employment patterns such as part-time jobs, non-fixed employing units employment as well as temporary, seasonal and flexible work should be encouraged and guided to adapt to the changes in employment needs of enterprises and employment patterns of workers. Policies on labour relations, wage payment and social insurance should also be improved so as to be compatible with flexible employment.

(3) Policies are made to encourage enterprises to absorb employment. The employment of enterprises is an important channel to solve the employment problem. Therefore, it is necessary to implement the following policies for qualified enterprises to absorb employment. ① Tax incentives policy. Sales tax, urban maintenance and construction tax, educational surtax and enterprise income tax shall be deducted in fixed amount within 3 years for business and trade enterprises, service-oriented enterprises (except those industries restricted by the State), labour service-oriented processing enterprises and small processing enterprises in streets and communities if they have newly recruited laid-off workers and unemployed persons, and have signed labour contracts with them for more than one year and paid social insurance contribution. ② Social insurance subsidies. All kinds of enterprises that employ people with difficulties in finding jobs and sign labour contracts with them for more than one year shall be given social insurance subsidies accordingly for some period. ③ Micro-secured loans. Eligible labour-intensive small enterprises shall be provided with a loan of no more than 2 million *yuan* if they recruit the hard-to-place workers to the required ratio.

(4) Assistance policies are provided to persons with employment difficulties. The following employment aid policies should be implemented for persons with employment difficulties. ① Social insurance subsidies and post subsidies to public welfare job. For the public welfare job created by local governments, priority should be given to those who meet the job requirements, and they should also be given subsidies for basic old-age insurance, basic medical insurance, unemployment insurance and appropriate post subsidies within the corresponding period. ② Social insurance subsidies to enterprises. If enterprises recruit persons with employment difficulties, sign labour contract and pay social insurance contribution, they should be given subsidies for basic old-age insurance, basic medical insurance and unemployment insurance within the corresponding period. ③ Social insurance subsidies to flexible employment. Persons with employment difficulties, who declare to be flexibly employed and pay social insurance contribution, should be given a certain amount of subsidies to the contribution. For persons with employment difficulties who are less than 5 years from the legal retirement age, the subsides to their social insurance contribution and post can be extended until they reach retirement age.

(5) Policies are made to support the large-and medium-sized SOEs to separate main business from the subsidiary business and reform the ownership of subsidiary business. In the process of structural adjustment, restructuring and ownership reform, and separation of main and subsidiary business, large-and medium-sized SOEs, if conditions permitting, are encouraged to make use of non-main business assets and idle assets to place redundant workers in enterprises. The potential of the enterprise should be fully used to resettle the redundant workers instead of directly pushing them to the society. In this case, the pressure of social employment can be released. The policies include: ① tax deductions and exemptions. In the separation and reforming subsidiary business ownership process, the economic entities (except for industries restricted by the State) established by large-and medium-sized SOEs for re-settling redundant workers should be exempted from corporate income tax within 3 years if they meet the conditions. ② Deduction of registered capital. The reformed enterprises are allowed to use state-owned net assets to pay the economic compensation to workers in case of terminating labour relations. As a result, the decreased book value of the state-owned assets shall be offset by the state-owned capital after approval according to the prescribed procedures.

(6) Policies are made to strengthen public employment services. In order to strengthen the employment service system, with public employment service being the main body, as well as to standardise the management of employment intermediary agencies and human resources market, the following requirements are proposed. ① Local governments at all levels should set up and improve public employment service system to undertake registration of employment and unemployment registration, and provide free public employment services such as consultation on employment policies and regulations, information about job supply and demand, guidelines on wages of different posts on the market and vocational training, as well as vocational guidance, job recommendation and employment aid. ② The funds for free public employment service provision should be incorporated into the government budget at the same level. ③ Efforts should be taken actively to promote the establishment of grass roots platforms in streets, communities, towns and villages, and basic administration services, deliver employment aid and conduct policy publicity activities should be carried out. ④ All kinds of job intermediaries which provide non-profit employment services should be encouraged and subsidised, and their service behaviours should be regulated according to law.

(7) Policies are made to reinforce vocational skills training. In order to enhance workers' initiative in participating in vocational training to improve their employability, the following policies are implemented. ① The unemployed persons and the eligible rural workers who have moved to cities for work should be subsidised for their participation in vocational training. ② The persons having difficulty in obtaining jobs and the rural migrant workers working in cities should be given a one-time subsidy when obtaining the vocational certificate through the first vocational skill appraisal (limited to specified types of work). ③ The departments of human resources and social security should identify a number of designated training institutes by bidding for all kinds of educational and training institutes to organise multi-level and multi-form skills training. ④ The mechanism of government purchasing training results should be established and improved. Subsidies shall be granted to vocational training according to the quality of training and the employment feedback after training. Guidance is available to training institutes on how to meet market and employment needs, as well as on how to improve the practicality and effectiveness of training.

(8) Policies on increasing funds input in employment are made. In order to ensure the implementation of the major policies and measures on employment and re-employment, the following provisions are made on the collection, use and management of funds. ① Governments at county level and above are requested to take into account the employment situation and employment objectives, and to allocate specific funds for employment to promote employment in the budget of the same level. It is mainly used for subsidies to job recommendation, vocational training, social insurance contribution, public welfare jobs, vocational skill appraisal, specific employment policy, small loan guarantee fund and subsidised interest to micro-secured loans, and for supporting public employment services. ② The central government should provide appropriate subsidies to local governments through special transfer payments and give priority support to the central and western part of China and old industrial bases. ③ While increasing financial input, according to the *Regulation on Unemployment Insurance*, unemployment insurance fund can be used to subsidise the workers who receive unemployment benefits to participate in vocational training and job recommendation.

(9) Do a good job in regulating and managing unemployment. Comprehensively use legal, economic and necessary administrative means to prevent unemployment at its source and to regulate unemployment. The policy stipulates: ① establish an unemployment alert system, on the basis of the goal of controlling unemployment rate in the national economic and social development plan and the actual situation of the each locality, gradually improve the unemployment monitoring system, determine a reasonable alert line for unemployment, formulate emergency plans, and take regulatory measures to deal with the possible unstable employment situation. For industries and enterprises directly affecting employment due to major changes in the domestic and international economic situation, as well as the difficult areas and industries with great unemployment pressure, guidance should be available for them so as to do a good job on unemployment control and to keep employment situation stable. ② Make good placement of the workers in SOEs that are re-organised, restructured and bankrupted and effectively protect workers' legal rights and interests. ③ Regulate enterprises' laying off activity. For enterprises with normal operation, the mass layoff plan shall be discussed by the workers' congress of the enterprise. In case of failing to pay economic compensation according to law and properly solving the debts owed by the enterprise to its employees, the enterprises should not lay off workers. If the one-time staff reduction of one enterprise exceeds a certain number or proportion, it should report to the local government in advance. (4) Guide business owners and managers to develop a sense of corporate social responsibility and strengthen the development of collective bargaining system. Through the development of tripartite consultation mechanism among government, enterprises (or employers) and workers (or employees), the interests of enterprises and workers should be well coordinated to increase the stability of workers' employment.

(10) Form an interactive policy between social security and employment promotion. In order to effectively link up the relationship between social security and employment promotion, further improve social security system, and establish the interactive mechanism, the policy stipulates: ① determine a reasonable unemployment benefit and urban residents' minimum living allowance level hierarchically and successively, so as to develop into a reasonably supporting system. ② Promote the development of incentive and restraint mechanism on employment promotion. The qualifications and procedures for claiming for unemployment benefits and minimum living allowances for urban residents should be strictly enforced. Qualifications for the said benefits shall be connected with the information of receiving job introduction, vocational training and participation in public welfare jobs, so as to gradually form the policy orientation for promoting employment. ③ Expand the coverage of social insurance, so that more urban and rural workers can participate in social insurance and are able to ensure the continuity and portability of social insurance even in migrating employment situation. Institutionally, it can be done just as the publicity says "no matter where you work, social insurance is portable."

3.2 Innovation and Development of Employment Policy in the New Era

Since the initiation of the proactive employment policy, along with the economic and social development and the deepening of employment reform, the policy has been continuously improved, interatively upgraded and continuously expanded. It becomes more and more valuable and has benefited more and more people, thus providing an important guarantee for the overall stability of employment. In particular, since the 18th CPC National Congress, the CPC Central Committee and the State Council have taken initiatives to adapt to and lead the new normal of economic development, and constantly promote the innovation and development of the proactive employment policy with Chinese characteristics.

(1) Stabilise and expand employment in the course of high-quality economic development. While adhering to market employment mechanism, the government should play its role, with the focus on promoting and stabilising employment, the following measures are proposed: ① to implement macro-control methods such as interval control, directional control and precise control, clearly put forward the stability and expansion of employment as the minimum limit of interval regulation and control, maintain the continuity and stability of macro-policies, promote the medium and high-speed economic growth, and enhance the ability of stimulating employment. ② To strengthen the connection between the economic policy and the employment policy, it clearly stipulates that a comprehensive evaluation of the impact on employment, employment environment and unemployment risk should be made in formulating major fiscal, taxation, financial, industrial and trade policies. ③ Keep on deepening structural adjustment, vigorously develop modern service sector, improve the diversified industrial system, support the development of labour-intensive industries, implement regional development strategies, and promote the synergy among industrial structure, regional structure and employment.

(2) Vigorously promote entrepreneurship-driven employment. The 18th National Congress of the CPC put encouraging entrepreneurship into the employment policy for the new era. It clearly requested for the combination of entrepreneurship and employment, creating a sound environment for mass entrepreneurship and innovation, and accelerating the cultivation of new growth drivers. A series of policies and measures have been formulated and implemented to promote entrepreneurship-driving employment, focusing on key groups, and strengthening education, training as well as employment and business start-up services.

(3) Widen employment channels for college graduates. The CPC Central Committee and the State Council have clearly put the employment of college graduates at the top of employment agenda, focusing on employment promotion, entrepreneurship driving and growing-up at the grass roots, and formulated and implemented specific policies and measures in many aspects, such as improving the policy system for promoting employment and entrepreneurship of college graduates, expanding diversified employment fields for college graduates, improving employment services and vocational guidance for the supply and demand of the employment market for college graduates, and improving the employment environment for college graduates.

(4) Make great efforts to promote poverty alleviation through employment. Poverty alleviation through employment has been included in the overall plan of employment and entrepreneurship. The important role of employment in targeted poverty alleviation should be brought into play, and various measures should be taken to promote the employment of poor workers and increase their income. In 2016, a pilot project was launched to coordinate labour services between the developed and poverty-stricken areas. It has worked out a set of replicable experience and working mechanisms such as in improving working mechanisms, strengthening docking and cooperation, promoting local employment, upgrading employment skills and increasing job security. From 2017 to 2018, policies and measures for poverty alleviation through employment were improved, and specific measures were put forward, such as mapping out basic information, promoting local and nearby employment, strengthening cooperation in labour services, strengthening skills training, and promoting stable employment. At the same time, an employment information platform for rural poverty-stricken families was established to centrally release information on jobs which supported the self-employment of poor labourers and organised out-going labour services. Poverty alleviation through labour services was strengthened by policy supports such as subsidies to job introduction, vocational training, social insurance contribution and transportation.

(5) Promote the resettlement of workers in enterprises reducing excess capacity in a smooth and orderly manner. A good job should be done in the process of reducing production capacity by minimising unemployment risk in structural adjustment, and creating a harmonious and stable social environment for reform and development. The main policy measures include encouraging the multi-channel redirection and resettlement of employees within enterprises, giving support policies to promote the employment and entrepreneurship of the shunted-off workers, implementing the entrepreneurship support policies for the shunted-off personnel who start up their own businesses, and giving priority to arrange public welfare jobs for people with employment difficulties.

(6) Vigorously strengthen vocational training. In order to meet the needs of economic transformation and upgrading, optimising the industrial structure as well as the employment and entrepreneurship of workers, we should accelerate the structural reform of human resources on the supply side, push forward lifelong vocational skills training system, and carry out large-scale training for in-service workers, corporate training, entrepreneurial training and job transfer training, strive to improve the pertinence and effectiveness of the training, and promote the continuous improvement of workers' capacity.

Implement the policy on overcapacity reduction issued by the Central Committee of CPC and the State Council, fastening the promotion of "closing, stopping, merging, transforming" overcapacity and making sure employee arrangement from overcapacity reduction in order and stable. (Photo taken by Xinhua News Agency reporter Yu Xu.)

(7) Establish an all-round public employment service system and promote the development of the human resources market. We should improve the public employment service system that covers both urban and rural areas, expand service supply, innovate operational mechanisms, so as to establish an all-round public employment service system. The main policy measures include clearly identifying the scope of universal public employment service, improving the public employment service function throughout the whole process, building up a public employment service system that is deliverable to the whole area, improving the convenient and efficient public employment service mode, and promoting employment growth with all-round public employment services. Vigorously promote the development of human resources service industry, and strive to improve the supply of human resources service. The main policy measures include realising the classified management of public services and commercial services, unifying and standardising the human resources market system, further expanding the pilot of human resources market open to foreign investors, actively promoting the development of human resources service industry, improving the government's policy on purchasing public human resources services, and steadily promoting the opening of human resources market to the outside world.

4. Achievements of Implementing the Proactive Employment Policy

The implementation of the proactive employment policy in China played an effective role in promoting employment and re-employment. It made great contribution to deepening system reform, facilitating economic development and maintaining social stability.

4.1 Solving the Re-employment Problems Properly and Successfully Easing the Remaining Problems Resulted from the State-owned Enterprises Reform

Through initiating and implementing the proactive employment policy, we have provided strong policy support for promoting re-employment, solved the problem of the laid-off and unemployed workers of SOEs, and successfully resolved the problem left over by the planned economic system for a generation. In the 5 years from 2003 to 2007, 25 million laid-off and unemployed persons from SOEs and urban collective enterprises were re-employed, and 7 million disadvantaged persons were assisted in re-employment. The registered urban unemployment rate fell from 4.3% in 2003 to 4% in 2007. At the same time, the number of employees in SOEs in China decreased from 71.31 million at the end of 1997 to 28.46 million at the end of 2007. A modern corporate system and a new employment system have also been established.

4.2 Improving the Employment Pattern, Promoting the Positive Interaction between Economic Development and Employment Expansion

The proactive employment policy was implemented. We accelerated the development of the service sector, no-public economy, such as individual business and SMEs by optimising the industrial structure, and actively explored ways of economic development conducive to employment expansion. Jobs continued to increase and the employment structure continued to improve. In 2003, urban employment rose from less than 8 million each year in the previous 5 years to more than 10 million in 2007 (Figure 3.1). The total number of employees reached 786.45 million in 2007 across the country, an increase of 32.85 million compared with 2002. The proportion of the unban employed population increased from 33.6% to 38.1%, and the proportion of the employed population in primary, secondary and tertiary industries changed from 50.0:21.4:28.6 to 40.8:26.8:32.4 respectively. During this period, individual entrepreneurship, private enterprise employment and flexible employment have also been greatly developed.

Figure 3.1 The Number of New Urban Employment (2003-2007)

(Unit: 10 thousand)

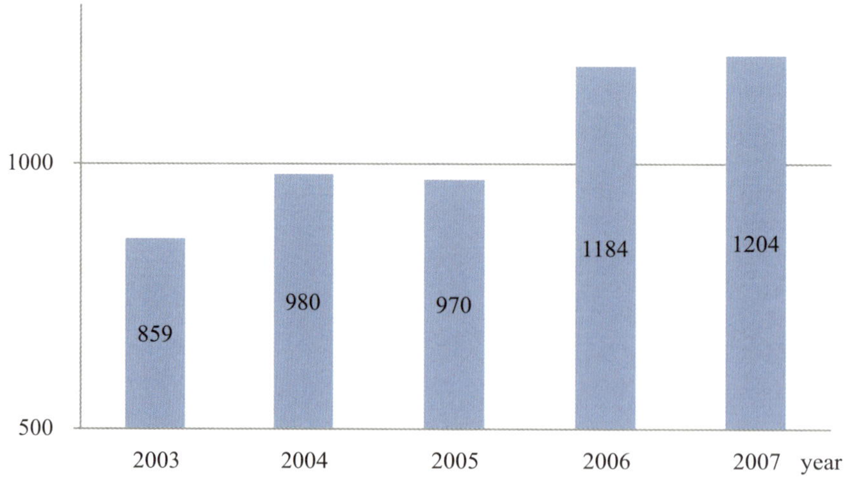

Source: *2003-2007 Statistical Bulletin*, the National Bureau of Statistics.

4.3 Establishing the Market-oriented Employment System and Facilitating the Employment System More Mature

The guideline of "employment chosen by workers independently, regulated by the market and promoted by the government" has been kept in the process of formulating and implementing the proactive employment policy. As an important part of the proactive employment policy, the encouragement of self-employment and self-entrepreneurship has given full play to the basic role of market mechanism in employment. At the same time, under the guidance of the proactive employment policy, the mechanisms of employment promoted by the government and regulated by the market have also been established and improved. Other mechanisms such as multi-departments joint meeting on employment, target responsibility on employment, as well as supervision and inspection on employment have been gradually established and played a positive role. Great progress has been made in public employment service system, either in terms of institutional development, or professional and socialised service delivery. Public employment service has been accessible at city, district (county), street (township) and community levels, preliminarily forming the four-level network.

4.4 Effectively Coping with the Severe Impact of the Financial Crisis and Maintaining the Basic Stability of Employment Situation

In 2008, in the face of unexpected international financial crisis, the State Council and relevant departments formulated and implemented a series of policies and measures to stabilise and expand employment, which constituted a new employment deal to cope with the financial crisis and led to the stabilisation and expansion of employment. The employment situation was relatively stable and the tide of unemployment was under control. In 2009, 11.02 million new urban jobs were created nationwide, representing 122 percent of the annual target of 9 million; 5.14 million laid-off workers were re-employed, representing 103 percent of the annual target of 5 million; and 1.64 million people having difficulties in finding jobs were employed, representing 164 percent of the annual target of 1 million (Figure 3.2). By the end of 2009, there were 9.21 million registered urban unemployed persons nationwide, and the registered urban unemployment rate stood at 4.3 percent, basically returning to the normal level. By 2010, 11.68 million new urban jobs were created nationwide, and arguably China was the first country in the world to get out of the unemployment trap.

Figure 3.2 The Situation of New Urban Jobs Created Nationwide, Re-employment of the Laid-off Workers and Employment of the People Having Difficulties in Finding Jobs in 2019

(Unit: 10 thousand)

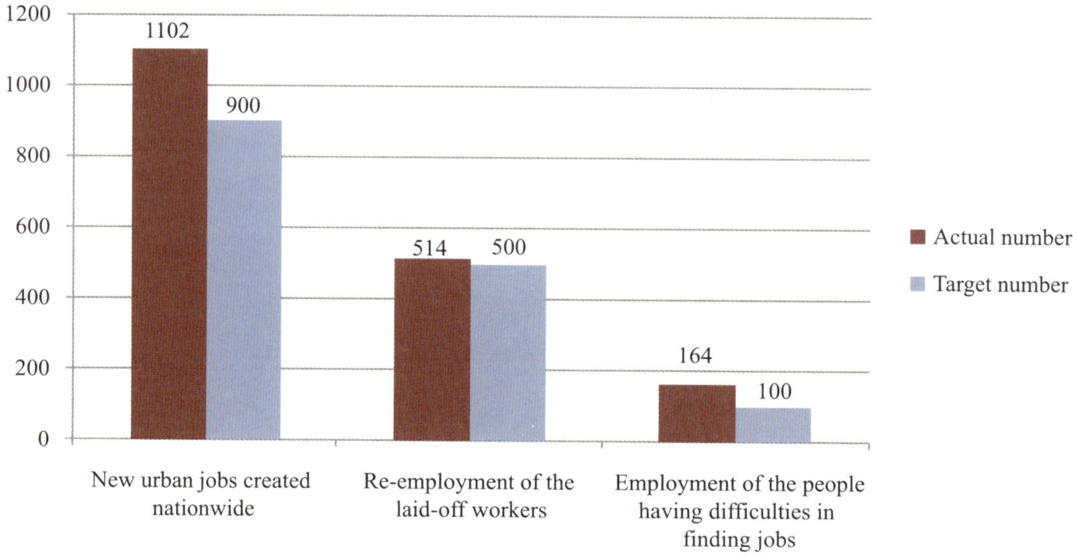

Source: *2009 Statistical Bulletin on the Development of Human Resources and Social Security*.

4.5 The Proactive Employment Policy Being Gradually Expanded, Enriched, Improved and Promoted, and Becoming the Policy Guarantee for the Continuous Promotion of Employment and Entrepreneurship

From the establishment of the initial framework of the proactive employment policy system in 2002, to further extension and expansion of the policy in 2005, then to the formal implementation of *Employment Promotion Law* in 2008, the employment promotion policy in China experienced a journey from initiation to development until being upgraded to legal system, forming the proactive employment policy system with Chinese characteristics. After 2008, the active response to the international financial crisis and major natural disasters made new progress and achievements in promoting employment. After 2012, with China's economic development into a new normal, in view of the new situation of employment, entrepreneurship and innovation to drive employment became a new driving force. In 2015, the State Council issued an important document on employment and entrepreneurship under the new situation, which enriched, enhanced and innovated the proactive employment policy. More than 13 million new urban jobs were created for 5 consecutive years. In 2017, the State Council issued another policy document on employment and entrepreneurship for the new era, which proposed policies and measures in 5 aspects, namely, adhering to the strategy of giving high priority to employment, supporting the development of new forms of employment, promoting entrepreneurship-driven employment, focusing on employment and entrepreneurship among key groups, and strengthening education, training as well as employment and entrepreneurship services. New platforms such as e-commerce and the sharing economy have led to a large number of new forms of employment, and entrepreneurial entities have registered significant growth for 5 consecutive years, so as to promote the national employment and entrepreneurship work up to a new level.

Specialists from the International Labour Organisation spoke highly of China's proactive employment policy, pointing out that China's proactive employment policy was a good example of a better combination of modern employment concepts, successful experience of various countries and China's national conditions. It included the three major elements of the proactive employment policies of all countries in the world, i. e. not only giving relief to the unemployed but also paying more attention to their re-employment, not only creating jobs for employment expansion but also paying more attention to the development of human resources, and encouraging the workers to start their own business in various forms of promoting employment. Relying on the proactive employment policy, China has succeeded in solving the serious problem of unemployment and semi-unemployment, which coexisted in both urban and rural areas. China has done what other countries cannot. In addition, the policy content and implementation results may worth recommending and learning for the rest of the world.

Chapter 4
Employment Promotion Law

1. Enactment of the Employment Promotion Law

1.1 Promulgation of the Employment Promotion Law

The Constitution clearly provides for ensuring the labour rights and obligations of the citizens, i. e. using various channels, the State creates conditions for employment, strengthens labour protection, improves working conditions and, on the basis of expanded production, increases remuneration for work and social benefits. The State provides necessary vocational training to citizens before they are employed.

Labour Law provides that the State shall take various measures to promote employment, to develop vocational education, to set up labour standards, to regulate social income, to improve social insurance system, to coordinate labour relationship, and gradually raise the living standards of labourers. However, in the face of China's long-term, arduous and complex employment problems, in order to do a better job in employment, it needs not only comprehensive laws such as the Constitution and *Labour Law*, but also a specific law to promote employment.

The Central Committee of CPC and the State Council have been attaching great importance to employment. At the national re-employment work conference held in 2002, the important idea of "employment being privotal to people's well-being" was put forward for the first time. It was clearly requested to put employment in a more prominent position in economic and social development, adhere to the people-centred principle, and realise a coordinated and sustainable development of the society. China's proactive employment policy was also formulated and implemented in the same year. During 2003-2007, the State Council, various departments and local governments successively formulated and implemented follow-up and supporting policies, which further extended, expanded, adjusted and enriched the proactive employment policy, and achieved remarkable results in implementation, which provided a rich and practical basis for the formulation of *Employment Promotion Law*. At the same time, the implementation of these reform measures also needed to be guaranteed by law. It was urgent to institutionalise and legalise the policies on promotion through legislation, and establish a long-term mechanism to promote employment. In 2007, *Employment Promotion Law* came into being after rounds of arguments. In August of the same year, the 29th Meeting of the Standing Committee of the 10th National People's Congress deliberated and passed *Employment Promotion Law*, which was promulgated by Presidential Decree No. 70 signed by the President of the People's Republic of China and went into effect in 2008. The enforcement of *Employment Promotion Law* was an important event in China's economic and social life and an important milestone in Chinese employment cause. It had a significant and

Employment Promotion Law **went into effect on January 1, 2008. (Photo taken by Xinhua News Agency reporter Xiaochuan Wang.)**

far-reaching impact on the establishment of a long-term mechanism for promoting employment, promoting a comprehensive, coordinated and sustainable development of human resources and social security, and building up a harmonious socialist society.

1.2 Guiding Ideology of Employment Promotion Law

In the process of law drafting, the most important thing was to determine the guiding ideology of legislation. First, it was necessary to fully embody the Party's and the State's policies on employment promotion and institutionalise them, and clarify the core position and role of employment in socioeconomic development, so as to establish a long-term mechanism to promote employment. The second was to clarify the decisive role of market employment and the government's responsibility to promote employment. The fundamental role of the human resources market on employment should be fully played to promote the employers' autonomy to choose workers and the workers' initiatives in seeking jobs, and guide the reasonable flow of workers. At the same time, the government should shift its role from the traditional centralised employment management model under the planned economy to accelerating the cultivation and regulation of market-oriented employment by formulating development strategies and implementing macroeconomic policies, as well as through policy guidance and service delivery to create a good environment for employment promotion and development. In order to make up for the shortage of the market, the government should also provide employment aid and other means to help the disadvantaged groups to achieve employment. Third, it was necessary to establish a clear employment system and policy system for all workers. *Employment Promotion Law* was to protect and serve all workers and all employers. The supporting policies should be inclusive, and the service and training should be impartial. It was necessary to build up a unified public employment service system and system between urban and rural areas, and develop the lifelong training system and policy for all workers. The fourth was to make clear the relationship between the specific law on promoting employment and the relevant laws. Before and after the promulgation of *Employment Promotion Law*, relevant laws and regulations such as *Labour Law, Labour Contract Law* and *Social Insurance Law* were promulgated one after another. At the same time, with the introduction of a series of departmental rules and regulations, the system of laws and regulations on employment promotion was gradually improved.

1.3 Legislative Purposes and Principles of Employment Promotion Law

(1) The legislative purpose of *Employment Promotion Law* was to promote employment, promote the coordination between economic development and employment expansion, and promote social harmony and stability.

(2) The legislative principles of *Employment Promotion Law* was first expanding employment. *Employment Promotion Law* clearly proposed that the State should put employment expansion in the prominent position of economic and social development. Local governments should take the expansion of employment as an important goal of economic and social development and economic structural adjustment, so as to realise the positive interaction between economic development and employment expansion. The second was market-oriented employment. *Employment Promotion Law* required deepening the reform of labour and employment system, improving the market-oriented employment mechanism, implementing market-oriented employment regulation, and ensuring the autonomy for both workers and employers in choosing jobs and in recruiting workers respectively. The third was equal employment. Discrimination in employment should be prohibited and fair employment opportunities should be provided to workers. The fourth was overall planning on employment. *Employment Promotion Law* requested the coordination among all departments and sectors of the society, social groups and organisations to promote employment; to coordinate industrial policies and employment policies; to do a good integrated job for the employment of new entrants in urban areas, the transfer employment of surplus rural labour force, and re-employment of the laid-off and unemployed people, so as to form a unified labour market between urban and rural areas step by step.

2. Contents and Characteristics of Employment Promotion Law

Employment Promotion Law consists of 9 chapters and 69 articles. It covers a wide range of issues, including government responsibility, working principles and mechanisms, policy support, fair employment, employment services and management, vocational education and training, employment aid, supervision and inspection, and legal responsibility.

2.1 Employment Guidelines

Employment Promotion Law emphasised the guideline of employment chosen by workers independently, regulated by the market and promoted by the government. In 2015, it further clarified the guideline of employment chosen by workers independently, regulated by the market, and employment promoted and entrepreneurship encouraged by the government.

(1) Make clear "employment chosen by workers independently". Workers are encouraged to achieve employment as soon as possible by setting up a correct concept of employment, fully mobilising their initiative and dynamic role, reaching their employment potential and their vocational skills, relying on their own efforts to apply for jobs, to be self-employed and to start up their own businesses.

(2) Make clear "employment regulated by the market". Bring the basic role of human resources market in promoting employment into full play. The information on supply and the demand in labour market should be used to guide the reasonable flow and employment of workers. The supply side and the demand side of the labour market can choose each other, thanks to the guaranteed autonomy of both employers and employees. The information of guidelines on wages of different posts in labour market can be used to adjust labour supply and demand.

(3) Make clear "employment promoted and entrepreneurship encouraged by the government". The government's important responsibility in employment promotion should be fully played by undertaking such important responsibilities as creating employment conditions, expanding employment opportunities, improving employment environment and providing employment aid, etc. Meanwhile, under the current situation of incomplete market mechanism and workers' insufficient initiative, government should assume more responsibility in improving market mechanism, regulating market behaviour and remedying market inefficiency. More efforts should be made to encourage workers to choose their own jobs and start up their own businesses, and support enterprises to increase jobs.

2.2 Fair Employment

It is not only an important principle to promote employment, but also an important issue of social concern to achieve fair employment, be against employment discrimination and protect the equal employment rights of workers. *Employment Promotion Law* holds high the banner of fair employment and creates fair employment environment. It is clearly stipulated that the workers enjoy the right to employment on an equal footing and to choice of jobs on their own initiative in accordance with law. In seeking employment, the workers shall not be subject to discrimination because of their ethnic backgrounds, races, gender, religious beliefs, etc. *Employment Promotoion Law* establishes a special chapter on fair employment, which emphasises that the disabled persons, the pathogen carriers of an infectious disease and rural workers who go to cities for employment shall enjoy equal right to work with other workers. When employing units hire workers and employment agencies deliver job intermediary services, they shall provide equal employment opportunities and fair employment conditions to the workers. Discrimination in employment is not allowed. *Employment Promotion Law* has provided strong legal protection in solving employment discrimination problem.

2.3 Government Responsibility

It is an important duty of the governments to promote employment and control unemployment, which is also an important goal for the governments around the world in exercising power. In China, it is the most important manifestation of the governments at all levels to govern for the people. *Employment Promotion Law* clearly defines the government's role in promoting employment in the following 6 areas.

(1) Create more jobs through economic development and industry structural adjustment. It is the government's primary responsibility to deal with the relationship among economic development, structural adjustment as well as expanding employment and reducing unemployment. *Employment Promotion Law* stipulates that governments at county level and above shall take employment expansion as an important goal and an important responsibility of economic and social development. Through economic development and industrial restructuring, various economic and social policies, such as industrial policies, fiscal policies and taxation policies, that are conducive to promoting employment, shall be implemented to expand employment and increase employment posts through multiple channels.

(2) Formulate and implement the proactive employment policy. Formulating and implementing systematic and active policy in line with the national conditions is a concrete manifestation of the government's duty performance. *Employment Promotion Law* has a special chapter on "policy support" to stipulate that the State shall implement various policies such as industrial, fiscal, taxation, financial, investment and trade policies, which are conducive to promoting employment. It requires the implementation of employment policies that integrate urban and rural areas, different regions and employment groups, and requests prevention, regulation and control of unemployment.

(3) Regulate the human resources market. Human resources market is a general summary of the existing labour market, professional market, graduate employment market and other markets. *Employment Promotion Law* clearly stipulates that governments at or above county level shall foster and improve a unitary, open, competitive and orderly market for human resources, intensify the development of information networks and relevant facilities for the market, establish a sound information service system for such market, and improve the market information disclosure system, so as to provide better employment services for workers.

(4) Improve employment services. In the chapter "employment services and management", *Employment Promotion Law* makes a clear provision for the improvement of employment services, especially strengthening public employment services. It requests that governments at or above the county level shall encourage all sectors of the society to carry out employment service activities in accordance with law, provide better guidance and exercise stricter supervision over public employment services and the services provided by job intermediaries, gradually improve the employment service system covering urban and rural areas, improve the quality and efficiency of services and facilitate an effective match for labour supply and demand, and fulfil the duty of providing free public employment services for workers.

(5) Strengthen vocational education and training. *Employment Promotion Law* has a special chapter on "vocational education and training", which stipulates that the State shall develop vocational education in accordance with law, promote vocational training and encourage the workers to improve their vocational skills and to increase their employability and capability of entrepreneurship. People's governments at or above the county level shall, in light of the need of economic and social development and market demand, formulate and implement plans for the development of vocational capabilities, encourage and support vocational skills training institutes and employing units to, in accordance with law, provide pre-employment training, on-the-job training, re-employment training and entrepreneurship training, establish a sound labour reserve system and apply a vocational certification system.

(6) Implement employment aid. *Employment Promotion Law* stipulates that governments at all levels are requested to establish a sound employment aid system and, in their support and assistance, give priority to the persons who have difficulty in finding jobs and regions with employment difficulties by all effective means, expanding the range of public welfare jobs, and ensuring that at least one member is employed in each urban family that needs employment. The implementation of employment aid to the disadvantaged groups is the basic requirement of guaranteeing citizens' right to employment, maintaining and improving the living conditions of workers, and promoting social equity and harmony. Meanwhile, *Employment Promotion Law* also stipulates that the range of persons who have difficulty in finding jobs shall be separately defined by governments at provincial level in light of the actual conditions of their respective administrative areas, so that all local governments can solve the problem of the persons with employment difficulties from the reality, which is more conducive to the full play of aid policy's effect.

2.4 Employment System

Employment Promotion Law institutionalises the employment work through legal form, so as to bring the work of employment into the legal track. It mainly includes 5 aspects.

(1) Strengthen government's responsibility in organising and leading employment. *Employment Promotion Law* clearly stipulates that the governments at or above the county level shall make employment increase one of their important goals in their endeavours for economic and social development, incorporate it into their plans for national economic and social development, and formulate medium- and long-term plans and annual work plans for employment promotion. People's governments at all levels and the relevant departments shall establish target responsibility system for employment promotion. People's governments at or above the county level shall, on the basis of the requirements of such a system, assess and supervise the work of its subordinate departments and governments at the next lower level. It not only requests the governments and relevant departments to establish the target responsibility system for employment promotion through legal form, but also further defines the important role of the system of inter-ministerial joint meetings on employment[1], and makes clear requirements for further improving the system so as to ensure that relevant departments work together to maintain a sustained and effective management on the work of employment. At the same time, the State shall establish workforce survey system as well as employment and unemployment registration system, in order to conduct statistical surveys on the workforce as well as employment and unemployment status and publish the statistical findings.

(2) Strengthen public employment services and employment aid system for workers. This system is an important embodiment of the government's public service function. *Employment Promotion Law* clearly stipulates that the governments at or above the county level shall establish public employment service institutions to provide free services to workers, and the funds shall be included in the financial budget at the same level. Through the institutional arrangement on the target groups, assistance channels, policies, measures and funds provision, the work of employment aid work has been normalised.

(3) Strengthen human resources market management systems that regulate market behaviour. *Employment Promotion Law* not only regulates the content of public employment services, but also sets out the conditions for the establishment of job intermediaries, their behaviour and management.

(4) Strengthen vocational skills development system to improve the competence of human resources. *Employment Promotion Law* further clarifies the institutional arrangements for vocational training for various groups such as the graduates from middle and high schools, the unemployed persons and the rural migrant workers to cities for employment, and the responsibilities and rights of employers and training institutes, so that the integration of human resources development and employment promotion is ensured by the institutional arrangement. At the same time, a network of vocational training, which takes technical schools as the backbone and employment training centres, enterprise training institutes and a large number of private training and education institutes as a complement, has been established. The system of training before employment and training before taking up a post has been basically established.

[1] Under the direct leadership of the State Council, the inter-ministerial joint meeting carries out work, regularly exchanges work progress, coordinates and solves difficult problems on policy implementation, supervises and inspects policy implementation of various departments, coordinates the actions of all departments, guides and promotes the national employment work, and timely reports to the State Council major problems on employment.

(5) Establish unemployment insurance and unemployment regulating and controlling system. The State establishes a sound unemployment insurance scheme to ensure the basic living standards of the unemployed and to prevent unemployment and promote employment. Meanwhile, an unemployment alert system should be established to prevent, regulate and control potential large-scale unemployment.

2.5 Employment Policy

Policies are the concrete embodiment that the government fulfils its responsibility. *Employment Promotion Law* has raised the proactive employment policy which has been tested by practice for years into a legal norm, which mainly includes 10 aspects.

The first is economic development policy conducive to employment promotion. *Employment Promotion Law* stipulates that the governments at or above the county level shall formulate overall plans for coordinating their industrial and employment policies. The governments shall provide more job opportunities by encouraging the development of labour-intensive industries and service industry, supporting SMEs, and encouraging, supporting and giving guidance for the development of non-public sectors. Moreover, the governments shall develop both domestic and foreign trade as well as international economic cooperation, bring into play the role of investment or major construction projects in promoting employment and create more channels for employment.

The second is fiscal policies conducive to the promotion of employment. *Employment Promotion Law* stipulates that the State implements the fiscal policies which are favourable for employment promotion, and increases funds input. People's governments at or above the county level shall appropriate special funds for employment promotion from their budgets. It also stipulates the specific expenditure items of the special funds. The audit organs and finance departments shall, in accordance with law, supervise and inspect the management and usage of the special funds.

The third is tax incentives conducive to job creation. *Employment Promotion Law* stipulates that the State encourages enterprises to increase employment, supports the employment of the unemployed persons and persons with disabilities, and gives tax preferences to enterprises and persons who meet the legal requirements according to law. The unemployed and the disabled who engage in self-employed business shall be exempted from administrative and institutional fees.

The fourth is financial policies favourable for employment promotion. *Employment Promotion Law* stipulates that the State shall open up more fund-raising channels for SMEs, and encourages financial institutions to improve financial services by giving such enterprises increasing support in credit loans and providing, within a given period of time, small credit loans, etc to support the labourers who start up their businesses independently.

The fifth is integrated employment policy between urban and rural areas. *Employment Promotion Law* stipulates that the State shall establish a sound system under which equal job opportunities for both urban and rural people are provided and guidance is given to the surplus rural labour force in their efforts to find other jobs in an orderly manner.

The sixth is regional overall employment policy. According to *Employment Promotion Law*, the State shall support the development of regional economy, encourage cooperation between different regions and comprehensively coordinate the efforts for a balanced increase of employment in different areas, so as to realise the balanced growth of employment in different regions and the coordinated development of regional economy.

The seventh is integrated group employment policy. *Employment Promotion Law* stipulates that governments at all levels shall make overall plans for the employment of the new labour market entrants in cities and towns, the transfer employment of the surplus rural labour force, and the re-employment of the unemployed.

The eighth is labour and social insurance policies conducive to flexible employment. *Employment Promotion Law* stipulates that the governments at all levels shall take measures to gradually improve and implement the labour and social insurance policies adapted to such flexible employment as part-time jobs, in order to provide assistance and services to the persons who look for flexible employment. It is conducive to promoting the healthy development of flexible employment.

The ninth is employment aid policy for the persons with employment difficulties. *Employment Promotion Law* stipulates that the State shall establish a sound employment aid system to help and support the persons who have difficulty in finding jobs.

The tenth is to implement unemployment insurance to promote employment policy. *Employment Promotion Law* clearly stipulates the function of unemployment insurance system in ensuring the basic living standards of the unemployed and promoting employment, and requires to strengthen the prevention, regulation and control of large-scale unemployment.

3. Implementation and Effectiveness of Employment Promotion Law

3.1 Implementation of Employment Promotion Law

(1) Accelerate the study of supporting laws, regulations and documents, and improve the inheritance of the proactive employment policy. The promulgation of *Employment Promotion Law* provided a good opportunity for the legalisation of employment, but some provisions of the law remained very general. Therefore, all functional departments studied and formulated relevant supporting laws and regulations to make the main contents of *Employment Promotion Law* more specific and operational. At the same time, local governments were guided and promoted to formulate corresponding local rules and regulations. Local employment promotion regulations or relevant measures were formulated according to their actual situation. The practice of the proactive employment policy has laid a solid foundation for the implementation of *Employment Promotion Law*. In order to better link the policy with the law, on the basis of retaining the core content of the current proactive employment policy system, more efforts should be made focusing on solving three problems. First, maintain the continuity of policies so as to make relevant policies such as vocational training, job recommendation, encouragement of self-employment and employment aid as long-term, universal and standardised policies. Second, on the basis of summarising the current policy implementation practices, the relevant policies were further enriched and adjusted, so that the target groups and projects of the policy support stipulated by law could be implemented. Third, the operability of the policy was enhanced to get the actual results of the legal provisions. In February 2008, *Notice on Further Doing Well in Promoting Employment* issued by the State Council made clear requirements on linking the current employment policy with the law, and implementing well the law. To implement this document, the Ministry of Human Resources and Social Security, the National Development and Reform Commission, the Ministry of Finance, the People's Bank of China and other departments strengthened coordination and cooperation, and formulated supporting policies such as fund management, micro credit, administrative fee reduction and exemption. All local governments also adjusted and improved their current employment policies and formulated local implementation opinions in light of the new situation and new tasks.

(2) Strengthen learning, training and publicity. The enactment and implementation of *Employment Promotion Law* not only provided the law basis for employment promotion and various supporting policies, but also put forward new and higher requirements for the administrative capacity of governments at all levels and departments concerned. To this end, special arrangements were made to strengthen the training of officials and related professionals at all levels. On the one hand, the training were organised for the personnel working with the department of human resources and social security as well as its employment service agencies at all levels, so as to develop a number of backbone professional teams who understood the law and were good at enforcing the law. On the other hand, study and training programmes were organised for the staff from the member organisation of the joint conference, so as to make them deeply

During September to December 2007, the Ministry of Labour and Social Security, the Ministry of Justice, All-China Federation of Trade Unions, All-China Federation of Industry and Commerce, China Enterprise Confederation and CCTV jointly hosted the National Television Contest on *Employment Promotion Law* and *Labour Contract Law*.

understand the content and requirements on implementing *Employment Promotion Law* relevant to their own work. Meanwhile, a variety of effective forms was taken to carry out extensive and in-depth publicity to popularise the law and to make governments at all levels, relevant departments, employers and all sectors of society, especially the broad masses of workers, fully understand the great significance and main contents of the law. Flexible and diversified legal publicity that was close to the reality of the society and daily life of the general public was organised to enhance the practical effect of law publicity and policy explanation. In particular, good practices in promoting employment and re-employment in some localities and units in recent years, were used for publicity. And some typical experience in self-employment and business start-up was used as well, so as to mobilise the whole society to work together to do a good job in employment and re-employment.

3.2 The Effectiveness of Employment Legislation

Employment Promotion Law has improved China's legal system on labour and social security, provided legal protection for the implementation of the proactive employment policy and for the promotion of employment reform and development. It has played a positive role in promoting a sound interaction between economic development and expanding employment, and promoting the realisation of social harmony and stability.

(1) Establish the important position of employment in the national economic and social development and make clear the important responsibilities of the government in promoting employment. Employment is pivotal to the common people's well-being and achieving fuller employment is an important task in building up a harmonious socialist society. *Employment Promotion Law* not only clearly stipulates that the State shall give priority to employment expansion in economic and social development, but also stipulates in a specific chapter the government's important responsibilities in employment expansion, as well as the establishment of a target responsibility system for employment promotion and its assessment and supervision. The government's important duty on employment promotion has been intensified by legal means.

(2) Carry forward the legalisation process of employment. A long-term mechanism on employment promotion was established by further enhancing the work of employment with legal means. *Employment Promotion Law* clearly stipulates to implement the proactive employment policy and adhere to the guideline of "employment chosen by worker independently, regulated by the market and promoted by the government". The proactive employment policy, which has been proved to be effective by practice, has not only been upgraded to a legal norm, but also further clarified that it is necessary to legalise the general policies and guidelines on employment promotion, to legalise the working mechanism and working system for promoting employment, and to institutionalise various policies, measures and funds for promoting employment. It has provided solid institutional support and legal guarantee for solving the country's employment problem in the long run.

(3) Strongly safeguard reinforced employment services and management. *Employment Promotion Law*, starting with improvement of the system and basic function, has made specific and clear provisions on policy support, fair employment, employment services and management, vocational education and training, employment aid, supervision and inspection, etc. It is necessary to combine the cultivation and development of the market with the regulation of market behaviour, combine the development of public employment services and vocational training with the development of relevant systems, and combine employment promotion with the strict implementation of policies. These combinations have not only ensured the solution of the problems such as poor implementation of policies, unavailability of basic function, non-standard or lack of guarantee operation, but also made the employment management service organisation system more complete and the safeguard measures more powerful.

(4) Further improve the legal system on labour and social security. *Employment Promotion Law* has not only filled the gap of national legal document on employment after the adoption of *Labour law* but also marked the further improvement of Chinese legal system on labour and social security with the Constitution as the fundamental basis and *Labour Law* as another principal document, and with *Employment Promotion Law*, *Labour Contract Law*, *Labour Disputes Mediation and Arbitration Law* and *Social Insurance Law* as the skeleton, complemented by some relevant laws and regulations.

With the continuous development of economy and society, the legislation in employment and related fields is also facing many new challenges. First, the existing laws and regulations lag behind the reform practice, while legislation and legislative amendment need to keep pace with the times. It is urgent to deal with the issues, for example, the establishment of a unified, open, fair and orderly human resources market for the overall planning of urban and rural employment, the impact of population aging on employment, the blank of relevant policies in response to sudden crises and major disasters, and the insufficient content of entrepreneurship-driven employment stipulated in law. Moreover, the achievement of fuller and higher quality employment needs the backstop of law enforcement. The Central Committee of CPC and the State Council regard employment as pivotal to the well-being of people, and set up the goal of achieving fuller and higher quality employment. However, the achievement of this goal needs not only further advancement by thorough implementation of *Employment Promotion Law*, but also a clearer reflection in the law amendment.

Chapter 5
Entrepreneurship-driven Employment

1. The Development Course of Entrepreneurship-driven Employment

1.1 The Initiation of Entrepreneurship-driven Employment

1.1.1 The Launch and Important Breakthrough of Entrepreneurship

In early 1980s, faced with the sharp increase of employment pressure caused by the return of 17 million educated youth to cities, the original policy of centralised employment allocation, which controled and restricted employment, was loosened to some extent. The "three-ways combined" employment guideline introduced, namely "job placement by labour departments, voluntary job-matching and self-employment", opened up a variety of employment channels. In particular, the promotion of self-employment and the development of individual economy enabled the workers to start up their own businesses. The reform of breaking the employment boundary between urban and rural areas was carried out in 1990s. The transfer of rural labour force brought about the development of individual economy and township enterprises. It broke through the original system of controlling the migration of rural workers, opened the door for them to get employment in cities and towns, and expanded the entrepreneurial opportunities for rural workers. After entering the 21st century, in the face of the outstanding contradictions of 30 million laid-off workers, in formulating the employment promotion policy, entrepreneurship was encouraged and supported as the important pillar, which made many laid-off workers re-employed by starting up their own businesses. After 2008, the sudden international financial crisis had a great impact on Chinese enterprises and employment. Among the policies and measures implemented in response to the crisis, major measures were taken to encourage and support migrant workers to start up their own businesses in their hometowns and to encourage the college students to start up their own businesses, which opened up a completely new world for employment, realised entrepreneurship-driven employment, and helped China out of employment difficulties in a short period of time. In 2015, the central government established a new employment guideline which could be put as "employment chosen by workers independently, regulated by the market, promoted by the government and entrepreneurship encouraged by the government", which further promoted new progress in China's entrepreneurship-driven employment.

1.1.2 Being Listed as an Important Part of the Proactive Employment Policy

One of the important elements of the proactive employment policy implemented since 2002 was to encourage and support workers to start up their own businesses by solving the financing problems through micro-secured loans with loan interest subsidised by finance, reducing the operation burden through tax and fee reductions and exemptions, enhancing entrepreneurs' capacity through entrepreneurship training and solving the problem of business premises by providing support accordingly. Over the past decade, business start-ups, self-employment and free migration of workers have become the mainstream of market employment. In particular, business start-ups have not only opened up a new world of employment, but also had a profound impact on the changing of employment pattern in China. The meaning of China's proactive employment policy includes three levels. First, the solution to unemployment cannot be just to passively provide unemployment benefit and living allowance, but also to actively promote more, faster and better employment. Second, promoting employment should try by all possible means to create jobs, and at the same time pay more attention to the development of human resources and improve workers' vocational skills and employability. Third, in the process of promoting employment, special encouragement and supports should be given to entrepreneurship development so as to promote entrepreneurship-driven employment. Therefore, the 17th CPC National Congress in 2007 clearly proposed to implement the development strategy of expanding employment, promote entrepreneurship-driven employment, improve policies on supporting entrepreneurship and self-employment, and strengthen the education on employment concept, so that more workers can become entrepreneurs. *Employment Promotion Law*, which came into effect in 2008, also makes it clear that workers should be encouraged to develop a correct concept on employment choice, improve their employability and entrepreneurial capacity, and start up their own businesses and become self-employed.

1.2 The Development of Entrepreneurship-driven Employment

1.2.1 Important Measures to Deal with the Impact of the Financial Crisis.

In September 2008, the State Council provided guidance on promoting entrepreneurship-driven employment, and made special deployments and specific arrangements for entrepreneurship and employment promotion. Especially in response to the impact of the international financial crisis, the first major initiative taken by the State Council was to promote entrepreneurship-driven employment. The initiative aimed at turning the pressure of the financial crisis into a driving force, so that more and more workers could tide over the employment difficulties brought about by the financial crisis by starting up their own businesses, creating more jobs in maintaining growth and protecting people's livelihood. While encouraging entrepreneurship-driven employment, the employment structure was actively adjusted and the development of SMEs and tertiary industry was further supported.

1.2.2 The New Polices to Promote Entrepreneurship in the New Era

After 2010, Chinese government has formulated policies and plans to promote employment and entrepreneurship, proposed the overall requirements and guiding ideology for employment promotion under the new situation, and made clear requirements on implementing the pro-employment strategies and the proactive employment policies, especially policies and measures to encourage and support entrepreneurship as an important element.

After 2012, with China's economic development entering the new normal, in view of the new situation faced by employment, entrepreneurship and innovation-driven employment has become a new engine. In April 2015, the State Council issued an important document on employment and entrepreneurship under the new situation. The greatest highlight of this document is to implement the new employment guideline, which was put as a combination of employment promoted by the government and entrepreneurship encouraged by the government, proposed by the 18th CPC National Congress, and the guideline's requirements. The proactive employment policy was expanded, enriched, upgraded and innovated timely by the document. It proposed the following: ① to support the development of new forms of employment and provide preferential policies on encouraging entrepreneurship and innovative development for emerging forms of enterprises; ② to implement entrepreneurship promotion plans and grass roots growth plans for the employment of college graduates by guiding and encouraging college graduates to get employment in urban and rural areas, micro-, small- and medium-sized businesses, social organisations and other sectors; ③ to expand the scope of subsidy policies for internship and job-seeking and entrepreneurship; ④ to emphasise streamlining administration and decentralising power, and pay attention to deliver convenient service to people; ⑤ to create an entrepreneurial environment by deepening the reform of "deregulation power, better management and optimising service", and promote the convenient registration and management for individual businesses; ⑥ to simplify the certification procedures of academic credentials for overseas students and encourage the overseas students to go back to China for employment; ⑦ and to refine service standards and procedures and establish "Internet Plus" public employment and entrepreneurship services platform. In order to vigorously promote mass entrepreneurship and promote entrepreneurship-driven employment, more policy supports and services shall be provided to create enabling entrepreneurship environment and to mobilise the enthusiasm and initiative of workers in starting up businesses.

In April 2017, the State Council issued a policy document on employment and entrepreneurship for the new era, i.e. adhering to the pro-employment strategy, supporting the development of new employment forms, focusing on employment and entrepreneurship of key groups, and strengthening education, training and the services for employment and entrepreneurship. New platforms, such as the network economy and the sharing economy, have brought about a large number of new forms of employment, and start-up entities have increased significantly for 5 consecutive years, thus promoting the national employment and entrepreneurship to a new level.

In September 2018, the State Council issued the guidance on promoting the high-quality development of innovation and entrepreneurship as well as creating an upgraded version of "mass entrepreneurship and innovation". The purpose was to deeply implement the innovation-driven development strategy, to further stimulate market vitality and social creativity, and to promote the high-quality development of innovation and entrepreneurship. The contents of the guidance were: first, policy upgrading, i.e. reducing costs through cutting down social security contribution rates for a certain period, streamlining administration and delegating powers and further deepening the reform of qualification and administrative approval in the field of human resources and social security, and solving financial difficulty by expanding the coverage of business start-up secured loans to more target groups. Second, training upgrading, i.e. organising more targeted entrepreneurship training for different entrepreneur groups, at different stages, or in different areas or sectors, and enhancing the training of leading entrepreneurs and developing their leading roles. Third, service upgrading, i.e. setting up specific counters/windows for entrepreneurship services and enhancing the role of public employment service institutions in offering entrepreneurship service guidance; improving the mechanism of government purchasing social services; building business incubation bases and parks to provide comprehensive supporting services. In this process, more policy support and efforts should be made to promote the entrepreneurship of key groups such as college graduates, returned migrant workers and returned overseas students. In April 2019, the State Council issued the guidance on promoting the healthy development of SMEs, to further stimulate the vitality and development momentum of SMEs, to ensure the implementation of *SME Promotion Law*, to ease the difficulties for SMEs, to stabilise and enhance the confidence and expectation of enterprises, to increase the support for innovation, to enhance the specialised development capacity of SMEs and the integrated development of large enterprises and SMEs, and to promote the healthy development of SMEs. It covered the following five aspects. First, create a good development environment, further relax market access, take the initiative to serve SMEs, and implement a fair and unified market supervision system. Second, solve the financing problem, improve the financing policy for SMEs, actively expand financing access, support direct financing by using capital market, reduce the financing burden for enterprises, and establish a classified supervision and assessment mechanism. Third, improve fiscal and tax support policies, improve fiscal and taxation support for SMEs financing, reduce the taxation and fee payment burden for SMEs, improve the government's procurement policy to support SMEs, and give full play to the leading role of various funds. Fourth, enhance the ability of innovation and development. Improve the environment for innovation and entrepreneurship, effectively protect intellectual property rights, guide the development of SMEs in their specialised and new direction, and provide information services for SMEs. Fifth, improve service guarantee system. Improve public service system, promote credit information sharing, attach importance to the cultivation of entrepreneurs, and support international cooperation and exchange. Sixth, strengthen organisation, leading an overall coordination. Strengthen support and overall guidance, strengthen supervision and evaluation, create a good public opinion atmosphere, and create a good environment conducive to the healthy development of SMEs.

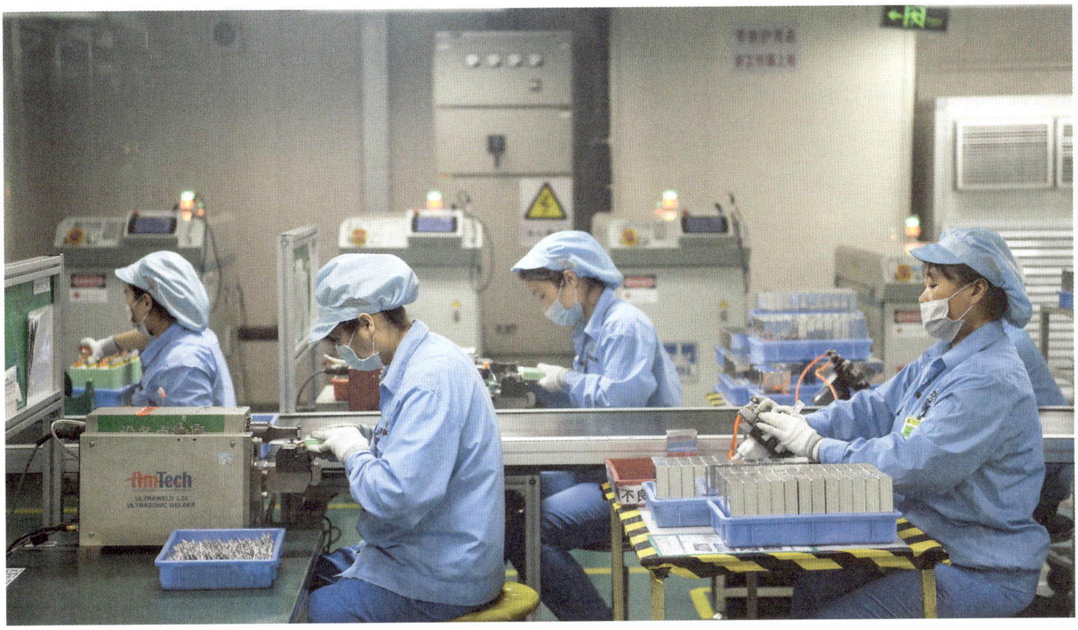

Various measures are taken to promote the development of small- and medium-sized enterprises. (Photo taken by Xinhua News Agency reporter Yu Bai.)

In December 2019, the Ministry of Human Resources and Social Security, the Ministry of Finance, and the Ministry of Agriculture and Rural Areas issued opinions on further promoting innovation and entrepreneurship by returning to and entering countryside, which supported rural migrant workers, college graduates and ex-servicemen to go back to or enter countryside to start up their own businesses, to promote the integrated development of primary, secondary and tertiary industries in rural areas, so as to achieve fuller and higher quality employment. It includes the following: first, to increase policy support, i.e. to implement the entrepreneurship support policy and business start-up secured loans policy. Second, upgrade entrepreneurship training, i.e. to expand training scale and to provide training subsidies. Third, optimise entrepreneurship services, i.e. to enhance service capacity, to strengthen institutional services, and to improve social insurance and social relief mechanisms. Fourth, strengthen professional support, i.e. to do a good job in employment services, and establish a contact mechanism for the people working out of their hometown. Fifth, strengthen the organisation and implementation, i.e. to strengthen organisational leadership, guidance and support, demonstration drive, and increasing publicity efforts. In light of local conditions, new progresses on such kind of innovation and entrepreneurship were made through active exploration and bold innovation in strengthening policy support and service delivery for the people who returned to and entered countryside to start up their own businesses.

2. Policy Measures on Entrepreneurship-driven Employment

2.1 Policy Content of Entrepreneurship-driven Employment

2.1.1 Policies to Encourage and Support Entrepreneurship

The proactive employment policy mainly encourages and supports more workers to be self-employed and start up their own businesses in four aspects. First, tax reduction and exemption policies as well as administrative fee reduction and exemption policies were implemented simultaneously to encourage and support more workers to start up their own businesses and reduce their burdens. With the changing of the situation, the target groups of this policy has gradually expanded from the laid-off and unemployed people to a variety of urban and rural entrepreneurship groups, including the unemployed, college students, returned migrant workers, ex-servicemen, scientific and technical personnel. The implementation period was also extended accordingly. Second, the policy of micro-secured loans was implemented to solve the problem of starting capital and working capital for workers to start up their own businesses. For the qualified self-employed persons, business starters or partners in business, if their self-financing was insufficient, and if the loan guarantee institution committed to guarantee the loan, they could apply for a micro-secured loan from the commercial bank or its branch. For the laid-off and unemployed persons who were engaged in partnership business and organised employment, the amount of the loan could be appropriately enlarged according to the number of such persons. For those who engaged in low profit business, the central finance would discount the interest in full amount according to the actual situation. With the changing of the situation, the beneficiaries of this policy gradually extended to the key entrepreneurship groups in both urban and rural areas, and the loan amount was increased several times. Third, the arrangements on business places and business administration were made to overcome the difficulties in getting business places and handling business administrative affairs. An overall arrangement was made on the production and operation venues for the entrepreneurs. Economic and technological development zones, industrial parks, high-tech parks, university science and technology parks, and small business incubators were used to build business start-up incubation bases. Better conditions were created for entrepreneurs through simplifying the business opening procedures with "all-in-one" service and "one counter" acceptance available, relaxing market access and creating comfortable and convenient business environment. Fourth, strengthen entrepreneurship training guidance services, explore the development of entrepreneurship training model and build up a platform for entrepreneurship services.

2.1.2 Multi-department Cooperation to Promote Entrepreneurship

In September 2008, the General Office of the State Council issued *Notice on Forwarding the Guiding Opinions of the Ministry of Human Resources and Social Security and Other Departments on Entrepreneurship-driven Employment*. As the first document specially for promoting entrepreneurship, it was jointly formulated by 11 departments to sort out the problems encountered in entrepreneurship one by one, proposed solutions and formed a joint force of multiple departments in making supporting policies and measures. The main contents are as follows.

(1) Improve the supporting policies and the entrepreneurial environment. First, liberalise market access. Various industrial, regional and operational barriers that hinder entrepreneurship shall be cleaned up and eliminated as quickly as possible. All regions and relevant departments may, according to the actual situation, properly relax the market access conditions for college graduates, unemployed people and returned migrant workers to start up their businesses. Second, improve administrative management. The fee charging disclosure system and enterprise fee payment registration card system shall be comprehensively implemented. The items of administrative approval related to business start-ups shall be further clarified and standardised and the procedures for project application, approval and certification shall be simplified so as to open up a "green channel" for starting up a business. Third, strengthen policy support. Supportive policies such as tax incentives, micro-secured loans, financial subsidies and venue arrangements that are conducive to workers' entrepreneurship shall be implemented to promote the development of SMEs and individual private enterprises, and support workers' entrepreneurship. Fourth, expand the financing channels. The innovation on financial products and financial services shall be actively promoted to support the advancement of entrepreneurship-driven employment.

(2) Strengthen entrepreneurship training and improve entrepreneurial ability. First, strengthen training. An entrepreneurship training system shall be established to meet the needs of all types of workers in urban and rural areas in starting up their own businesses, and gradually all workers with entrepreneurial aspirations and training needs shall be included in such training. The entrepreneurship curriculum and teaching staff of colleges and vocational schools shall be strengthened to carry out entrepreneurship training and practical training. Entrepreneurs participating in entrepreneurship training shall be given vocational training subsidies in accordance with relevant policies and regulations. For those who receive unemployment benefits, in case of participating in entrepreneurship training, the training subsidy shall be paid by the unemployment insurance fund. Second, improve the quality of training. The quality of entrepreneurship training shall be constantly improved through regulating the training standards, enhancing the teachers' capacity and improving the training mode. Third, establish incubation base. Local governments at all levels shall make overall arrangements for the production and operation venues needed by entrepreneurs. The infrastructure and supporting construction shall be built up well and priority shall be given to secure start-up places.

Entrepreneurial guidance services are provided for entrepreneurs. (Photo taken by Xinhua News Agency reporter Chang Xu.)

(3) Improve the service system and provide high quality services. First, improve the service organisation. Relying on the public employment service system, the organisation of entrepreneurship guidance service shall be improved to develop entrepreneurial guidance techniques, improve the entrepreneurial service function, improve the efficiency of entrepreneurship service, and take the responsibilities of organising, serving and implementing entrepreneurship-driven employment. Second, improve service content. "All-in-one" entrepreneurship services such as idea development, business planning, risk assessment, business opening guidance, financing services, and follow-up support, shall be organised and carried out for the entrepreneurs. An effective channel for entrepreneurs to exchange information and help each other shall be developed by establishing a platform for releasing information and policies on entrepreneurship. An evaluation and recommendation system for entrepreneurial projects that is developed and run by market with the government's support shall be established. A resource bank for entrepreneurial projects shall be established so as to develop an effective project collection and regular information release system. Third, provide employment services. Public employment services shall be provided to entrepreneurs, new businesses and their employees. All kinds of training institutes shall be organised to conduct targeted training and order-based training according to the employment demand, so as to provide the start-up enterprises with suitable staff. The entitled persons participating in the vocational skill training shall be given the corresponding vocational training subsidy and the vocational skill appraisal subsidy according to regulations.

(4) Strengthen organisational leadership and promote the development of work. First, strengthen government responsibility. Local governments at all levels should take promoting entrepreneurship as an important task and put it on the important agenda of employment, and actively facilitate the comprehensive development of entrepreneurship-driven employment. Second, improve the working mechanism. A working group shall be established with the participation, responsibilities sharing and coordination of such departments as human resources and social security, development and reform, as well as small- and medium-sized enterprises administration to jointly study and formulate policies and work plans to promote entrepreneurship-driven employment. The main indicators on measuring entrepreneurship-driven employment shall include the improvement of the entrepreneurial environment, the improvement and implementation of the entrepreneurship policy, the improvement of the effectiveness of entrepreneurship training, the quality of entrepreneurship services, the initial success rate of new businesses, the stability rate of new businesses and the employment rate created by entrepreneurship. All these indicators shall be included when conducting employment assessment to the localities. Third, create a good atmosphere. It is necessary to strengthen entrepreneurship education, give full play to the positive role of all stakeholders of society in supporting and promoting entrepreneurship, strengthening the guidance of public opinion, and setting up entrepreneurship models. Organisations and individuals that have made remarkable achievements on entrepreneurship-driven employment shall be praised or commended.

2.2 Implementation and Effect of SIYB Project

In 2004, the Ministry of Labour and Social Security (MOLSS) of the People's Republic of China officially cooperated with International Labour Organisation (ILO) to launch Start and Improve Your Business (SIYB) training programme. After nearly 20 years of development, the SIYB training programme has become the largest, most well-known, most widespread, most effective and most sustainable business start-up training brand in China, and played an important role in promoting entrepreneurship-driven employment.

2.2.1 Development Stage of the SIYB Project

(1) Exploration and development stage (1997-2003). Through cooperation with ILO, MOLSS implemented the "ILO/Japan/China Inter-country Project on Strategic Approaches toward Rural Employment Promotion" to carry out entrepreneurship training for the surplus labour in the national poverty-stricken counties of Gansu, Hebei and Jiangxi provinces. Due to the success of the project, with ILO's support, MOLSS continued to implement the "ILO/Japan/China Inter-country Project on Strategic Approaches toward Urban Employment Promotion" to carry out entrepreneurship training for the laid-off workers from SOEs in Baotou city Inner Mongolia autonomous region, Jilin city Jilin province and Zhangjiakou city Hebei province. The most important achievement of this stage was having introduced international advanced training technology through international cooperation, and carried out localisation and revision of "Start Your Business" (SYB) training courses and materials. At the same time, in order to better meet the needs of China's national conditions, the government launched the proactive employment policy, and explored the work mode of combining government subsidised entrepreneurship training with micro-secured loan policy. The laid-off workers mastered the entrepreneurial methods, tided over the financial difficulties and reduced the entrepreneurial risks.

(2) Consolidation and improvement stage (2004-2007). MOLSS cooperated with ILO again to introduce and implement SIYB China project nationwide. It introduced a full set of SIYB training technology and project management methods, and trained millions of small business starters with strong entrepreneurial ability. The targeted trainees also expanded from the laid-off workers to the returned migrant workers, university graduates, ex-servicemen and the disabled. The SIYB training became a brand in promoting entrepreneurship-driven employment for local authorities based on practice. At the same time, the achievements of this international project were expanded through the implementation of the proactive employment policy and the implementation of the "The Plan of Ability to Promote Entrepreneurship". Employment training centres and employment service centres set up entrepreneurial service windows to carry out "all-in-one" entrepreneurship services, based on providing micro-secured loans, with business guidance, projects display, entrepreneurship incubation and follow-up support as the main body. Gradually, a "Trinity" work mode of policy support, entrepreneurship training and entrepreneurship service in line with China's national conditions was created after pilot practices. As a result, the multiplier effect of entrepreneurship-driven employment was growing and people's sense of entrepreneurship was getting stronger and stronger.

(3) Sustainable development stage (2008-2013). The State placed encouraging entrepreneurship in a more prominent position in facilitating employment. Pushed by the proactive employment policy, another new wave of entrepreneurship-driven employment was set off. On the basis of summing up the achievements and experience, MOHRSS explored a point-to-side employment promotion pattern in entrepreneurial cities. In other words, by means of developing entrepreneurial cities, stimulating the social vitality of major cities to establish a national entrepreneurial brand. At the same time, a series of activities, such as entrepreneurship theme forum, entrepreneurship training camp, entrepreneurship contest, was conducted to boost entrepreneurship-driven employment. In addition, the technical system of entrepreneurship training was improved through the cooperation with new projects. Entrepreneurship practical training technology suitable for China was developed, which was based on the technology learnt from the European Simulation Company. In cooperation with ILO, Emergency Start and Improve Your Business (E-SIYB) project for Wenchuan post disaster reconstruction, Get Ahead project for female entrepreneurship and Green Business Option (GBO) project for green environmental entrepreneurship were implemented one after another. Moreover, by learning the advanced experience from foreign countries, the national occupational qualification named as "Entrepreneurial Consultant" was issued. The functional standards of entrepreneurship service were developed to guide the establishment of entrepreneurship guidance centres in various parts of the country. The public entrepreneurship service system fitting in with China's national conditions was established. At this stage, the entrepreneurial environment and entrepreneurial atmosphere were significantly improved, and the entrepreneurial training mode and technical methods were more matured.

(4) Promotion and innovation stage (2014 to date). The State raised mass entrepreneurship and innovation up to the national strategy level, and clearly proposed the idea of entrepreneurship and innovation-driven employment. On the one hand, the good situation of entrepreneurship and innovation was developed through implementing the new employment policy, relaxing the policy, opening the market and freeing up the enterprises. On the other hand, the business start-up service was optimissd. A "1+X" business start-up training brand was created. That is, apart from the SIYB core training courses, which can build up the generic capacities on business start-up and management, "X" additional courses such as those on vocational skills (e.g. beauty, hairdressing, etc), professional skills (e.g. 3D printing, etc), industrial development (e.g. Internet, etc) and regional economy (e.g. e-commerce village) can be added to them, depending on the entrepreneurial groups, entrepreneurs at different stages and in different industries. Meanwhile, on the basis of constructing public entrepreneurship service system, efforts have been made in strengthening the sharing of network information resources, optimising new financing mode, and expanding and strengthening the crowd innovation space, so as to make it into an important platform of entrepreneurship services.

2.2.2 Achievements and Effects of SIYB Project

(1) Achievements in promoting employment through entrepreneurship. During the implementation period of SIYB project, 60,000 entrepreneurial trainers were trained and more than 3,000 entrepreneurship training institutes were established. The targeted groups of SIYB project were constantly expanded, and finally nearly 10 million entrepreneurs were helped to participate in the training and realise their entrepreneurial dreams. The introduction and implementation of SIYB project met the needs of China's employment and re-employment. The entrepreneurship training system organised and promoted by the government has been initially established, and combined with a series of proactive employment policies such as micro-secured loans, which has laid a solid foundation for promoting entrepreneurship-driven employment in China.

(2) Achievements in the construction of national entrepreneurship training system. While consolidating the achievements of SIYB project, MOHRSS further pursued sustainable and innovative development in line with the national conditions of China. By improving technical standards, enriching curriculum resources, improving trainers' ability, organising trainers' contests, building an information platform and innovating service means, the entrepreneurship training system, consisting of multi-training providers, multi-training models and covering different stages of entrepreneurial activities was basically established. And the "Malanhua China Entrepreneurial Training" brand demonstration project under MOHRSS was created. Up to now, the project has trained 700,000 trainees yearly and more than 60,000 trainers in total.

3. Achievements of Entrepreneurship-driven Employment

In accordance with the strategic plan of the CPC Central Committee and the State Council on promoting employment driven by business start-ups, creating entrepreneurial cities was taken as a key task by all localities. Entrepreneurship-driven employment was promoted effectively through developing an efficient organisational promotion mechanism, improving policy system according to local conditions, implementing effective entrepreneurship training and well targeted entrepreneurship services, and creating a pro-entrepreneurship public atmosphere.

3.1 Demonstration and Driving Role of Entrepreneurial Cities

In September 2008, the State Council made specific arrangements on entrepreneurship-driven employment, and proposed as follows: focusing on guiding and promoting cities with good work foundation and relatively mature conditions; implementing relevant supporting policies to promote entrepreneurship-driven employment; actively exploring in the aspects of organisation and leadership, entrepreneurship training, entrepreneurship service and social participation; and establishing entrepreneurial cities with entrepreneurship-driven employment. At the beginning of 2009, MOHRSS, as the leading ministry, set up a leading group to promote entrepreneurship-driven employment. It made overall plans for the entrepreneurship of university graduates, the laid-off and unemployed people, returned migrant workers, ex-servicemen and returned overseas students, and actively coordinated relevant departments to directly guide provinces and cities in promoting entrepreneurship-driven employment.

The first group of 82 national-level entrepreneurial cities was published after selection based on the recommendation of all provinces. In March 2009, a national working conference on creating entrepreneurial cities was held in order to plan and promote such work. In November of the same year, a training programme was conducted in Shanghai for the mayors from entrepreneurial cities to strengthen their understanding and responsibilities, so that they could play a leading role in this area. In November 2011, the national promotion meeting on entrepreneurship-driven employment was held to summarise and exchange experience, facilitating work progress and implementing new measures.

3.1.1 Bringing the Entrepreneurial Cities' Leading Effect into Full Play

Summarising successful experience and starting fresh from cities, a breakthrough was first achieved. Some projects conducted in the pilot cities in the past years showed the successful experience that for some work it was relatively easier to break the ice in cities, so it was decided that nationwide entrepreneurship-driven employment would be first started from cities. For those institutional and policy problems that could not be solved at national or provincial level for the moment, a breakthrough could be tried first at city level.

Cities had more entrepreneurial opportunities than the countryside and they were also the main battlefield for entrepreneurship-driven employment. So, developing entrepreneurial cities was not only conducive to the increase of entrepreneurs and employment promotion in these cities, but also conducive to the expansion of the city's new economic growth point and the improvement of its development environment. The common features of the first group of 82 national level entrepreneurial cities were economic development environment being relatively good and having a good public employment service system as well as a solid foundation on entrepreneurship training. In addition, the proactive employment policy achieved good results, in particular, the micro-secured loan policy and the taxation and fee reduction policy were well implemented there.

By starting with developing entrepreneurial cities, it was expected to get some breakthroughs and better results so as to create a new work situation on entrepreneurship-driven employment. At the same time, using typical cases and individual cities as examples to lead both the work and the whole country to a new step at national level.

3.1.2 Guiding Entrepreneurial Cities to Establish and Improve Five Systems

(1) Establish the organisational leadership system. The work content and the key examination points include the following four aspects. First, the government leaders should command in the frontline and place the work in an important position. Second, the relevant departments should form a joint force with an effective coordination and promotion mechanism. Third, the social partners, such as the federation of industry and commerce, trade unions, the Communist Youth League, women's federation, the disabled persons' federation, industrial associations and entrepreneurs' associations, should actively participate in it and give full play of their roles, so as to establish a socialised operation mechanism for entrepreneurship-driven employment. Fourth, responsibilities and tasks should be clearly described, and objectives and responsibilities should be well implemented at all levels.

(2) Improve the policy support system. The work content and the key examination points include the following four aspects. First, relax the market access, registration conditions and premise arrangement by the principle that all is accessible unless prohibited. Second, effectively improve the administration and certification procedures and build up a green channel. Third, vigorously strengthen policy support, improve and implement supportive policies such as tax deduction, micro-secured loans, premise arrangement, etc. Fourth, broaden financing access, set up special funds to support entrepreneurship and develop a long-term effective mechanism for micro-secured loans.

(3) Improve the entrepreneurship training system. The work content and examination focus on the following three aspects. First, expand the scope of entrepreneurship training, including all the new entrepreneurs in the training rotation, and improve the training quality. Second, make full use of the existing conditions and idle resources to establish and improve business incubator bases and promote practical training for start-up business. Third, implement subsidy policy for training and integrate business start-up training with project development, small loans and business start-up guidance.

(4) Build up an entrepreneurial service system. The work content and the examination focus on two aspects. First, according to the needs of the creating entrepreneurial city, establish and improve the entrepreneurship guidance service organisation based on the existing public employment service system, strengthening the development of entrepreneurship service team, building or rebuilding the entrepreneurship guidance service centres. Second, actively study the form and content of entrepreneurship service, and establish a public platform on entrepreneurship service, improving the service means and establishing the entrepreneurship information service network and information release mechanism.

(5) Improve the performance assessment system. There are four major indicators. "Government behaviour" is the first indicator to examine whether the five major systems are complete or not. "Questionnaire survey" is a tool to objectively understand and reflect whether people and organisations' satisfaction to the city's entrepreneurial environment has been raised or not. "The start-up activity index" is to see whether the entrepreneurial proportion of urban employees is really increased, and whether the growth and development of small enterprises and micro enterprises have been improved than before. "The entrepreneurial contribution index" is to see whether the multiplier effect of entrepreneurship-driven employment has been achieved or not.

3.1.3 Breakthroughs and Achievements Made by the Entrepreneurial Cities

In order to test the effectiveness of the work and further push it forward, in 2012, commissioned by the Ministry of Human Resources and Social security, China Employment Promotion Association set up an expert evaluation group, together with other non-governmental professional investigation institutes and authoritative research institutes, made an evaluation of the first group of entrepreneurial cities. The evaluation showed that these cities obtained remarkable achievements in promoting entrepreneurship-driven employment. It could be seen that in order to promote entrepreneurship-driven employment in the whole country, the most practical and effective way was to implement the strategic plan of promoting entrepreneurship-driven employment by starting with a group of cities to take the lead in building up a system, breaking through difficulties and achieving good results, and then to extend it gradually.

(1) Establish the five major systems. First, in terms of developing organisational leadership system, entrepreneurship leading groups have been set up and worked actively in all the entrepreneurial cities. The CPC Party Committee at city level and the city government have closely worked together and played their front-line leading roles, which has ensured the joint efforts of all relevant departments and social organisations in employment promotion. Second, in terms of constructing policy support system, employment promotion is now supported by comprehensive economic and social policies, rather than just by employment policy as it used to, and the linkage effect of multiple policy support has started to emerge. The entrepreneurial cities have introduced favourable support policies in such areas as easing market access, improving administration, solving financing bottlenecks, implementing tax incentives, increasing entrepreneurial premises, and encouraging employment promotion, which has not only promoted entrepreneurship, but also achieved institutional breakthrough and innovation. Third, regarding the establishment of an entrepreneurial training system, a preliminary training system has been set up for all types of workers in urban and rural areas who have the desire to start up their own businesses, and various forms of entrepreneurial training have been carried out. This has laid a good foundation for the improvement of their entrepreneurial capacity and quality. Fourth, in terms of developing start-up service system, public platforms for start-up services and social intermediary organisations have been generally set up, and the "all-in-one" all-round service has been carried out for different groups of people. These measures have greatly improved the start-up environment, facilitated entrepreneurs, and realised the transformation of passive services to active services. Fifth, with regard to the development of job evaluation system, a scientific and objective performance evaluation mechanism and a corresponding statistical index system have been set up to evaluate, inspect and supervise the work of entrepreneurship-driven employment.

(2) Make a breakthrough in solving the difficult problems such as the high threshold of starting up a business and financing. In order to solve the problem of high threshold and difficulty in handling affairs related to starting up a business, the cities cleaned up all kinds of barriers by further lowering the market threshold, implementing the principle of "accessible unless prohibited", simplifying the registration procedure and reducing the cost of starting up a business. In view of the financing and premises difficulty, many provinces and cities took granting micro-secured loans as an important breakthrough point. After innovation, they set up a good mechanism for it which could be put as "loans easy to get, to be well used and recoverable." It enabled micro-secured loan policy to play its full role and provide strong support for workers to start up their businesses, breaking the bottleneck of financing. Many cities provided entrepreneurs with "start-up premises" by relying on various parks, making use of idle factories and building incubation bases so as to gradually alleviate the business space problem. In view of the low success rate of college students in starting up their businesses, each entrepreneurial city vigorously promoted "the College Students' Entrepreneurship Leading Plan", actively explored the fields of intellectual entrepreneurship, and increased incubation services and policy support. As a result, such rate increased substantially.

(3) The number of entrepreneurs and start-up entities increased sharply. Each of the entrepreneurial cities actively removed market barriers, stopped unjustifiable charges and funds-raising, and strictly prohibited interference with the normal operation of start-up enterprises. Joint examination and approval, approval for the request before the deadline and "one-stop" commitment service were implemented for project initiation, filing, examination and approval, and certificate handling. In 2011, the number of new private enterprises and the self-employed increased by 109% and 66% respectively, compared with 2008. In 2011, the number of individual and private economic entities per 10,000 economically active population in the entrepreneurial cities increased by 33% compared with 2008, 3 percentage points higher than the national level in the same period; while the number of such entities in the entrepreneurial cities actually increased by 42%, 10 percentage points higher than the national level in the same period; and the number of employees in individual and private economic entities in these cities increased by 52%, exceeding the national level by 18 percentage points.

(4) Entrepreneurship training was gradually launched. More than 80% of the entrepreneurial cities established an elementary entrepreneurship training system and an entrepreneurship service system for various types of entrepreneurs in urban and rural areas, with the active participation of various stakeholders. In 2011, 1.455 million workers nationwide participated in entrepreneurship training, 80% more than that in 2008, and the training quality was also improved accordingly. The entrepreneurial cities witnessed an obvious effect, with target groups generally focusing on college graduates, the unemployed people and the returned migrant workers. In terms of specific practices, it could be generalised as follows: formulating entrepreneurship training plans; introducing subsidy policies; integrating education and training resources within the city; promoting entrepreneurship training into campuses, communities and rural areas; strengthening the development of teaching staff and practical training bases; and adopting advanced courses and training technology to enhance training quality. From 2009 to 2011, about 76% of the entrepreneurial cities made big progress on both "the qualified rate of entrepreneurship training" and "the business opening rate in a half year after entrepreneurship training" or at least remained a high level for these two indicators.

3.2 Entrepreneurship and Innovation Gradually Forming a New Upsurge of Employment

3.2.1 Entrepreneurship and Innovation Becoming the Two Engines of Economic Development under the New Normal

"Mass Entrepreneurship and Innovation" was an important decision to meet the needs of economic and social development. Since the 18th CPC National Congress, China's economic development has entered a new normal. While the economy entering the medium- and high-speed development stage, the industrial development also stepped into a new development stage in China. In accordance with the current situation and future economic development trend in China, the CPC and the State put forward "Mass Entrepreneurship and Innovation" as a strategic nationwide call, which became a strong driving force for China's reform and development in the new era.

In June 2015, the State Council issued *Opinions on Several Policies and Measures to Vigorously Promote Mass Entrepreneurship and Innovation*, proposing to vigorously promote mass entrepreneurship and innovation, which was of great significance. First, it is an inevitable choice to cultivate and instil new driving forces for economic and social development. When economic development enters the new normal, it needs to shift from factor-driven and investment-driven to innovation-driven. The purpose of promoting mass entrepreneurship and innovation is to support all kinds of market entities to continuously start up new enterprises, to develop new products, to open up new markets, and to cultivate emerging industries by structural reform, institution and mechanism innovation, and by eliminating various institutional constraints and barriers that are not conducive to entrepreneurship and innovation. Second, it is a fundamental measure for expanding employment and making people rich. At present, China is under huge employment pressure and prominent structural employment contradictions. Promoting mass entrepreneurship and innovation is to create an fair competitive entrepreneurial environment, so that all kinds of entrepreneurs in the market with dreams, readiness and abilities can increase their income through starting up businesses, just like brining a duck to water and ending up with an interactive development between starting up businesses and promoting employment. Third, it is an effective way to stimulate the innovation potential and entrepreneurial vitality of the whole society. At present, the concept of entrepreneurship and innovation is far from being deeply rooted in the hearts of the Chinese people. The entrepreneurship education and training system is not complete. The ability to be creative and the courage to be entrepreneurial are insufficient. And a favourable environment of encouraging innovation and tolerating failure has not yet been nurtured. To promote mass entrepreneurship and innovation, it is necessary to intensify the whole society's entrepreneurship education with innovation as the core, to carry forward the entrepreneurial spirit which can be generally put as daring to be the first, pursuing innovation and never giving up in spite of reverses. Constantly enhancing the awareness of entrepreneurship and innovation may possibly ensure entrepreneurship and innovation to become the common value and good manner pursued by the whole society.

3.2.2 The New Policy of Mass Entrepreneurship and Innovation Providing Better Services for Innovators and Entrepreneurs

Since the initiation of promoting mass entrepreneurship and innovation, a series of policies and measures has been issued at both national and local level to support mass entrepreneurship and innovation. The multiplier effect of entrepreneurship-driven employment has been further unleashed, the employability driven by entrepreneurship has been continuously enhanced, and the employment of key groups has been steadily moved forward.

Thoroughly implement the innovation-driven development strategy, promote the in-depth development of "mass entrepreneurship and innovation", and promote fuller and higher quality employment. (Photo taken by Xinhua News Agency reporter Xiaoguang Luo.)

(1) Unblock the way of starting up a business and expand the effect of entrepreneurship-driven employment. Institutional and mechanic barriers that restrict workers from starting up businesses should be removed through continuously deepening the reform to streamline administration and delegate power, improve regulation and upgrade services, so as to constantly improve the environment for starting up businesses, deepen the reform of administrative examination and approval systems as well as business system, and lower the threshold for market access. The preferential tax and fee policies should be implemented to encourage college graduates, ex-servicemen, the disabled and the registered unemployed to start up their own businesses. More policy supports for start-up beginners such as premise support, facilities provision, rent reduction and housing concessions should be provided to reduce the cost of starting up a business, and accelerate the formation of a policy environment conducive to workers' participation in starting up businesses.

(2) Mobilise workers' initiatives in starting up businesses. Many programmes, such as innovative and entrepreneurial talents attracting plan, entrepreneurship training plan, and the pilot programme supporting the returned migrant workers to start up businesses in their hometowns were implemented. College and secondary school graduates and professionals were supported and encouraged to change their employment and career value and to become entrepreneurship leaders by giving full play of their knowledge and technology advantages. More overseas high-end talents could be attracted to start up businesses and innovate in China by further relaxing the conditions for foreign talents to apply for visa, work permit, residence permit and permanent resident permit, simplifying the examination and approval process, and increasing funding support for starting up businesses. It is necessary to vigorously promote entrepreneurship, cultivate the sense of entrepreneurship, and create a favourable social atmosphere of encouraging entrepreneurship and being tolerant to failure in the whole society.

(3) Strengthen the service for business start-ups and improve the success rate of starting up businesses. The "mass entrepreneurship and innovation" demonstration bases at a high standard with distinctive features were established in regions, universities, research institutes and enterprises in order to enhance the entrepreneurial service ability. The new incubation mode was promoted in the development of maker spaces, incubation bases and entrepreneurial parks for providing "all-in-one" services such as project development, business guidance and financing to support the successful entrepreneurship of workers. Small and micro enterprise entrepreneurship and innovation bases were established to form an open and comprehensive service platform that combined online with offline, and incubation with investment. The platform provided entrepreneurs at different stages with different needs, with targeted, specialised, differentiated and customised guidance services. It also provided start-up enterprises with low-cost and convenient services for business start-up and growth to promote their rapid development. Meanwhile, an entrepreneurial service platform aiming at everyone would be developed to further promote the development of entrepreneurial cities, and actively cultivate the entrepreneurial ecosystem.

3.2.3 Further Developing the Role Played by Small and Micro Enterprises of Being the Main Channel for Employment

With the promotion of mass entrepreneurship and innovation, small and micro enterprises are blooming everywhere. Supporting the development of small and micro enterprises has become one of the important issues in the context of mass entrepreneurship and innovation. The purpose of promoting mass entrepreneurship and innovation and optimising the policy environment is actually to promote and optimise the policy environment for the healthy development of small and micro enterpries. To promote mass entrepreneurship and innovation, it is necessary to let social forces play a greater role so that small and micro enterprises can really survive and grow well. Only in this way can the market vitality and social creativity be better stimulated, so that the supply and demand for jobs can be connected in a wider area. The business environment can be optimised by expanding market access, implementing a series of policies to support small and micro enterprises, including tax and other burden reduction, and clearing up and standardising related policies on enterprise charges. The efforts have been made to promote the innovative development of small and micro enterprises, to promote the development of entrepreneurship and innovation demonstration bases of small and micro enterprises and to utilise e-commerce platforms to open up new markets, so that small and micro enterprises can increase their employment capacity and become the main force in offering job opportunities and a new engine for China's economic growth.

3.2.4 Rapidly Developing New Forms of Employment

It is estimated that new driving forces may contribute to about 70% of the total increased employment. The research shows that the new driving forces represented by new industries, new forms and new models shall have a positive effect on promoting entrepreneurship-driven employment, which has formed the most active and dynamic mechanism. In order to adapt to the characteristics of the new forms of employment pattern, policies have been put forward to support its development. The first is to support the development of emerging business forms. Policy orientation shall be adjusted rapidly to promote the efficient and full utilisation of social resources through co-sharing and improving policies and regulations on taxation and social security, and to promote a rapid development of new economic forms such as sharing economy for creating more new employment opportunities. The second is to improve the employment and social security systems that adapt to the features of the new employment forms. Workers shall be supported to get diversified jobs through new business forms. If employees sign labour contracts with emerging business enterprises, enterprises shall participate in social insurance schemes for employees according to law, and the eligible enterprises can enjoy the supportive policy if they meet the requirements of job creation. It is needed to explore specific unemployment insurance and work injury insurance schemes suitable for flexible workers, and those entitled workers can enjoy the supportive policies on flexible employment and entrepreneurship.

3.3 Main Achievements of Entrepreneurship-driven Employment

3.3.1 Stimulating Market Vitality and Innovation Power, and Expanding New Space for Employment

In recent years, the State has vigorously promoted the reform to "streamline administration and delegate power, improve regulation and upgrade services". The dividend of reform has been continuously unleashed, and the vitality of various market entities has been bursting. Since the business system reform was implemented in 2014, by the end of 2018, the number of newly established enterprises increased from 6,900 in 2013 each day on average to 18,400, and the number of enterprises with more than one thousand workers increased from 11.4 every day in 2013 to 23.9, more than doubled. The number of real market entities in China reached 106 million in 2018, 73% of which were established in the past 5 years.

Practice has proved that mass entrepreneurship and innovation are important measures to cultivate new driving forces, to develop emerging industries and to increase new jobs. Market vitality and innovation power have been fully activated. New economy and new employment are springing up, which has become an important source of employment growth. By the end of 2018, 31.433 million private enterprises and 73.286 million self-employed businesses registered in industry and commerce departments, increased by 24.859 million and 44.113 million, compared with 6.574 million and 29.173

million respectively in 2009. The number of employees in private enterprises was 213.754 million and the number of workers in self-employed businesses was 160.376 million, an increase of 134.714 million and 102.612 million, compared with 79.04 million and 57.764 million in 2009 respectively.

3.3.2 The Entrepreneurship of Key Groups Continuing to Grow, and Online Entrepreneurship Becoming a New Growth Point

In recent years, more than 13 million new urban jobs have been created in China for 7 consecutive years, and the surveyed unemployment rate in 31 major cities has remained at a low level. The proactive employment policy has been continuously improved, and remarkable achievements have been obtained for the employment of key groups. Since 2013, college graduates have witnessed "double growth" in the number of employment and entrepreneurship for 4 consecutive years, and millions of college students have registered as market entities. From 2013 to 2016, there were 0.359 million, 0.478 million, 0.559 million and 0.615 million college graduates registered as entrepreneurs at the industrial and commercial administrations (Figure 5.1). The policy of encouraging migrant workers to return home starting up their own businesses has become a new trend. According to statistics, by the end of 2018, there were 7.8 million people returning or entering countryside to start up businesses.

Figure 5.1 The Number of Registered College Graduates Starting up Businesses from 2013 to 2016

(Unit: 10 thousand)

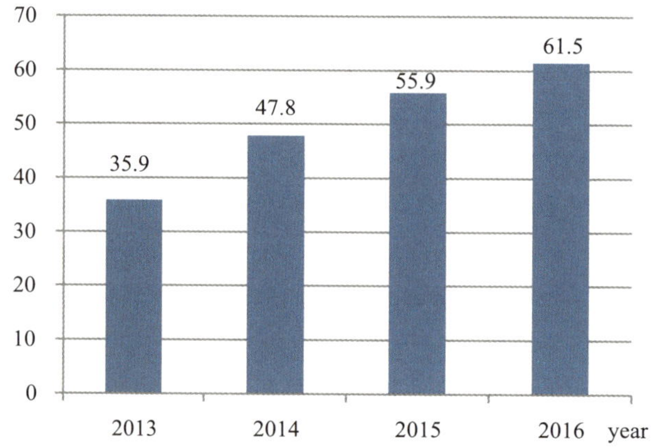

With the rapid development of network economy and e-commerce, a large number of new jobs emerged. By the end of 2018, the platform economy directly created 5.98 million jobs and about 75 million service providers were involved, which expanded job opportunities and career development possibilities for many grass roots entrepreneurs. First, employment scale was expanded and employment areas were extended. Online start-ups had a low threshold, low start-up costs, rapid development possibility, flexible business forms, a long business chain, and large room for growth. It not only promoted direct employment expansion in related industries, but also effectively boosted employment in the industrial chain such as logistics, payment, customer service and others. At the same time, starting up a business online might lead to the development of many new careers, providing the expansion space for employment. Second, the employment structure was optimised and the employment mode was innovated. Workers had to constantly improve their cognitive character and the ability to master the latest knowledge, and gradually became the workers with the capacity of mastering new technologies and new knowledge at any time requested by the era of knowledge economy, so that a lot of intelligent employment would be created, which would promote the rise of intelligent intensive industries and the optimisation of the employment structure. Third, the quality of employment was improved and fair employment was promoted. Online start-ups offered more employment choices, which not only extended employment forms, enriched employment contents and increased employment rate, but also improved employment elasticity, met various employment demands and greatly improved employment flexibility.

3.3.3 Changing the Entrepreneurship Concept and Improving the Entrepreneurship Environment

Entrepreneurship has brought about a fundamental change in the concept of employment. Especially after the financial crisis, more and more workers have changed their employment concept and realised that they should depend on themselves to find jobs. Workers have changed their ideas from "getting a job" from the government or other organisations to "creating a job" by starting up their own businesses with full responsibility for profits and losses themselves. Chinese entrepreneurs have set up five kinds of spirits. The first is daring to smash the bonds of traditional ideas, pioneering and innovative. The second is pragmatic, self-reliant, working hard and persevering. The third is progressive, never giving in despite reverses. The fourth is professional, faithful and with integrity. The fifth is dedicating to reward the society after success. These five spirits have become the source of motivation for workers to start up their own businesses, and have played a positive role in promoting the changing of employment concept for the new generation of workers. It is of great significance to cultivate and encourage more entrepreneurial workers to have these spirits, carry it forward in the whole society, and change their employment concept.

By building up entrepreneurial cities, the government explored the way to establish the five systems, i.e. organisational leadership, policy support, entrepreneurial training, entrepreneurial service and job evaluation, so as to provide a better entrepreneurial environment for entrepreneurs. Business start-up premises were expanded and incubation bases were established. Family residences, houses rented and temporary commercial premises were allowed to be the premises for starting up businesses. Many cities built incubation bases by using existing idle factories and various parks, and provided business guidance services and a certain period of policy support. By broadening the financing channels and taking the micro-secured loans as an important source of financing, the amount of loans granted was increased and the efficiency of loan service was improved. Entrepreneurship guidance agencies and public service platforms were set up in large, medium and small cities across the country. According to the business environment assessment report of the World Bank, China's overall business environment assessment in 2018 jumped to the 46th place among 190 economies in the world, with 50 places up from 2013. Among them, the convenience of starting up enterprises substantially rose to the 28th place, up by 130 places in 5 years.

Chapter 6
Employment Service

1. Overview of Employment Service

Employment service refers to a series of service measures provided by specific institutions to meet the needs of workers to seek employment or employing units. The main contents include providing employment information, vocational guidance, job recommendation, employment training, entrepreneurship guidance, human resources and social security agencies, and other related services. The core business of employment service is to provide intermediary service for job matching between employees and employers.

Employment service institutions refer to those organisations specialised in employment service activities. Employment service institutions can be divided into two categories by their basic nature, i.e. public employment service institutions and job intermediary agencies. According to the requirements of relevant laws, regulations and policies, the public institutions undertake the responsibility of providing free public welfare employment services to workers, and are set up by the government at or above the county level. The job intermediary agencies are set up by social organisations or individuals in accordance with the provisions of *Company Law of the People's Republic of China* and *Employment Promotion Law*. According to the operation and management rules of human resources market, relevant paid job intermediary services are provided to employees and employers through business operation.

Employment service system is the general name, including all kinds of employment service agencies and intermediary organisations. At present, China's employment service system is mainly composed of public employment service institutions affiliated to human resources and social security departments and job intermediary agencies run by other departments and the society.

The Chinese government attaches great importance to employment, constantly increases policy support, strengthens employment services, and actively builds a broad platform for the employment of workers. (Photo taken by Xinhua News Agency reporter Xiao Liu.)

1.1 The Development Course of Public Employment Service

Employment Promotion Law stipulates that people's governments at or above the county level shall set up public service agencies for employment. With the continuous development of economy and society, the network of public employment service institutions has gradually developed, and the public employment service system has been gradually established and improved, which has initially formed a public employment service system with Chinese characteristics. There are five stages in its development history.

1.1.1 Initial Stage (1980s)

At the beginning of China's reform and opening-up policy, the urban employment system developed under the planned economy started to reform, featured by government controlling employment quotas and assigned jobs exclusively to urban residents. The employment guideline implemented for that period was put as job placement by labour departments, voluntary job-matching and self-employment (the so-called "three-ways combined"). The market mechanism started to played a role in allocating labour resources, and labour service companies emerged, which were the embryonic form of employment service agencies. Labour service companies belong to social organisations, initiated by the government's labour department, integrating the placement of employment and training. Gradually, these companies assume the multiple functions of organising and managing the social labour force and promoting employment. By the end of the 1980s, labour service companies were widespread throughout the country. At the same time, with the reform of personnel system, starting from early 1980s, personnel departments in some regions began to set up talent exchange centres to provide exchange services and talent management for local recruitment of talents.

1.1.2 Gradually Forming Stage (1990s)

Since mid 1980s, the market has played an increasingly important role in allocating labour resources. In 1990s, with the development of the human resources market, various kinds of employment agencies emerged. The employment service organisations run by the labour department gradually developed into employment service system with job recommendation, employment training, unemployment insurance and organising the unemployed to take up production as four main businesses. Accordingly, the labour departments at province, municipality, major district and county level set up agencies specialising in the administration of employment services, and set up service entities such as job recommendation centres, employment training centres, unemployment insurance offices and labour service corporate management centres, and so on. A set of systems was initially established for the registered unemployed with service items of providing living allowance, job recommendation, training organisation and employment promotion. The public employment service network began to take shape. At the same time, governments at all levels encouraged social organisations and individual citizens to set up employment agencies in accordance with law. All types of employment agencies developed rapidly and became an important complement to the employment service system. During this period, personnel exchange service agencies were also established at provincial, municipal and county levels throughout the country, mainly responsible for file management, graduates' employment procedures, market information release, organising job fairs and so on.

1.1.3 Establishment and Improvement Stage (Late 1990s)

In 1998, the Central Committee of CPC and the State Council issued a circular, requesting all localities to ensure the basic livelihood of the laid-off workers in SOEs and their re-employment, to make the development of a market employment mechanism as one of the working objectives, and to make more efforts to develop the human resources market. Public employment agencies should open specific service counters to offer vocational guidance for the laid-off workers free of charge. To this end, since 1999, the Ministry of Labour and Social Security organised 100 large- and medium-sized cities in China to carry out a pilot project on developing a scientific, standardised and modernised labour market with a view to improve the functions of public employment services. At the end of 2000, *Labour Market Management Regulations* promulgated by the Ministry of Labour and Social Security clearly set out the nature, content and target of free public employment services, as well as the responsibilities of the government organisations in providing public employment services.

1.1.4 Rapid Development Stage (Early 21st Century)

Since the beginning of the 21st century, with the implementation of the proactive employment policy, China's public employment service system and institutional development entered a fast track. In 2002, China began to implement the proactive employment policy, which explicitly required governments at all levels to establish a public employment service system, to provide free job recommendation to all the urban registered unemployed and laid-off workers from SOEs, and to provide free re-employment training for the urban unemployed workers and laid-off workers from SOEs. The funds needed were mainly borne by local finance, while the central finance gave appropriate subsidies to the regions in financial difficulty. In 2003, on the basis of summing up the above-mentioned pilot projects on the labour market, the Central Committee of CPC and the State Council further proposed that employment services should be institutionalised, specialised and socialised. In 2005, according to the requirements of the State Council, public employment service institutions were opened to all job seekers free of charge, and the vocational training subsidy was extended to rural workers entering urban areas for work. In 2007, the Ministry of Labour and Social Security issued *Notice on Improving the Functions of Public Employment Service*, which specified the six service functions of public employment services (comprehensive service, information release, job recommendation, vocational guidance, training and business start-up service, employment and unemployment management), and vigorously promoted the one-stop service. Through the institutionalised, specialised and socialised employment services, in terms of institutional construction, the process of organic connection among the registration system for the unemployed, the employment aid system for people with employment difficulties, employment and unemployment registration and employment services were further strengthened. In terms of specialisation construction, the construction of diversified service functions, people-centred service concept, professional staff and the IT service means were further strengthened. In terms of socialisation, it was reflected in the fact that all kinds of job seekers and employers, such as rural migrant workers, highly skilled talents and college graduates, were included in the service target. All kinds of private service agencies such as all job intermediaries, labour dispatch, vocational consultation and vocational training institutes were encouraged to deliver public welfare employment services. A service evaluation system based on the satisfaction of service recipients was established.

1.1.5 Enriching and Improving Stage (After 2008)

Employment Promotion Law, which was implemented in 2008, further clarifies that governments at or above the county level shall do the following: incorporating the funds for public employment service institutions into the government budget at the same level; establishing and improving public employment service system; setting up public employment service institutions; and providing workers with free services, including consultation on employment policies and regulations, information about supply and demand of jobs, information on guiding wages on the labour market and vocational training, vocational guidance and job recommendation, employment and unemployment registration, and employment aid, etc. In the same year, the Ministry

Provide employment services for college graduates. (Photo taken by Xinhua News Agency reporter Ying Liu.)

of Labour and Social Security also promulgated *Regulations on Employment Service and Employment Management*. In 2009, among the six major initiatives launched by the Ministry of Labour and Social Security in response to the impact of international financial crisis on employment, multiple departments jointly carried out a series of employment service activities and special vocational training programmes, as well as employment aid for the disadvantaged groups. These measures not only mitigated the impact of the crisis, but also enriched the public employment service function and further improved the service system. For example, the Ministry of Human Resources and Social Security, together with the Ministry of Education, All-China Federation of Trade Unions (ACFTU), Central Committee of the Communist Youth League, All-China Women's Federation and China Disabled Persons' Federation, jointly organised a series of employment service activities, mainly including: re-employment assistance focusing on promoting the employment of zero employment families; recruitment week for private enterprises and employment service month for college graduates to promote the employment of college graduates; and the "Spring Breeze Action" to facilitate the rural workers to work in cities after the Spring Festival every year. Another example was implementing employment aid system for the disadvantaged groups. It mainly relied on public employment service institutions such as streets and communities to open special service counters for the groups with employment difficulties, provide special aid services such as policy consultation, job recommendation, skills training, agency affairs, and provide one-to-one tracking service and guidance for particularly hard-to-put workers. It should be specially pointed out that China would move forward to an equal public employment service for both urban and rural workers. Since 2005, equal employment service policy was implemented nationwide, which improved the employment environment for rural labourers to work in cities.

At city and district level in large-and medium-sized cities and some small cities where conditions permitted, comprehensive service places were set up, normally named as public employment agencies, and at the grass roots level, i.e. sub-district and residential communities, labour security working platforms were set up. A public employment service network with five management levels, i.e. central, provincial, city, district (county), sub-district (township), and six service delivery levels, i.e. the former five plus residential community, was gradually established. It integrated the services of employment policy, job recommendation, vocational guidance and agency services, and connected with vocational training, management of the unemployed, job post development, business start-up training and business start-up guidance so as to provide the one-stop convenient service. In 2018, the number of public employment and talent exchange service institutions at and above the district/county level totalled 5,618 nationwide. Most of the sub-districts and townships set up grass roots working platforms, and most of the residential communities and villages had staff to deal with labour and social security affairs. In 2018, public employment and personnel service institutions at all levels handled 55.18 million cases of registered recruitment and 37.74 million cases of registered job-seeking, provided 17.19 million vocational guidances, 18.59 million job recommendations, 4.36 million business start-up guidances and 2.01 million business start-up trainings.

1.2 The Status of Private Employment Service

Private job intermediary agencies refer to the commercial organisations which are run by corporate organisations such as non-governmental departments and social organisations or by individual citizens to provide intermediary services and other related services for employing units to recruit workers and workers to seek jobs.

Since 2002, a series of proactive employment policies was promulgated by the Chinese government. On the one hand, private job intermediary agencies were regarded as an important force in promoting employment and thus they were encouraged for development. Policy support was available for them if they participated in employment services for the laid-off workers and migrant workers. On the other hand, job intermediaries were strictly regulated. The illegal job intermediary agencies and the infringement on job seekers' rights and interests were severely cracked down.

Employment Promotion Law stipulates that governments at all levels should encourage private job intermediary agencies to carry out employment service activities in accordance with law, and provide subsidies for public welfare employment service activities. *Employment Promotion Law* also makes clear provisions on the conditions for setting up job intermediary agencies, approval procedures, prohibited activities and punishment on illegal acts. *Labour Contract Law* and *Provisional Regulation on Labour Dispatch* have made corresponding provisions on the rights, responsibilities and obligations of private employment service agencies to carry out labour dispatch business and the rights and interests protection of the dispatched workers. *Government Procurement Law* clearly defines government procurement activities. *Administrative Measures for Government Purchase of Services* stipulates in detail such as the purchasing party and the supplying party, purchasing items and scope, guided purchasing catalogue, purchasing methods and procedures, budget and financial management, performance evaluation and supervision management. It meets people's needs for public services by optimising the allocation of social resources, reducing costs, promoting fair competition, improving the quality and efficiency of service.

By the end of 2017, China had set up about 30,200 human resources service agencies, increased by 13% over the previous year, including 21,990 private service enterprises, accounting for 72.9% of the total (Table 6.1). The total number of employees of these agencies reached 0.584 million, increased by 5.6% over the previous year. The number of employees in private service enterprises was 0.396 million, accounting for 67.8% of the total (Table 6.2).

Table 6.1 Changing of Various Human Resources Service Institutions (2016-2017)

Year	Public employment and talent service institutions	Proportion	State-owned service enterprises	Proportion	Private service enterprises	Proportion	Hong Kong, Macao, Taiwan and foreign-funded service enterprises	Proportion	Other human resources service organisations	Proportion
2016	5,262	19.7%	1,493	5.6%	18,859	70.6%	227	0.9%	854	3.2%
2017	5,259	17.4%	1,793	6.0%	21,990	72.9%	235	0.8%	885	2.9%

Source: SUN J. China Human Resources Services Development Report (2018) [M]. Beijing: China Personnel Publishing House, 2018.

Table 6.2 Employees in Human Resources Services (2016-2017, by Nature of Institution)

(Unit: 10 thousand, %)

	Total number of people		Proportion in the total number of employees in the industry	
	2016	2017	2016	2017
Human resources service agencies under governmental organisations	9.1	8.8	16.5	15.1
State-owned service enterprises	6.0	6.6	10.8	11.3
Private service enterprises	37.0	39.6	66.9	67.8
Hong Kong, Macao, Taiwan and foreign-funded service enterprises	1.9	2.1	3.4	3.6
Other human resources service organisations	1.3	1.3	2.4	2.2

Source: SUN J. China Human Resources Services Development Report (2018) [M]. Beijing: China Personnel Publishing House, 2018.

1.3 Cooperation Between Public and Private Employment Service Agencies

Internationally, it has become a trend that many countries encourage cooperation between public and private employment service agencies when implementing labour market policies. Facing the new employment challenges in the new era, China needs to reform the current public employment service system, mechanism and operation mode. At the same time, it shall vigorously explore ways to promote cooperation between public and private employment service agencies, and gradually establish a "three-in-one" employment service structure, i.e. cooperation between public employment service institutions, employment service agencies run by social partners and private employment service agencies.

1.3.1 Significance of Promoting Cooperation Between Public and Private Employment Service Agencies

The first is to help the government change its functions, expand and extend the scope and field of public employment services, and form a diversified and multi-level employment service supply system. The second is to make up for the deficiency of the current public employment service system and function, and improve the overall quality and efficiency of public employment services. The third is to reduce the operation cost of public employment services and improve the efficiency of public funds for maximising the efficiency of government input funds. The fourth is to help public and private employment service agencies complement each other and form a joint force to provide comprehensive and high-quality employment and training services for job seekers and employers efficiently and conveniently.

1.3.2 Responsibilities, Rights and Interests of Public and Private Employment Service Agencies in the Cooperation

At present, the cooperation between public and private employment service agencies in some regions in China is conducted mainly in accordance with the provisions of *Government Procurement Law* and *Administrative Measures for Government Purchase of Services*, and the contracts signed by the two parties based on the specific contents of the cooperation. The contract stipulates the responsibilities, rights and interests of both parties.

(1) Responsibilities and obligations of public employment service institutions and their competent authorities. First, formulate and carry out the service purchasing plan. According to the requirements of laws and regulations and the needs of the general public for diversified employment services, define the framework of the cooperation system, and formulate the overall plan, specific programme/project and implementation rules on the purchasing. Second, establish the principles, objectives and tasks of purchasing services. It should not only comply with the relevant national laws, regulations and policies, but also select qualified and competent private employment service agencies and other social forces to deliver public employment services or even operate public employment service institutions. Third, determine the basic conditions and standards of partners. It stipulates that the cooperative service organisation must be an independent corporate entity, and its business areas include entrepreneurship and employment services;

it must have full-time staff, corresponding facilities, equipment and financial resources for the service business; it should have the ability and practical experience in organising various employment and entrepreneurship service activities, as well as good cooperation foundation with other partners, and recognised performance of efficiently carrying out service activities. Fourth, establish the procedures and methods of purchasing services. An open, fair and impartial bidding and tendering procedure in accordance with law should be formulated and implemented to select cooperative service institutions, and sign contracts with them for the purchase, which stipulates the responsibilities, rights and obligations of both parties. Fifth, be responsible for the calculation and allocation of government purchase service funds, as well as the inspection and supervision of the use of funds. Sixth, be responsible for the evaluation, supervision, reward and punishment of cooperation projects. According to the regulations and the service content, scope, quantity and quality standards stipulated in the service contract, the cooperative project should be evaluated and supervised in advance, during and after the event, and reward and punishment should be implemented according to the performance evaluation results.

(2) Responsibilities and obligations of private employment service agencies and their competent authorities. First, operate and manage the public employment and entrepreneurship service institutions or projects stipulated in the contract. In accordance with the requirements of national laws and policies, under the guidance and supervision of competent government departments, public employment and entrepreneurship service resources, including personnel, funds, information, facilities and equipment, should be well managed and used according to the contract. Second, establish and develop network services. Provide a communication and service matching platform for the market supply and demand sides for the purpose of communication, exchange, connection and matching services. Meanwhile, improve the traditional service mode by providing integrated online and offline employment and entrepreneurship services. Third, organise a team of experts to provide employment and entrepreneurship services. The guidance and consulting services should be provided by mobilising and attracting other social forces to participate in the cooperation projects. Fourth, hold large-scale employment and entrepreneurship activities to build up a service platform for job seekers and entrepreneurs. The activities include job fairs, entrepreneurial projects promotion meeting, entrepreneurship salons, skills training etc. Fifth, actively summarise the cooperation projects, conduct regular self-inspection and customer return visits, timely report to the public employment service institutions and competent government departments, and cooperate well in the performance evaluation process.

1.3.3 Forms of Cooperation Between Public and Private Employment Service Agencies

(1) Integrate employment information resources and establish an employment information platform. In order to realise the sharing of recruitment information and job-seek information, make full use of the public employment and talent service information system owned by the public employment service institutions, and incorporate the employment position information scattered at the private agencies into the public information system for centralised management, information release and application.

(2) Jointly carry out special employment service activities and expand the effectiveness of such service activities. Joint activities such as "Spring Breeze Action" and the employment service month for college graduates are carried out to provide job seekers, such as rural migrant workers and college graduates, with job information matching services, so as to expand the coverage of employment services and improve the efficiency of job recommendation service.

(3) Strengthen exchanges and cooperation to raise professional standards together. Relying on public employment service resources, private employment service agencies shall take the initiatives to carry out business discussions and interactive exchanges to jointly promote the development of employment services.

2. Public Employment Service System

2.1 Distribution of Public Employment Service and Its Organisation

2.1.1 Public Employment Service Institution

Public employment service institutions are the carriers that undertake the public employment service activities, and they are specific organisations set up by the government in accordance with the requirements of relevant laws and regulations to provide employment services for employees and employers. There are three types of public employment service institutions in China: public employment service management organisations, public employment service delivery organisations and grass roots public employment service offices. The public employment service management organisations undertake the planning of the service, the management of service organisations and the labour market within their jurisdiction area. The public employment service delivery organisations focus on job recommendation services. According to the requirements of integrating service counters, they set up specific comprehensive service delivery places directly providing services to job seekers and employers, undertaking various employment services such as policy consultation, information release, job recommendation, vocational guidance, vocational training, entrepreneurship service and agency affairs. The grass roots public employment service offices mainly refer to the labour and social security working platform at sub-district/ township and residential community level, which undertake the basic and general work, such as providing public employment services to the people and providing employment aid to the groups with employment difficulties under their jurisdiction.

The public employment service institution staff introduces preferential policies to entrepreneurs. (Photo taken by Xinhua News Agency reporter Yang Yang.)

The public employment service institutions have three characteristics. First, the public employment service institutions perform the public employment service function on behalf of the government, which is of public welfare nature. Second, public employment service institutions are specialised agencies responsible for providing employment services to workers, with corresponding professional service capabilities, including basic service functions, service places, service personnel and service technology and equipment. Third, the services with public welfare nature provided by the public employment service institutions are realised through free services and employment aid to workers.

2.1.2 Public Employment Service System

Public employment service system is a working system for providing employment services for citizens, which is established by the State according to the overall policy requirements on employment promotion. It consists of various public employment service institutions at all levels. According to the service content, the public employment service system includes comprehensive service institutions, specialised service institutions and grass roots service counters. Comprehensive service institutions are responsible for providing various employment services for all kinds of workers. Specialised service institutions are responsible for providing special services in some specific items or fields, such as employment services for college graduates and the disabled, and entrepreneurship services. Grass roots service counters are responsible for basic human resources and social security services, employment aid and human resources survey and statistics.

Public employment service institutions at or above the county level shall, in accordance with the employment objectives and tasks determined by the government, formulate annual employment service plans, and annual objectives and tasks for public employment service institutions. It undertakes the work relevant to the implementation of laws, administrative regulations and policies on promoting employment, and it participates in the formulation and implementation of various employment policies. It is directly responsible for the overall planning of employment services for the urban unemployed, new entrants to the labour market, college graduates and rural surplus labour force.

2.2 The Items, Content, Function and Role of Public Employment Service

Employment Promotion Law stipulates that public employment service institutions shall provide six basic services to workers free of charge: ① consultation on employment policies and regulations; ② release of information about supply and demand of jobs, guidance rates of wages on the market and vocational training; ③ vocational guidance and job recommendation; ④ employment aid to people who have difficulty in finding jobs; ⑤ registration of employment and unemployment; and ⑥ other public services for employment.

2.2.1 Consultation on Employment Policies and Regulations

The public employment service institutions shall provide consultation and guidance services on the general laws, regulations and policies on labour and social security for employers, job seekers and other service clients, mainly related to employment support policies, social security policies, protection of labour rights and interests.

2.2.2 Information Collection and Release

The public employment service institutions shall collect and release the human resources market information related to job seeking and recruitment of the service clients through various forms. The information mainly include: supply and demand of jobs, guidance rates of wages on the human resources market and vocational training. In addition, they shall provide information on the analysis and prediction of supply and demand of jobs, employment service items, policies and regulations on social security and employment, and other relevant information on employment services.

2.2.3 Vocational Guidance

The public employment service institutions shall provide professional vocational guidance for job seekers in choosing jobs and preparing for employment, and for employing units in recruiting workers. In accordance with service clients, vocational guidance can be divided into the guidance to individual job seekers and that to employers.

In accordance with guiding methods, it can be divided into one-to-one individual guidance and group guidance. In accordance with the service delivery time and employment stages, it can be divided into pre-employment guidance, on-the-job/in-service guidance and post-employment guidance. The guidance service contents mainly include investigating and analysing the trend of occupation changes and the status quo of supply and demand in the human resources market; carrying out assessment on workers' vocational quality and employability; and helping the workers understand the vocational situation, master job-seeking methods, determine job direction and career plan; proposing vocational training and recommending vocational training programmes to workers; providing special vocational guidance services to groups, such as women, the disabled, ex-servicemen, college graduates and persons with employment difficulties; giving guidance to employers in selecting recruitment methods and determining employment qualifications; and providing consultation services on business start-up and operation for the self-employed people and people ready to start up their own businesses.

2.2.4 Job Recommendation

Job recommendation is to promote employment by providing intermediary services for both supply and demand sides of the market, including collecting and releasing information on job supply and demand, and providing intermediary services for employers in recruiting workers and for workers on how to seek jobs. The main tasks are job-seeking registration, corporate employment survey and registration, the information collection and dissemination of market supply and demand, job-seeking and recruitment guidance and consultation.

The public employment service institutions should deliver job recommendation services in the following procedure. First, register for both job seekers and employers who apply for the service in the institutions. Second, recommend and provide possibly matching information on job supply and demand according to the needs and qualifications of job seeking or recruitment. At the same time, according to the requirements and conditions of the registered job seekers and employers, actively match the corresponding job supply and demand information. Third, based on the job supply and demand information registered by job seekers and employers, match job supply and demand information for job seekers and employers, and take the initiative to contact both job seekers and employers, providing them with on-site recruitment so that they can make the face-to-face two-way-selection. Relying on the Internet and other modern technical means, develop the human resources market information database to carry out the analysis and forecast on human resources supply and demand. Collect, sort out and regularly release the market information.

2.2.5 Employment Aid

Special measures and special employment policies shall be made to give priority support and focused help to the persons with employment difficulties in order to promote and stabilise their employment.

The public employment service institutions should provide employment aid services in the following procedure. First, provide specific guidance to the people with employment difficulties and provide one-to-one services. Second, provide follow-up services and guidance to those receiving job recommendation, so as to continuously understand their employment situation. Third, actively contact local employers to develop public welfare posts suitable for those with employment difficulties. Fourth, establish employment aid system, regularly carry out special service activities for the groups with employment difficulties, and combine daily assistance with concentrated assistance.

2.2.6 Registration of Employment and Unemployment

The public employment service institutions should undertake employment and unemployment management affairs commissioned by government departments, such as making employment registration for the employees recruited by the employing units, the self-employed and those in flexible employment forms, and establishing corresponding accounts for them; making registration for the unemployed who have the labour capacity and employment expectation within the legal working age, and providing them with consultation services on employment policies and employment services. They should also provide services such as approving unemployment benefits and file management for the unemployed, administration of the employment and unemployment registration certificate (later renamed as employment and business start-up certificate), approval of subsidies, and supporting services relating to business start-up secured loans. The public employment service institutions also guide the employing units in making good record on dismissal and recruitment.

2.3 Building up a Comprehensive Public Employment Service System

The 19th CPC National Congress put forward the task of employment in the new era and the goal of achieving higher quality and fuller employment. Speeding up the construction of a comprehensive public employment service system is an important measure to achieve the goal of employment.

2.3.1 Main Connotation and Basic Elements of the Comprehensive Public Employment Service System

Comprehensive public employment services imply the all-round, convenient and efficient services with the purpose of promoting employment and entrepreneurship, which are guided by the implementation of employment and business start-up policies, with the main line of meeting workers' diversified needs on employment and entrepreneurship and the basic needs of employers so as to match labour supply and demand.

(1) The main connotation of a comprehensive public employment service system. It includes: ① Services cover all clients, i.e. full coverage of service clients. First, employment and entrepreneurship services are available to all urban and rural workers with employment and entrepreneurship willingness. Second, employment services are available to all kinds of employment units with recruitment needs. Third, support services are available to all social training and intermediary institutes with such service demand. ② Services are available throughout the whole employment process, i.e. full availability during service process. First, services are available in each step of implementing employment policy. Second, services are available at all stages of workers' career. Third, services are available in all aspects of unit/organisation employment. ③ Services are equipped with complete functions, i.e. full range of service items. First, provide vocational guidance services and job recommendation services. Second, provide employment skills training services. Third, provide specific assistance services. Fourth, provide poverty alleviation via employment and labour export services. Fifth, provide entrepreneurship services for the whole process. Sixth, provide unemployment security services. Seventh, provide employment cooperation services. Eighth, provide information and data analysis services. ④ Use a variety of service tools, i.e. full range of service means. The first is the offline window service. The second is the online network service. The third is the integration of online and offline integrated services. The fourth is the publicity and consultation service. ⑤ Offer effective and convenient services, i.e. full promotion of service efficiency. First, deliver services on the spot or nearby or through internet. Second, simplify the service procedure. Third, offer accurate and targeted services.

(2) Building up a comprehensive employment service system includes six basic elements. The first is institutional standards, including the construction of a basic and equal service system and a public service standard system. The second is hardware construction, including the planning and construction of service agencies and reasonable layout of service outlets. The third is intelligent construction, including the service function setting and the information service platform construction. The fourth is organisation components, including the construction of a public employment service organisation system and a cooperative organisation network. The fifth is capacity building, including the development of professional work team, job responsibility description and performance management. The sixth is institutional guarantee, including the implementation of the legal status of employment work and the provision of funding security.

2.3.2 Key Work

(1) Promote equal services and achieve universal services. It includes promoting equal services for all urban and rural workers, promoting equal services for all types of employers, and promoting equal services in different regions in China.

(2) Promote standardisation and realise regulation. It includes speeding up the establishment and improvement of national and local standard system, implementing these standards and promoting standardised and well-regulated services.

(3) Promote specialisation and provide refined services. It includes creating intelligent matching, accurate and efficient job recommendation services; exploring accurate identification and judgment to offer refined vocational guidance services; providing services linked with the entrepreneurship training and guidance with focus on capacity building, entrepreneurship nurturing, guidance and supporting; providing services connected with vocational skills training which should be market and demand oriented and focusing on effectiveness; providing unemployment insurance services which should be closely linked with the three-in-one functions of unemployment insurance, i.e. ensuring livelihood, promoting employment and preventing unemployment; and delivering employment aid services which are differentiated by people and precisely targeted.

(4) Make every effort to enhance the level of informatisation and realise intellectual service. It includes developing a unified national public employment service information platform, vigorously promoting information interconnection and data sharing, and further strengthening the development and application of employment information big data.

(5) Make full use of market mechanism and realise service delivered by social service providers. It includes using market mechanism to integrate market resources, exploring the development of purchasing service mechanism, strengthening cooperation between public and non-public institutes to form joint force in employment service, strengthening inter-departmental coordination to form a favourable and interactive service delivery mechanism.

2.3.3 Safeguard Measures

(1) Strengthen organisation and leadership. It includes formulating an overall plan of employment and business start-up services covering the integrated urban and rural areas; improving system, mechanism and institutional building; determining annual targets and tasks as well as clarifying responsibilities; and carrying out an all-round evaluation on the progress and quality of public employment services promoted by all localities.

(2) Strengthen the development of professional team. Build up a platform for public employment service personnels which is conducive to their stable career development, and accelerate the improvement of personnel development mechanism and promote the development and stability of a professional team. Formulate and implement the capacity upgrading plan for public employment service personnels; accelerate the establishment of training mechanism for full-time service personnels at all levels; and comprehensively improve their professionalism and service ability.

(3) Strengthen the financial support. In line with the need to achieve the employment objectives and tasks of the new era and to provide all-round employment services, governments at each level have continuously increased budget input at the same level, integrated existing resources by pooling all employment-related funds so as to increase funds efficiency, and strengthened supervision and guidance on how to use the specific employment funds.

(4) Strengthen the performance evaluation. The service evaluation and efficiency assessment should be strengthened by combining with promoting standardised and well-regulated services. Service staff should be motivated to improve their service behaviour and performance. Timely discover and solve problems so as to improve service efficiency and quality.

2.4 Construction of the Public Employment IT Service

According to the overall plan of human resources and social security IT construction, the public employment service information system shall be improved.

2.4.1 Content of Information System Construction

(1) The employment IT service system. It includes the database of the clients' information and service resources (such as employment posts), the sub-system of searching and matching supply and demand information, and the self-service information sub-system for the clients.

(2) The management information system of employment service. It covers the sub-system of business operation information management of various employment service institutions, and the sub-system of storage, analysis and statistics of service effectiveness information, etc.

(3) The information release system of human resources market. It includes analysis and forecast sub-system of supply and demand information, sub-system

Deepen the integration of the"Internet Plus" innovation and employment services, and continuously expand the service contents and innovate the service mode. (Photo taken by Xinhua News Agency reporter Shaopeng Li.)

of specific information release and sub-system of public information release.

2.4.2 The Function of the Public Employment IT Service

(1) Information network is an effective tool for employment services. Through the construction of information network, more and more information is provided to the clients in time; through expanding information network to sub-districts, residential communities and villages, services are more accessible to the clients; through the analysis and automatic matching of the network, individualised or packaged services can be provided to clients.

(2) Information network is a powerful means in managing service business. Through the construction of information network, information management and information sharing can be achieved, which has effectively improved the management of each service business and the coordination of different services, and provide timely and accurate resource information and management information, so as to ensure a good management of all the employment service businesses.

(3) Information network can provide a useful support for macro-decision-making. It is an important source of information for governments at all levels and relevant departments to make relevant decisions. Through information technology, a lot of information on the integrity and unity of the human resources market has been summarised and refined. On the basis of statistical analysis, this summarised information can serve relevant departments for their policy and decision-making.

2.4.3 Establishment and Improvement of the Employment Information Service System

The establishment of a sound employment information service system refers to the working system that can provide the society with the supply and demand information of the human resources market and related information. First, information service can effectively guide and regulate the flow and allocation of market resources. On the one hand, it can help workers to find their jobs on their own and assist employers to achieve successful recruitment. On the other hand, it can effectively guide the flow of human resources and improve the efficiency and quality of human resources allocation. At the same time, market information plays a guiding role for vocational training institutes in selecting training direction, for workers in getting prepared for entering the market, and for employing units in rationally determining the recruitment scope and labour remuneration. Second, through releasing market supply and demand information, the government has effectively improved the disadvantaged workers' understanding and mastering of market information, which can better solve the problems caused by the late or incorrect information or misunderstanding. Third, improving the information service system not only serves the public, but also serves as an important channel for governments at all levels and relevant departments to learn about the current situation and development trends of the human resources market, it is an important source of information for macro-decision-making on employment.

3. Development of Private Employment Service

Private employment agencies are part of China's employment service system. *Employment Promotion Law* stipulates that people's governments at or above the county level shall encourage all sectors of the society to carry out employment service activities in accordance with law; provide better guidance in and exercise stricter supervision over public employment services and the services provided by job intermediaries, and gradually improve the employment service system covering urban and rural areas. This not only provides the legal basis for private employment agencies, but also points out their development direction.

3.1 Characteristics of Private Employment Service

As something new emerged with the development and improvement of market economy, the private employment intermediary agencies share the following characteristics. First, they are organised and operated as companies. Most of them go through the registration procedures at the industrial and commercial administration, carry out business in the capacity of the company, operate independently and assume full responsibilities for their own profits and losses. Second, they have diversified service modes and wide service contents. Their service modes aim at meeting the customers' requirements and they act as a talent broker. The service contents include organising various talent exchange activities, recruiting talents for enterprises, recommending jobs for talents, carrying out talent quality assessment, organising professional and technical training, carrying out talent consultation services, etc. Third, they differentiated their services to different clients. Some agencies serve all talents and employers, while some only serve high-end professionals; some pave the way for domestic talents to go abroad, and some provide enterprises with HR management suggestions. Fourth, their services are delivered in modernised means or tools. Many private employment agencies use high-tech and Internet to establish talent pool and information network, and release the information on talent supply and demand through the media.

3.2 Main Contents of Private Employment Service

3.2.1 Contents of Service

The first is information service. Information service includes labour market information collection, information exchange and information release.

The second is human resources management and consultation service. By using the theory and methodology on human resources development and management to analyse the corporate human resources development and management, the service is to find out the weak link and improve it, so as to help the enterprise to develop human resources correctly and effectively, manage human resources reasonably and scientifically, and create sustainable competitiveness for the enterprise.

The third is talent assessment service. Talent assessment refers to measuring and evaluating the basic quality and performance of a person by a series of scientific means and methods. It includes vocational ability test and assessment, vocational analysis and evaluation, etc.

The fourth is recruitment service. Recruitment service is a kind of activity that uses labour market mechanism to provide intermediary services for workers to seek jobs and employers to recruit and employ workers according to law. It includes job seeking and interview, job introduction and recommendation, and holding recruitment fair, etc.

The fifth is personnel outsourcing service. Personnel outsourcing service refers to the enterprises outsourcing one or several human resources management tasks or functions according to the actual needs to other enterprises or organisations, so as to reduce their labour cost and maximise the efficiency. It includes organising recruitment commissioned by the employing units, keeping files or archives entrusted by job seekers, and handling of labour and social insurance affairs commissioned by the labour administrative departments.

The sixth is headhunting service. Headhunting service is to help excellent enterprises to find the talents they need, also known as senior talent search. Headhunting can also refer to the act of hunting for talents, i.e. finding, tracking, evaluating, selecting and providing senior talents. Headhunting service has become an important channel for enterprises to obtain high-level talents, and it has developed into an industry.

3.2.2 Service Standards

The first is civilised service. It includes clean and neat site with convenient facilities; staff deliver services by hanging a card to identify oneself; using words politely and properly; respecting privacy, keeping secrets, being honesty and reliable.

The second is fair service. It refers that all kinds of job seekers and employers are treated equally for fair service and without discrimination.

The third is efficient service. It refers to making every effort to provide comprehensive, fast and accurate service to satisfy job seekers and employing units; paying attention to enhance job seekers' capacity, competitiveness and employability, and cultivating their sense of taking initiatives in seeking employment.

The fourth is flexible service. The service modes are diversified, which can meet the service needs of different job seekers and employing units. The service content and service agreement are based on mutual consultation with job seekers and employing units.

3.2.3 The Role of Private Employment Service

The first is to offer personalised services to job seekers. Public employment service agencies provide basic employment services for all workers, especially for vulnerable groups in the labour market. Private intermediaries provide differentiated and personalised employment services, which can meet the specific needs of job seekers, improve workers' competitiveness in the job market, and promote private intermediary agencies to become increasingly rich and perfect in offering service businesses.

The second is to make up for the deficiency of public employment service institutions. It has been proved by years of practices that opening up the labour market, allowing or even encouraging the private intermediary to carry out job recommendation service under legal framework, giving full play to the advantages of the private intermediary in employment service, such as flexible mechanism, strong market development ability, fast application of new technology, and providing specialised and personalised service for the clients, can effectively make up for the shortcomings of public employment service institutions. In 1997, the International Labour Organisation adopted *Private Employment Agencies Convention* (No. 181) and *Private Employment Agencies Recommendation* (No. 188), which abolished the government monopoly on employment agencies, revitalised labour market and realised the reasonable allocation of labour resources, which also complied with this development trend.

The third is to promote the achievement of full employment. The achievement of full employment needs the joint efforts of various parties. The standard operation and efficient service of private intermediary agencies will help to achieve the goal. Under the modern market economy system, in the course of conducting their daily business activities, private intermediary agencies have not only got many job vacancies and job seeking information, but also mastered more diversified service modes and more flexible working mechanisms. They place emphasis on applying network technology and improving efficiency, so as to promote the rapid matching and docking between employees and employers, and thus making contributions to the realisation of full employment.

Chapter 7
Vocational Training

1. Vocational Training and Employment Promotion

1.1 Development Process of Vocational Training in China

(1) During the recovery period of national economy (1950-1952), vocational training focused on job transition training for the unemployed workers. When the People's Republic of China was founded in 1949, there were more than 4 million unemployed workers and other unemployed people in cities across the country. The government adopted a variety of methods for resettlement, such as work-relief programmes, self-help production projects, return-to-countryside for production and delivering relief benefits. Meanwhile, a large number of job transition training courses were organised to train the unemployed workers in accordance with the actual needs of local production and construction. The training period was usually from 3 months to 6 months or 1 year, or a combination of short- and long-term, but mainly short-term. The training content focused on vocational skills with necessary political and cultural education. This kind of vocational training not only played a good role in solving the unemployment problem at that time, but also accumulated some experience on vocational training in China.

(2) During the period of large-scale economic construction (1953-1966), vocational training focused on training the reserved skilled workers. In 1953, China began to implement the first Five-year Plan and entered a period of large-scale economic construction. A large number of new technical workers were demanded in various industrial sectors. As a result, the planned training of the reserved technical workers became the main task of vocational training in this period. Technical school education and apprenticeship training were two key models for the training of the reserved technical workers. After rectification, consolidation, improvement and enrichment, some transition training classes with better conditions turned into technical schools, whose main mission was to train the talents with complicated skills (major) for generally 2-3 years. The students were requested to reach the standard for middle-level technical workers in terms of operation skills when they graduated. The main target group of apprenticeship training was the urban youth over the age of 16. According to the national requirements on apprenticeship period and training objectives, the apprenticeship training was carried out at workplaces in the form of apprentices following master workers, so as to train the junior technical workers. Apprenticeship used to be the main form to train the reserved skilled workers in China. During this period, the State had also established an eight-level wage system and a corresponding eight-level skill-grading system. Through apprenticeship assessment and workers' skill upgrading, China began to establish the assessment system for workers.

(3) After China's reform and opening up (1979-2000), vocational training stepped into a vigorous development stage. In late 1970s, China began to reform and open up, entering a new historical period of modernisation. During this period, vocational training witnessed an unprecedented and all-round development. Technical schools were rapidly restored and developed. The apprenticeship training continued to play its due role, and employment training centres emerged. The workers' in-service technical training became increasingly well regulated, and the workers' assessment system was restored and improved. After about 20 years of reform, the socialist market economic system was initially established, and labour market mechanism began to play a fundamental role in the allocation of labour resources. The market-oriented employment mechanism was gradually developed. The mechanism of developing workers' vocational skills according to the needs of the labour market began to establish, and the working system of vocational training including occupations classification, vocational demand forecasting, formulation of vocational skill standards, vocational training, vocational skill appraisal, vocational guidance, vocational skills competition and so on, initially took shape.

(4) From 2001 to 2010, vocational training began to adjust and reform. At the end of 20th century, due to the economic structure adjustment and the large-scale laid-off workers, vocational training was impacted to a certain extent. In order to meet the needs of economic and social development for skilled workers, vocational education and vocational training shall be strengthened. The State Council held the national vocational education working conference in 2002 and 2005 respectively to analyse the situation and problems faced by vocational education, and further clarified the objectives, tasks and policies on strengthening vocational school education and vocational training. In 2010, the State Council, for the first time since the founding of the People's Republic of China in 1949, issued *Opinions on Strengthening Vocational Training and Promoting Employment*, a specific document on strengthening vocational training. Later, the State Council again held a national vocational training working conference. It was proposed in the document issued by the State Council and the national vocational training working conference that we should thoroughly implement the scientific outlook on development, take serving employment and economic development as the purpose, establish a new vocational training mechanism with a wide range of trainees, various forms of training, standardised management and operation, and sound safeguard measures, on the basis of adhering to the principles of integrated development of urban and rural areas, employment-oriented, skill-based and lifelong training, so as to improve vocational training system for all workers and accelerate the cultivation of millions of high quality skilled workers. The main tasks of vocational training were to meet the needs of expanding employment scale, improving employment quality and enhancing enterprises' competitiveness; to improve the system, innovate mechanism, and increase fund input; to carry out large-scale employment skills training, occupational skills upgrading training and entrepreneurship training; to effectively improve the pertinence and effectiveness of vocational training; and to strive to realise the goal of "employing one person after training one person" for pre-employment training, and "training one person after employing one person" for in-service training, so as to provide strong skilled talents with support for promoting employment and economic and social development. Every effort should be made to provide the new entrants to human resources market with the opportunity to receive appropriate vocational training, and to provide enterprise workers in skilled positions with at least one skill upgrading training, and to provide at least one entrepreneurial training for every entrepreneur who desired to attend training, so that the training of high-skilled personnel could meet the needs of industrial structure optimisation and upgrading and enterprise development.

(5) During the 12th Five-year Plan (2011-2015), vocational training started to further develop and improve. The 12th Five-year Plan on Employment Promotion made specific arrangements for vocational training. In 2014, the Ministry of Human Resources and Social Security issued *Several Opinions on Promoting the Reform and Innovation* *of Technical Schools and Colleges* in view of the prominent problems encountered by technical schools and colleges, such as having difficulty in enrol students, the lack of operation funds and poor payment of both staff and graduates. It made clear that the reform and development of technical schools and colleges at present and for the period to come should aim to meet the needs of the market, and adhere to the school-running philosophy which could be put as high-end leading, schools-enterprises cooperation, multiple stakeholder running and intensive development mode at the same time, insisting on paying equal attention to both schooling system education and vocational training, deepening the reform of the school-running system, innovating the training mode of skilled workers, comprehensively improving the capacity on skilled workers training and exploring the development of a national standard and a framework on the training of skilled workers. In 2015, the General Office of the Ministry of Human Resources and Social Security and the General Office of the Ministry of Finance jointly issued *Notice on Carrying out the Pilot Work of New Apprenticeship in Enterprises*. By implementing the new enterprise apprenticeship system with the main content of "recruitment equalling enrolment, workers equalling students, and joint training by enterprise engineers (technicians) and school teachers", the new recruited workers and job transition workers in enterprises should be organised to participate in the new apprenticeship training, so as to speed up the development of young skilled workers in enterprises. At the same time, the Ministry of Human Resources and Social Security issued a series of documents aimed at upgrading the vocational skills for the unemployed college graduates, rural workers and the disabled. An inclusive vocational training service system for all urban and rural workers was initially set up. Through promoting the development of vocational skills practical training bases, carrying out the pilot project of the new apprenticeship in enterprises, and increasing the intensity of occupational skills upgrading and training, the system for training skilled workers basically took shape, with enterprises and industries as the main body, technical schools and colleges as the basis, meanwhile school vocational education closely linking with enterprise training, and assisting with the joint efforts of government promotion and social support. The vocational training system has been established that covers all urban and rural workers, goes throughout their study and work life, and meets the workers' needs on vocational training.

1.2 Vocational Training and Employment Promotion

Vocational training must be employment-oriented, while expanding employment must take improving the quality of workers as the fundamental starting point. Both of the above should be closely integrated, taking market demand as the core. Practices have proved that vocational training has played a vital role in promoting employment.

1.2.1 Vocational Training as an Important Way to Promote Employment

(1) Vocational training has enhanced workers' employability and promoted their employment. On the one hand, the trained workers have improved both their skills and market awareness. Therefore, they are quite competitive in the labour market, and have some employability correspondingly. On the other hand, enterprises require workers to have necessary qualifications for the post, and the workers who have received vocational training and thus have the corresponding skills would have more opportunities to get employed by enterprises.

(2) Vocational training has a positive effect on employment and labour productivity. In labour-intensive and technology-intensive industries, workers' skills determine the production efficiency and product quality. At the same time, high-competence workers who have received vocational training would improve the social productivity, increase output and national revenue, so as to increase the overall social consumption, and help to stimulate investment growth and expand the scale of social employment.

(3) Vocational training has played a role in preventing unemployment. With the upgrading of industries and the changing of production technology, new industries and occupations emerge in large numbers, traditional industries and occupations are eliminated, and thus unemployment coexists with job vacancies. However, the trained workers, especially those with multi-skills, can adapt to the needs of different employment positions and greatly reduce the risk of unemployment.

1.2.2 Expanding Employment Based on Improving Workers' Competence

First, it is an important way to expand employment and an effective way to improve the quality of employment by improving workers' competence, so that they have higher employability and better technical skills.

Second, great Great efforts should be made to strengthen the training of employment skills and improve the employability of the new labour forces. Necessary pre-job training and on-the-job training are conducive for workers to find jobs as early as possible, and make them better adapted to the requirements of employment.

Third, on-the-job training should be vigorously strengthened to develop high-competence industrial workers. The adjustment of economic structure and the development of enterprise technology have made higher requirements for workers' technical skills. To cope with these challenges, in accordance with the requirements of the life-long training, it is necessary to constantly strengthen on-the-job skill training, continuously enhance the working ability of the staff, promote their steady development in their posts, and constantly improve the quality of employment.

Fourth, strengthening the re-employment training and improving the ability of the unemployed to change jobs will help the laid-off and the unemployed to realise re-employment. Entrepreneurship training should be organised to strengthen the development of workers' entrepreneurial awareness and entrepreneurial ability, so as to promote entrepreneurship through training and promote employment through entrepreneurship.

1.3 Important Action Plan of Vocational Training in Recent 30 Years

(1) Vigorously carry out employment training. In the late 1970s, with a large number of educated young people returning to the city, the employment pressure was unprecedented. According to the requirements of the central government, the State Administration of Labour established labour service companies to carry out employment training for the unemployed, which has made great contributions to relieving the employment pressure, enhancing the employability and solving the unemployment problems. In 1994, the Ministry of Labour issued *Regulations on Employment Training* to standardise the employment training. In 1990, the State Council proposed the establishment of labour reserve system. Employment training, as a specific form of training, was developed under new conditions. *Employment Promotion Law* implemented in 2008 clearly requires that the State should take measures to improve labour reserve system and improve the vocational skills of urban and rural middle and high school graduates; local governments at all levels should encourage and support employment training to help the unemployed to improve their vocational skills; effective measures should be taken to organise and guide rural workers to participate in skills training so as to enhance their employability and entrepreneurial ability.

(2) Implement re-employment training programmes. During 1998-2000 and 2001-2003, the Ministry of Labour and Social Security successively organised and implemented two "three-year ten million" re-employment training programmes. From 2004 to 2005, the ministry continued to implement the re-employment training programme in depth by widely mobilising social resources and strengthening vocational guidance and skills training. On the basis of a comprehensive assessment on training pass rate and employment rate, the government purchased the training outputs by paying subsidy to training expenditure with government budget. Through the development and improvement of this mechanism, the expectation of this programme was achieved, i.e. combing the training supply of social institutes with workers' needs, training projects adaptable to the employment demand of the market, and subsidy linking with training effects.

(3) Actively explore entrepreneurship training mode. In 1999, the Ministry of Labour and Social Security, on the basis of summing up the pilot experience of Beijing, Shanghai and Suzhou, vigorously promoted entrepreneurship training. By 2003, entrepreneurship training was extended to more than 100 cities in China. From 2005 to 2007, the Ministry of Labour and Social Security, in cooperation with the International Labour Organisation and the British government, organised a wide range of entrepreneurship training programmes in China to provide entrepreneurial assistance for the unemployed. Based on local practices and international experience, entrepreneurship training gradually developed into an all-in-one entrepreneurship policy and service system, including training and business start-up guidance, business idea development, micro loan, tax deduction and business incubation, which helped the unemployed and other employees to realise entrepreneurship with the skills they mastered and laid a foundation for the State to formulate policies for entrepreneurship and employment promotion.

(4) Improve employability programme by enhancing vocational training. In 2002, the Ministry of Labour and Social Security launched this programme, which emphasised to improve the employability, working ability and career change ability for the unemployed, the new labour force, the enterprise employees and the surplus rural labour force. The main tasks were to strengthen re-employment training with a view to achieve 90% pass rate in training evaluation and 50% employment rate after training; to promote entrepreneurship training with a view to achieve 40% success rate in entrepreneurship; and to accelerate the training of technical skilled workers, so that the number and proportion of technical skilled workers, especially senior technical skilled workers, technicians and senior technicians could be significantly increased; to implement vocational certification system nationwide, and vigorously promote employment permit system.

(5) Implement vocational training "5 + 1" action plan. In 2005, the Ministry of Labour and Social Security, in coordination with the formulation of the national 11th Five-year Plan, comprehensively launched the "5 + 1" action plan on vocational training for accelerating the training of skilled workers in general sense and millions of high-quality skilled workers. This plan includes five sub-plans, namely new technicians training and promotion sub-plan, urban re-employment sub-plan through skills, the competence-driven entrepreneurship sub-plan, employment sub-plan of rural labour through skills, and the skills leading sub-plan through national vocational certification, as well as skill-job docking action. This is a systematic programme of promoting employment by training, aiming at all kinds of groups in different employment status. It has comprehensively improved the targeted groups' employability, entrepreneurial ability, working ability and job transfer ability through pertinent vocational training and employment services.

(6) Implement special vocational training programme. The global financial crisis at the end of 2008 had a significant impact on the employment situation. In order to maintain a stable employment situation and give full play to the important basic role of vocational training in promoting all-round employment and serving the stable development of the economy, the Ministry of Human Resources and Social Security, the National Development and Reform Commission and the Ministry of Finance jointly launched and implemented a special vocational training programme in 2009 and 2010 according to the general deployment of the CPC Central Committee and the State Council. The planned training tasks would be well completed by relying on technical schools and colleges as well as all kinds of vocational training institutes, and the training results would be purchased by the government. The general idea was to expand training scale, extend training period, increase training input, improve training ability and maintain employment stability.

(7) National high-skilled talent revitalisation plan. The CPC Central Committee with Comrade Xi Jinping as the core attached great importance to the work of talent, emphasised that the talent was the first resource to support development. In 2011, the Ministry of Human Resources and Social Security, together with the Ministry of Finance, issued *Notice on Printing and Distributing the Implementation Plan of National High-skilled Talent Revitalisation Plan*, which specified that from 2011 to 2020, the construction project of high-skilled personnel training bases, the construction project of skilled master studio and the technician training project should be implemented. In 2011, the Ministry of Human Resources and Social Security and the Ministry of Finance launched the construction of the first group of 20 high-skilled talent training bases and 50 skilled master studios. Since 2016, the supply side structural reform under the new normal of the economy has created new requirements on developing a high-skilled contingent. In 2016, the Ministry of Human Resources and Social Security and the Ministry of Finance issued a *Circular on Further Promotion of the National Plan for the Revitalisation of Highly Skilled Talent*, which proposed that during the 13th Five-year Plan period (2016-2020), it was necessary to closely combine the development needs of strategic emerging industries, advanced manufacturing industry and modern service industry, with the focus of developing a large number of high-skilled workers with superb techniques, exquisite skills and craftsmanship spirit, and thus to steadily improve the overall competence of the Chinese industrial workers.

(8) Implement national large-scale vocational skills upgrading campaign. At present and for the period to come, the structural employment contradiction is prominent. The domestic and foreign economic environment may bring profound influence to employment, and put forward new requirements on promoting industrial upgrading and the competence of workers. The CPC Central Committee and the State Council have attached great importance to vocational skills training. The government work report in 2019 proposed that implementing the vocational skills upgrading campaign, and allocating 100 billion *yuan* from the surplus in unemployment insurance funds to provide skills upgrading and job transfer training for more than 15 million employees. In the same year, the General Office of the State Council issued *Vocational Skills Upgrading Scheme (2019-2021)* (hereinafter referred to as the scheme), which is a guiding document for large-scale vocational skills training for the current and future period. The scheme has identified three training priorities for enterprise employees, key employment groups and the poor labour force. The training has been vigorously carried out through three types of training providers, i.e. enterprises, vocational schools and colleges (including technical schools and colleges), and social training and evaluation institutes. It has effectively increased the supply of training and aroused the enthusiasm of various training institutes. The key point of the vocational skills upgrading campaign is to motivate the workers and the training providers to participate in vocational skills training on a large scale through policy guidance and incentive.

2. Improvement of Vocational Training System

2.1 Overview

China's vocational training system includes occupational classification and vocational standards, vocational training and institutes, skilled workforce evaluation system, vocational skills competition and skilled talent awarding system.

2.1.1 Occupational Classification and Vocational Standards

In 1988, the Ministry of Labour, together with 45 competent departments of the State Council, carried out the third revision of the national technical grading standards for workers. In 1992, China's first *Directory of Job Classification of the People's Republic of China* was completed. In 1999, the Ministry of Labour and Social Security, the State Bureau of Quality and Technical Supervision and the National Bureau of Statistics jointly promulgated the first authoritative document on the classification of Chinese occupations, i.e. *Occupational Classification Code of the People's Republic of China*. At the end of 2010, the Ministry of Human Resources and Social Security, together with relevant departments, initiated the revision of *Occupational Classification Code of the People's Republic of China*, and officially released the latest version in 2015. Vocational standards and vocational skill appraisal standards were guadually formulated and promulgated in batches. A dynamic national occupational classification and vocational standard system has been initially established. At the same time, a national vocational certification system composed of five levels, namely, junior worker, intermediate worker, senior worker, technician and senior technician, has been established. The development of occupational classification and vocational standards provided a scientific basis for labour forces management and vocational training.

2.1.2 Vocational Training and Institutes

Vocational training includes employment skills training (including labour reserve training, re-employment training and rural labour transfer training), occupational skills upgrading training and entrepreneurship training. According to the vocational skills standard, the trainings are divided into three levels, i.e. primary, intermediate, senior vocational trainings and other adaptive training, focusing on developing technical and skilled talent. The training programmes are mainly undertaken by technical schools and various vocational training institutes.

2.1.3 Skilled Workforce Evaluation System

Skilled workforce evaluation is the recognition of the knowledge, technology and ability of skilled workers engaged in certain occupations. Different from academic education, skilled workforce evaluation is closely combined with the specific requirements on vocational work, which reflects more of the actual working standards and norms of a specific occupation, as well as the actual ability of workers engaged in this occupation.

2.1.4 Vocational Skills Competition and Skilled Talent Awarding System

Vocational skills competition is divided into three levels: national, provincial (including autonomous regions and municipalities) and prefecture level. The national vocational skills competition is usually held every two years. At the same time, skilled talent awarding system has been established. The establishment of vocational skills competition and skilled talent awarding system has improved the social status of skilled talent, motivated the enthusiasm of the majority of employees to participate in vocational training, and created a social environment conducive to the growth of skilled talent.

2.2 Technical School and College and Vocational Training Institute

2.2.1 Technical School and College

Skilled worker education is an important part of the national education system and human resources development, which undertakes the important task of training high-quality skilled talent for economic and social development. Technical schools and colleges become the comprehensive technical education and training base which undertakes the work of technician education, vocational training, vocational skill appraisal, competition training, public practice training, employment service and so on. They are the important carrier to develop the lifelong vocational training system for workers and the important platform for training skilled workers. Technical schools and colleges are divided into the following three types.

(1) General technical school. General technical school is mainly to train intermediate skilled workers. The length of schooling for middle school graduates is generally three years, and for high school graduates it is generally two years.

(2) Senior technical school. Senior technical school is mainly to train senior skilled workers. The length of schooling for graduates with the same or similar majors in technical schools and other secondary vocational schools is generally two years, and for high school graduates it is generally three years.

(3) Technical college. Technical college undertakes schooling education to train preparatory technician, the training programme for technicians from enterprises before promotion or upgrading, the assessment and evaluation of technicians, and the training of teachers from technical schools and colleges. Technical college is generally to train senior technical workers and preparatory technicians. For training preparatory technicians, the schooling system is generally seven years for middle school graduates, five years for high school graduates, and two years for senior technical school graduates and other vocational college graduates with senior technical skilled worker qualification.

Technical schools and colleges are characterised by school-enterprise dual system and work-study integration, and they have become the main training venue for technical workers as well as the training base for high-skilled talent. Schools and colleges are well integrated and co-developed with enterprises, with distinct characteristics in terms of school running and unique advantages in terms of cultivating skilled talent (Table 7.1).

Table 7.1 Comprehensive Situation of Technical Schools and Colleges over the Years

Year	Number of technical schools and colleges	Enrolment (unit: 10 thousand)	Number of students (unit: 10 thousand)	Number of graduates (unit: 10 thousand)	Number of teaching staff (unit: 10 thousand)	Number of non-student trainees (unit: 10 thousand)	Number of non-student trainees finishing the training programme (unit: 10 thousand)
1999	4,098	51.5	156.0	66.2	26.9	149.1	144.6

Continued

Year	Number of technical schools and colleges	Enrolment (unit: 10 thousand)	Number of students (unit: 10 thousand)	Number of graduates (unit: 10 thousand)	Number of teaching staff (unit: 10 thousand)	Number of non-student trainees (unit: 10 thousand)	Number of non-student trainees finishing the training programme (unit: 10 thousand)
2000	3,792	50.4	140.1	64.6	24.0	158.5	156.7
2001	3,470	55.1	134.7	47.7	22.0	151.7	163.9
2002	3,075	73.3	153.0	45.4	20.3	208.6	196.9
2003	2,970	91.6	193.1	45.3	20.2	226.9	226.7
2004	2,884	109.7	234.4	53.5	20.4	265.6	257.5
2005	2,855	118.4	275.3	69.0	20.4	273.3	270.1
2006	2,880	134.8	320.8	86.4	21.5	337.7	330.2
2007	2,995	158.5	367.1	99.7	24.0	380.7	369.8
2008	3,075	161.4	397.5	109.0	24.7	400.0	389.8
2009	3,064	156.4	414.3	115.2	25.8	484.1	382.9
2010	2,998	158.6	421.0	121.3	26.5	468.4	371.3
2011	2,914	163.5	429.4	118.9	26.5	527.5	416.1
2012	2,892	156.8	422.8	120.2	26.7	551.3	441.6
2013	2,882	133.5	386.6	116.9	26.9	525.3	397.1
2014	2,818	124.4	339.0	106.8	26.5	508.5	372.3
2015	2,545	121.4	321.5	94.6	26.0	476.6	378.9
2016	2,526	127.2	323.2	93.1	26.5	451.6	349.9
2017	2,490	130.9	338.2	90.5	26.9	456.4	326.1
2018	2,379	128.5	341.6	90.3	26.7	420.6	301.6

Source: National Bureau of Statistics.

2.2.2 Vocational Training Institute

Vocational training institutes mainly undertake all kinds of vocational training tasks to train workers with vocational skills for the society. China's vocational training institutes mainly include employment training centres, private vocational training institutes, Sino-foreign cooperative vocational training institutes and enterprise training institutes.

(1) Employment training centre. The employment training centre is a vocational training base which mainly provides employment skills training for the new labour force and the unemployed. With the development of employment situation, the centre also provides entrepreneurship training for urban and rural entrepreneurs. The characteristics of the employment training centre are as follows: mainly delivering short-term, single skill training with seeking employment after training as the main task; with the training content mainly based on operational skills, supplemented by relevant theoretical knowledge, which belongs to non-schooling education; the training funds mainly relying on production and operation income and tuitions. After years of development, some employment training centres have become training entities with considerable strength and scale.

(2) Private vocational training institute. Private vocational training institutes refer to schools or other training institutes run by social organisations or individuals other than state institutions, which use non-state financial funds. The State implements the policy of actively encouraging, vigorously supporting, correctly guiding and administering private vocational training institutes according to law. Private vocational training institutes play an important role in re-employment training and rural labour transfer training.

(3) Sino-foreign cooperative vocational training institute. The Sino-foreign cooperative vocational training institute is jointly organised by foreign educational and training institutes and such Chinese institutes within the territory of China, with main target groups being Chinese citizens. The guideline policy of the State for them are expanding and opening up, well-regulated in school-running, management by law, promoting development, and encouraging high-quality foreign educational and training resources to conduct vocational training activities in China.

(4) Enterprise training institute. Enterprise employee training is an important part of vocational training. China has always attached great importance to on-the-job training for enterprise employees and the development of skilled workers. In the process of developing learning enterprises and learning society, the operation mechanism of overall planning made by the government, guided by industries, regulated by the market, and training programmes delivered by enterprises independently should be gradually formed by fully relying on enterprises while industry playing its due role.

2.3 Vocational Certification System and Vocational Skill Level System

2.3.1 Vocational Skill Appraisal

Vocational skill appraisal is a testing activity on vocational skill level, which belongs to standard referenced test. It is an objective measurement made by the assessment institute on the technical and theoretical knowledge and practical operation ability that workers should master in a certain occupation. China's vocational skill appraisal is an objective, fair, scientific and standardised evaluation and accreditation activity on workers' skill level or vocational qualification by the assessment and appraisal institutes, which are accredited by the government's human resources and social security administrative department according to the national occupational standards or qualifications. It mainly includes the assessment of primary, intermediate and senior skills, technician and senior technician qualification assessment. Vocational skill appraisal is an important part of the national vocational certification system. The vocational certificate is the proof of the bearers' skill level.

2.3.2 Vocational Certification System

The vocational certification is the national recognition on workers' knowledge, technology and ability in certain occupation. It is the main basis for the worker to apply for a job, hold a post, start up business independently and get employed by the employing unit. The vocational certification is closely related to the specific requirements of vocational work, which reflects more of the actual working standards and norms of a specific occupation, and workers' actual ability in this occupation. The vocational skill level is generally divided into five levels, i.e. junior worker, intermediate worker, senior worker, technician and senior technician, which corresponds to national vocational qualification level 5, level 4, level 3, level 2 and level 1 respectively. Vocational certification system is a kind of internationally accepted certification system for technical skilled talent.

2.3.3 Vocational Skill Level System

The vocational skill level recognition is a talent evaluation system carried out by employers and social evaluation organisations, based on national vocational skill standards or industrial and enterprise evaluation standards. The qualified employing units can carry out vocational skill level recognition service independently for their employees or for the workers outside according to the actual situation. In contrast, qualified social evaluation organisations can carry out vocational skill level recognition service for all workers according to market and employment needs. The vocational skill level certificate is issued by the employer and social evaluation organisations, with coding rules formulated by the Ministry of Human Resources and Social Security to standardise the certificate (or electronic certificate) style. The vocational skill level system is an important part of diversified talent evaluation.

2.4 Basic Work of Vocational Capacity Building

Vocational capacity building includes the development of relevant personnel and teaching materials as well as teaching and research work.

2.4.1 The Development of Relevant Personnel

(1) The development of faculty team in technical schools and colleges. The development of faculty team is an important basis for strengthening the education and vocational training of skilled workers. With the gradual deepening of the school-enterprise cooperation system, in order to further improve the quality of skilled workers' education and vocational training, more and more technical schools and colleges have begun to attach importance to train "integrated" teachers who can teach vocational theory and guide internship at workplace, and to continuously strengthen the training and further study of teachers, so as to enhance the capacity of vocational training teachers, having them constantly adapt themselves to the new needs of reform and development.

(2) The development of trainers for entrepreneurial training. Entrepreneurship training is an important means to improve workers' entrepreneurial ability and an important content of promoting entrepreneurship and employment. In order to promote the development of entrepreneurship training, the Ministry of Human Resources and Social Security has set up a steering committee for entrepreneurship training, which is responsible for the overall planning, coordination and promotion of national entrepreneurship training services. The trainers of entrepreneurship training are divided into trainers and master trainers, which have the following characteristics: ① wide coverage. Most provinces have their own trainers who can basically meet the training needs of localities. ② Diversified training providers. In addition to the human resources and social security departments, more and more people from trade unions, women's federation, youth league, universities, private institutes, consulting companies and other organisations have joined in the team of trainers, many of whom have rich experience in business management. ③ Follow the technical standards strictly. In terms of the trainer management, the technical standards are strictly implemented at any project stage including selection, training, dispatch and evaluation of trainers.

(3) The development of vocational skill appraisal personnel. Vocational skill appraisal personnel refer to the persons who, within the scope of specified occupations (type of work), levels and categories, examine and evaluate the vocational skills for candidate workers in accordance with a unified assessment method, standards and requirements. The vocational skill appraisal personnel include assessors and senior assessors.

(4) The development of the vocational skill appraisal supervisors. The supervision on the quality of vocational skill appraisal refers to the supervision and inspection action or activities on vocational skill appraisal institutions' implementation of the relevant national laws, regulations and policies on the vocational skill appraisal and on the implementation of national vocational standards, examination administration, certificate administration, etc. The supervisors shall be authorised by the departments of human resources and social security or the relevant departments of the State Council to carry out the supervision in their respective regions and industries.

2.4.2 Development of Teaching Materials and Teaching Research

The development of teaching materials is an important part of vocational training, a carrier that reflects educational thoughts, educational concepts and teaching contents, and a necessary tool for workers' self-study and on-the-job study. In 2000, the Ministry of Labour and Social Security established the Working Committee of Vocational Training Teaching Materials, which was responsible for studying and formulating the general idea and development plan on the development of vocational training materials, and coordinating the development of vocational training materials in various regions and departments.

3. Development of Lifelong Vocational Skill Training System

According to the different trainees and training contents, vocational training can be divided into employment skill training (including labour reserve training, re-employment training, rural labour forces transfer training), post skill upgrading training and entrepreneurship training. It basically covers all the stages of workers' career, and can also meet workers' requirements on improving their vocational competence and employability. It has become a lifelong vocational skill training system for Chinese workers.

3.1 Employment Skill Training

3.1.1 The Function and Role of Employment Skill Training

Employment skill training generally refers to the necessary vocational ethics, specialised theory, vocational skills and other aspects of training and training activities for all the urban and rural workers with employment expectation and training desire to improve their employability. It is mainly implemented by vocational schools at all levels, employment training centres and private vocational training institutes.

The target groups of employment skill training mainly include first-time employment workers such as new arising labour forces in urban and rural areas and rural workers who transfer to non-agricultural industries or to urban areas for employment; workers changing from employment to unemployment, and other workers who need to learn and improve vocational skills before employment or on the job.

The roles of employment skill training are as follows. The first is to vigorously develop employment skill training, implement the strategy of invigorating the country through science and education, and transfer economic construction to the track of relying on scientific and technological progress and improving the quality of workers. The second is to improve the employability of workers, promote employment, and create conditions for them to participate in market competition and employment. The third is to improve the competence of the back-up technical workers in enterprises to meet the higher requirements made by the quickening pace of industrial restructuring and the deepening of enterprise reform on workers' competence.

3.1.2 Labour Reserve Training

The labour reserve system is a regulated system that young workers must be trained before they get employed. Its basic connotation is to organise urban new arising labour forces and other job seekers to receive vocational training and education for a certain period of time before employment, so that they can obtain corresponding vocational qualifications or master certain vocational skills, and then realise employment in the labour market under the guidance and help of national policies. By extending the time for these workers to enter the labour market, it can reduce labour supply, regulate labour supply and demand, and ease employment pressure.

In 1990s, China entered a new round of employment peak. The structural unemployment problem that workers' competence did not fit in with the development of production was becoming increasingly prominent. In addition, a large number of middle and high school graduates entered the labour market or employment positions without the necessary vocational training, which not only resulted in huge employment pressure, but also affected the increase of the labour productivity and economic efficiency of the enterprises. To some extent, training and employment are disconnected or misplaced.

In 1996, the Ministry of Labour put forward the proposal of adding 1-2 years of vocational training to the new arising labour forces in order to ease the employment pressure and improve the competence of the work forces, which was highly valued by the central leadership. In 1997, the pilot work of labour reserve system was organised and implemented in 36 cities in China, and good results were achieved. In 1998, in the work arrangement of promoting national employment and re-employment, all localities were requested to universally implement the labour reserve system, and provide vocational and technical training for 1-3 years to middle and high school graduates in cities and towns who failed to continue their studies. In 1999, in *Decision on Deepening Education Reform and Comprehensively Promoting Quality Education*, the CPC Central Committee and the State Council once again reiterated that labour reserve system should be actively implemented and the training before work employment system should be adhered to. Starting from 1999, labour reserve system should be widely implemented in cities and towns throughout the country. Through promotion and publicity activities, a large number of middle and high school graduates have been mobilised to participate in labour reserve training.

3.1.3 Re-employment Training

Re-employment training refers to the training on vocational guidance, vocational skills, vocational ethics and vocational discipline for the unemployed with more than one working experience. The trainees of re-employment training are mainly the laid-off and unemployed people.

In late 1980s, with the implementation of the labour contract system for all the employees and the optimisation of the labour organisation, redundant workers began to emerge in enterprises. In order to help the redundant workers who needed to change their jobs to realise re-employment as soon as possible, the Ministry of Labour requested that the redundant workers of SOEs should take part in the job transfer training, and the trainees were entitled for training expense deduction or exemption and they were given priority to employment. In the mid-1990s, in the context of unemployed workers increasing year by year, in order to reduce unemployment and promote employment, China began to implement re-employment project. One of the important contents of the project was to require the unemployed workers to take part in job transfer training during the period of unemployment, and the government formulated a free training policy for such trainees. Since 1998, the problem of the laid-off workers in SOEs has become increasingly prominent. The CPC Central Committee and the State Council attached great importance to the livelihood and re-employment of these workers. It was requested to enhance re-employment training while ensuring the basic living standards of workers in SOEs, and to clarify the target groups, objectives and tasks of re-employment training. The labour and social security departments formulated a series of policies and measures to promote re-employment training, which had gradually standardised the re-employment training and played a positive role. The organisation and implementation of re-employment training are as follows.

(1) Make re-employment training plan after a thorough survey. For organising re-employment training, the first is to carry out in-depth investigation and research to understand the basic situation of local laid-off and unemployed persons, the development trend of social production, the market demand on workers' skills and the situation of various vocational training institutes. Subsequently, the re-employment training plans and overall arrangements can be made accordingly.

(2) Select training institutes from the society. Re-employment training should fully mobilise the strength of the whole society and make use of the resource advantages of various education and training institutes at all levels to carry out the training. It is needed to select a group of qualified education and training institutes with good training facilities, strong training capacity and high training quality as designated re-employment training institutes. Guiding them to strengthen their contacts with the enterprise re-employment service centres, job recommendation agencies and employers in order to provide the laid-off and unemployed persons with training and guidance in line with market demand.

(3) Organise flexible and diverse skills training based on market demand. According to the needs of the labour market and the characteristics of the laid-off and unemployed workers, the designated re-employment training institutes should determine training programmes, make training plans and carry out targeted training programmes. In terms of the training form, combined with the actual situation of the laid-off workers, it should be flexible and diverse, either a combination of full-time centralised training with half day training and night school decentralised training, or centralised classes in training institutes or joint classes between enterprises and training institutes not far from the laid-off workers' home or workplace. Also, take full advantage of the remote vocational training with large quantity, wide range and low cost, and the widely use of radio and television, audio-visual education and Internet, developing a remote vocational training network to deliver training programmes to classroom, to enterprises and to workers' families.

(4) Provide personalised vocational guidance according to the characteristics of the laid-off workers. In re-employment training, special vocational guidance courses should be set up to help the unemployed to recognise the employment situation, update their employment concepts, raise their awareness of independent employment, provide them with job information and job seeking methods, guide them to make personal re-employment plans and measures, and actively guide them to realise re-employment.

(5) Strengthen the training on entrepreneurial ability and develop a group of small bosses. For the laid-off workers who have strong entrepreneurial awareness and some entrepreneurial possibilities, entrepreneurship training should be organised to guide them to make feasible business plans on the basis of market survey. Continuous consultation, guidance and services should be provided to help them solve the problems encountered in the start-up and operation process, and thus cultivate and bring up a number of successful small bosses.

(6) Ensure training funds and training results purchased by the government. Funds availability is the key for carrying out re-employment training. The funds for re-employment training should be raised through various channels and used reasonably. The sources of funds include: first, financial input from the central and local governments at all levels, which is mainly borne by local finance, with the central finance giving appropriate subsidies to the areas with difficulty. Second, unemployment insurance fund can be used to subsidise the vocational training for the unemployed persons during the insured period. Third, the funds needed for the training programmes which are organised by industries and enterprises shall be paid from their financial account of education funds. The fourth is social donation. The subsidies to re-employment training shall be in connection with the training effect on promoting employment, and free training shall be provided to eligible unemployed persons. If training institutes undertake free training, relevant government departments shall approve and allocate financial subsidies to the institutes according to the number and duration of training, the pass rate of training, and the re-employment rate after training. Through the mechanism of government purchasing training results, training institutes are effectively guided to carry out training in accordance with market demand, strive to improve the quality of training, actively contact with employers, broaden employment channels after training, and improve the efficiency of funds.

(7) Provide good employment services and closely link training with employment. One-stop service mechanism shall be established for job demand forecasting, unemployment registration, vocational training, job recommendation and vocational guidance so as to promote a close combination of training and employment. For workers who are interested in self-employment and start-up businesses, employment service agencies shall, jointly with relevant departments, help them to enjoy preferential policies such as industrial and commercial registration, tax deduction and exemption, premise arrangement, capital and credit loan.

3.1.4 Rural Labour Forces Transfer Training

Rural labour forces transfer training refers to the targeted training on vocational skills, vocational ethics, vocational disciplines, relevant laws and regulations, rights protection and common knowledge of urban life when rural workers shift from agriculture to non-agricultural industries. This kind of training can effectively enhance the job-transition skills for the rural workers, and it is an important means to enhance their employment competitiveness and work ability. In accordance with the requirements of the CPC Central Committee and the State Council on keeping expanding the scale of rural labour forces transfer training, improving the quality of training, and making overall use of training funds, since 2006, the labour and social security departments have actively taken measures to carry out large-scale transfer training for rural workers, improve the vocational skills and overall competence of migrant workers, and guide them to obtain employment in non-agricultural industries.

(1) Implement the special work plan for rural labour force transfer training. Since 2006, the labour and social security departments have organised and implemented the Rural Labour Force Skills Employment Plan throughout the country. In 5 years, 40 million rural labourers were trained in non-agricultural vocational skills, and 8 million people were trained every year. According to the characteristics of the rural labour forces, the training is divided into three categories: labour reserve training for the middle and high school graduates in rural areas who will not go on to recieve further education, and veterans and other new arising labour forces in rural areas; labour export training for the rural surplus labour forces with willingness to go out for work; and skill upgrading training for rural workers already working in cities and towns. From 2009 to 2010, the special vocational training programmes were focused on new arising labour forces and returned migrant workers in rural areas, as well as newly recruited migrant workers by enterprises. According to statistics, from 2006 to 2009, more than 37 million rural workers participated in the training.

(2) Select the best training institutes from the society. The departments of human resources and social security at all levels have identified a number of institutes with good training quality and good social reputation as designated training institutes by way of bidding, which are open to all the qualified education and training institutes in society. Directing them to organise labour reserve training and various short-term practical technical training or vocational qualification training in a flexible and diversified manner in accordance with the needs of the labour market, so as to help rural workers to master a skill or obtain the relevant vocational qualifications before entering the labour market to compete for employment.

(3) Ensure training funds and improve the funding subsidy mechanism. According to the requirements of the State Council, the transfer training for rural workers is implemented with training input shared by the government, employers and individuals. In order to improve the efficiency of funds, local governments have also developed a mechanism by linking financial subsidies with training quality and employment effects to improve the subsidy methods. The taining institute can apply for the corresponding subsidy from the human resources and social security department by presenting the list of eligible trainees, training certificates or vocational qualification certificates or employment situation materials after the training if the training is organised by the institute. The employer can apply for the training subsidy as well if the training is organised by the employer. In addition, some areas have also explored ways to issue training vouchers and set up training accounts to mobilise the rural workers to actively participate in training and encourage training institutes to organise the training.

3.2 Post Skill Upgrading Training

The post skill upgrading training refers to the education and training activities for workers on ideological, political and management knowledge, vocational ethics, technical skills, operational skills, etc, which are organised by enterprises based on the needs of production and operation. There are three ways to conduct the training task: first, staff training institutes set up by enterprises; second, joint efforts by enterprises and education and training institutes outside enterprises; third, vocational training institutes outside at the request of enterprises with payment given by enterprises.

Strengthen technical education and vocational training, and promote the development of high-quality skilled personnel. (Photo taken by Xinhua News Agency reporter Zhiyong Bai.)

The purpose of organising the post skill upgrading training for enterprise workers is to develop three talent teams for enterprise development by establishing system, improving mechanism and innovating mode. The three talent teams are as follows. The first is a modern management talent team familiar with domestic and foreign business management, with strong management ability, professional capacity and social competence. The second is a scientific research and development talent team with high theoretical level, scientific and technological attainments, and proficient in relevant professional technology. The third is a team of skilled workers with excellent skills, fine working style and professionalism. In order to achieve these goals, the enterprise should mainly make efforts in the following eight aspects.

(1) Establish a training management system suitable for the modern corporate system. In accordance with the requirements for the establishment of a modern corporate system, starting from the need of maximising employees' enthusiasm to become talent in their posts, corresponding corporate staff training and management system shall be established to realise the smooth running of the four-in-one operation mechanism, i.e. tra ining→examination→position→compensation and provide organisational guarantee for promoting the deep development of enterprise human resources.

(2) Make a training plan according to the training needs. Based on the actual needs of the enterprise and the demand of employee types and the skill level created by the development strategy of the enterprise and the overall layout of production and operation, it is necessary to make a scientific and reasonable training plan, clarify the objectives and tasks of the short-term and medium-term staff training, develop a training system, and take effective measures to promote the development of corporate training.

(3) Establish training bases for enterprise workers. Relying on enterprise worker training bases, public practical training bases, and vocational schools, inclusive of senior technical schools and technician colleges, as the bases for enterprise worker training, various levels and types of vocational training and continuing education have been organised to provide workers with practical and efficient training by using a variety of means and channels.

(4) Achieve the echelon development of skilled workers driven by the high-end talents. On the basis of carrying out the training of workers in an all-round way, enterprises have focused on training high-skilled workers and speeded up the training of high-skilled talents through developing the study and training system for technicians, the system of leading apprentices by famous teachers, the enterprise trainer system and the skill leader system. The overall development of the skilled worker team should be promoted through extensively carrying out on-the-job training and various vocational skill competitions, selecting and awarding a number of skilled and outstanding technical leaders, and give full play to their demonstration and leading role.

(5) Strengthen basic work. It includes selecting personnel with high level of professional knowledge and skills to serve as teachers, developing teaching curricula in light of the actual situation of production lines and the latest technological development of the enterprise. Enterprises with good conditions shall vigorously develop and use multimedia teaching materials, simulation teaching equipment and software to better carry out training.

(6) Increase fund inputs in training and ensure the availability of training funds. The expenses for conducting vocational education and staff training shall be borne by relevant organisations in accordance with the provisions of *Employment Promotion Law*and *Vocational Education Law of the People's Republic of China*. The earmarked funds for the education and training of staff and workers should be guaranteed, especially those on the front line.

(7) Adhere to the system of working with certificates. Vocational qualification certificate is closely connected with staff training and corporate employment system. When recruiting workers, priority should be given to those who have obtained corresponding diploma or certificate from vocational schools and the qualification certificate of vocational training. When the job vacancy applicable to national employment permit system, applicants must obtain the corresponding vocational qualification certificate.

(8) Promote the practice of job arrangement based on training and assessment with compensation based on performance and contribution. Wage and post allowance are linked with the skill level so as to give preference to high-skilled workers in key technical posts in terms of wage, benefits and training.

3.3 Entrepreneurship Training

Entrepreneurship training is a kind of basic knowledge and ability training for those who have entrepreneurial desire and corresponding conditions to start up a small business or for self-employment. There are three modes of entrepreneurship training.

3.3.1 SIYB Training Mode

SIYB training mode is a training project specially developed by the International Labour Organisation (ILO) to meet the needs of training micro (small) enterprise owners, and it has been promoted in more than 80 countries in the world. SIYB training technology was introduced into China in 2001 by the pilot project jointly implemented by the Ministry of Labour and Social Security and ILO, and later on it has been implemented in most cities in China. The training adopts the small class training, using knowledge training, case studies, role play, free discussion and other forms, and the training effect is obvious.

3.3.2 Three Stage Training Mode

The whole entrepreneurship training process is divided into theoretical learning stage, consultation and guidance stage, and follow-up support stage. At the theoretical learning stage, it mainly carries out the education on entrepreneurship awareness, entrepreneurship basic knowledge and relevant economic laws and regulations. At the consultation and guidance stage, the experts of the advisory committee or the teachers from training institutes give classified guidance and consultation to the entrepreneurship plan made by the trainees, so as to help them to determine the business projects with development prospects and meeting the market demand, and modify and improve the business plan. At the follow-up support stage, the experts and teachers mainly aim at the problems encountered by the trainees in the actual business start-up process, and provide consultation and services.

3.3.3 Local Self-created Mode

According to the actual needs, all localities can develop teaching plans and organise entrepreneurship training. For example, according to the different needs of the trainees in Shanghai, the training is divided into three types, i.e. entrepreneurial introductory class, entrepreneurial practical training class and entrepreneurial improvement class. Modular training mode is adopted to organise training, and the start-up guidance, personalised guidance and follow-up services are strengthened for the trainees. Aiming at the psychological problems and skills situation of the unemployed, Yunnan province has launched a simulated entrepreneurship training mode to help students to learn the experience and lessons, that cannot be summed up only through a long-term practice, in the shortest time, and provide them with necessary policy support to help them successfully start up businesses.

Although each of the above-mentioned entrepreneurship training models has its own characteristics with different focuses on both contents and methodologies, these models have one thing in common, i.e. they all combine entrepreneurship training with relevant activities such as vocational guidance and micro-loans, to provide entrepreneurs with a full range of services.

4. Development of High-skilled Talent Team

4.1 Overview

High-skilled talents are those who have excellent technologies and exquisite skills, capable of carrying out creative work, and making contributions to the society. It mainly refers to skilled workers who have obtained the vocational qualifications of senior worker, technician and senior technician, and the corresponding level of personnel. High-skilled talents can be divided into three types.

4.1.1 Technical Skilled Talents

Technical skilled talents refer to those engaging in technical operation in the production and processing line at enterprises, having high skill level and being capable of solving operational problems. They are mainly distributed in processing, manufacturing, service and other vocational fields.

4.1.2 Compound Skilled Talents

Compound skilled talents refer to those who master more than one operation skill in the production and processing line at enterprise, and can engage in complex work of multiple types of job and multiple positions in production, and solve production operational problems, such as the technician of CNC machining centre, talent of electro-mechanical integration, talent of comprehensive service, and talent of emerging creative and operational integration.

4.1.3 Knowledge and Skill Talents

Knowledge and skill talents refer to those who have both high level of professional theoretical knowledge and high level of operational skills. They can use their theoretical knowledge to guide production practice and creatively carry out their work. They are mainly distributed in high-tech industries and emerging occupational fields.

4.2 Policy Measures

(1) Further strengthen organisational leadership and improve relevant laws and regulations. The development plan of high-skilled talent team should be formulated and included in the overall plan of economic and social development and the development plan of talent team. The government set up a coordination mechanism for the work of high-skilled talents, participated by various government departments, trade unions, Communist Youth League, women's federation and other people's organisations, responsible for macro-guidance, policy coordination and organisational promotion of the work of high-skilled talents. The legislation on vocational skill training should be accelerated to make more explicit and specific provisions on the responsibilities of the government, enterprises and colleges in terms of vocational skill training and skilled talent training, and bring the work of skilled talents into the legal track.

(2) Improve the training system and speed up the development of high-skilled talents. Combined with the needs of regional economic development, industrial structure adjustment and technology upgrading for high-skilled talents, the role of enterprises and vocational schools and colleges should be brought into full play to accelerate the training of high-skilled talents. Relying on the large-scale, high-level and distinctive senior technical schools, technician colleges, higher vocational colleges and large-scale backbone enterprises (groups), a demonstration base for developing and training high-skilled talents should be established to further improve teaching facilities and training conditions, and enhance their training ability. At the same time, vocational schools and enterprises are encouraged to carry out various forms of cooperation on the basis of mutual benefit and win-win results, so as to continuously enhance the pertinence of skilled talent training. It is encouraged to build public practical training bases in accordance with the needs of local industrial distribution and pillar industry development through financial inputs and various financing methods, so as to provide public welfare and high-level skill training and skill appraisal services for the workers from various enterprises, college students and other workers.

(3) Improve the evaluation and incentive system, and smooth the growth channel of skilled talents. By breaking through the restrictions of age, qualification, identity and proportion, a diversified evaluation system in line with the growth law of high-skilled talents should be actively explored and improved. Relying on qualified large- and medium-sized SOEs, the evaluation of high-skilled talents should be advanced continuously. The evaluation model of high-skilled talents, which is close to the production practice of enterprises, focuses on professional ability and performance, and pays attention to the level of professional ethics and professional knowledge, should be improved. According to the national vocational skill standards and the teaching practice of vocational schools and colleges, the vocational skill education and training standards should be developed to guide vocational schools and colleges to adjust the curriculum and teaching content, standardise the skill appraisal activities, and enable graduates to obtain the diploma and corresponding vocational qualification certificates at the same time.

Order-based vocational training such as integration of school and enterprise and learning by working speeds up the training of high-skilled talents. (Photo taken by Xinhua News Agency reporter Bohan Shen.)

(4) Improve the talent management mechanism and give full play to the role of high-skilled talents. Enterprises are encouraged to establish a leading system of high-skilled talents according to their own development needs, giving full play to the important role of high-skilled talents in solving technical problems, carrying out technological innovation and passing on skills to apprentices. Encouraging governments, industries and enterprises at all levels to select the winners of "Grand Skill Award of China", "National Technical Expert" and other high-skilled personnel with unique skill from the production lines and service positions to set up skill master studios, so as to create favourable conditions for skill master to conduct skill research and training, make technical breakthrough, technical or skill innovation and other activities. At the same time, it also provides opportunities and environment for young workers to learn from famous teachers, upgrade their skills and participate in innovative activities, so as to speed up the inheritance and promotion of the unique skills and innovative achievements of the skill masters.

(5) Carry out skill competition extensively to promote the emergence of more high-skilled talents. The role of vocational skills competition (Figure 7.1) in discovering and selecting excellent and high-skilled talents should be further played. The coordinated development of domestic and international vocational skills competitions should be comprehensively promoted on the basis of on-the-job training, with domestic competitions as the main body and led by the World Skills Competition. The employees and college students should be guided and driven to actively participate in on-the-job training and skills competition and continuously improve their skills, so as to build up a platform for more excellent and high-skilled talents.

(6) Strengthen the commendation and awarding, and raise the economic and social status for high-skilled talents. The commendation and awarding system should be improved which is guided by government commendation and awarding but mainly relies on the awarding of employers and social forces. The incentive system and mechanism for high-skilled talents should be improved. The high-skilled talents who have made outstanding contributions should be commentated and awarded. In brief, the awarding system for high-skilled talents should be developed, with government awards as the guidance, enterprise awards as the main body, and necessary social awards as the supplement so as to constantly improve the economic benefit and social status of high-skilled talents.

Figure 7.1 Categories and Operation Diagram of Vocational Skills Competition

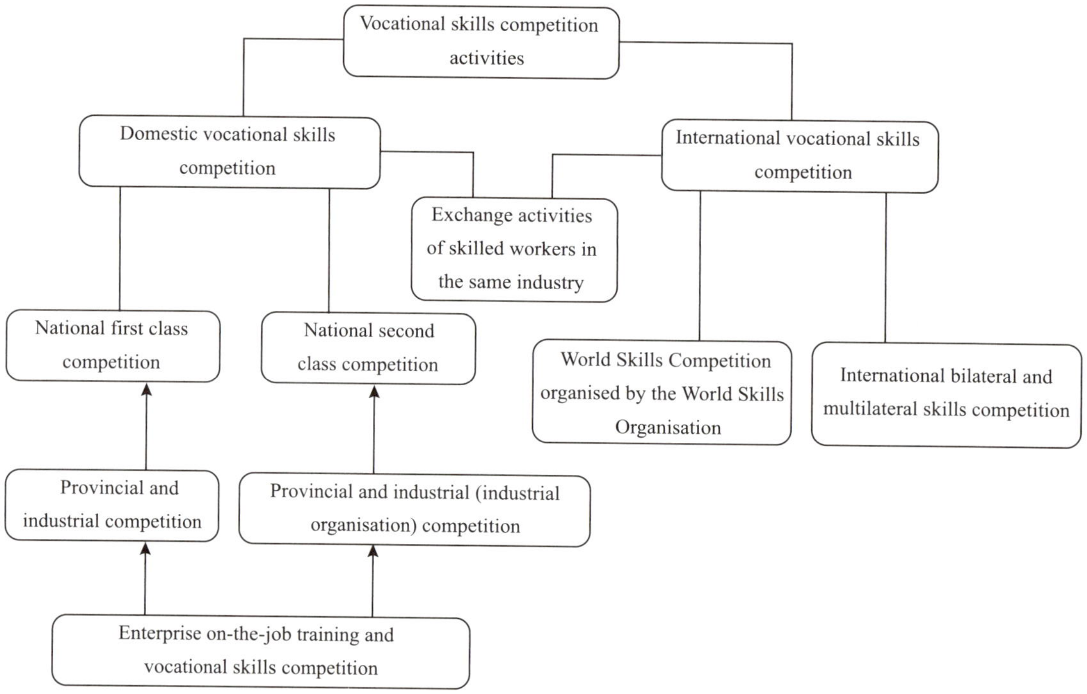

(7) Strengthen technical support and consolidate work foundation. According to the needs of economic and social development, the scientific classification of occupations can provide the basis for the training and evaluation of high-skilled talents. The training of teachers for high-skilled talents should be further strengthened and the structure of teachers should be optimised. Furthermore, it is necessary to strengthen the research on the development law of high-skilled talents, deepen the teaching reform of vocational schools and colleges, strengthen the development of modern training technology suitable for high-skilled talents, develop distinctive teaching materials, speed up the compilation and revision of national vocational skill standards for technicians and senior technicians, and improve the examination question bank of vocational skill appraisal, so as to meet the needs of cultivating high-skilled talents.

(8) Increase fund input and provide financial guarantee. It is necessary to establish a multi-funding mechanism for high-skilled talents by government, enterprises and the society. Governments at all levels should support the training of high-skilled talents, and support the best vocational schools and colleges that have achieved remarkable results in training high-skilled talents with additional input from the earmarked funds for basic vocational education construction given by the State. The development of practical training bases for high-skilled talents should be included in the national plan on supporting the development of vocational education. Enterprises should be guided to fulfil their responsibilities and obligations on the training of skilled workers and to ensure the funds for training skilled workers. More efforts should be made to create a policy environment for the broad participation of social forces in developing high-skilled talents as well as vocational education and training. People from all sectors of society and overseas are encouraged to provide donations and other training services for the development of skilled workers. Financial institutions are encouraged to provide financing services for public practical training bases and vocational schools that cooperate with enterprises to train skilled workers.

4.3 Major Achievements

The CPC Central Committee and the State Council have attached great importance to the work of high-skilled talents. The National Talent Conference held in 2003 brought the construction of high-skilled talents into the overall plan on the national talent team construction, and made a series of strategic arrangements and deployment. Over the years since then, the central and local authorities took effective measures to optimise the policy environment, establish working mechanism, improve the atmosphere of public opinion, closely follow up all the stages in constructing a high-skilled contingent, and promote the work of high-skilled talent into a fast track. The scale of high-skilled talent training has been continuously expanded. It can be seen in the following four areas.

(1) The quality and quantity of high-skilled talent supply have been improved obviously. Craftsmen are constantly emerging. By the end of 2016, the number of high-skilled workers had reached 47.91 million. 476 training bases for high-skilled talents and 594 skill master studios had been set up at national level to conduct training programmes for technicians. The central government had invested 2.05 billion *yuan* in total.

(2) The development system has been gradually formed. A high-skilled talent training system has been essentially established with enterprises and industries as the main body, vocational colleges as the basis, school education closely linked with enterprise training, and with joint efforts between government promotion and social support. Up to now, there are more than 2,500 technical schools and colleges, which are important places for training reserve middle-level and senior-level skilled workers, with more than 3 million students nationwide. Many cities have also built a number of public practical training centres. Under the guidance of government departments, some large- and medium-sized enterprises have gradually established and improved the training system, and actively carried out the training of enterprise skilled workers, which plays an important role in the cultivation of skilled talents.

(3) Skills competition wins honour for China and the Chinese people. After China joined the World Skills Organisation in 2010, more attention has been paid to the leading role of the World Skills Competition so as to promote the improvement of domestic competition and vocational education and training. In 2011, 2013, 2015, 2017 and 2019, China successively participated in the 41st to 45th World Skills Competition, winning 36 gold medals, 29 silver medals, 20 bronze medals and 58 excellence prizes in total (Figure 7.2). In 2017, China won 15 gold medals, 7 silver medals, 8 bronze medals and 12 excellence prizes in the 44th World Skills Competition in Abu Dhabi, United Arab Emirates, ranking first in terms of the number of gold medals, the overall number of medals and the total score of the team. In 2019, China won 16 gold medals, 14 silver medals, 5 bronze medals and 17 excellence prizes in the 45th World Skills Competition in Kazan, Russia, again ranking first in the number of gold medals, the overall number of medals and the total score of the team, creating the best result since China participated in the World Skills Competition. Later, the 46th World Skills Competition will be held in Shanghai, China.

(4) Unlock career paths by evaluation and awarding. High-skilled talent selection and recognition are organised every two years. Each time, 30 winners of "Grand Skill Award of China" and 300 winners of "National Technical Expert" award are commended, apart from some material rewards to them. Since 1995, a total of 260 winners of "Grand Skill Award of China" have been awarded, and 3,028 persons have been granted the title of "National Technical Expert" (in addition, 5,349 persons have been granted the title of "National Technical Expert" through competitions). The practice of high-skilled talents entitled for the special government allowances of the State Council has been promoted constantly. Since 2008, 400 high-skilled talents have been selected every two years for the entitlement of the special government allowances (since 2012, 500 persons have been selected each time). Apart from the certificates of honour, a lump-sum special allowance will be given to them as well. By the end of 2018, 2,729 high-skilled talents entitled for the special government allowances of the State Council were selected.

Figure 7.2 Statistics of the Number of Awards of Chinese Team in the 41st to 45th World Skills Competition

Source: the Ministry of Human Resources and Social Security.

The Chinese delegation performed very well in the 45th World Skills Competition, winning 16 gold medals, 14 silver medals, 5 bronze medals and 17 excellence prizes, once again ranking first in terms of the number of gold medals, the overall number of medals and the total score of the team.

Chapter 8

Group Employment

1. Youth Employment

1.1 Overview of Youth Employment

Youth employment is a global employment problem. According to the results of the 2007 sample survey on population changes in China, the population aged 15-34 accounted for 28.7% of the total population in China. At the end of 2008, China's youth (16-34 years old) accounted for 32.5% of the total employment in China.

With the development of education in China, people with higher education have become the mainstream of young workers. The number of college graduates has increased year by year, reaching 8.2 million in 2018, an increase of 2.61 million from 5.59 million in 2008, increased by nearly 46.7 percent (Table 8.1). According to preliminary estimates by the National Bureau of Statistics of China, the proportion of people with college or higher education rose from 0.9% to 20.1% in 2018 compared with 1982; the proportion of people with high school education rose from 10.5% to 18.0%; and the proportion of people with middle school education increased from 26.0% to 43.2%. [①] To better adapt to the changes in the labour market, China has also taken various measures to vigorously

[①] Data are extracted from *A Series of Report on Economic and Social Development Achievements of the 70th Anniversary of the Founding of the People's Republic of China* issued by the National Bureau of Statistics.

develop vocational education and training, which are important measures to prevent unemployment, stabilise employment and promote re-employment.

Table 8.1 Number of College Graduates in China (2008-2018)

(Unit: 10 thousand)

Year	College graduates
2008	559
2009	611
2010	631
2011	660
2012	680
2013	699
2014	727
2015	749
2016	756
2017	795
2018	820

Source: the Ministry of Education.

In China, some college graduates and other youth groups still have employment problems. On the one hand, the total employment pressure is great. Each year, more than 15 million new entrants to the labour market need to be employed in cities and towns, more than half of whom are college graduates. And many young labourers from the rural areas need to transfer for employment as well. On the other hand, the structural contradiction of employment is prominent. At present, China remains in the middle stage of industrialisation and in the middle and low end of the industrial chain. Most of the job vacancies in the market are for general workers in manufacturing industries and waiters in service industries, with relatively insufficient high-quality jobs. However, the new generation of young job seekers pays more attention to career development, salary and working conditions, so naturally, there is a mismatch between the supply and demand of jobs. Some young labourers' ability and competence do not meet the needs of the enterprises, and the number of innovative and technical talents is far less than the need of economic transformation and upgrading.

1.2 Major Policy Measures to Promote Youth Employment

1.2.1 Major Measures to Promote Youth Employment

Promoting youth employment relates to the well-being of many families and the development future of the country. The Chinese government insists that the employment of young people, with focus on university graduates, should be the top priority in the work of employment, and has adopted a series of measures to promote youth employment and entrepreneurship.

(1) Take comprehensive measures to promote youth employment and entrepreneurship. The Chinese government has taken effective measures in the following four areas. First, develop the economy and expand the space for employment. The government implements pro-employment policy, regarding employment as the minimum limit of a reasonable range of economic operation, strengthening the inter-linkage among employment policy and macroeconomic, industrial, fiscal, and financial policies, and ensuring a positive interaction between promoting economic development and expanding employment. It is necessary to foster new drivers of growth, promote the rapid development of new industries, new forms of business and new models, and expand diversified employment opportunities suitable for young people. Second, encourage entrepreneurship and innovation to create jobs. The government continues to streamline administration and delegate power, lower the threshold for starting up businesses, and increase policy support for starting up businesses. Young people are encouraged to start up businesses by reducing or waiving taxes and fees, providing loans, and strengthening the building of incubators. Third, strengthen vocational skill training. The government implements vocational skill upgrading action and accelerates the development of knowledge-based, skill-based and innovation-based labour force. Fourth, accelerate the building up of public employment service system, which is convenient and efficient, covering all people, throughout the whole process, and accessible to the whole city. It provides free services, such as policy consultation, job recommendation, employment and business start-up guidance, and assistance to the persons with employment difficulties, to all workers including young people, especially in light of the characteristics of young people, making more use of micro-blogs, WeChat, mobile phone Apps and other means to provide more flexible and convenient employment services.

(2) Formulate specific plans. In recent years, the Chinese government has formulated and implemented *the Medium- and Long-term Youth Development Plan (2016-*

2025), putting forward the goals, tasks and key measures to promote youth employment and entrepreneurship. The development goals of youth employment and entrepreneurship proposed in the plan are as follows: relatively full employment for youth, the employment rate of college graduates remaining at a high level; better employment rights protection for youth, such as their salary benefit, labour protection and social insurance being fully protected; the youth entrepreneurship service system being further improved, and the entrepreneurial vitality being significantly improved. The development measures include: promoting the improvement of youth employment and entrepreneurship policy system, strengthening youth employment service, promoting youth to participate in entrepreneurship practice, and strengthening the protection of youth employment rights and interests.

(3) Implement specific plans for targeted group. In recent years, the Ministry of Human Resources and Social Security has issued a series of document measures to implement a number of specific plans to promote youth employment, such as "Internship Programme for 1 Million Youth in 3 Years" for the unemployed graduates and unemployed youth, "Youth Employment Sailing Plan" for the long-term unemployed youth, the special vocational skill upgrading plan for the rural new generation of young workers, the labour reserve training programme for middle and high school graduates in urban and rural areas who have not continued their school studies, the entrepreneurship training programme for young entrepreneurs with training desire, and the new apprenticeship training for the newly recruited and newly transferred workers in enterprises.

In "Internship Programme for 1 Million Youth in 3 Years", five work contents are put forward. The first is to clearly identify the trainees. The trainees are unemployed college graduates within two years after leaving school and 16 to 24-year-old unemployed youth. The second is to develop internship posts, and determine a number of enterprises, institutions and social organisations as youth employment internship units according to the development of advantageous industries and youth internship needs, fully tapping the internship positions and providing internship services. The third is to organise the recommendation of internship positions and negotiation activities for two-way selection, and help the matching between the supply and demand sides of the internship by various measures. The fourth is to strengthen the internship management to ensure that the internship activities are arranged in a standardised and orderly manner. The fifth is to implement follow-up support, encourage the trainee units to retain the trainees after the internship period, and continuously provide employment and entrepreneurship services for those who have not been retained.

In "Youth Employment Sailing Plan", five main measures are proposed. The first is to find out the basic situation, understand and master the basic information of youth's family situation, unemployment reasons, job seeking intention, skill level, etc. The second is to carry out practical guidance to encourage the unemployed youth to go out of their homes for creating more opportunities to understand the society. The third is to improve the employability according to the unemployed youth's ability and employment intention, providing them with targeted training programmes for mastering at least one special skill. The fourth is to support independent entrepreneurship, organise the unemployed youth with entrepreneurial intention to visit the entrepreneurial park and to sense the entrepreneurial atmosphere, and motivate them to start up their own businesses. The fifth is to carry out the bottom-line support. Priority shall be given to poverty-stricken families, low-income families in urban and rural areas, zero-employment families and unemployed youth with disabilities. Special vocational guidance and psychological counselling services shall be provided. Special recruitment activities shall be organised and these people shall be recommended first to enterprises.

1.2.2 Policies and Measures to Promote the Employment and Entrepreneurship of College Graduates

The Chinese government attaches great importance to the employment of college graduates. Since 2009, a series of policies and measures has been formulated to promote the employment of college graduates. In 2011, 2013 and 2014, the General Office of the State Council continuously issued documents to promote the employment and entrepreneurship of college graduates. In 2016, the General Office of the CPC Central Committee and the General Office of the State Council issued opinions on further guiding and encouraging college graduates to work at the grass roots level. In 2016, the Ministry of Human Resources and Social Security and the Ministry of Education launched the employment and entrepreneurship promotion plan for college graduates. In 2019, the Ministry of Human Resources and Social Security, the Ministry of Education, the Ministry of Public Security, the Ministry of Finance and the People's Bank of China jointly issued new documents on the employment and entrepreneurship of college graduates, so as to promote the employment and entrepreneurship of college graduates in an all-round way.

(1) Actively expand the field of employment for college graduates. Combining the development of strategic emerging industries, the transformation of the economic development pattern and the adjustment of the economic structure, major efforts should be devoted to develop intelligence-intensive and technology-intensive industries that have a strong ability to absorb employment. Great efforts should also be made to develop production services and consumer services with growth potential, promote the development of "Internet Plus" new technologies, new forms of business and new models, and continue to develop service jobs in social management and public education, health and culture, so as to continuously broaden the employment channels for college graduates and strive to expand the scale of economic development to absorb college graduates.

In the process of China's economy upgrading from labour-intensive to intelligence-intensive, the industrial workers dominated by Chinese youth are developing rapidly. (Photo taken by Xinhua News Agency reporter Yi Tang.)

(2) Increase policy support to guide multiple-channel employment. The Chinese government has continuously improved the policy system for promoting the employment of college graduates, making full use of various policies such as fiscal, taxation, financial and capital subsidies to guide college graduates to seek employment in urban and rural grass roots units as well as micro-, small- and medium-sized businesses, and support new forms of employment and flexible forms of employment. Policies on tuition and student loans compensation, higher wages, financial subsidies and favourable conditions for professional titles shall be implemented for those who are employed at the grass roots units, especially in the central and western regions, and in the hard and outlying areas. The grass roots service projects such as "*Three Supports and One Assistance Plan*" and "*Special Post Programme for Rural Teachers*" are implemented to guide college graduates to provide volunteer services in such fields as urban and rural grass roots education, medical care, and public health. When service period expires, they can enjoy preferential policies such as bonus points for postgraduate entrance examination and targeted recruitment. Tax relief, social insurance subsidies, vocational training subsidies and other policies should be implemented for small- and medium-sized enterprises absorbing employment of college graduates. College graduates working at private enterprises can enjoy the same treatment as those in SOEs and institutions in terms of professional and technical title evaluation. For flexible employment, social security subsidies and other policies should be implemented.

(3) Encourage college graduates to start up their own businesses. The first is to optimise the entrepreneurial policy environment. For qualified college graduates who start up their own businesses, a tax reduction of 12,000 *yuan* per household per year shall be available within 3 years, and a maximum of 150,000 *yuan* of interest subsidy for business start-up secured loans shall be provided, and a one-time business start-up subsidy shall be issued. These places with good conditions should be supported to establish employment and entrepreneurship funds for college graduates to assist graduates in entrepreneurship and innovation. The second is to strengthen innovation and entrepreneurship education. It should be incorporated into the whole process of talent cultivation in colleges and universities. Colleges and universities should be guided to develop innovative entrepreneurship education courses formulate measures such as credit conversion, flexible schooling system, and retain student status to suspend school for start-up business, carrying out various entrepreneurial activities, enhancing college students' innovative spirit, entrepreneurial consciousness and innovative entrepreneurial ability. The third is to strengthen the cultivation of ability and quality. College graduates with entrepreneurial intention should be organised to participate in entrepreneurship training with training subsidies available according to regulations. Relying on various training institutes and enterprise training centres, high-quality, distinctive and targeted training courses should be innovated and developed to meet the needs of graduates in different stages of entrepreneurship, different fields and different business forms. The fourth is to provide excellent entrepreneurial services. According to the characteristics and needs of college graduates, it is necessary to provide one-stop entrepreneurship services, such as policy consultation, project development, risk assessment, business guidance, financing services, follow-up support and entrepreneurship incubation, etc. The business start-up of college graduates should be supported in an all-round way by actively building entrepreneurship incubation carriers such as a maker space and a college students' entrepreneurship park, holding various activities such as "the Wing of Entrepreneurship and Innovation in China" entrepreneurship and innovation competition.

(4) Support college graduates to participate in employment internships and vocational skill training programmes. In combination with the development of competitive industries in various regions and the needs of young people for internships, enterprises, institutions and social organisations with good reputation and standardised management should be organised as employment internship units, and the internship subsidy policy should be implemented to help the unemployed youth to enrich their practical experience and enhance their employment competitiveness. College graduates with training needs should be actively organised to participate in vocational skill training and vocational skill appraisal in order to help them improve their employability. Subsidies should be provided to them for their vocational skill training and vocational skill appraisal. If the enterprise recruits fresh graduates and carries out post skill training within one year after graduation, vocational training subsidies shall be given according to regulations.

(5) Strengthen employment guidance and employment service for college graduates. Career development and employment guidance curriculum system should be established throughout the university education period. Regular employment service activities such as specific job fairs, supply and demand fairs, and campus recruitment should be organised. The network should be actively used to provide employment services so as to adapt to the needs and characteristics of college graduates. The college graduates who have not been employed should be included in the employment aid system, and services such as job vacancy information, vocational guidance and vocational training should be provided according to the needs of the position. College graduates with difficulties in employment should be included in the employment aid system to provide one-to-one employment assistance. The regulation of human resources market should be strengthened to protect the employment rights and interests of college graduates.

1.3 Achievements in Promoting Youth Employment

In recent years, the Chinese government has implemented a series of policies and measures to promote the overall stability of youth employment. The employment rate of college graduates has remained at a high level, and the scale of independent entrepreneurship has been expanding. The number of trainees increased, with 330,000 college graduates taking part in vocational training in 2018, 22,000 of whom successfully started up their own businesses in the same period after the training. More than 370,000 high school graduates from urban and rural areas who did not continue their studies also took part in vocational training, with 21,000 of them becoming successful entrepreneurs in the same period after the training.

2. Women's Employment

2.1 Overview of Women's Employment

By the end of 2017, women accounted for 49% of China's population, and they were an important part of labour resources. The majority of women have actively participated in national construction and made great contributions to economic development and social progress. Women's economic and social status has also been significantly improved. Since China's reform and opening-up policy, with the sustained and stable development of the national economy, the State has formulated and implemented a series of supporting policies to promote employment and re-employment. The employed women increased from 170 million in 1978 to 340 million in 2018, accounting for 43.7% of the total employed population.

Since the founding of the People's Republic of China in 1949, China has enacted a series of laws and regulations to protect women's rights and interests in labour and employment. *Common Programme for Chinese People's Political Consultative Conference*, the provisional Charter issued in 1949, explicitly states that the feudalism which binds women shall be abolished and that women shall have the same rights as men in all aspects of political, economic, cultural, educational and social life. At present, China has basically formulated a whole set of legal and regulatory systems to protect women's labour rights and interests and promote women's employment, which take the Constitution as the basis, with *Law on the Protection of the Rights and Interests of Women*, *Labour Law* and *Employment Promotion Law* as the main lines, and *Provisions on the Labour Protection of Women Workers*, *Provisions on the Scope of Forbidden Work for Women Workers*, *Provisions on Labour and Health Care for Women Workers*, *Interim*

Measures on Maternity Insurance for Enterprise Workers and other regulations as specific measures. These laws, regulations, and policies have effectively protected the rights and interests of women in labour and employment.

2.2 Policy Measures to Promote Women's Employment

Since the founding of the People's Republic of China in 1949, the Chinese government has always attached great importance to women's employment, formulated and implemented various laws and regulations to guarantee women's employment rights, and adopted various measures to promote women's employment. Since the 18th National Congress of the Communist Party of China, China has implemented the pro-employment strategy and actively promoted equal employment between men and women. In 2019, nine departments, including the Ministry of Human Resources and Social Security, issued *Notice on Further Standardising Recruitment and Promoting Women's Employment*, which defined six kinds of gender discrimination in employment, and improved three mechanisms, i.e. joint interview, human resources market supervision and judicial relief to provide strong support for ensuring women's equal right for employment.

(1) Actively develop employment positions and improve employment policies to promote women's employment. In recent years, China has made great efforts in developing tertiary industry, in particular the community services, which is suitable for women's employment, continuously enhancing the ability of labour-intensive enterprises, small- and medium-sized enterprises and non-public-owned enterprises for women's employment, and expanding employment fields for women. By the end of 2017, 65.453 million women had been employed in urban units nationwide.

(2) Increase policy support and encourage women to start up their own businesses. Entrepreneurship training and one-stop entrepreneurship services such as policy consultation, project recommendation, business start-up guidance and follow-up support should be actively provided to women who are willing to start up their own businesses. Preferential policies such as micro-secured loans and interest discount should be given to those who meet the requirements. In recent years, the human resources and social security departments with other relevant departments have jointly carried out publicity activities on some outstanding female employment and entrepreneurship cases to guide and encourage more female workers to become entrepreneurs.

(3) Strengthen education and training to improve women's competence. Since the founding of the People's Republic of China in 1949, the Chinese government has empowered women with equal rights to education as men by law, which has substantially changed the previous situation that women's illiteracy rate was much higher than that of men. Since China's reform and opening-up policy, high school education has been vigorously popularised. With the increase of financial support for students in central and western regions and families in these regions with financial difficulties, the opportunities for women to receive high school education have been increased significantly. As of 2017, female students in senior high school education accounted for 47.7% of the total number of students. In 2017, female students in colleges and universities accounted for 52.5% of the total number of students in colleges and universities, 28.4 percentage higher than that in 1978; female students in graduate schools accounted for 48.4%, 29.8 percentage higher than that in 1985.

(4) Actively provide targeted employment services for female job seekers. Public employment service agencies at the provincial, municipal, county and township levels are open to female job seekers free of charge. Many urban public employment service agencies even set up specific counters and hold specific job fairs for female job seekers. The departments of human resources and social security and the women's federation jointly organised specific activities for female rural workers named as "Spring Breeze Sending Jobs", and provided targeted employment services free of charge to rural women working in cities.

(5) Improve the maternity insurance system and improve women's employment environment. In order to avoid employers' unwillingness to employ female workers because of their bearing burden, China has vigorously promoted the establishment of maternity insurance system in recent years. The participants of national maternity insurance increased from 108.76 million at the end of 2009 to 204.34 million at the end of 2018, and such insurance beneficiaries increased from 1.74 million to 10.89 million.

(6) Strengthen law enforcement and supervision to protect the legitimate rights and interests of female workers. Labour and social security inspection institutions have strengthened inspection on the industries or enterprises that use more female workers, actively carrying out special inspection activities to standardise the market order and special labour protection for female workers, and focusing on investigating and punishing some illegal acts that infringe the rights and interests of female workers. It is necessary to regulate the recruitment and employing behaviour of employers, guide enterprises to conscientiously implement the provisions on equal employment in laws and regulations, actively deal with the complaints from female workers, and correct all kinds of discriminatory behaviours.

2.3 Achievements in Promoting Women's Employment

With the rapid economic and social development of the country, women have more and diversified employment choices, as well as a wider road to entrepreneurship. Female workers and entrepreneurs have increased substantially. In 2017, 340 million women were employed, double that of 1978. In 2017, there were 15.297 million female professionals in enterprises and institutions of the public sector, accounting for 48.6% of the total, with an increase of 9.5 percentage points over 1982. From 2009 to 2018, the country granted a total of 383.77 billion *yuan* of micro-secured loans for women's employment and entrepreneurship, with 6.569 million women receiving such loans, giving strong support to women's employment and business start-ups. In 2017, All-China Women's Federation held China Women's Entrepreneurship and Innovation Competition, with 560,000 female participants. The women's federation has trained 100,000 women as e-commerce leaders

The majority of women actively participate in national construction and make great contributions to economic development and social progress. (Photo taken by Xinhua News Agency reporter Yu Mu.)

to drive more than 15 million women to increase their incomes and become rich. A service system named "Internet Plus Women Entrepreneurship" has initially taken shape, with women accounting for 55% of the total number of Internet entrepreneurs. In 2017, 71.2% of the enterprises implemented labour protection for women workers, increased by 35.2 percentage points over 2002. Nearly 300,000 grass roots enterprises and institutions have established women workers' rest and nursing rooms, covering 18.494 million women workers.

3. Employment of Rural Workers

China has a large rural population and abundant labour resources. In the early days when the People's Republic of China was founded in 1949, rural workers were mainly engaged in agricultural production. From 1950s to 1970s, through the active development of rural economy, the employment situation gradually improved. In 1978, there were 306.38 million rural employed persons[①]. Since China's reform and opening up policy, the State has implemented the household contract responsibility system with remuneration linked to output and encouraged the development of diversified economy in agriculture sector and township enterprises, which boosted the enthusiasm of rural workers in production and management, greatly improved their efficiency, and resulted in a lot of surplus labour in the countryside. With the rapid development of township enterprises and the gradual establishment and improvement of the labour market, the surplus rural labour force began to shift to non-agricultural industries and move to the city for employment. As of 1997, rural employed persons reached 490.39 million. Entering the 21st century, the Chinese government vigorously promoted the employment and entrepreneurship of rural workers. Rural workers engaged in non-agricultural employment continued to increase. And those moving to cities for employment and becoming new urban residents increased as well. They devoted themselves to manufacturing and service industries, participated in urban construction and development, and played an important role in China's economic and social development.

[①] The rural employed persons refer to the persons above the age of 16 who actually participate in production and business activities and obtain income in kind or currency. The rural employed persons include both workers within the working age, and those over the working age yet actually remaining working, but excluding the students who are registered at their hometowns or villages, the in-service military personnel, people losing the ability to work, and the unemployed and the household workers.

With the rapid development of township enterprises and the gradual establishment and improvement of the labour market, surplus rural labour began to transfer to non-agricultural industries.

3.1 Basic Situation of Employment of Rural Workers

3.1.1 Employment Structure of Rural Labour Force in China

Employment structure and industrial structure are closely related. Since the founding of the People's Republic of China in 1949, the employment structure of the rural labour force has shown the following changes. The employment proportion of the labour force in the primary industry showed a downward trend, while the employment proportion in the secondary and tertiary industries showed an upward trend. At the end of 2018, 341.67 million people were employed in rural areas, 288.36 million of whom were engaged in non-agricultural sectors (including 172.66 million rural workers engaged in non-agricultural sectors outside their hometowns). For the rural employees in non-agricultural sectors, 141.58 million (49.1%) worked in the secondary industry, while 145.62 million

(50.5%) working in the tertiary industry. In other words, only 0.4% of rural employees worked in the primary industry.

3.1.2 Employment Channels of Rural Labour Force

Since the reform and opening-up policy was implemented, the practices in China show that the rural labour force has three main channels for employment: employment in agricultural sector, mainly engaged in planting and breeding; transitioned employment locally and nearby in non-agricultural sector; and employment outside the hometowns or home villages, including cross-regional urban work and doing business.

(1) Agricultural employment. Since 1980s, China's agricultural employment has shown a rapid growth trend. The household contract responsibility system with remuneration linked to output in rural areas has stimulated the autonomy and enthusiasm of rural workers in production, greatly emancipated the rural productivity, and significantly increased employment opportunities in agriculture. In recent years, all regions have actively expanded rural employment space through: ① accelerating the development of forestry, aquaculture, animal husbandry and other industries by vigorously developing high-yield, high-quality and high-efficiency agriculture; ② developing industrialised agricultural operations to extend the agricultural industrial chain; ③ accelerating the development of the depth and breadth of agricultural production, especially exploring ways to exploit non-cultivated land resources such as barren mountains, barren gullies, barren hills and barren beaches, and further tapping the potential for employment within agriculture.

(2) Local and nearby transfer employment. It is an important direction to develop non-agricultural industries in rural areas and promote the local and nearby transfer employment of rural workers. Since China's reform and opening-up policy was implemented, the coastal and relatively developed areas in East China have created a large number of jobs and taken the lead in realising the local transfer of a large number of rural labourers, thanks to the vigorous development of township enterprises, private economy and county economy. In recent years, with the development of the central and western regions and the coordinated development strategy of regional economy, rural labour force transferring to nearby areas has also expanded on a large scale. It has played a positive role in accelerating the overall socioeconomic development of the county economy and underdeveloped areas, and promoting the construction of new socialist countryside.

The township and village enterprises have become the main channel to absorb the rural labour force employment, which increases the income of the rural workers and promotes the transfer employment of the rural labour force.

(3) Cross-regional migrating employment. At the end of 1970s, a large number of rural workers began to engage in home-based industry and commerce. In the early days, migrating employment was mainly in outbound marketing and construction industry. At the end of 1984, the number of migrant workers was less than 2 million nationwide. However, in the following years, as the township and village enterprises grew rapidly, rural workers moving across regions increased rapidly to about 10 million by 1988. Since then, the rapid development of the national economy, especially the economic development of the eastern seaboard, did drive the sharp increase of rural migrant workers moving across regions, especially to cities. It rose from 40 million in 1994 up to 288.36 million in 2018.

3.1.3 The Basic Situation of Rural Workers Engaged in Non-agricultural Employment

(1) The overall amount of employment and the geographical distribution of employment. In 2018, 288.36 million rural workers were employed in non-agricultural industries, according to a national survey of household visits in rural areas conducted by the National Bureau of Statistics of China (Figure 8.1). 172.66 million of them (including 135.06 million rural workers entering cities and towns) worked in non-agricultural industries outside their hometowns, while 115.7 million employed within the townships.

Figure 8.1 Total Number of Rural Workers Engaged in Non-agricultural Employment (2014-2018)

(Unit: 10 thousand)

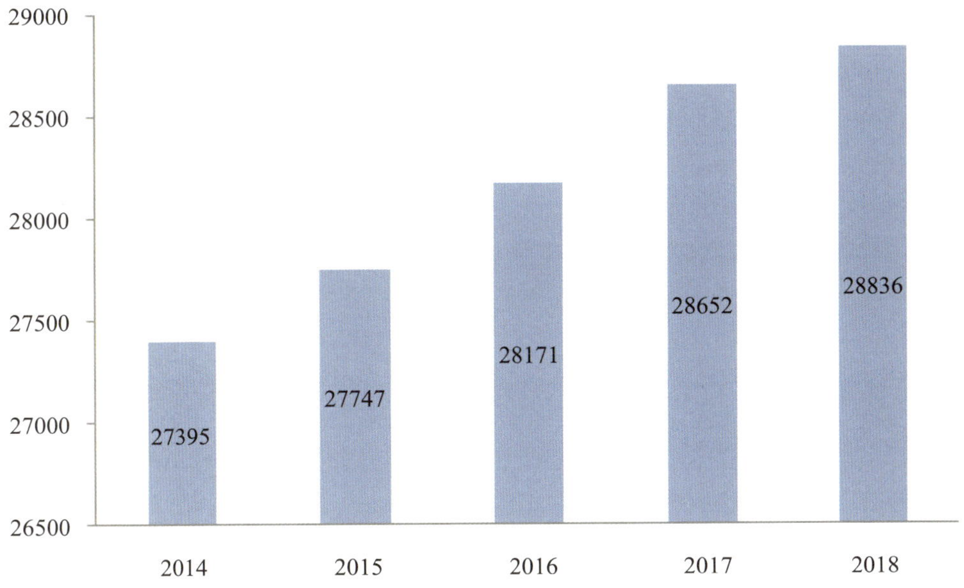

Source: the website of the National Bureau of Statistics.

(2) Main features. First, of all the rural workers engaged in non-agricultural employment, 65.2% were male and 34.8% were female. Women accounted for 30.8% of the outbound non-agricultural rural workers, and 38.6% of the local non-agricultural rural workers. Second, the average age of rural workers engaged in non-agricultural employment is 40.2 years old. In terms of age structure, 52.1% of rural workers engaged in non-agricultural employment are under the age of 40, and 22.4% are over 50 years old. Third, of all rural workers engaged in non-agricultural employment, 15.5% of them have finished primary school education, 55.8% finished middle school education, 16.6% finished high school education, and 10.9% finished junior college or above.

(3) Wage income. The results of special survey conducted by the National Bureau of Statistics showed that in 2006, the average monthly wage of rural workers engaged in non-agricultural employment was 966 *yuan*. Since the 18th National Congress of the Communist Party of China, the income of rural workers engaged in non-agricultural employment increased rapidly. According to the survey of the National Bureau of Statistics, in 2018 the average monthly income of rural workers engaged in non-agricultural employment was 3,721 *yuan*, increased by 2,755 *yuan* or 285.2% compared with 2006.

(4) Rural education. In the early days when the People's Republic of China was founded in 1949, rural education fell far behind the city in China. Since China's reform and opening-up policy was implemented, compulsory education in rural areas achieved comprehensive development as its funding has been guaranteed by public financial budget. Since the 18th National Congress of the Communist Party of China, the State has vigorously supported rural education, implemented major projects such as constructing rural boarding schools and poverty alleviation through education. According to the statistics of the Ministry of Education, in 2018 more than 90% of the counties in China achieved balanced development in terms of compulsory education, with more rural teenagers enjoying better and fairer education. Rural residents finishing middle school education accounted for 42.5%, those of senior high school or technical secondary school education accounted for 11.0%, and those of junior college or above accounted for 3.9%. The improvement of rural residents' cultural competence promotes the overall quality of rural labour force, so that high-quality labour forces are provided for economic development.

3.2 Policies and Measures to Promote the Transfer Employment of Rural Workers

3.2.1 The Evolution of Rural Labour Migrating Employment Policy

The state policy on the migrating employment of the rural labour force has undergone three stages. From late 1970s to late 1980s, it gradually changed from controlled migration into allowing the migration. From late 1980s to late 1990s, the policy changed from disorderly migration into orderly migration. From the end of 1990s to present, differentiated policies between urban and rural areas turned into overall planning of urban and rural employment.

3.2.2 Introducing Policies to Promote Overall Planning of Urban and Rural Employment

First, in In order to give equal treatment to rural workers engaged in non-agricultural industries, the Ministry of Labour and Social Security issued regulations to eliminatethe restriction of migration and unreasonable charges, and improve the working environment for rural workers in cities.

Second, strengthen employment services and promote the transfer of rural labour. ①Establish a public employment service system for all workers, including rural workers. The State clearly proposed that in terms of employment services, free job recommendation services should be available at public employment service institutions for rural workers who registered for employment in cities and towns. In case of unemployment, the rural workers who lived in the cities permanently could make unemployment registration in their residences of the city and enjoy equal public employment services as well as inclusive employment policies. ② Implement the Spring Breeze Action to strengthen the employment services for rural workers who enter the city to seek employment. During the peak period of rural labour migration after the Spring Festival, the Spring Breeze Action is carried out nationwide. During this period, public employment service institutions in cities provide free services for rural workers. At the same time, they recommend a number of honest private employment agencies, cracked down on illegal job intermediary agencies and improved the employment environment. ③ Build up labour export demonstration counties and transfer employment demonstration counties, and promote the in-depth development of rural employment. In order to further improve the labour exporting services, it is suggested that the three-in-one work mode, i.e. vocational training, employment service and labour rights protection, should be vigorously promoted, and the effective matching of labour exporting and labour importing should be strengthened. After that, more than 190 labour export demonstration counties were determined for focusing on summing up and promoting the experience of the demonstration counties. It has promoted the transfer employment of rural labour force at national level and the employment service in counties and townships. ④Establish and improve the county and township public employment service system. In 2002, it was clearly stated in the national employment policy that organisations in charge of labour and social security affairs could be set up or selected in the streets and townships with heavy tasks in this field. Subsequently, the Ministry of Labour and Social Security put forward requirements on the establishment of work platform in sub-districts (townships) and residential communities, which could be simply put as six availabilities, i.e. institutions, personnel, funds, service delivery place, systems and routine work. By the end of 2009, 89% of the townships in China had established corresponding working institutions, and 41% of the villages employed full-time or part-time staff who mainly engaged in labour resource statistics, job recommendation, labour export and guiding training. As of 2018, most of the grass roots sub-districts and townships across the country established work platforms, set up special service places or service counters to undertake the basic responsibilities of employment work. Specific service counters were set up in residential communities and villages, and door-to-door services were carried out. ⑤ Organise and implement the rural labour force's skill plan for employment to improve the rural labour force's vocational skills. Since 2006, the rural labour force's skill plan for employment has been organised and implemented nationwide, and one-time vocational training subsidies have been provided for rural workers working in cities. Since then, a number of national vocational skill training programmes have also covered rural workers.

Third, carry out pilot projects to coordinate urban and rural employment and improve the integrated urban-rural labour market. In order to further promote the transferred employment of rural labour force, in 2006, the Ministry of Labour and Social Security, the National Development and Reform Commission, the Ministry of Finance and the Ministry of Agriculture jointly decided to select some areas with good employment foundation, strong management and service ability, as well as high enthusiasm for reform and innovation to carry out the pilot work of balancing urban and rural employment, establishing an integrated labour market between urban and rural areas, and developing a system to guarantee the equal employment of urban and rural workers, and promoting full employment of urban and rural workers. The pilot areas should establish and improve the organisational system for the management of urban and rural employment, establish both vocational training and public employment service systems covering urban and rural areas, improve the labour and employment management system, and properly solve the social security problems for rural workers. On the basis of achievements and experience obtained, it will be extended to the whole country.

Fourth, support rural migrant workers to start up their own businesses in their hometowns. In 2008, in order to implement the development strategy of expanding employment and promote entrepreneurship-driven employment put forward by the 17th National Congress of the Communist Party of China, the General Office of the State Council forwarded *Guiding Opinion on Promoting Entrepreneurship-driven Employment*, which aimed at promoting entrepreneurship from the aspects of improving supporting policies, improving the entrepreneurial environment, strengthening entrepreneurship training, improving the entrepreneurial ability, improving the service system and providing high-quality services. It is clearly specified that the policy is applicable to all groups including rural workers. Also, it proposes to provide relevant policies to support rural migrant workers to start up their own businesses in their hometowns, actively do a good job in providing financial and entrepreneurship services for their entrepreneurship at hometowns.

3.3 The Contribution of Promoting the Transfer Employment of Rural Labour Forces to the Economic and Social Development

Since the founding of the People's Republic of China in 1949, the CPC and the State have promoted rural reform and development in accordance with the national conditions and agricultural conditions. From the land reform to the implementation of agricultural cooperation in 1950s, from the establishment of household contract responsibility system with remuneration linked to output in 1980s to promoting the separation of the three rights of rural contracted land in 2014, and from fighting the battle of poverty alleviation since the 21st century to implementing the rural revitalisation strategy since 2018, a series of reform and construction initiatives has promoted the continuous innovation of rural system and mechanism, and promoted the liberation of agriculture and the development of secondary and tertiary industries in rural China. Since the 18th CPC National Congress, the CPC Central Committee with Comrade Xi Jinping as its core has persisted in making it the top priority of the whole Party's work to solve "Three Rural Issues" [①], and continued to strengthen the policy of strengthening agriculture, benefiting farmers and enriching farmers, established and improved the mechanism and policy system for urban-rural integration development, comprehensively deepened rural reform, steadily implemented rural revitalisation strategy, and achieved remarkable results in targeted poverty alleviation, agriculture industry and rural development.

[①] "Three Rural Issues" refer to the problems of agriculture, rural areas and farmers.

First, the transfer employment of rural migrant workers is another great creation in China after the household contract responsibility system with remuneration linked to output and the rise of township enterprises, which is also a great initiative to liberate rural productivity. The rural migrant workers connect cities and developed areas with rural and less developed areas. The transfer employment of rural migrant workers works effectively in promoting the optimal allocation of labour resources and productivity between urban and rural areas, closely linking the solution of the "Three Rural Issues" with the development of industrialisation, urbanisation and modernisation, and it has paved a new way of urban-rural integrated development. Second, rural workers' going out for work has become the main channel to expand employment and increase income. It has also become an effective form to have the development of industry drive the development of agriculture, to have the development of cities drive that of rural areas, and developed areas drive less developed areas. Through employment in cities and developed areas, the rural migrant workers have brought billions of funds back to rural areas every year, which have become an important source of purchasing agricultural means of production and improving living conditions, and also provided the capital accumulation for agricultural and rural development. These workers have mastered techniques, improved their competence, broadened their vision, accumulated experience, enriched social network, and increased rural human capital. A group of rural workers with capital, techniques and the concept of market economy have become a new force in driving the development of rural economy, which has promoted the growth of county economy in underdeveloped areas and directly promoted the construction of new socialist countryside. Third, the rural migrant workers have become an important force to push China's urbanisation construction and urban development, providing endless labour force for the development of secondary and tertiary industries in urban China, and they have become new urban residents with productivity and consumption power. It has promoted the overall development of the market economy and made an important contribution to the national economy.

4. Employment of People with Employment Difficulties

Employment Promotion Law stipulates that the persons who have difficulty in finding jobs refer to those persons who have difficulty in getting employed because of their physical condition, level of skills, family factor, loss of land, etc, or who cannot get re-employed after being unemployed for a continuous period of time. The specific range of such persons shall be separately defined by the people's governments of provinces, autonomous regions and municipalities in light of the actual conditions of their respective administrative areas. Meanwhile, it also clearly stipulates that governments at all levels shall establish a sound employment aid system and give priority to the persons who have difficulty in finding jobs, by means of exemption and deduction of taxes and fees, discount interest loans, social insurance subsidies, post subsidies, by providing public welfare jobs and through other channels.

4.1 Policy Measures and Achievements in Promoting the Employment of the Persons in Urban Areas Who Have Difficulty in Finding Jobs

The employment aid system refers to the special system established by the government, which takes the persons who have difficulty in finding jobs as the main target group, formulates various special support policies, develops public welfare jobs through multiple channels, and provides targeted assistance measures to help them to get re-employed as soon as possible. At present, China has basically established a relatively complete employment aid system. As an institutional arrangement for the government to provide priority support and key assistance to the persons who have difficulty in finding jobs and zero employment families, it has played an important role in promoting and stabilising employment and maintaining the overall stability of the employment situation.

4.1.1 Employment Aid Policy

(1) Encourage the persons who have difficulty in finding jobs to be self-employed and start up their own businesses. The first is the policy of exemption and deduction of taxes and fees. For qualified workers engaged in self-employed business, sales tax, urban maintenance and construction tax, education surcharges and individual income tax shall be reduced or exempted within the prescribed limits, and shall be exempted from the administration business charge. The second is the policy of discount interest loans. For qualified workers who are self-employed, start up their own businesses or engage in partnership business and organised employment, the government shall establish a guarantee fund to provide loan guarantee for the insufficient part of self-raised funds, and banks shall grant micro-secured loans, and the government finance shall provide a certain or full amount of loan interest discount. The third is the policy of social insurance subsidies. For eligible workers who are re-employed by means of flexible employment, a certain proportion of social insurance subsidies shall be given to enhance the employment stability. Fourth, local governments also take various measures to solve the problem of business premises and to facilitate the portability of social insurance. Various policies have been adopted to reduce the production and operation costs if those persons who have difficulty in finding jobs seek self-employment or start up their own businesses, which would not only solve the financing problems, relieve the worries behind, but also enhance their career development potential and sustainability of employment.

(2) Encourage enterprises to absorb the persons who have difficulty in finding jobs. The first is preferential tax policies. If the eligible enterprises recruit hard-to-place people as new employees in new job vacancies, sign labour contracts with them for more than one year, and pay social insurance contribution for them, sales tax, urban maintenance and construction tax, education surcharges and enterprise income tax shall be deducted or exempted in accordance with the actual number of employees the enterprises have recruited within the corresponding period. The second is social insurance subsidy policy. If the eligible enterprises recruit hard-to-put people as new employees in new job vacancies, sign labour contracts with them for more than one year, and pay social insurance contribution for them, social insurance subsidies shall be given within the corresponding time limit. The third is business start-up secured loans policy. For the labour-intensive small enterprises that meet the conditions of the loans, if the number of newly recruited hard-to-place people in the new job vacancies reaches a certain proportion of the enterprise employees and the enterprise signs labour contracts with them for more than one year, the loan granted can be up to 1 million *yuan* according to the number of such newly recruited employees.

(3) Give priority to put the persons who have difficulty in finding jobs at the public welfare jobs funded and developed by the government. The first is to develop more public welfare jobs, especially the service posts and management assistant posts, which are mainly funded and supported by the government or developed by socially raised funds. The posts are developed mainly for resettling these had-to-place people to meet the needs of social public interests. The second is to give priority assistance. Public employment service agencies at all levels should, under the same conditions, give priority to provide the persons who have difficulty in finding jobs with employment services such as job information, job recommendation and vocational guidance, and recruit them or arrange job opportunities for them. The third is to implement relevant supporting policies. According to the number of hard-to-place people in public welfare jobs, social insurance subsidies shall be given within the corresponding period, and appropriate post subsidies shall be provided at the same time.

4.1.2 Implementation of Special Employment Services Measures

(1) Job-seeking registration and vocational guidance. Tailor-made service programmes should be made for the persons with job hunting difficulties and in urgent need of employment. The specific service content should be tailored to their different needs in terms of seeking employment and accessing to re-employment support policies and other policies relating to labour and social security. Targeted services should be provided through the comprehensive use of job recommendation, vocational guidance, employment training, public welfare jobs and other related services.

(2) Job assistance and development. It is necessary to get information of a number of employment posts suitable for the persons with job hunting difficulties, organise them to participate in recruitment activities, or deliver the information to them individually and to their homes, so as to ensure that they understand the job information and get jobs in time. At the same time, the social insurance subsidy and post subsidy policies should be available for them if they are put in public welfare jobs. For those who have been flexibly employed, they shall be organised to make employment registration and participate in social insurance, and they shall be assisted to get social insurance subsidies.

(3) Vocational skills training. According to the needs of the job, combined with the characteristics of the people with employment difficulties, these people should be referred to vocational skills training, be guided in selecting the courses, and be organised to participate in vocational skills training based on the recommendation. Some localities provide not only training subsidies, but also living subsidies, transportation subsidies and other measures to encourage and support these people to actively participate in the training.

(4) Following up the implementation of various service measures. The information on the recommended persons, such as placement in post, recruitment progress and files, social insurance contribution and wage payment should be followed up in time. Regular aid and irregular aid should be combined. With the improvement of employment aid services, other forms of assistance activities should be actively organised.

Relying on grass roots public employment service organisations, Chinese government has combined daily and centralised aid to help the persons who have difficulty in finding jobs through various channels. In 2018, the Chinese government helped 1.81 million people with employment difficulties to find jobs nationwide, 55,000 of whom were from 50,000 zero-employment households, and realised the dynamic clearing of zero-employment households.

4.2 Policies and Measures to Promote the Employment of the Rural Poor and Achievements

It is the most effective and direct way to eliminate poverty if one person gets employed implying that the whole family gets out of poverty. The Chinese government attaches great importance to poverty alleviation through employment. In 2017, the government proposed that efforts should be made in encouraging those able to work to participate in work and employment, and the public should be guided to work hard for lifting themselves out of poverty through production incentives and subsidies as well as work relief programmes. In order to implement the central government's overall plan on poverty alleviation, the Ministry of Human Resources and Social Security formulated a three-year action plan on poverty alleviation from the ministry perspective, made specific arrangements for intensified and precise implementation of policies, and clarified relevant requirements and work measures.

4.2.1 Seven Basic Requirements for Poverty Alleviation through Employment

(1) Develop job positions locally and nearby with multi-channels. Efforts should be made to strengthen the construction of poverty alleviation carriers, such as poverty alleviation workshops and community workshops, explore operational mechanisms in light of local conditions, increase policy support, promote sustainable development, and guide poverty alleviation workshops to absorb more poor people into employment. It is necessary to train the getting-rich leaders through business start-up in poverty-stricken villages, support the development of rural e-commerce, and support poverty-stricken counties in building business start-up parks. The employment potential of agriculture should be tapped by encouraging more business owners to absorb the poor labour force into employment. Combining with local traditional culture, natural ecology and industrial base, work-at-home flexible employment should be encouraged. Overall plans on developing public welfare jobs should be made, guiding poor counties and townships to actively develop employment posts, such as road maintenance, forest protection, grass protection and ecological management, for poverty alleviation.

(2) Deepen labour cooperation. Coordinate the labour cooperation between the eastern developed areas and the western underdeveloped areas. Developed regions are requested to timely adjust the contents of supplementary agreements according to the progress of labour cooperation, improve the cooperation measures and the effectiveness of cooperation, widely collect job information suitable for the poor labour force, build a matching platform for the employers and poor workers, and guide more poor workers to participate in labour service cooperation to realise transfer employment.

(3) Vigorously strengthen employment services. Focusing on the combination of supporting the ambition and wisdom, all-round, accurate and refined employment services should be provided. Vocational guidance should be actively provided to guide the poor workers to establish a correct employment concept, enhance the employment readiness, stimulate the endogenous power of work to become rich, mobilise the employment enthusiasm of the poor labour force, and increase the labour participation rate of the poor labour force. At the same time, combining with the advantages of local typical industries and human resources, a number of labour service brands should be created and be promoted to drive the transfer employment.

(4) Promote poverty alleviation through skills. in order to ensure the accessibility of vocational skill training to the poor workers with training desire, all kinds of vocational colleges, vocational training institutes and enterprises at all levels should be widely mobilised to carry out vocational skill training for the poor labour force. The training subsidy policy should be implemented. The project-based training should be promoted to purchase the employment skill training packages from the training institutes recognised by the government. And the goal should be realised, which can be put as "one person starting up a business after participating in the training and attributing to one household getting out of poverty or even becoming well off".

(5) Do a good job in poverty alleviation through employment in deep poverty-stricken areas. Taking poverty alleviation through employment in deep poverty-stricken areas as top priority, special work programmes on poverty alleviation through employment should be developed to specify objectives and tasks, determine the number and channels of employment promotion for the poor labour force each year, and establish a work responsibility system. It is necessary to coordinate the development and reform, finance and other departments to provide favourable policies for deep poverty-stricken areas in terms of funds allocation and project arrangements so as to help solving practical problems.

(6) Strengthen the work style of poverty alleviation through employment. The gorernment should further implement the policies, improve the operation methods, lower the policy threshold, and enhance the operability, so as to ensure that the qualified poor labour force and employers can enjoy the policy support. In-depth field visits and investigations should be done to give the guidance on how to solve outstanding problems in the routine work.

(7) Create a good social atmosphere. It is necessary to strengthen the publicity on poverty alleviation through employment, vigorously publicise the policies and measures on employment poverty alleviation, good experience and best practices, and outstanding individuals and typical cases of poverty alleviation through employment and entrepreneurship, so as to create a good social atmosphere to support the poor labour force in employment and entrepreneurship, building up the value that it is glorious to become rich through honest work.

4.2.2 Five Measures to Promote Poverty Alleviation through Employment

(1) Strengthen employment services. All regions should make practical employment poverty alleviation plans, have an accurate understanding on poor workers' basic information, strengthen employment services, carry out one-to-one precise assistance, and fully mobilise the poor workers'enthusiasm for employment. Local public employment service agencies should deeply explore the situation of the poor labour force, take into account their poverty characteristics, actively carry out vocational guidance, strengthen job recommendation, promote accurate matching among employment expectations, employment skills and posts, and expand the coverage of poverty-alleviation through employment. Human resources service agencies should play its full role to strengthen the monitoring of supply and demand information in human resources market, and organise activities such as special recruitment, employment and entrepreneurship guidance and skills training.

(2) Support the development of poverty alleviation workshops and other carriers to absorb employment. A number of carriers of poverty alleviation through employment such as poverty alleviation workshops, community factories and satellite factories should be established in poor townships and villages. Cooperating with the poverty alleviation departments, the establishment of poverty alleviation workshops and other carriers should be integrated into the construction planning of poverty alleviation projects, and the construction standards should be constantly improved. Enterprises, farmers' specialised cooperatives, poverty alleviation workshops and other types of employing units are encouraged to absorb the employment of the poor labour force. Those carriers replacing training with work shall be given vocational training subsidies, and the enterprises with such practice shall be given a certain amount of social insurance subsidies according to the regulations. The employment poverty alleviation bases with good employment results shall be given one-time fund subsidies.

(3) Encourage entrepreneurship-driven employment by people returning and going to the countryside. We shall actively promote the construction of entrepreneurship parks in poverty-stricken counties, increase entrepreneurship support policies and service support, guide all kinds of people to start up businesses in poor counties, and promote the employment of poor labour force. A number of entrepreneurial projects should be developed in poverty-stricken areas by undertaking industrial transition, developing rural e-commerce, creative agriculture, rural tourism and other measures. Supporting policies for small and micro enterprises shall be available for those entrepreneurial projects registered with industrial and commercial administration according to the regulations. The supporting policies shall be implemented first for those enterprises absorbing more poor workers. One-time entrepreneurship subsidy shall be given to the poor labour force, migrant workers and other entrepreneurs who return to the countryside to set up small and micro enterprises for the first time or engage in self-employed business and have been in normal operation for more than 6 months. For those entrepreneurship incubation carriers in poor counties with a large number of on-incubation businesses and good incubation effect, the amount of awarding and subsidy for the entrepreneurship incubation base shall be increased.

(4) Deepen labour service cooperation for poverty alleviation. The labour service cooperation between the labour flow-out and flow-in areas should be strengthened to improve the implementation of labour services agreements, strive to expand the scale of labour export and improve the degree of the organised labour services. The governments of the labour flow-out areas should be encouraged and supported to set up labour stations in cities or regions receiving a large number of poor labourers, so as to provide continuous assistance for the migrant workers. The governments of the labour flow-in areas should do a good job in providing matching and connecting services with the labour flow-out areas, focusing on the development and provision of employment posts, and providing three-in-one services, i.e. an integrated service of vocational training, employment services, and labour rights protection for the poor labourers, so as to enhance their employment stability. For enterprises employing poor labourers from other places, policies such as social insurance subsidies, business start-up secured loans and interest discount shall be available with reference to policies applicable to the local people with employment difficulties.

(5) Develop public welfare jobs as a last resort. Considering the actual needs of rural construction, public welfare jobs such as cleaning, public security, road maintenance, water management, supporting the disabled and elderly care should be developed to help poor labourers' employment. The newly created and vacated public welfare jobs in poverty-stricken areas shall be used first of all to place the poor labour force, which can be given a certain period of post subsidies by employment subsidies. The departments of forestry, grassland, transportation and poverty alleviation shall actively coordinate each other to develop all kinds of public welfare jobs to resettle the poor labour force. All localities are encouraged to mobilise more poor labour force to participate in the small-scale infrastructure project and project of rural human settlement environment improvement by means of work relief, award-for-subsidy and labour subsidy.

4.2.3 Effectiveness of Poverty Alleviation through Employment

After years of hard work, poverty alleviation through employment has made positive progress. First, an effective employment poverty alleviation mechanism has been established. Relying on the working mechanism of poverty alleviation, a precise assistance mechanism and a fund guarantee mechanism have been established. Second, the poverty alleviation through employment policy system has been developed. The Ministry of Human Resources and Social Security, the Ministry of Finance, the Poverty Alleviation Office of the State Council and other departments have issued a series of supporting policies to promote the employment and entrepreneurship for the poor labour force. Various localities have also formulated many policies according to the local conditions and developed a policy system covering the vast number of poverty-stricken labour force, employers and employment service agencies. The third is to build up a work pattern of poverty alleviation through employment. All localities, proceeding from the reality, have constantly innovated their ideas and methods of paying equal attention to local employment and migrant work so as to alleviate poverty. Some places have connected major projects with the aid to targeted poor labour force from the target areas. Through these efforts, at the end of 2019, China helped 12.13 million poverty-stricken labourers to be employed, and the poverty-stricken population decreased from 98.99 million in 2012 to 5.51 million, with the poverty incidence rate dropping from 10.2% in 2012 to 0.6%[1] in rural China.

Take precise employment measures to help the poor and send jobs to villagers' homes. (Photo taken by Xinhua News Agency reporter Xiang Wan.)

4.3 Laws and Policies to Promote the Employment of the Disabled and the Achievements

China has 85 million disabled people. Protecting the employment rights and interests of the disabled and helping them to achieve employment and business start-up are

[1] The data are from the National Bureau of Statistics and the Ministry of Human Resources and Social Security.

fundamental for improving their economic conditions and social status, which are also the basic conditions and the main path for them to realise equality, participation and sharing.

4.3.1 Guaranteed by Laws and Regulations

The Chinese government has always attached great importance to the employment of the disabled and has formulated a series of laws and regulations to protect their employment rights and interests. For instance, it is stipulated in the Constitution that the State and society shall help to make arrangements for the work, livelihood and education of the blind, deaf-mutes and other handicapped citizens. *Law of the People's Republic of China on the Protection of Disabled Persons* provides that the State shall guarantee disabled persons' right to work. Employment of disabled persons shall follow the principle of combining collective arrangement with individual arrangement. Preferential policies and measures of support and protection shall be adopted with a view to gradually popularising, stabilising and rationalising employment of disabled persons through multiple channels, at various levels and in a variety of forms. At the same time, the welfare enterprises shall be entitled for corresponding supporting policies in terms of financial support, tax reduction and exemption if they reach the assigned proportion for employment of disabled persons. *Employment Promotion Law* stipulates that people's governments at all levels shall make overall plans for the employment of the disabled and create conditions for their employment. When an employing unit recruits persons, it shall not discriminate against disabled persons. *Regulations on Employment of Disabled Persons* make more specific provisions on the responsibilities of employing units and the governments. Enterprises shall reach the assigned proportion for employment of disabled persons, while the governments at all levels shall ensure the employment of disabled persons, and provide free employment services for them.

4.3.2 Promoted by Policy Measures

(1) Expand employment forms and create jobs suitable for disabled persons. On the one hand, while setting up welfare enterprises and institutions to provide employment for the disabled, employing units are required to arrange employment for the disabled in certain proportion, and the disabled persons are supported to start up their own businesses and seek jobs on their own. On the other hand, community service businesses are actively developed, with priority given to the employment of the disabled. Great efforts have been made to develop public welfare jobs to ensure the employment of the disabled, laid-off and unemployed people with employment difficulties. In rural areas, the disabled persons are organised to engage in planting, breeding, handicraft industry and other production activities by providing production services, technical guidance, agricultural material supply, purchase of agricultural and sideline products, credit and other support for the disabled. At the same time, the State has formulated and implemented a series of poverty alleviation and benefiting agriculture policies, which have also played a positive role in promoting the employment of the disabled.

(2) Improve public employment service system and provide employment services for the disabled. In terms of employment services, public employment service institutions run by the governments at all levels are accessible to the disabled free of charge, providing them with employment services such as vocational guidance and job recommendation. The disabled persons are included in the group with employment difficulties. Standing books for the disabled are set up through public employment service institutions at sub-district, township and residential community level. One-to-one employment assistance is implemented to them, and policies such as social security subsidies and post subsidies are available to them. Disabled persons' federations all over the country have set up employment service institutions, which are responsible for collecting information about disabled job seekers, recommending disabled persons to employing units, organising training for disabled persons, and making unemployment registration for the disabled at the request of human resources and social security departments.

(3) Implement labour protection to improve the employment quality of the disabled. When employing disabled workers, the employing unit shall sign a labour contract or service agreement according to law. The employing units shall provide the disabled workers with working conditions and labour protection suitable for their own conditions, and shall not discriminate against disabled workers in terms of position promotion, professional upgrading, evaluation of professional titles, remuneration, social insurance and social welfare. In case of any disputes between disabled workers and employing units, local legal aid institutions shall provide legal assistance for them according to law, and disabled persons' federations at all levels shall provide support and play their due role as well.

(4) Strengthen inspection on the law enforcement to protect the legitimate employment rights and interests of the disabled. Through labour inspection, labour and social security inspection institutions at all levels should timely discover and correct the employers' violation of the laws and regulations and their infringement on the disabled persons' legitimate rights and interests, focusing on investigating and punishing such behaviours as not signing labour contracts with the disabled, unreasonable deduction or arrears of wages, and failing to pay social insurance contributions for the disabled.

(5) Improve social security system to raise the social security benefits of disabled persons. In recent years, social insurance policies for disabled persons have been continuously improved, and the coverage of social insurance has been extended. Urban employees with disabilities have been encouraged to participate in basic old-age insurance, unemployment insurance, work injury insurance and maternity insurance in accordance with regulations. The urban poor self-employed persons with disabilities are encouraged to participate in social insurance, and the subsidising policy has been actively implemented if they participate in basic old-age insurance. Since 2009, the new rural social pension insurance has been implemented throughout the country, and the rural disabled persons have been actively helped to participate in the system.

4.3.3 Achievements

Since 2011, China has supported nearly 13 million disabled persons to develop production, 6.76 million of whom have been lifted out of poverty. As of 2018, the number of workers with disability certificates reached 9.484 million. In 2018, 494,000 disabled persons were trained under the real-name registration system in urban and rural areas, and 367,000 people with disability certificates in urban and rural areas gained new jobs, including 118,000 in urban areas and 249,000 in rural areas. At the same time, 2,811 employment service institutions for the disabled persons have been set up throughout the country, with 34,000 employees. 5,490 poverty alleviation bases for the disabled persons have been set up, and 881,000 disabled persons have been placed in employment, which have facilitated the income increase of 1.769 million families with disabled persons.

Chapter 9
Unemployment Insurance and Unemployment Prevention

China's current unemployment insurance system was established under the background of carrying out labour system reform in 1986. Its initial purpose was to solve the basic living problems of enterprise employees in case of unemployment and provide help for them to realise re-employment. Since then, the unemployment insurance system has been constantly improved, and has actively exercised its three-in-one functions, i.e. ensuring basic livelihood of the unemployed, preventing unemployment and promoting employment. Great efforts have been made in focusing the formulation and implementation of preferential policies for enterprises and the people, such as expanding unemployment insurance coverage, increasing unemployment benefits, reducing contribution rate, assisting enterprises for job retention, and upgrading skills, which have achieved remarkable results.

1. Unemployment Statistics and Dynamic Monitoring of Unemployment

1.1 Unemployment Statistics

Unemployment statistics are part of employment statistics, which are generally divided into four stages: statistical design, survey registration, data collection and analysis. Unemployment statistical indicators mainly include the number of unemployed people and unemployment rate.

1.1.1 The Unemployed Persons

The data of the unemployed are obtained through registration and survey. The registered unemployed persons refer to those who are within working age, having the ability to work but with no job, and get registered at the local public employment service institution to seek employment. The surveyed unemployed persons refer to those who are over 16 years old (without upper age limit), having the ability to work and not yet getting engaged in work with an income during the survey period, but they are looking for jobs in some way and will probably get employed.

1.1.2 Registered Urban Unemployment Rate

It refers to the proportion of the registered urban unemployed persons in the total number of urban employees plus the registered urban unemployed persons at the end of

Workers can register their unemployment in the public employment service institutions in their permanent residence. (Photo taken by Xinhua News Agency reporter Jianghua He.)

the reporting period. Among them, the number of registered urban unemployed persons comes from the public employment service institutions.

Since the establishment of the unemployment registration system in early 1980s, China has been using the registered urban unemployment rate as an important indicator for macroeconomic regulation and control, which does provide an important basis for the State to formulate policies and make decisions. Honestly, since not all the unemployed persons are registered in the public employment service institutions, and lots of rural workers entering urban areas are not included as the registered urban unemployed persons, the registered urban unemployment rate is not sensitive enough to reflect the overall unemployment situation in some regions or the country.

1.1.3 Surveyed Urban Unemployment Rate

It covers all the economically active population (including rural workers who have lived and worked in cities and towns for more than six months). It is the proportion of the eligible unemployed persons (i.e. the surveyed urban unemployed persons) in the total number of employed persons in cities and towns and the surveyed urban unemployed persons. The survey on unemployment rate is conducted by the National Bureau of Statistics.

In 2016, the National Bureau of Statistics officially released the monthly surveyed unemployment rate. Thanks to scientific sampling and ensured sample size, the statistical data for surveyed unemployment rate can reflect the employment and unemployment situations of the regions and the country more sensitively than the registered unemployment rate, and can also reflect the employment and unemployment status of rural workers who have lived in cities and towns for more than six months.

1.2 Dynamic Monitoring of Unemployment

1.2.1 Concept and Evolution

In June 2008, the Ministry of Human Resources and Social Security established the unemployment dynamic monitoring system. Through monitoring the changing of employment population affected by bankruptcy, closure, relocation, serious difficulties in production and operation, production transition, and major technological innovation or adjustment of business mode in some urban enterprises, the increase and decrease of enterprise jobs during the economic fluctuation period are known for the relevant government organisations, which provide the basis for taking measures to prevent and control unemployment, and for establishing an early warning system for unemployment.

The monitoring results are made into three-level (i.e. national, provincial and city) unemployment dynamic monitoring reports on regular basis. National unemployment dynamic monitoring report is made by the Ministry of Human Resources and Social Security. The provincial report is done by the provincial human resources and social security department, on the basis of the dynamic monitoring data in the region, the registered unemployment rate of cities and towns under the province, the record of enterprise labour and employment, and the supply-demand ratio of human resources market in the province, which will be reported to the provincial government and submitted to the Ministry of Human Resources and Social Security. The city report on unemployment is made in a similar way as the provincial one, with focus on the analysis of the reasons for the increase or decrease of employees. The city report will be delivered to the city government, and submitted to the provincial human resources and social security department.

1.2.2 The Purpose and Significance of Establishing Unemployment Dynamic Monitoring and Reporting System

(1) It is an effective way to comprehensively understand the situation of employment and unemployment. The unemployment dynamic monitoring and reporting system directly investigates and collects the changing information on enterprise positions, analyses the causes of job losses in some key industries and enterprises. As an effective means to comprehensively understand the unemployment situation, the unemployment dynamic monitoring and reporting system helps to reflect the employment and unemployment situation more accurately and timely.

(2) It helps to provide important information to support policy making. On the basis of comprehensively understanding the employment and unemployment situation of some key enterprises, the unemployment dynamic monitoring and reporting system helps to study and judge the overall local employment situation, provides support for the formulation of stabilising employment policies, and improves the pertinence and effectiveness of the policies. The effect of the implementation of employment policies and measures will also be confirmed by relevant monitoring data.

(3) It helps to lay the foundation for developing unemployment early warning system. The unemployment dynamic monitoring and reporting system has further improved the employment and unemployment information survey system. By collecting and analysing the data needed for unemployment early warning, related departments can timely grasp the information of job losses in some key industries and enterprises in the period of economic fluctuation under the complex and changeable economic situation, and enhance the predictability, pertinence and effectiveness of unemployment control policies. It is useful for judging and understanding the unemployment situation timely and accurately, and providing the basis for taking more effective measures in time, preventing and resolving the large-scale unemployment risk.

1.3 Effectiveness of Unemployment Dynamic Monitoring and Reporting System

In November 2009, the Ministry of Human Resources and Social Security decided to establish the unemployment dynamic monitoring system in the whole country on the basis of the effectiveness of the pilot practice of unemployment dynamic monitoring and reporting system carried out in some cities of six provinces. At the end of 2019, 52,000 enterprises were included in the monitoring system.

2. Unemployment Insurance System

2.1 Establishment and Development of Unemployment Insurance System

2.1.1 Unemployment Relief in the Early Days of the People's Republic of China

On the eve of the founding of the People's Republic of China in 1949, the unemployment situation in China was very serious. There were 4.72 million unemployed persons in urban areas, and the unemployment rate was as high as 23.6%. After the founding of the People's Republic of China, the Chinese government has adopted a series of policies and measures to solve the problem of urban unemployment. One of the important measures is to establish the unemployment relief system to ensure the basic livelihood of the unemployed. This is the earliest embryonic form of the unemployment insurance system in China.

2.1.2 Basic Principles for Establishing Unemployment Insurance System in Line with China's National Conditions

(1) Wide coverage. Social security system aims at protecting the basic rights and interests of every worker. The unemployment insurance system shall cover all kinds of employing units and their employees in urban areas.

(2) Moderate benefit. The benefit for guaranteeing the basic livelihood of the unemployed should be adapted to the economic and social development level, instead of being too low or too high. Unemployment benefits should be adjusted timely, according to the improvement of people's living standards at different stages of economic and social development to ensure the basic livelihood of the unemployed.

(3) Paying equal attention to ensuring the basic livelihood, preventing unemployment and promoting employment. Different from social relief, unemployment insurance shall not only guarantee the basic livelihood of the unemployed, but also provide employment services for the unemployed and give financial subsidies to help the unemployed to be re-employed. At the same time, it can stabilise the workforce and prevent large-scale unemployment by refunding contributions to the insured enterprises for their job retention action (i.e. no or less layoffs), and offering skill upgrading subsidies to the insured employees who have obtained the corresponding vocational qualification certificates or vocational skill level certificates.

(4) Contributions shared by employing units, workers and the state. The unemployment insurance contributions shall be jointly paid by the employing unit and the individual worker, and be subsidised by public finance. This contribution co-sharing mechanism is conducive to enhance workers' awareness to participate in social insurance, and it can also disperse the fund-raising pressure and increase the fund sources, so as to ensure the normal use of unemployment insurance fund.

(5) Equality between rights and obligations. Only employers and employees participate in unemployment insurance according to law and fulfil the obligation of paying contributions can the employees be entitled for the unemployment benefits.

2.1.3 Establishment, Development and Significance of the Current Unemployment Insurance System in China

China's current unemployment insurance system was established in 1986, and its establishment can be roughly divided into three stages.

The first stage is 1986-1993. In July 1986, the State Council issued *Interim Provisions on Awaiting Job Assignment Insurance for Workers of State-owned Enterprises* (hereinafter referred to as *Interim Provisions*), which marked the formal establishment of the current unemployment insurance system in China, established the basic framework of the system, and initially played its role.

The second stage is 1993-1999. In April 1993, the State Council issued *Provisions on Awaiting Job Assignment Insurance for Workers of State-owned Enterprises*, which indicated that *Interim Provisions* changed into the formal one on the basis of adjusting *Interim Provisions* issued in 1986.

The third stage is 1999 to present. In January 1999, the State Council issued *Regulations on Unemployment Insurance* and *Provisional Regulations on the Collection and Payment of Social Insurance Premiums*, marking that the reform of Chinese unemployment insurance system has entered a new stage, and the unemployment insurance system has been further improved. In July 2011, *Social Insurance Law* went into effect, which further clarified the coverage of unemployment insurance, the conditions and period for benefit claim, benefit level and portability of participation record, and identified the status of unemployment insurance system from the legal perspective.

The establishment and gradual improvement of the unemployment insurance system imply an important reform of China's employment system. As an important part of the market-oriented employment mechanism, the unemployment insurance system has played a positive role in the reform of the employment system. At the same time, the establishment of this system has filled the gap of Chinese social security system. It has created favourable conditions for the transition of labour system from planned economy to market economy, opened a good beginning for the development of social security system independent from enterprises, and made contributions to promoting development and stability.

2.2 Raising, Using and Managing Unemployment Insurance Fund

2.2.1 Raising Unemployment Insurance Fund

Unemployment insurance fund is raised by collecting unemployment insurance contribution. The fund is shared by the insured units, employees and the State.

(1) Composition of fund income. The collection of unemployment insurance fund follows the principles of determining revenue by expenditure, moderate and fairness. According to *Regulations on Unemployment Insurance*, unemployment insurance fund includes unemployment insurance contribution interest of unemployment insurance fund, financial subsidy and other funds that shall be included in unemployment insurance fund according to law.

(2) Contribution of unemployment insurance. The contributors of unemployment insurance include urban enterprises and institutions and their employees, who shall pay unemployment insurance contributions according to the regulation, and individual payment shall be withheld by the employing unit. Urban enterprises, institutions and other insured units take the total payroll of their employees as the premium payment base, the employees take their own wages as the premium payment base. The insured units and individuals pay 2% and 1% of their premium payment base respectively. The insured units must declare the amount of unemployment insurance contribution that shall be paid to the unemployment insurance agency on monthly basis, and pay within the prescribed time limit after verification. The unemployment insurance contribution to be paid by the insured individual shall be withheld and paid by their employing units. The unemployment insurance contribution must be paid in currency, not in kind. The collecting institutions shall be prescribed by the governments of provincial/autonomous regions/municipal government. Since 2015, in order to relieve the burden of enterprises and promote employment stability, related departments have implemented a series of unemployment insurancecontribution reduction policies (Table 9.1).

(3) Financial subsidies to unemployment insurance funds. In order to cope with the possible payment difficulties, it is stipulated to establish unemployment insurance adjustment fund at provincial level. If the city fund is insufficient, it shall be supplemented by the provincial adjustment fund. If it still cannot meet the payment needs, the local finance shall give subsidies, and if necessary, the unemployment insurance contribution rate can be adjusted according to the specified conditions and procedures. Among them, the financial subsidy to unemployment insurance fund is the government's direct support to unemployment insurance under specific circumstances, including regular subsidies and temporary subsidies, thus ensuring the normal and stable operation of the unemployment insurance system in the institutional arrangements.

Table 9.1 Unemployment Insurance Contribution Reduction Policies Since 2015

Release time	Document name	Contents
February 2015	*Notice of the Ministry of Human Resources and Social Security and the Ministry of Finance on the Adjustment of Unemployment Insurance Contribution Rate* (No.24, 2015, issued by the Ministry of Human Resources and Social Security)	It is clearly specified that the unemployment insurance contribution rate shall be lowered by 1 percentage point as a whole. The unemployment insurance contribution rate shall be temporarily reduced from 3% to 2%, and the specific proportion of payment by units and individuals shall be determined by the people's governments of all provinces, autonomous regions, and municipalities.
April 2016	*Notice of the Ministry of Human Resources and Social Security and the Ministry of Finance on Periodic Reduction of Social Insurance Contribution Rate* (No. 36, 2016, issued by the Ministry of Human Resources and Social Security)	The total unemployment insurance contribution rate shall be reduced to 1%-1.5% (of which the individual contribution rate shall not exceed 0.5%).
February 2017	*Notice of the Ministry of Human Resources and Social Security and the Ministry of Finance on Issues Related to Periodic Reduction of Unemployment Insurance Contribution Rate* (No. 14, 2017, issued by the Ministry of Human Resources and Social Security)	Provinces, autonomous regions and municipalities with the total unemployment insurance contribution rate of 1.5% can reduce to 1% in total.

Continued

Release time	Document name	Contents
April 2018	*Notice of the Ministry of Human Resources and Social Security and the Ministry of Finance on the Continuation of the Phased Reduction of Social Insurance Contribution Rates* (No. 25, 2018, issued by the Ministry of Human Resources and Social Security)	Provinces, autonomous regions and municipalities that implement the unemployment insurance contribution rate of 1% shall extend the period of periodic reduction of the rate until 30 April, 2019.
April 2019	*Notice of the General Office of the State Council on Printing and Distributing the Comprehensive Scheme for Reducing Social Insurance Rate* (No. 13, 2019, issued by the General Office of the State Council)	Provinces that collect 1% of the total unemployment insurance contribution rate shall extend the period of periodic reduction of unemployment insurance contribution rate to 30 April, 2020.
December 2019	*Opinions of the State Council on Further Improving Employment Stability* (No. 28, 2019, issued by the State Council)	The implementation period of the policy of periodic reduction of unemployment insurance contribution rate shall be extended to 30 April, 2021.

2.2.2 Use of Unemployment Insurance Fund

The expenditure of unemployment insurance fund includes basic livelihood expenditure, re-employment promotion expenditure and other expenses. The use of unemployment insurance fund should follow the regulations in accordance with the expenditure items which should not be randomly increased or decreased, and the expenditure standard should not be changed. The expenditure of unemployment insurance fund is also not allowed to be diverted to any other purpose.

(1) Basic livelihood expenditure. It is directly used to guarantee the basic livelihood of the unemployed and other relevant persons, including expenditure on jobless claims, expenditure on medical subsidies (adjusted as basic medical insurance contribution after the implementation of *Social Insurance Law* in 2011), expenditure on funeral benefits, expenditure on lump-sum living allowances for rural contract-based workers and expenditure on basic living allowances for laid-off workers from SOEs (implemented in 1998, but cancelled in 2006).

(2) Re-employment promotion expenditure. This expenditure is for the purpose of helping the unemployed to be re-employed as soon as possible. It is covered by the unemployment insurance fund, including subsidies for both vocational training and job recommendation services for the unemployed. These two subsidies can be paid to the institutions concerned or to the unemployed individuals directly who have participated in training or received job placement services.

With the further improvement of the unemployment insurance system in promoting employment and preventing unemployment, the expenditure items and scope for promoting employment are further expanded. Apart from paying the subsidies for vocational training and job recommendation for the unemployed, the unemployment insurance fund aims at stabilising employment, and it can also be used for providing social insurance subsidy for employees of insured enterprises, post subsidy and subsidy for the interest of the micro-secured loans for entrepreneurs.

(3) Other expenses. The items of other expenses refer to the expenditures related to unemployment insurance as prescribed or approved by the State Council in addition to the above-mentioned expenditure items.

2.2.3 Management of Unemployment Insurance Fund

(1) Budget and settlement management of unemployment insurance fund. The unemployment insurance fund budget is an annual unemployment insurance fund revenue and expenditure plan which is prepared according to employment, unemployment situation and fund demand, and submitted to the government for approval according to the regulations. It mainly includes budget preparation, approval, implementation and adjustment. The settlement of unemployment insurance fund is a financial report which is compiled according to the prescribed procedures and submitted to the government for approval, summarising and reflecting the actual operation of the fund in the current year, and mainly including balance sheet, fund income and expenditure statement, relevant attached tables and financial statement, etc. The budget and settlement management of unemployment insurance fund is an important means of fund management, which is conducive to strengthening the prediction and supervision of fund income and expenditure, strengthening budget restraint, realising fund revenue and expenditure balance and ensuring fund safety.

(2) Financial management of unemployment insurance fund. The financial management of unemployment insurance fund is a supervision on the overall operation of the fund. Its task is to raise and use unemployment insurance fund according to law. The main work is to establish and improve the financial system of the fund, and do a good job in the planning, control, accounting, analysis and assessment of the fund, which includes the management of fund income and expenditure, fund investment management, fund assets and liabilities management, and financial statement management.

(3) Accounting of unemployment insurance fund. The accounting of unemployment insurance fund is a sequential reflection and supervision on the income, expenditure and management of the fund. In order to strengthen the supervision of unemployment insurance business activities, accurately and comprehensively reflect and supervise the collection, expenditure, balance and investment of the unemployment insurance fund, and ensure the safety of the fund, the unemployment insurance fund shall keep separate accounts and keep accountability independently. The accounting of unemployment insurance fund shall be standardised according to the requirements of relevant systems. The characteristics of unemployment insurance fund accounting are as follows. First, it adopts cash basis accounting system. Second, the accounting elements include assets, liabilities, fund balance, income and expenditure, etc. In order to effectively carry out the accounting, apart from strengthening the organisation and management of the accounting work, unemployment insurance agencies should also strengthen accounting supervision and restraint, and establish internal audit system and accounting files.

2.3 Unemployment Benefits

2.3.1 Composition of Unemployment Benefits

Unemployment benefits refer to various kinds of assistance provided by unemployment insurance fund to the workers participating in unemployment insurance in cash as the basic form, in case of unemployment and thus losing sources of income temporarily. It plays an important role in guaranteeing the basic life of the unemployed and promoting their re-employment as soon as possible.

Benefits related to unemployment insurance include: unemployment benefit for basic life; medicare subsidy during the benefit entitlement period (adjusted as basic medical insurance contributions paid by the unemployment insurance fund after the implementation of *Social Insurance Law* in 2011); funeral subsidy and bereavement allowance for the eligible dependents in case that the insured unemployed persons die during the unemployment benefit claims period; and subsidies for vocational training and job recommendation during the unemployment claims period.

2.3.2 Conditions for Unemployment Benefits

The applicants can apply for unemployment benefits if they meet the following conditions at the same time. First, participating in unemployment insurance in accordance with the provisions, both the employing unit and the individual applicants have fulfilled their obligation to pay contributions for at least one year. Second, the applicants lost jobs not because of their own will. Third, the applicants have made unemployment registration and are seeking jobs. During the period of receiving unemployment benefits, the unemployed shall enjoy other benefits related to unemployment insurance at the same time according to regulations.

2.3.3 Standard of Unemployment Benefits

Unemployment benefits shall be no less than the minimum living allowances of urban residents, and the specific standard of unemployment benefits shall be determined by the people's government of a province, autonomous region or municipality.

(1) Become members of the basic medical insurance for employees and recieve basic medical insurance benefits. In order to improve the medical insurance benefits for the unemployed, *Social Insurance Law* stipulates that the unemployed participate in the basic medical insurance for employees. In 2011, a specific policy was formulated by the Ministry of Human Resources and Social Security for the unemployed to participate in the basic medical insurance for employees, stipulating that the unemployed should participate in the basic medical insurance for employees, and the expenses needed should be paid from the unemployment insurance fund, and the unemployed persons are not liable for basic medical insurance contributions. The unemployed persons receiving unemployment benefits are entitled to corresponding hospitalisation and outpatient medical insurance benefits from the month when they participate in the basic medical insurance for employees, and the length of entitlement period shall be consistent with the unemployment benefit period. The contribution years of the unemployed persons participating in basic medical insurance for employees shall be calculated cumulatively with that before their unemployment.

(2) Funeral subsidy, bereavement allowance and the payment standards. If the unemployed persons die during the period of receiving unemployment benefits, funeral subsidy and bereavement allowance shall be paid to their family members in lump sum according to the local regulations on in-service employees.

(3) Vocational training subsidies, job recommendation subsidies and the payment standards. During the period of receiving unemployment benefits, in order to help the unemployed persons to be re-employed, the unemployment insurance fund pays subsidies for their vocational training and job recommendation. Specific measures and standards shall be formulated by the people's government of a province, autonomous region or municipality.

(4) The lump-sum living allowance for contracted rural workers. If the contract-based rural migrant workers employed by the employing unit have worked continuously for one year, after rescission or termination of their labour contract, a lump-sum living allowance will be paid to them according to their working hours. Specific methods and standards for subsidies shall be formulated by the people's government of a province, autonomous region or municipality.

2.3.4 Unemployment Benefit Entitlement Period

Social Insurance Law and *Unemployment Insurance Regulations* stipulate that the unemployment benefit entitlement period is divided into three grades according to the accumulated contribution years of both the employer and the unemployed person before unemployment. First, those who have paid contributions for more than 1 year but less than 5 years, can get no more than 12 months' unemployment benefits. Second, those who have paid contributions for more than 5 years but less than 10 years, can get no more than 18 months' benefits. Third, those who have paid contributions for more than 10 years, can get no more than 24 months' benefits.

2.3.5 Termination of Unemployment Benefits

Any of the following circumstances occurs during the benefits receiving period, both unemployment benefits and other benefits related to unemployment insurance shall be suspended: ① re-employment; ② enrolment of military service; ③ emigration to foreign countries; ④ receiving basic old-age insurance benefits; and ⑤ refusal of the appropriate job arrangement or training programmes recommended by the department or institution designated by the local government without justifiable reasons.

At the end of 2018, the number of people covered by unemployment insurance was 196.435 million with 2.231 million beneficiaries, and the average monthly unemployment benefits reached 1,266 *yuan*. The annual income of unemployment insurance fund was 117.11 billion *yuan*, and the fund expenditure was 91.53 billion *yuan* (Table 9.2).

Table 9.2 Development of Unemployment Insurance (2014-2018)

Year	Number of insured persons at the end of the year (unit: 10 thousand)	Number of benefit receivers at the end of the year (unit: 10 thousand)	Fund income of the year (unit: 100 million *yuan*)	Fund expenditure of the year (unit: 100 million *yuan*)	Accumulated fund balance (unit: 100 million *yuan*)
2014	17,042.6	207.2	1,379.8	614.7	4,451.5
2015	17,326.0	226.8	1,367.8	736.4	5,083.0
2016	18,088.8	230.4	1,228.9	976.1	5,333.3
2017	18,784.2	220.2	1,112.6	893.8	5,552.4
2018	19,643.5	223.1	1,171.1	915.3	5,817.0

Source: the National Bureau of Statistics.

3. Unemployment Prevention

The main measures of unemployment prevention are to control unemployment and implement job retention programmes to assist the enterprises.

3.1 Initiation of Unemployment Control and Work Focus

3.1.1 Unemployment Control

Unemployment control means to control the growth of unemployed persons by legal, economic and necessary administrative means, and carry out employment services to promote their re-employment through various policies and measures formulated by the State to promote their re-employment as soon as possible.

The core goal of unemployment control is to control the rise of unemployment rate. Specific objectives also include: ① the number of unemployed persons should not exceed a certain proportion of the economically active population; ② the emergence time and area of the unemployed persons should not be too concentrated; and ③ the individual's unemployment period should not be too long. At the same time, on the basis of ensuring their basic life, the unemployed persons who are temporarily unable to get employment shall be organised into various employment preparation activities, so as to alleviate the risks brought about by the increase of unemployment and create favourable social environment for the sustained and healthy development of economy and society.

3.1.2 Main Policy Measures of Unemployment Control

(1) The quantity of employed persons to be unemployed should be regulated and controlled from the source. The governments should fully play their role in controlling the quantity of employed persons to be unemployed at the socially acceptable level in the course of adjusting economic structure, in particular, in regulating the lay-off behaviour of enterprises and doing a good job in the allocation of employees from closed and bankrupt enterprises.

(2) Do a good job in helping the unemployed persons and strive to reduce the negative impact of the increase in unemployment. Employment services should be strengthened and improved to provide assistance to the unemployed persons and families, in particular, making special emphasis on the persons with special difficulties in finding jobs. Supportive policies such as social insurance and post subsidies should be implemented to help the long-term unemployed persons to take up public welfare jobs for re-employment. The unemployed persons should be encouraged and guided to find jobs in a variety of flexible forms, including part-time, temporary, seasonal and flexible work. The social security system should be improved and efforts should be made to reduce the negative impact of increased unemployment.

(3) Give full play to the role of unemployment insurance in promoting the re-employment of the unemployed. Unemployment benefits should be given to eligible unemployed persons in full amount and on time, and the unemployment insurance fund should be increased in its input for promoting the re-employment of the unemployed.

3.2 Implementation and Effect of Job Retention Programmes

3.2.1 Initiation and Development of Job Retention Programmes

Supporting enterprises to stabilise their jobs refers to encouraging enterprises not to lay off workers or lay off fewer workers and ensure stable employment at enterprises during a specific period through expanding the use of unemployment insurance funds and using unemployment insurance funds to pay social insurance contribution subsidies and job retention subsidies to enterprises in difficulty. Stabilising employment and controlling unemployment at the source is an important means to keep the employment situation stable as well as an important measure to protect the legitimate rights and interests of workers.

(1) Supporting enterprises to stabilise job positions so as to prevent unemployment is a new measure to cope with the international financial crisis. At the end of 2008, the impact of the international financial crisis on Chinese enterprises was serious, so ensuring stable employment for enterprises became increasingly urgent. In order to stabilise employment, the "five deferring, four reducing and three subsidies" policy was adopted to stabilise both jobs and workers at enterprise. In addition, the employment of flexible workers was stabilised through social insurance subsidies. Apart from the above policy, enterprises were also encouraged to assume social responsibilities to stabilise labour relations and to make efforts not to reduce or lay off employees in special periods. The measures of delaying the collection of social insurance contributions and using unemployment insurance funds to help enterprises to reduce their burdens and stabilise their jobs not only stabilised the employment of enterprise employees, but also led other economic policies to strengthen the protection and support for enterprises. It greatly enhanced the confidence of enterprises in coping with the financial crisis, which not only enabled a number of enterprises to tide over the most difficult days, but also saved a number of jobs, and achieved the effect of unemployment prevention. Meanwhile, relavant departments obtained good experience in dealing with emergency events and large-scale unemployment problems, and laid a good foundation for establishing the long-term unemployment contingency plan. To some sense, using unemployment insurance funds to stabilise jobs is a kind of innovation of China's more proactive employment policy.

Give full play to the role of unemploy-ment insurance in stabilising and promoting employment, and give priority to enterprises with operation difficulties. (Photo taken by Xinhua News Agency reporter Shirao Yang.)

(2) Supporting enterprises and stabilising jobs to prevent unemployment played an active role again in the process of resolving overcapacity. In order to resolve the potential risks of large-scale unemployment and collective labour disputes in key areas with excess capacity in steel and coal industries, properly resettling employees and promoting re-employment, in November 2014, the State took measures to support corporate merger and re-organisation, resolve excess capacity as well as eliminate backward production capacity, and do a good job in stabilising the workforce. Unemployment insurance funds provided subsidies for stabilising jobs, which were not more than 50% of the total amount of unemployment insurance contributions actually paid by the enterprise and its employees in the previous year. In April 2015, the State Council issued *Opinions on Further Improving the Employment and Entrepreneurship Work under the New Situation*, requiring that the coverage of the policy of using the unemployment insurance funds to support enterprise job stability should be expanded from three types of enterprises stated above to all qualified enterprises.

(3) Supporting enterprises and stabilising jobs to prevent unemployment took continuous effects in stabilising employment. In April 2017, according to the policy requirements of the State Council to lower the threshold of subsidy for stabilising jobs and increase the subsidies for stabilising jobs in the iron, steel, coal, coal-powered industry with no or less layoffs, the Ministry of Human Resources and Social Security decided to implement the so-called escort operation, i.e. job retention plan, by using unemployment insurance funds to support enterprises for stabilising jobs across the whole country from

2018 to 2020. It did push the comprehensive and standardised implementation of the unemployment insurance policy to support enterprises to stabilise their jobs, and realise the full coverage of policies in all regions with pooled unemployment insurance funds as well as the full coverage of enterprises that met the application conditions, so as to escort enterprises to extricate themselves from difficulties, reduce unemployment and stabilise employment.

Several Opinions on Promoting Employment at Present and in the Future (No. 39, 2018, the State Council) issued in 2018 specified that 50% of the unemployment insurance contributions actually paid in the previous year should be refunded to the insured enterprises that do not lay off or lay off less workers. Meanwhile, it was specified that in 2019, the insured enterprises with temporary production and operation difficulties but promising to return to normal were entitled for refunding 6-month unemployment benefits or 3-month social insurance contributions. In March 2019, the Ministry of Human Resources and Social Security, together with the Ministry of Finance, the National Development and Reform Commission, and the Ministry of Industry and Information Technology, issued *Notice on Unemployment Insurance Supporting Enterprises to Stabilise Employment Posts* (No. 23, 2019, the Ministry of Human Resources and Social Security), which put forward detailed requirements for the implementation of stabilising employment policies such as unemployment insurance contribution refund.

3.2.2 Achievements of the Policy by Supporting Enterprises to Stabilise Jobs

Practice has proved that the policy of using unemployment insurance funds to support enterprises to stabilise jobs has played an indispensable role in helping enterprises in trouble to tide over the difficult days, stabilising employment and keeping a basically stable employment situation. From 2015 to 2019, a total of 131.1 billion *yuan* was refunded to nearly 2.83 million enterprises for stabilising jobs, benefiting 250 million workers and having achieved very positive results.

3.2.3 New Measures of Unemployment Insurance

In order to give full play to the role of the unemployment insurance system, the Chinese government has formulated some new policies and measures based on the implementation of the above policies and measures.

(1) Use unemployment insurance funds to support skills upgrading of insured employees. Skills upgrading subsidy policy is the concrete indication of the function of unemployment insurance system to prevent unemployment and promote employment. The purpose is to encourage the insured workers to improve their vocational skills and employment competitiveness, reduce unemployment risk, enhance employment stability, and reduce unemployment from the source. In 2017, the State decided to disburse subsidies for employees' skills upgrading of insured enterprises from the unemployment insurance fund, clarifying the application conditions, audit procedures and subsidy standards. In 2018, the government further launched the so-called "ready-for-flight action" on vocational skills upgrading nationwide. Namely, it is to encourage all localities to actively, comprehensively and standardisedly implement the policy of using unemployment insurance funds for skills upgrading subsidy, so that all the qualified employees of the insured enterprises can enjoy the subsidy for skill upgrading. To further exert the policy effect, in 2019, with the approval of the State Council, from 1 January 2019 to 31 December 2020, the application conditions for subsidies could be relaxed from enterprise employees participating in unemployment insurance for 3 years or more to those for 1 year or more. By the end of 2019, the government have provided 3.26 billion *yuan* in subsidies, benefiting nearly 2 million insured employees.

(2) Reduce the unemployment insurance contribution rate to mitigate the burden on enterprises. In order to implement the decision and arrangement of reducing tax and fees made by the central government, since 2015, the central government has reduced unemployment insurance contributions in three consecutive phases and extended the deadline for implementing the rate reduction policy for three times. The overall rate has been reduced from 3% to 1%, and the policy implementation period is extended to 2021. Such policy has reduced the burden of enterprises by nearly 400 billion *yuan*, effectively reducing the cost of enterprises, and making positive contributions to the development of the real economy and supply-side structural reform.

(3) Provide the unemployed with temporary price subsidies to ensure their basic livelihood. In 2016, the State stipulated that temporary price subsidies should be given to unemployment benefit recipients by using unemployment insurance funds. A linkage mechanism between unemployment benefits and price increases has been established to give temporary price subsidies by using unemployment insurance funds. It has played a positive role in mitigating the impact of price increases and ensuring the basic livelihood of the unemployed.

(4) Support poverty alleviation and increase support for the deeply poverty-

stricken areas. In order to implement the national plan in winning the battle against poverty, in June 2018, the Ministry of Human Resources and Social Security and the Ministry of Finance jointly made a policy of using unemployment insurance fund to support poverty alleviation, which requests to give full play of unemployment insurance to support the targeted and precise poverty alleviation. Three adopted measures are as follows: first, to raise the unemployment benefits in deeply poverty-stricken areas to 90% of the minimum wage. Second, for the enterprises participating in unemployment insurance in deeply poverty-stricken areas, the job retention subsidy can be raised to 60% of the total amount of unemployment insurance contributions actually paid by the enterprises and their employees in the previous year. Thirdly, the conditions for applying for skills upgrading subsidies should be relaxed from three years of accumulated contributions to one year, so as to encourage the employees in these areas to improve their vocational skills, enhance the endogenous driving force for poverty alleviation, and achieve employment and income stability. In addition, the public institutions that employ the registered poverty-stricken persons and sign labour contracts with them are entitled to the job retention refund and skills upgrading subsides, so as to stimulate the enthusiasm of all employers in deeply poverty-stricken areas to employ poverty-stricken labourers.

(5) Improve the unemployment insurance system for the elderly insured workers. In December 2019, in view of the fact that it was difficult for the elderly insured workers to find new jobs in case of unemployment, the State Council issued *Opinions on Further Doing a Good Job on Stabilising Employment*. It is clearly stated that those, who have not been employed when the unemployment benefit entitlement period expires and have less than 1 year to reach the statutory retirement age, can continue to receive unemployment benefits until the statutory retirement age. For the elderly insured workers who are unemployed, a seamless connection between unemployment benefits and pension benefits is available, which is an innovation of the institutional guarantee mechanism for the people with employment difficulties, and it fills in a blank of social security policy coverage.

Chapter 10
The Goal of Employment Development Planning: Fuller and Higher Quality Employment

1. The Goal of China's Employment Development Plan[1]

The Chinese government has always attached great importance to employment. The significance of employment has been stated that employment is of greatest importance to people's well-being. It is the basis for people's livelihood, the source of wealth and the foundation of stability, which has been considered as an important governing philosophy. Accordingly, employment has been put in a prominent position in economic and social development, and the Chinese government has formulated development plans and work objectives to promote employment and reduce unemployment.

1.1 Arrangement of Employment in the National Economic and Social Development Plan

The national economic and social development plan is the general outline for the economic and social development of the country, drawn up by the Chinese government on a five-year cycle in accordance with the conditions of different periods. It is an important document that provides strategic guidance for the nation's social and economic development, people's livelihood and cultural development. It is also an important basis

[1] The plans listed in this section are mainly employment-related development plans implemented under the market economy system in the 21st century.

for the government to fulfil its responsibilities in economic regulation, market supervision, social management and public service.

1.1.1 Put Employment Expansion at the Forefront of Economic and Social Development

With a population of more than 1.4 billion, China's employment problem is more complex than that of any other country in the world. The Chinese government attaches great importance to it, adheres to the principle that employment is pivotal to people's well-being, and considers the expansion of employment as an important element in formulating economic and social development plans. *The Outline of the 10th Five-year Plan for National Economic and Social Development of the People's Republic of China* (hereinafter referred to as the 10th Five-year Plan) was promulgated in March 2001, which was the first five-year plan implemented under the market economy system when China entered the 21st century. Different from the previous plans which put more emphasis on economic growth rate, the main objectives of the 10th Five-year Plan covered economic growth, reform and opening up, social progress and other fields, giving more emphasis on balanced development. It was the first time that employment expansion was made as an important goal of economic and social development in the 10th Five-year Plan, under which economic and social policies conducive to employment expansion were implemented. Moreover, in the main expectation of macro-control, laying equal stress on economy and employment was clearly described that the average annual economic growth rate was about 7%. The number of both new urban employment and transferred agricultural labour force in five years reached 40 million, and the registered urban unemployment rate was controlled at about 5%. It was required to maintain a faster economic growth rate and create more jobs. *The Outline of the 11th Five-year Plan for National Economic and Social Development of People's Republic of China* (hereinafter referred to as the 11th Five-year Plan) was promulgated in March 2006, which attached more attention to the coordinated development of economy and society, and clearly put forward the general goal of expanding employment by all means. The 11th Five-year Plan stated that the main targets of economic and social development were the average annual growth of GDP reaching 7.5%, the number of both new urban employment and the transferred agricultural labour force reaching 45 million respectively, and the registered urban unemployment rate being controlled at 5%. The 11th Five-year Plan also requested to place the expansion of employment in a more prominent position in economic and social development and implement the proactive employment policy. *The Outline of the 12th Five-year Plan for National Economic and Social Development of the People's Republic of China* (hereinafter referred to as the 12th Five-year Plan), was promulgated in March 2011, which took the protection and improvement of people's well-being as the fundamental starting point and foothold of accelerating the transformation of the economic development mode, and clearly requested to put employment promotion in the priority position in economic and social development. The 12th Five-year Plan requested that the main target of economic and social development was to achieve steady and rapid economic growth. In detail, the average annual growth of GDP reached 7%, and 45 million new jobs were created in urban areas, keeping the registered urban unemployment rate within 5%. Moreover, plans on how to implement the pro-employment strategy should be made so as to improve the employment quality and strive for fuller employment. *The Outline of the 13th Five-year Plan for National Economic and Social Development of the People's Republic of China* (hereinafter referred to as the 13th Five-year Plan) was issued in March 2016, which proposed to adhere to the people-centred development idea and to take improving people's well-being and promoting people's all-round development as the starting point and foothold of development. The 13th Five-year Plan requested to continue to develop scientifically and accelerate the transformation of the economic development model, and strive for higher-quality, more efficient, more equitable and more sustainable development. The main target of economic and social development was to maintain medium-high speed of economic growth. The main economic indicators should be balanced and coordinated. The quality and efficiency of development were significantly improved, and people's living standards and quality were generally improved, with relatively sufficient employment positions. Furthermore, it was clearly requested to implement pro-employment strategy, implement more proactive employment policies, create more jobs, focus on solving structural employment contradictions, and encourage entrepreneurship-driven employment, so as to achieve fuller and higher quality employment.

1.1.2 Take Promoting Employment as an Important Objective of the Macroeconomic Regulation and Control

The four major indicators of the macro-control, i.e. economic growth rate, inflation rate, unemployment rate and balance of international payments, are interrelated, influencing and restricting each other. History also shows that it is not easy to fight inflation, and it is even harder to fight unemployment. So, apart from keeping an open eye on GDP growth, inflation, balance of international payments, fixed asset investment and money in circulation, using the unemployment rate as a "barometer" of economic and social performance, we must pay close attention to the changes in employment rate and unemployment rate and take timely and effective measures to expand employment and reduce unemployment. To this end, *Notice on Furthering the Re-employment for the Laid-off and Unemployed Persons* (No. 12, 2002, the CPC Central Committee, the State Council) proposed that unemployment rate control and job creation should be regarded as important indicators of the macro-control and incorporate them into the national economic and social development plan (Table 10.1). In 2003, the Chinese government started to use "newly increased urban employment" and "registered urban unemployment rate" as an important part of economic and social development indicators, and formally incorporated them into the annual plan for national economic and social development in order to strengthen the macroeconomic regulation and control and ensure coordinated economic and employment growth. *Employment Promotion Law* which went into effect in 2008 also makes special provisions on this, requiring governments at or above the county level to make employment increase as one of their important goals in their endeavours for economic and social development, incorporate it into their local economic and social development plan, and formulate medium- and long-term plans and annual work plans on employment promotion.

1.2 Employment Arrangements Made by Employment Promotion Plan and Annual Employment Plan

1.2.1 Employment Arrangements Made by Employment Promotion Plan

Employment promotion plan is the work plan made by the Ministry of Human Resources and Social Security (i.e. the Ministry of Labour and Social Security before the institutional reform of the State Council in 2008) in accordance with the overall requirements of the national economic and social development plan. The employment promotion plan was issued in the name of the State Council after 2012. However, before 2012, the objectives and arrangements were specified mainly in the ministry level document named as the Labour and Social Security Development Plan.

In April 2001, the Ministry of Labour and Social Security issued *the Outline of the 10th Five-year Plan for the Development of Labour and Social Security Undertakings* (hereinafter referred to as the 10th Five-year Plan for Labour and Social Security). The main objectives of employment during the 10th Five-year Plan period were to form a

Table 10.1 Arrangement on Employment in the Outline of the National Economic and Social Development Plan

	The 10th Five-year Plan	The 11th Five-year Plan	The 12th Five-year Plan	The 13th Five-year Plan
Objective	Take employment expansion as an important goal of economic and social development, and implement economic and social policies conducive to employment expansion.	Put employment expansion in a more prominent position in economic and social development and do everything possible to expand employment.	Give priority to employment promotion in economic and social development.	People's living standards and quality of life are generally improved, and employment positions are relatively adequate.
Task	In each of the five years, 40 million new urban jobs are created and 40 million agricultural labourers are transferred, and the registered urban unemployment rate is kept at around 5 percent. The proportion of employed persons in primary, secondary and tertiary industry in 2015 was 44%, 23% and 33% respectively. The urbanisation level is raised.	Maintain a relatively fast economic growth rate and create more jobs; formulate and implement the Five-year Plan to create 45 million new jobs in urban areas and transfer 45 million agricultural labour force, and control the registered urban unemployment rate at 5%. The proportion of employed persons in the service sector increases by 4 percentage points.	45 million new jobs are created in urban areas in 5 years, and the registered urban unemployment rate is controlled within 5%. The urbanisation rate increases by 4 percentage points. The per capita disposable income of urban residents and the per capita net income of rural residents increase respectively by more than 7% annually.	The main economic indicators are balanced and coordinated, and the quality and efficiency of development are significantly improved. Employment, education, culture and sports, social security, medical care, housing and other public service systems are improved, and the accessibility of equal basic public services is steadily improved. Employment positions are relatively sufficient. Under the current standard, the rural poverty-stricken population is lifted out of poverty, and all poverty-stricken counties are no longer named as poverty-stricken counties and the regional overall poverty is solved.

Continued

	The 10th Five-year Plan	The 11th Five-year Plan	The 12th Five-year Plan	The 13th Five-year Plan
Arrangement	Maintain a faster economic growth rate and create more jobs; formulate and implement preferential policies to develop labour-intensive industries which have the comparative advantage, and service enterprises, SMEs and non-public enterprises with high employment capacity. Encourage self-employment and flexible employment, strengthen on-the-job training and re-employment training, and improve the employment service system.	Implement the proactive employment policy, coordinate urban and rural employment, and strive to control the scale of unemployment. Continue to implement and improve favourable policies to encourage enterprises to expand employment and enhance employment training. Encourage labourers to obtain various forms of employment such as self-employment and business start-up, and improve the employment service system. Build up the vocational skill training mechanism supported by the governments with social participation at a fast pace, and improve the employment aid system.	Implement pro-employment strategy; improve the employment mechanism with the combination of employment chosen by labour force independently, regulated by the market and promoted by the government; create equal job opportunities, improve the quality of employment, and strive for full employment. It also puts forward specific requirements on implementing more proactive employment policies, strengthening public employment services and vocational training, and building a harmonious labour relationship.	Implement more proactive employment policies, create more jobs, focus on solving structural employment contradictions, and encourage entrepreneurship to drive employment, so as to achieve full and high-quality employment. It also puts forward specific requirements for expanding the scale of urban employment, strengthening the support for flexible employment and new forms of employment, improving the service capacity of public employment and entrepreneurship, improving employment and entrepreneurship service system, implementing the lifelong vocational skill training system, improving the statistical index system of employment and unemployment, and improving the unemployment monitoring and early warning mechanism.

Source: relevant contents are extracted from the website of the Chinese government.

market-oriented employment mechanism, expand the employment scale, improve the employment structure and improve workers' competence. The 10th Five-year Plan for Labour and Social Security also defined the main tasks of this period and made clear arrangements on doing a good job in employment and re-employment (Table 10.2). In October 2006, the State Council approved and forwarded *the Outline of the 11th Five-year Plan for the Development of Labour and Social Security Undertakings (2006-2010)* (hereinafter referred to as the 11th Five-year Plan for Labour and Social Security), and determined that the main goal of employment during the 11th Five-year Plan period was to achieve sustained employment growth. It was required that apart from focusing on solving the re-employment problem for the laid-off and unemployed people left over by the system transition, efforts should be made in the employment of new urban labour force and the transfer of rural surplus labour force, and to broaden employment channels, increase employment positions, improve employment structure and quality, strengthen unemployment control, and maintain stable employment situation. The 11th Five-year Plan for Labour and Social Security further clarified the main tasks of this period, and made clear arrangements on implementing long-term strategies and policies to promote employment and to expand employment by all means. In January 2012, the State Council issued *Notice on Approval and Transmission of Employment Promotion Plan (2011-2015)* (hereinafter referred to as Employment Promotion Plan). This is the first employment plan issued in the name of the State Council, which made it clear that the goal of promoting employment during the 12th Five-year Plan period was to achieve sustained expansion of employment scale and more reasonable employment structure. The 11th Five-year Plan for Labour and Social Security also proposed the main tasks and policy measures to promote employment in the next five years from eight aspects, such as improving the ability of economic development to stimulate employment, implementing more proactive employment policies, coordinating the employment of labourers in urban and rural areas and the key groups. In January 2017, the State Council issued *the 13th Five-year Plan for Employment Promotion*, which clearly pointed out that by 2020, the employment scale should be steadily expanded, the employment quality should be further improved, the employment structure should be continuously optimised, the equal public employment and entrepreneurship service system between urban and rural areas should be more complete, and the protection system of workers' rights and interests should be improved continuously. In addition, *the 13th Five-year Plan for Employment Promotion* proposed the key tasks of promoting employment in the next five years from five aspects, such as enhancing the ability of economic development to create jobs, enhancing the ability of entrepreneurship-driven employment, and strengthening the ability of key groups to secure employment.

Table 10.2 Arrangements on Employment Made in the Employment Promotion Plan

	The 10th Five-year Plan for Labour and Social Security	The 11th Five-year Plan for Labour and Social Security	Employment Promotion Plan	The 13th Five-year Plan for Employment Promotion
Objective	Form a market-oriented employment mechanism, expand employment scale, improve employment structure, enhance workers' competence.	Employment continues to grow. Increase the number of jobs, improve employment structure, improve the quality of employment, strengthen the control of unemployment.	The employment scale continues to expand, and employment structure is more reasonable. Unemployment is effectively controlled; the level of human resources development is significantly improved; employment quality is further improved; a unified, standardised and flexible human resources market is basically formed; and the mechanism for safeguarding workers' rights and interests is further improved.	The employment scale is steadily expanded, and the quality of employment is further enhanced. The environment for starting up businesses is significantly improved, and the ability of driving employment continues to increase. The human resources structure is continuously optimised, and workers' employability and entrepreneurial capacity are significantly enhanced.
Task	Create 40 million new jobs in urban areas and realise the task of 40 million transferred agricultural labour force across the country. The registered urban unemployment rate is controlled at about 5%. By the end of the 10th Five-year Plan, the proportion of employment in the three industries shall be adjusted to 44:23:33.	45 million new jobs in urban areas are created across the country, and the registered urban unemployment rate is controlled within 5%, with 45 million agricultural labour force being transferred.	Create 45 million new jobs in urban areas and realise the task of 40 million transferred agricultural labour force. The proportion of urban employment is gradually increased, and the employment structure of the three industries is optimised. Unemployment is effectively controlled, and the registered urban unemployment rate is controlled within 5%.	Create over 50 million new jobs in urban areas, and the registered urban unemployment rate is controlled within 5%, lifting 10 million people out of poverty.

Continued

	The 10th Five-year Plan for Labour and Social Security	The 11th Five-year Plan for Labour and Social Security	Employment Promotion Plan	The 13th Five-year Plan for Employment Promotion
Arrangement	Specific arrangements are made for continuing to carry out the proactive employment policy, broadening employment channels, further cultivating and developing the labour market, improving the employment service system, adapting to the adjustment of rural economic structure and the acceleration of urbanisation process, doing a good job in developing and employing rural labour force, solving the employment problem for surplus rural labour force through multiple channels, and doing a good job in guaranteeing the life of the laid-off workers and promoting re-employment.	Specific arrangements are made for implementing the strategy of developing economy and promoting employment at the same time; establishing the economic growth mode which is conducive to expanding employment; continuing to implement the proactive employment policy to promote the re-employment of the laid-off and unemployed people; constantly improving the market employment mechanism to promote the overall employment of urban and rural areas; establishing an institutionalised, specialised and socialised public employment service system; strengthening unemployment control; and improving the employment management system, etc.	Specific arrangements are made from eight aspects, such as improving the ability of economic development to stimulate employment, implementing more proactive employment policies, coordinating the employment of labourers in urban and rural areas and the key groups, vigorously developing human resources, strengthening the prevention and control of unemployment, and strengthening the construction of human resources market.	Specific arrangements are made from five aspects, such as enhancing the ability of economic development to create jobs, enhancing the ability of entrepreneurship-driven employment, strengthening the ability of key groups to secure employment, improving the ability of matching supply and demand in the human resources market, and strengthening the ability to improve workers' competence.

Source: relevant contents are extracted from the website of the Ministry of Human Resources and Social Security.

1.2.2 Determination and Completion of Annual Employment Objectives and Tasks

In accordance with the general requirements and arrangements outlined in the national economic and social development plan, at the end of each year, the Ministry of Human Resources and Social Security, together with the National Development and Reform Commission, the Ministry of Finance and the National Bureau of Statistics of China, take into account factors such as the predicted growth rate of the national economy, the supply of urban labour resources, and the employment growth law in recent years, to predict and judge the situation and tasks faced by employment and re-employment in the coming year, and after consultation with the provinces, put forward to the State Council proposals for the target tasks in the new urban employment and unemployment rate in the coming year. When confirmed by the State Council, commitment will be made to the public in the form of government work report at the National People's Congress in the coming year.

When the annual employment targets and tasks are determined, the Ministry of Human Resources and Social Security will refine and decompose them to provinces, autonomous regions and municipalities directly under the central government. On the basis of a careful analysis of the employment situation in the regional perspective, each region shall study and determine the objectives, tasks and concrete measures for the employment in the region in accordance with the unified set of objectives and tasks, and divide them layer upon layer and clarify their responsibilities. The effect of employment work shall be used as an important indicator in evaluating the performance governments and departments at all levels in the field of labour and employment. *Employment Promotion Law* specifically stipulates that governments at all levels and the relevant departments shall establish target responsibility system on employment promotion. The governments at or above the county level shall, on the basis of the requirements of such a system, assess and supervise the work of their subordinate departments and the governments at the next lower level.

Among the target tasks, the number of new urban employment[①] is an indicator that has been adopted since 2003 in order to keep track of the achievement on employment target in various regions of China (Table 10.3). The surveyed urban unemployment rate was used for the first time in 2018, in parallel with the previously used registered urban unemployment rate, as a macroeconomic target. The surveyed urban unemployment rate

[①] The number of new urban employment in the year = the total number of new urban employment in the year − the total number of urban natural attrition in the year.

covers the permanent population migrating from rural areas to urban areas. The surveyed unemployment rate is adopted to facilitate international benchmarking and make a more comprehensive understanding on the situation and changing of unemployment in the society.

Table 10.3 Achievement of the Main Employment Targets for the Calendar Years in China

Year	The number of new urban employment (unit: 10 thousand)		The registered urban unemployment rate at year-end (%)		The surveyed urban unemployment rate at year-end (%)	
	Target	Accomplished	Target	Accomplished	Target	Accomplished
2003	800	850	4.5	4.3	—	—
2004	900	980	4.7	4.2	—	—
2005	900	970	4.6	4.2	—	—
2006	900	1,184	4.6	4.1	—	—
2007	900	1,204	4.5	4.0	—	—
2008	1,000	1,113	4.5	4.2	—	—
2009	900	1,102	4.6	4.3	—	—
2010	900	1,168	4.6	4.1	—	—
2011	900	1,221	4.6	4.1	—	—
2012	900	1,266	4.6	4.1	—	—
2013	900	1,310	4.6	4.1	—	—
2014	1,000	1,322	4.6	4.1	—	—
2015	1,000	1,312	4.5	4.1	—	—
2016	1,000	1,314	4.5	4.0	—	—
2017	1,000	1,351	4.5	3.9	—	5.0
2018	1,000	1,361	4.5	3.8	5.5	4.9
2019	1,000	1,352	4.5	3.6	5.5	5.2

Source: government work reports in the website of the Chinese government and the statistical bulletin of the website of the Ministry of Human Resources and Social Security.

Since the implementation of the proactive employment policy in 2003, China has created 11.893 million new urban jobs every year on average. In particular, since 2013, the number of new urban jobs has exceeded 13 million annually. The total number of employees reached 774.71 million at the end of 2019. The registered urban unemployment rate was 3.6%. The unemployment rate in 31 big cities has remained basically stable at about 5%, and the employment situation has been stable generally.

2. The Goal of Fuller and Higher Quality Employment

2.1 Initiation of Fuller and Higher Quality Employment

2.2.1 Background

fuller and Higher quality employment is the inherent requirement for China's economic development from high-speed growth to high-quality development, as well as the indication of implementing the people-centred development concept and meeting people's expectation of better employment.

(1) Meet the requirements of economic transformation. Since China's reform and opening-up policy, the economy has achieved a rapid growth for 40 years. However, there are some remaining problems, such as slow pace of structural optimisation and quality improvement, lack of power for sustainable development, low quality employment and small share of labour income. The 12th Five-year Plan requested that the transformation of economic development mode should be taken as the main line. The 18th CPC National Congress report also stipulated that the foothold of promoting economic development should be shifted to improving quality and efficiency, driven by scientific and technological progress, improvement of workers' competence and management innovation. The 13th Five-year Plan further proposed to speed up the transformation of economic development mode to achieve higher quality, more efficient, more equitable and more sustainable development. With the economy shifting from extensive expansion to quality benefit, employment also needs to change from quantity expansion type to the improvement of quality while ensuring the corresponding quantity.

(2) Meet the requirements of employment transformation. Under the background of a new era, employment presents many new characteristics, especially with the acceleration of China's economic transformation and urbanisation, industrialisation, marketisation and internationalisation, China's employment is facing many new challenges. From the macro-perspective, the employment pressure on aggregate, i.e. the total supply of labour force exceeding the total demand, still persists; the structural contradiction of employment is more prominent; the employment situation of college students remains very severe, accompanied with the problems of hundreds of millions of rural-to-urban migrant workers needing jobs and their urbanisation and citizenisation; entrepreneurship-driven employment turns into the new engine for economic development; and with the shifting of driving force, new industries and new business forms are emerging. From the micro perspective, some deep-seated contradictions and problems are gradually revealed through the micro level, such as slow wage growth of enterprise employees, frequent occurrence of extra-long overtime work, insufficient social security, workers' competence in need of improvement, and the jobs losses intertwined with unstable employment. The employment contradiction mainly focuses on employment quality. Therefore, great efforts should be made to improve the quality of employment while ensuring employment growth.

(3) Meet the needs of coping with the domestic and international situations. At present, in order to cope with the crowding out effect in employment caused by machine replacement, the contradiction between the new business forms and traditional employment, and the influence of domestic and international uncertainties, the Chinese government has made the strategic requirement of maintaining stable growth and ensuring people's livelihood by stabilising employment. To stabilise employment, more efforts should be made not only in guaranteeing employment quantity, but also improving employment quality step by step. Only by improving employment quality can we give full and effective play to the efficiency of human resources and truly guarantee the continuity and stability of employment. At the same time, in the face of global trade friction and employment competition, the employment in China must be upgraded and employment quality must be improved.

(4) Meet workers' expectation. To achieve fuller and higher quality employment is the expectation of Chinese people. A better and more stable job is the greatest hope of all workers and their children. In the long run, it is the embodiment of putting people first philosophy in the process of employment transformation. At present, solving the problem of low quality employment is also the task of further promoting employment reform and innovative development. Therefore, we must adhere to the people-centred philosophy and take meeting workers' expectation in higher quality employment as the starting point and foothold so that the overall employment can be upgraded to a higher level.

2.2.2 Goal Setting Process

From the 16th CPC National Congress (2002) to the 19th CPC National Congress (2017), the setting of China's employment goals has advanced and improved step by step. The 16th CPC National Congress took "achieving a higher rate of employment" as an important goal in building up a well-off society in an all-round way by 2020. The 17th CPC National Congress made an important decision on building up a well-off society in an all-round way and put forward the goal of "creating more employment opportunities". The 18th CPC National Congress put forward the goal of "creating more employment opportunities" and explicitly requested to promote the realisation of higher quality employment. At the 19th CPC National Congress, the goal of "achieving fuller employment and creating better quality jobs" was proposed. It can be seen that the goals of each period are closely related to the employment situation, economic context and social development at that time (Table 10.4). In 2002, there were still a large number of laid-off workers in China. The Chinese government put forward the goal of full employment, which reflected the determination of the Chinese government in solving the problem of re-employment for the laid-off workers, and making Chinese people have full confidence in a bright future. However, due to insufficient conditions at that time, it could only be put as achieving a higher rate of employment. By 2007, China's urban and rural employment entered a new stage, and *Employment Promotion Law* has been promulgated, so it was put as creating more employment opportunities. By 2012, China has created more than 11 million new jobs annually for many consecutive years. The contradiction of total labour supply exceeding total labour demand has been eased to some extent, and workers have made a higher expectation of the quality of employment. Hence, it is necessary for the State to create more jobs of better quality. By 2017, along with the socialism with Chinese characteristics entering a new era, China's economic development has shifted from high-speed growth to high-quality development. The main social contradiction to be solved at the time was the unbalanced and inadequate development, which needed to further enhance people's sense of fulfilment by improving the quality of employment. Therefore, the 19th CPC National Congress proposed to the new goals of "achieving fuller employment and creating better quality jobs".

Over the past decade or so, the changing of employment objectives and tasks have been in line with the progress of China's economic and social development and the transformation of major social contradictions. They have also fully reflected the Chinese people's aspiration for a better life and better jobs. In order to solve the major social contradictions in the new era, increase the sense of fulfilment, happiness and security of the broad masses of workers, and promote social fairness and justice, the attainment of fuller and higher quality employment must be set as the priority target to be pursued continuously in employment promotion, and every effort must be made to realise it.

Table 10.4 Employment Objectives, Requirements, Principles and Policies of the 16th CPC National Congress to 19th CPC National Congress

	16th CPC National Congress (2002)	17th CPC National Congress (2007)	18th CPC National Congress (2012)	19th CPC National Congress (2017)
Objectives	Achieving a higher rate of employment	Creating more employment opportunities	Creating more employment opportunities	Achieving fuller employment and creating better quality jobs
Requirements	Try every possible means to expand employment and constantly improve people's livelihood.	Implement the development strategy of expanding employment and promote entrepreneurship-driven employment.	Promote higher quality employment.	Improve employment quality.
Principles and policies	Employment has a vital bearing on the people's livelihood. It is a long-term strategy and policy to expand employment. Encourage people to find jobs on their own or become self-employed.	Employment is vital to people's livelihood. Continue to follow a proactive employment policy. Strengthen government guidance, improve the market mechanism for employment, and improve policies to encourage people to start up businesses or find jobs on their own.	Employment is crutial to the people's well-being. Implement the principle of promoting self-reliant employment, market-regulated employment and government-backed employment and entrepreneurship, and the strategy of giving top priority to employment and a more proactive employment policy.	Employment is pivotal to people's well-being. Give high priority to employment and pursue a proactive employment policy, striving to achieve fuller employment and create better quality jobs.

Source: relevant contents are extracted from the website of the Chinese government.

2.2 Basic Connotation of Full Employment and Quality of Employment

2.2.1 Full Employment

Full employment means that under a certain wage level, all people who are willing to work have the opportunity to obtain employment. Full employment does not mean that everyone has a job. Structural unemployment and frictional unemployment remain even in the state of full employment, i.e. temporary unemployment remains in the process of career change caused by technological progress, industrial structure adjustment, working age and demand preference.

2.2.2 Quality of Employment

The quality of employment refers to the advantages and disadvantages of the relevant factors in the process of engaging in social work and the suitability of the work to the individual. It mainly involves such factors as remuneration, social security, working conditions, employment stability, protection of workers' rights and interests, workers' personal feelings, career development space and social evaluation.

2.2.3 Fuller and Higher Quality Employment

Fuller and higher quality employment means that through economic development, more jobs shall be created, with employment structure and workers' competence being improved. Barriers to workers' migration shall be removed, and employment and business start-up services shall be optimised. All these shall enable workers to have fuller and more equitable access to employment and career development opportunities, and continuously optimise the allocation of human and other resources. At the same time, with the development of economy and society, the increase of labour productivity, and the progress of science and technology, workers' labour remuneration and social security benefits have been continuously raised, and their working conditions inclusive of occupational safety have been continuously improved. While maintaining the employment stability, workers' rights and interests have been protected, and labour relations have become more harmonious and stable. As a result, the sense of fulfilment, happiness and security of workers and their families shall be enriched, more secure and more sustainable. The goal of fuller and higher quality employment is an organic unity, one complementing the other to facilitate the achievement of the general requirement and primary target on employment promotion.

2.3 Measurement of Fuller and Higher Quality Employment

2.3.1 Measurement Standard of Full Employment

In China, full employment is a status compatible with the development of a harmonious society, which mainly refers to the macro and meso level, i.e. the national and regional level. It can be seen in the following four aspects. First, the labour resources should be more fully developed and utilised, which is the starting point of realising full employment. There are more employment opportunities in the society; the total amount of employment continues to expand; employment structure has been further optimised; and urban and rural employment has been better integrated. All the urban and rural workers should get education, training and employment opportunities. A complete vocational skills training system is available for all workers. Second, the mechanism of market employment is sound and the employment channels are smooth, which are the pre-conditions for full employment. Workers have a favourable environment to choose their own jobs, migrate freely and start up their own businesses easily. The behaviours of the government, employers, workers and social intermediary organisations are regulated according to law. A unified and open human resources market mechanism plays its fundamental role. The public employment and talent service system covers both urban and rural areas. Third, unemployment rate and the average unemployment cycle can be controlled at a level bearable to the society, which is a symbol of full employment. The unemployed can get unemployment benefit and be organised into the corresponding employment preparation activities through employment service, and the people in difficult groups can get effective employment aid. Unemployment insurance plays an important role in guaranteeing basic life, promoting employment and preventing unemployment. Fourth, the employment stability has been further improved, and workers' employment rights and interests are effectively protected, which is the result of full employment. Labour relations are more harmonious; a steady adjustment mechanism is available for labour income; and social security system covers all workers.

2.3.2 Measurement Standard of the Quality of Employment

It is measured mainly from the macro, meso and micro levels. The macro level implies national and regional perspectives. The measurement indicators are as follows. First, whether the expansion of employment scale is in balance with the labour supply. Second, whether the improvement of workers' competence matches the industrial development. Third, whether the optimisation of employment structure is compatible with the expansion of employment. Fourth, whether the improvement of employment environment meets the requirements on independent and fair employment and entrepreneurship. Fifth, whether the labour relations can facilitate a win-win situation between the employee and the employer. The meso level [1] refers to the enterprises perspective, since the enterprise is the market subject. It can be measured as follows. First, whether the working environment and cultural identity are recognised. Second, whether the labour remuneration keeps increasing and the insurance benefit and welfare meet the demand. Third, whether the capacity building system is available and the career development channel is smooth. Fourth, whether the job stability is sustained and the employment is well regulated. The micro level refers to the perspective of individual workers. The measurement standard is composed of five core elements. The first is more employment choices and career development channels, including the improvement and optimisation of employment environment, and the workers getting better employment and business start-up opportunities. The second is the continuous increase of labour remuneration and welfare benefits, including remuneration for work being increased, employment equity being ensured and employment discrimination being effectively prevented. The third is employment stability and reliable social security, including the stability of employment being enhanced, the employed being entitled to social security benefits. The fourth is higher vocational competence and working capacity, including the improvement of workers' competence, effective education and training, and the growth of talent team. The fifth is safe and healthy labour conditions and harmonious labour relations, including the harmonious labour relations and the rights and interests of employers and employees being guaranteed, and whether the occupational safety and health condition as well as workers' safety and health being improved.

[1] The relevant standards at the meso level are derived from the research on improving the employment quality of enterprises jointly carried out by China Employment Promotion Association and McDonald's China in 2018.

3. Policies and Measures to Achieve Fuller and Higher Quality Employment

3.1 Key Elements to Push the Work Forward

At present and in the future, in the process of promoting fuller and higher quality employment, we should grasp three key elements.

(1) Insist on the consistency of employment objectives with the process of economic and social development. Being an important component of the economic and social development goal, the employment goal is complementary to other economic and social development goals. Therefore, achieving fuller and higher quality employment requires healthy and stable economic development with higher quality, as well as continuous improvement in efficiency and social responsibility of enterprises. It is necessary to achieve the simultaneous growth of residents' income and labour remuneration as well as the increase of labour productivity. To achieve fuller and higher quality employment, we should do our best and do what we can to meet the needs of the vast number of workers for better life through their work.

(2) Adhere to the principle of proceeding from reality, and implement policies according to different categories. When measuring the quality of employment, we should also fully consider the imbalance of development in different regions, such as the differences among the eastern, central and western regions, and the differences between economically developed cities and resource exhausted cities. The attributes of enterprises in different industries should be also taken into consideration, such as coal and steel industry affected by structural transformation, retail and service industry affected by Internet technology, and manufacturing sector affected by new intelligent technology. Measurement may vary among different employment forms, e.g. salary workers in the traditional economy would be different from individual workers, and the new forms of employees under the sharing economy. The differences between different groups should be taken into consideration as well, such as young and older people, and male and female workers. In order to provide the basis for delivering accurate service and carrying out classified support, the targeted, representative and measurable indicators should be selected for carrying out the survey and evaluation of the quality of employment and full employment.

(3) Mobilise the strength of the society to push it forward together. First of all, the government departments should further improve policies, strengthen services, make efforts in management and provide guarantees. Enterprises and employers should also vigorously improve the level of human resources management and work hard in building up a harmonious labour relation and promoting career development for employees. Workers should strive to improve their competence and ability to adapt to the requirements of higher quality employment. The strategic goals, guidelines and policies of the State to promote fuller and higher quality employment should be closely combined with addressing the workers' concerns about their vital interests, so that improving the quality of employment becomes the common goal of the society.

3.2 Policies and Measures to Promote the Work and the Effects

In order to achieve fuller and higher quality employment, the Chinese government has not only set clear objectives and requirements at different stages, but has also adopted a series of policy measures to facilitate the realisation of the objectives. Through long-term efforts, obvious results have been achieved. To be specific, according to the basic requirements in achieving fuller and higher quality employment, implementation measures have been taken in the following six areas and good results have been achieved.

(1) Improve employment structure and employment environment, and find the growth point of employment. Reasonable employment structure and good employment environment are the important conditions for expanding employment and promoting the development of entrepreneurship, as well as the important basis for increasing employment opportunities and improving employment quality. Through policy support and guidance, the Chinese government has gradually improved the employment structure and constantly optimised the employment environment. In terms of improving employment structure, by encouraging the development of tertiary industry and modern agriculture, guiding the transfer of surplus rural labour force into the urbanisation process, the employment in secondary industry has been steadily improved, and the employment scale of tertiary industry has been expanded, with employees in primary industry being reduced. As a result, the employment structure of the three major industries has become more reasonable. By promoting the transformation of economic development mode, adjusting the economic structure and promoting the development of emerging industries, new growth points of employment have been found and more employment opportunities have been created. In terms of improving employment environment, lots of fiscal and monetary policies have been implemented, such as granting loans, providing subsidies to the interest of micro-loans and tax (fee) reductions (exemptions) to support the development of private and micro enterprises and to encourage individual workers to start up their own businesses. Relevant government departments have simplified procedures to provide convenient and good services when promoting workers' employment and entrepreneurship. Public employment service institutions have provided job seekers and entrepreneurs with timely labour supply and demand information by continuously strengthening and improving the labour market information system, so as to help them realise employment and entrepreneurship as soon as possible. The strong policy support and comprehensive public services have facilitated the creation of a good employment environment, and remarkable results have been achieved in promoting full employment and improving employment quality. The number of new employment in urban China has remained over 13 million for six consecutive years. More entrepreneurs and bosses of small and micro enterprises have made great progress, and employment has been doubled.

The integration and improvement of new technology to traditional forms, i.e. modern warehouse workshops not only help to improve labour efficiency, but also reduce labour cost.

(2) Control the growth of unemployment rate and keep the employment situation stable. The inherent requirement of controlling the growth of unemployment rate is to keep the unemployment rate within the range of social affordability, and to have the number of unemployed people not exceeding a certain proportion of the economically active population. Unemployment groups should not emerge too concentrated either in terms of time or areas, and the individual labourers should not stay unemployed for too long. To this end, the Chinese government, in accordance with the pro-employment strategy, has formulated and implemented an proactive employment policy that, apart from promoting economic growth, has created jobs, expanded employment demand and enabled more labourers to obtain employment. This is the most important factor in controlling the rise of unemployment. At the same time, starting from unemployment prevention and keeping stable employment, the job retention policy has been implemented to help enterprises to overcome temporary difficulties, stabilise the staff team and reduce unemployment. In particular, during the international financial crisis, there was no mass unemployment, and arrangements were made to guarantee the livelihood of the laid-off and unemployed persons and to encourage support for re-employment, thus maintaining the overall employment stability. Over a long period of time, the unemployment rate has been kept at about 5% and relatively full employment has been achieved.

(3) Reform the income distribution system to promote employment equity. Labour remuneration is an important factor to measure the quality of employment, and fair employment is the basic guarantee to improve employment quality, which is directly related to workers' vital interests. It is important to realise employment equity, income equity and equal pay for equal work. Therefore, the Chinese government has made positive efforts to promote employment equity. Since China's reform and opening-up policy, the Chinese government has taken a series of policy measures to reform the income distribution system. This includes: first, according to the development of the national economy, the governments of all localities shall determine and raise minimum wage in a timely manner. Second, the wages of employees from SOEs shall be linked to economic performance. Third, the wages of employees from private enterprises shall be decided by the enterprises themselves. Fourth, for public welfare jobs, the government provides wage subsidies and social insurance subsidies to ensure that workers receive reasonable remuneration for their work. Fifth, equal pay for equal work is introduced for different workers in the same position. Through these measures, a new mechanism of income distribution has been established, making the remuneration for workers more reasonable and increasing year by year, so as to improve employment quality. In promoting fair employment, by formulating laws, regulations and policies, strengthening supervision and inspection as well as other measures, employment discrimination has been prevented, and all workers are equal in employment rights and interests regardless of their identity of urban or rural residents, gender or ethnic group. Enterprises can recruit employees on demand. The proactive employment policy implemented and the public employment services provided cover both urban and rural workers and various groups, achieving equal treatment in policy support and in employment services. These measures have guaranteed the realisation of employment equity.

E-commerce platforms have lowered barriers to employment and promoted fair employment. A disabled online merchant is granted the Top 10 Global Netrepreneur of the Year Awards at Alibaba's Global E-commerce Conference.

(4) Strengthen education and training to enhance employability. Improving the competence and employment ability can create favourable conditions for workers to obtain employment and for their career development, which is the key to improve employment quality. The Chinese government has made great efforts to improve workers' competence and ability to find jobs by deepening the reform of educational system and, in particular, strengthening vocational skills training. The measures include that in terms of improving the training supply, according to the demand of the labour market, the faculty and specialty setting of colleges and universities are adjusted and innovated to enable college students to receive vocational education that is favourable for employment, and to open up the career development channel for college students after graduation. Meanwhile, the integration of enterprises, vocational schools and colleges and social training institues are guided to organise various types of vocational training for urban and rural workers on large scale. In terms of innovating the contents and methods of training, it is necessary to enhance the pertinence, effectiveness, practicability and sustainability of training, to build up a lifelong vocational training system for all urban and rural workers, and to innovate training forms and methods by means of order-based or designated-based, online and offline training. In terms of strengthening policy guidance and support, the government provides vocational training subsidies to promote vocational skills training. In terms of improving training quality, through implementing vocational skill appraisal system, the workers are encouraged to actively participate in the vocational training and obtain the qualification, so as to improve the training quality. The above measures have strengthened vocational training, created conditions for improving the employability and professional quality of workers, and laid a good foundation for the realisation of high-quality employment.

(5) Stabilise employment and improve social insurance system. Maintaining employment stability is the greatest expectation of Chinese workers in the period of economic and social development and transformation, and social security is an important guarantee condition for stabilising employment and improving employment quality. Since China's reform and opening-up policy, the Chinese government has made great efforts to strengthen the construction of social security system and has gradually established a social insurance system covering urban and rural workers and various enterprises, including basic old-age insurance, medical insurance, unemployment insurance, work injury insurance and maternity insurance. Workers, whether they are employed or unemployed, whether they move to urban or rural areas for employment or cross-regional employment, can enjoy the corresponding insurance benefits according to the regulations, which has protected their legitimate rights and interests. By eliminating the worries behind them, the workers can settle down in their jobs and seek career development. The continuous improvement of China's social security system has played an important role in improving employment quality. At the same time, the Chinese government has implemented a number of policies and measures to stabilise employment, and has made great efforts to maintain the stability of the workforce. Although unemployment and job losses have increased in the face of serious natural disasters and financial crisis, measures have been taken to resolve the above problems in the short term. On the whole, the workers' employment situation is basically stable, which also reflects the improvement of employment quality.

(6) Maintain harmonious labour relations, and create good working conditions. Labour relations and working conditions are related to the legitimate rights and interests of both employers and employees, and to the occupational safety and physical and mental health of workers. To maintain harmonious labour relations and create good working conditions is an important part of improving employment quality. The Chinese government attaches great importance to the handling of labour relations. It guides enterprises and workers to establish harmonious labour relations by formulating policies and regulations and establishing corresponding systems, and to properly settle labour disputes in accordance with law. The specific measures include: first, when enterprises recruit employees, both employers and employees should sign labour contracts to clarify their respective rights and strictly implement them. Second, enterprises and entrepreneurs should participate in social insurance and pay social insurance contributions in a timely and fixed manner. Third, enterprises are required to refer to the wage guidelines to determine the wage level and not to reduce labour remuneration. Fourth, enterprises are required to regulate layoffs and not to lay off workers at will. Fifth, in case of labour dispute, employers and employees should apply to labour dispute arbitration institutions for mediation and arbitration in accordance with the prescribed procedures. At the same time, it is necessary to guarantee the employing units to employ workers independently and to carry out human resources management according to law. These measures have a good effect on the establishment of harmonious labour relations, the protection of the legitimate rights and interests of both employees and employers, and also help to improve employment quality. In terms of creating good working conditions, the main measures taken are to promote the enhancement of occupational safety awareness and the construction of safety facilities in enterprises through the formulation and implementation of policies and regulations, and to guide enterprises to make the best efforts to improve working conditions in accordance with their own conditions, and to create a good environment for workers to secure employment. At the same time, through supervision and inspection, and promoting the implementation of the policies, relevant departments can find problems and solve them in accordance with law. These measures strongly urge enterprises to strengthen the management of occupational safety protection, to increase input, and to gradually improve working conditions. Good results have been achieved in stabilising people's employment and ensuring their health and safety in production.

References

China Employment Promotion Association. Establishment and development of China's proactive employment policy [M]. Beijing: China Labour and Social Security Publishing House, 2016.

China Employment Promotion Association. Research programme on employment [M]. Beijing: China Labour and Social Security Publishing House, 2015.

China Employment Promotion Association. Latest theoretical research results of China's employment (2003-2012) [M]. Beijing: China Labour and Social Security Publishing House, 2012.

China Employment Promotion Association. The road of China's employment to the world [M]. Beijing: China Labour and Social Security Publishing House, 2016.

China Employment Promotion Association. Focus on China's employment (2010) [M]. Beijing: China Labour and Social Security Publishing House, 2011.

China Employment Promotion Association. Focus on China's employment (2011) [M]. Beijing: China Labour and Social Security Publishing House, 2012.

China Employment Promotion Association. Focus on China's employment (2012) [M]. Beijing: China Labour and Social Security Publishing House, 2013.

China Employment Promotion Association. Focus on China's employment (2013-2014) [M]. Beijing: China Labour and Social Security Publishing House, 2014.

China Employment Promotion Association. Focus on China's employment (2014-

2015) [M] . Beijing: China Labour and Social Security Publishing House, 2015.

China Employment Promotion Association. Focus on China's employment (2015-2016) [M] . Beijing: China Labour and Social Security Publishing House, 2016.

China Employment Promotion Association. Focus on China's employment (2016-2017) [M] . Beijing: China Labour and Social Security Publishing House, 2017.

China Employment Promotion Association. Collection of unemployment insurance [M] . Beijing: China Labour and Social Security Publishing House, 2015.

Department of Population and Employment Statistics of the National Bureau of Statistics of China, Department of Planning and Finance of the Ministry of Human Resources and Social Security. China labour statistics yearbook (2018) [M] . Beijing: China Statistics Press, 2019.

LAI D, LI C, ZHANG Q. China employment in the last 70 years (1949-2019) [M] . Beijing: China Labour and Social Security Publishing House, 2017.

Leading Group of Legal Popularisation for Human Resources and Social Security Departments in China. A handbook on human resources and social security legal systems [M] . Beijing: China Labour and Social Security Publishing House, 2013.

LIU Y. Connotation and measurement of higher quality and fuller employment [J] . China's Employment, 2017 (12).

MA Y T, TIAN G Z. Research report on the cooperation between public and private employment service institutions in China [J] . China's Employment, 2018 (1).

Ministry of Human Resources and Social Security. Promoting people's well-being and promoting people's all-round development [M] . Beijing: China Labour and Social Security Publishing House, China Personnel Publishing House, 2017.

Ministry of Human Resources and Social Security. China human resources and social security yearbook (2009) [M] . Beijing: China Labour and Social Security Publishing House, China Personnel Publishing House, 2009.

Ministry of Human Resources and Social Security. China human resources and social security yearbook (2010) [M] . Beijing: China Labour and Social Security Publishing House, China Personnel Publishing House, 2011.

Ministry of Human Resources and Social Security. China human resources and social security yearbook (2011) [M] . Beijing: China Labour and Social Security

Publishing House, China Personnel Publishing House, 2011.

Ministry of Human Resources and Social Security. China human resources and social security yearbook (2012) [M] . Beijing: China Labour and Social Security Publishing House, China Personnel Publishing House, 2012.

Ministry of Human Resources and Social Security. China human resources and social security yearbook (2013) [M] . Beijing: China Labour and Social Security Publishing House, China Personnel Publishing House, 2013.

Ministry of Human Resources and Social Security. China human resources and social security yearbook (2014) [M] . Beijing: China Labour and Social Security Publishing House, China Personnel Publishing House, 2014.

Ministry of Human Resources and Social Security. China human resources and social security yearbook (2015) [M] . Beijing: China Labour and Social Security Publishing House, China Personnel Publishing House, 2016.

Ministry of Human Resources and Social Security. China human resources and social security yearbook (2016) [M] . Beijing: China Labour and Social Security Publishing House, China Personnel Publishing House, 2017.

Ministry of Human Resources and Social Security. China human resources and social security yearbook (2017) [M] . Beijing: China Labour and Social Security Publishing House, China Personnel Publishing House, 2017.

Ministry of Human Resources and Social Security. China human resources and social security yearbook (2018) [M] . Beijing: China Labour and Social Security Publishing House, China Personnel Publishing House, 2019.

MO R, CHEN Y, XIONG Y. China employment development report (2009) [M] . Beijing: Social Science Academic Press, 2019.

National Bureau of Statistics of China. China statistical yearbook (2019) [M] . Beijing: China Statistics Press, 2019.

National Bureau of Statistics of China. Economic and social development achievements of the 70th anniversary of the founding of new China [R] . 2019.

Research Group of China Employment Promotion Association. Research report on employment statistics in China [R] . 2017.

Research Group of China Employment Promotion Association. Research report on speeding up the construction of a comprehensive public employment service system [R]. 2018.

The State Council Information Office. Equal development and sharing: the development and progress of women's cause in the past 70 years [M]. Beijing: People's Publishing House, 2019.

The State Council Information Office. Equality, participation and sharing: protection of the rights and interests of the disabled of new China in the past 70 years [M]. Beijing: People's Publishing House, 2019.

WANG X C, XIN C X. Employment promotion and vocational skills development [M]. Beijing: China Labour and Social Security Publishing House, 2012.

XIN C X. Unemployment insurance [M]. Beijing: China Labour and Social Security Publishing House, 2011.

ZHANG H. On the role and improvement path of private job intermediary agencies [J]. Jiangxi Social Sciences, 2010 (8).

ZHANG X J. Reform and development of employment in China [M]. Beijing: China Labour and Social Security Publishing House, 2008.

ZHANG X J. China's employment reform and development in the last 40 years [M]. Beijing: China Labour and Social Security Publishing House, 2016.

中国的就业

中华人民共和国人力资源和社会保障部　组织编写

中国劳动社会保障出版社

图书在版编目（CIP）数据

中国的就业：汉、英 / 中华人民共和国人力资源和社会保障部组织编写．-- 北京：中国劳动社会保障出版社，2021

ISBN 978-7-5167-5120-6

Ⅰ.①中… Ⅱ.①中… Ⅲ.①就业政策 - 研究 - 中国 - 汉、英 Ⅳ.①F249.20

中国版本图书馆 CIP 数据核字（2021）第 266699 号

中国劳动社会保障出版社出版发行

（北京市惠新东街 1 号　邮政编码：100029）

*

北京华联印刷有限公司印刷装订　　新华书店经销

787 毫米 × 1092 毫米　16 开本　32 印张　545 千字

2021 年 12 月第 1 版　　2021 年 12 月第 1 次印刷

定价：138.00 元

读者服务部电话：（010）64929211/84209101/64921644

营销中心电话：（010）64962347

出版社网址：http://www.class.com.cn

编辑工作委员会

前言

就业是民生之本。

国际劳工组织在2001年《全球就业议程》中提出：就业已成为人们生活的核心，这不仅是因为人们需要依靠就业而生存，而且就业还是人们融入社会、实现自身价值以及为后代带来希望的手段。因此就业已经成为社会和政治稳定的关键因素。中国人口众多，民生问题首当其冲。就业关乎劳动者的生存和发展，关系亿万劳动者及其家庭成员的切身利益，既是保障和改善民生的经济社会基础和重要条件，又是全面建成小康社会以满足人民对美好生活向往的重要标志，因此促进就业就成为保障和改善民生的头等大事。中华人民共和国成立70年来，中国共产党和中国政府一直高度重视就业工作，千方百计促进就业和减少失业，并为此付出了巨大努力，实现了就业总量持续增长、就业结构调整优化、就业质量逐步提升、就业公平更好体现，推动了人民收入稳步增长和贫困人口大幅减少，取得了举世瞩目的成就。2017年，国际权威机构对世界各国进行多项发展指标综合评估，将中国就业表现列为世界第一。

中国就业在发展中经历了许多重大挑战。从20世纪50年代迅速解

决旧中国遗留下来的几百万失业人员问题，到70年代及时处理上千万下乡知青返城就业问题，到世纪之交妥善化解3 000万下岗职工再就业问题，到21世纪应对突发自然灾害和国际金融危机对就业的冲击……中国政府针对不同时期面临的不同压力，及时采取了相应的政策措施，使就业矛盾得到了妥善化解，使就业形势保持了基本稳定，并由此保证了经济持续发展和社会政治稳定。

中国就业制度在20世纪80年代改革开放后进行了一系列改革，从原来的计划经济体制下“统包统配”的管理制度逐步改变为现在以市场机制为导向的就业制度，培育和建立起统一规范的人力资源市场。同时，在法律法规体系上逐步健全，在就业政策和服务体系上不断完善，保证了就业事业持续健康发展。特别是21世纪以来，中国政府坚持实行就业优先的发展战略，制定实施积极的就业政策，从而推动就业和创业在新的时期取得新的发展。

伴随中华人民共和国70年发展，特别是在改革开放40年的前进历程中，中国政府学习借鉴了各国成功的做法，探索出了做好就业工作的规律，并积累了许多宝贵的经验。正是在总结这些经验的基础上，近几年，中国共产党和中国政府明确提出要坚持就业优先战略和积极的就业政策，将实现更加充分更高质量就业作为新时代的任务目标，并为此作出了一系列战略部署，出台了更加全面系统的促进就业和创业的政策措施。这既体现了中国政府为改善民生和全面建成小康社会对就业工作提出的新要求，也顺应了广大人民群众对美好生活的向往。就业事业必将沿着中国特色社会主义道路继续砥砺前行。

《中国的就业》一书系统介绍了中华人民共和国成立70年以来，就业的改革发展历程和基本概况，阐述了中国就业经历的数次挑战和取得的历史性成就，全面总结了中国政府在实践中取得的经验，并展望了中国就业事业未来的发展。本书为国内外读者提供深入了解中国就业的窗口，也为国际国内有关专业人士研究中国就业制度沿革、政策框架和工作体系提供重要的参考资料。我们期待，《中国的就业》一书可以从一个侧面向世界展示中国政府在坚持以人民为中心的发展道路上作出的不懈努力，同时让读者们看到中国人民实现更加幸福美好生活的前进步伐。

2019年12月

目录

第一章
中国就业概况

一、中国就业基本情况

（一）概述

就业是民生之本。中国人口众多，劳动力资源丰富（见表1-1），解决好劳动者就业的问题，不断扩大就业，减少失业，一直是中国政府面临的重大任务。中华人民共和国成立70年来，中国政府始终对就业工作给予高度重视，把就业工作摆在经济社会发展的优先位置，为此作出了巨大努力，使就业形势保持长期平稳，对稳定经济社会全局和改善人民生活发挥了重大积极作用。特别是改革开放40多年来，伴随着经济体制改革以及劳动就业制度改革不断深化，计划经济体制下统包统配制度造成的就业门路狭窄、就业形式单一、就业活力不足的格局彻底改变。中国政府在大力发展经济的同时，采取多种措施创造就业岗位，扩大劳动者就业，经过几十年的努力，基本形成了适应社会主义市场经济发展要求的就业管理体制，市场机制在劳动力资源配置中的决定作用逐步显现，城乡劳动者的就业渠道明显拓宽，促进了就业总量持续增长，就业结构调整优化。在此过程中，根据《中华人民共和国宪法》（以下简称《宪法》）以及《中

表 1-1 人口数量和构成

年份	总人口 / 万人	16 岁以上人口 / 万人	经济活动人口 / 万人	按性别分				按城乡分			
				男性		女性		城镇		乡村	
				人口数 / 万人	比重 /%	人口数 / 万人	比重 /%	人口数 / 万人	比重 /%	人口数 / 万人	比重 /%
1952	57 482	—	—	29 833	51.9	27 649	48.1	7 163	12.5	50 319	87.5
1957	64 653	—	—	33 469	51.8	31 184	48.2	9 949	15.4	54 704	84.6
1962	67 295	—	—	34 517	51.3	32 778	48.7	11 659	17.3	55 636	82.7
1965	72 538	—	—	37 128	51.2	35 410	48.8	13 045	18.0	59 493	82.0
1970	82 992	—	—	42 686	51.4	40 306	48.6	14 424	17.4	68 568	82.6
1975	92 420	—	—	47 564	51.5	44 856	48.5	16 030	17.3	76 390	82.7
1978	96 259	—	40 682	49 567	51.5	46 692	48.5	17 245	17.9	79 014	82.1
1980	98 705	—	42 903	50 785	51.5	47 920	48.6	19 140	19.4	79 565	80.6
1985	105 851	—	50 112	54 725	51.7	51 126	48.3	25 094	23.7	80 757	76.3
1990	114 333	—	65 323	58 904	51.5	55 429	48.5	30 195	26.4	84 138	73.6
1995	121 121	—	68 855	61 808	51.0	59 313	49.0	35 174	29.0	85 947	71.0
2000	126 743	—	73 992	65 437	51.6	61 306	48.4	45 906	36.2	80 837	63.8
2002	128 453	—	74 492	66 115	51.5	62 338	48.5	50 212	39.1	78 241	60.9
2003	129 227	—	74 911	66 556	51.5	62 671	48.5	52 376	40.5	76 851	59.5

续表

年份	总人口 / 万人	16 岁以上人口 / 万人	经济活动人口 / 万人	按性别分				按城乡分			
				男性		女性		城镇		乡村	
				人口数 / 万人	比重 /%	人口数 / 万人	比重 /%	人口数 / 万人	比重 /%	人口数 / 万人	比重 /%
2005	130 756	—	76 120	67 375	51.5	63 381	48.5	56 212	43.0	74 544	57.0
2010	134 091	—	78 388	68 748	51.3	65 343	48.7	66 978	49.9	67 113	50.1
2011	134 735	110 932	78 579	69 068	51.3	65 667	48.7	69 079	51.3	65 656	48.7
2012	135 404	111 586	78 894	69 395	51.3	66 009	48.7	71 182	52.6	64 222	47.4
2013	136 072	112 197	79 300	69 728	51.2	66 344	48.8	73 111	53.7	62 961	46.3
2014	136 782	112 825	79 690	70 079	51.2	66 703	48.8	74 916	54.8	61 866	45.2
2015	137 462	113 296	80 091	70 414	51.2	67 048	48.8	77 116	56.1	60 346	43.9
2016	138 271	113 833	80 694	70 815	51.2	67 456	48.8	79 298	57.3	58 973	42.7
2017	139 008	114 289	80 686	71 137	51.2	67 871	48.8	81 347	58.5	57 661	41.5
2018	139 538	114 678	80 567	71 351	51.1	68 187	48.9	83 137	59.6	56 401	40.4
2019	140 005	115 028	—	71 527	51.1	68 478	48.9	84 843	60.6	55 162	39.4

资料来源：《中国统计年鉴》和国家统计局网站。

华人民共和国劳动法》(以下简称《劳动法》)、《中华人民共和国就业促进法》(以下简称《就业促进法》)等法律法规，国家在保证劳动者的就业权利的同时，采取各种政策措施积极促进就业，不断满足劳动者的就业需求，就业质量显著提升。特别是近十年来，在以习近平同志为核心的党中央领导下，全面实施就业优先战略和更加积极的就业政策，深化就业创业体制机制改革，不断强化各方面重视就业、支持就业的导向，实现经济发展与扩大就业良性互动，在推动经济高质量发展中创造更多高质量就业机会，为经济社会持续健康发展发挥了重要支撑作用。

（二）就业规模的扩大和就业结构的优化

1. 就业规模不断扩大

中华人民共和国成立 70 年来，就业总量从 1949 年的 1.8 亿人增加到 2019 年的 7.8 亿人，扩大了 3.3 倍，其中城镇就业人数达到 4.4 亿人，比 1949 年增加了 27.9 倍。

（1）从中华人民共和国成立到 1957 年，就业人数迅速增长。中华人民共和国成立（1949 年 10 月，以下同）时，全国就业人员达 18 082 万人，其中城镇就业人员 1 533 万人，城镇大量劳动力处在失业状态。各级人民政府在采取多种措施控制失业的同时，积极发展经济，努力扩大就业。1952 年，城镇就业人员迅速增加到 2 486 万人。1953—1957 年第一个五年计划期间，国家开始了大规模经济建设，有效带动了就业规模的迅速扩大。到 1957 年，全国就业人员达到 23 771 万人，比 1949 年增加了 5 689 万人，年均增长 3.5%；城镇就业增长更快，1957 年城镇就业人员达 3 205 万人，比 1949 年增长 1 倍以上，年均增长 9.7%。

从 1958 年开始，中国经济建设遇到曲折，就业规模波动较大、增长缓慢。其中 1961 年和 1962 年，每年减少就业近 800 万人。1978 年，全国就业人员为

40 152 万人，其中城镇就业人员为 9 514 万人，20 年间年均分别只增长了 2.1% 和 3.0%。

（2）改革开放后，城镇就业持续较快增长。改革开放（1978 年 12 月开始，以下同）以来，党和政府坚持以人民为中心，采取多种措施创造就业岗位，同时实现了经济发展与扩大就业。2019 年，全国就业人员达 77 471 万人，其中城镇就业人员达 44 247 万人，比 1978 年增长了 3.7 倍，年均增长 3.9%。尤其是中共十八大（2012 年 11 月召开，以下同）以来，在经济发展进入新常态的背景下，由于国家大力实施就业优先战略，落实积极的就业政策，推动创业带动就业，全国城镇就业总量增加了 7 145 多万人，平均每年增加 1 000 万人以上。

中国政府高度重视就业工作，每年都通过举办招聘会等多种形式为求职者提供就业岗位。

（新华社记者赵圣健摄）

2. 就业结构不断优化

中华人民共和国成立 70 年来，中国就业的城乡结构、产业结构、所有制结构不断优化，实现了就业的可持续发展。

（1）城镇就业逐年上升，比重已过半。1949 年，全国城镇就业人员仅占全国就业人数的 8.5%，大部分劳动者在乡村就业。中华人民共和国成立后，随着国民经济的逐步恢复，特别是工业化进程的加快，大量农村劳动力被吸引到城镇就业。1978 年，城镇就业人员达 9 514 万人，占全国就业人员比重升至 23.7%。30 年间，城镇就业比重增加 15.2 个百分点，平均每年提高 0.5 个百分点。

改革开放极大地解放和发展了生产力，释放了劳动力市场的活力，城镇就业人员数量迅速增加。2014 年，城镇就业比重首次超越乡村，达到 50.9%。2019 年，城镇就业人员达 44 247 万人，占全国就业人员比重进一步提高到 57.1%，较改革开放之初增加了 33.4 个百分点，平均每年提高 0.8 个百分点。

（2）第二、第三产业吸纳就业稳定增长。中华人民共和国成立之初，国家工业基础薄弱，服务业发展滞后，绝大多数劳动者从事农业劳动。1952 年，第一产业就业人员占比达 83.5%，第二、第三产业就业人员占比分别为 7.4% 和 9.1%。随着门类比较齐全的现代工业基础初步形成，第二、第三产业就业人员迅速增加。1978 年，第一产业就业人员占比降至 70.5%，第二、第三产业就业人员占比分别提升至 17.3% 和 12.2%。

改革开放以来，第二、第三产业吸纳就业人数逐年上升，到 1997 年就业总量超过了第一产业；到 2011 年分别达到 29.5% 和 35.7%，第三产业首次超过第一产业，成为吸纳就业人数最多的产业。自 2014 年以来，第一产业成为就业人数最少的产业，其就业人数占全国就业人员比重逐年下降。2018 年，全国三次产业就业人员分别为 20 258 万人、21 390 万人和 35 938 万人，占比分别为 26.1%、27.6% 和 46.3%（见图 1-1）。服务业蓬勃发展占主导的现代模式逐步形成，就业结构更加优化。2013—2018 年，服务业就业人数占全国就业人员比重

平均每年增加 1.7 个百分点，比 1978—2012 年的平均年增长率高约 1.0 个百分点。

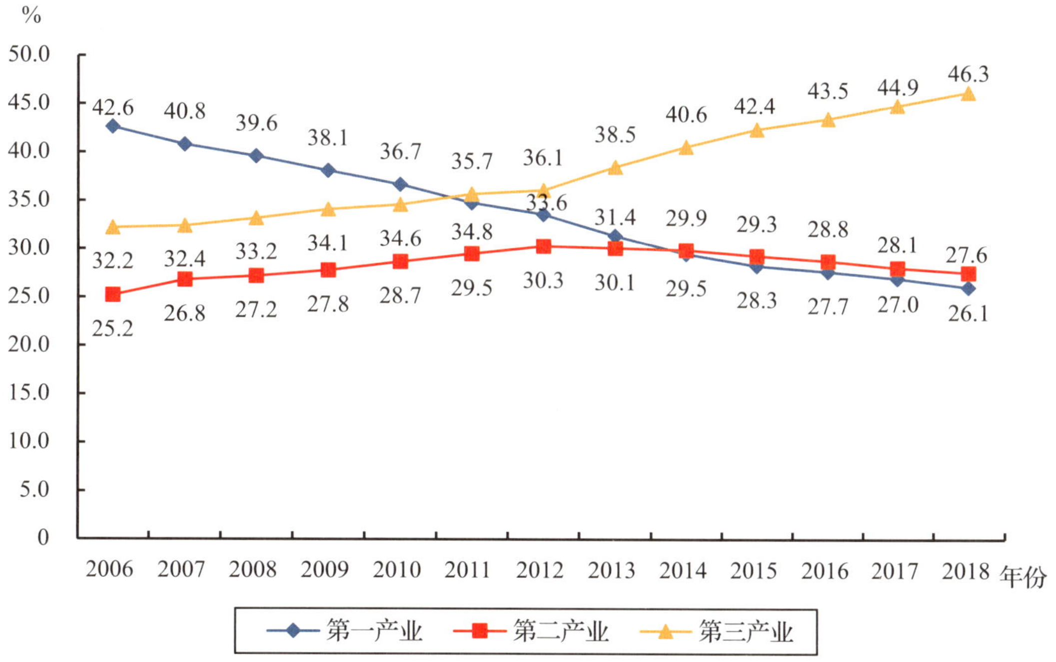

图 1-1　2006 年以来历年年末分产业就业人员构成情况

资料来源：《中国统计年鉴》和国家统计局网站。

（3）非公有制经济成为城镇就业主渠道。中华人民共和国成立时，个体私营经济在国民经济中还占有较大比重，个体劳动者占城镇就业人员的 47.2%。1956 年以后，公有制经济成为中国的经济基础，个体私营经济全面萎缩。1978 年，城镇 9 514 万名就业人员中仅有个体就业人员 15 万人，其他就业人口都集中在国有和集体单位。

改革开放以来，非公有制经济就业人数迅速增长。2018 年，城镇非公有制经济就业人员占比从 1978 年的 0.2% 提高到 83.6%，其中，城镇私营企业就业人员和城镇个体就业人员分别为 13 952 万人和 10 440 万人（见表 1-2），分别占城镇就业人员的 32.1% 和 24.0%。

表 1-2

就业基本情况

单位：万人

年份	就业人员合计	按产业分就业人员			按城乡分就业人员		按登记注册类型分城镇非私营单位就业人员								工商登记注册的私营个体就业人员			
		第一产业	第二产业	第三产业	城镇就业人员	乡村就业人员	国有单位	城镇集体单位	股份合作单位	联营单位	有限责任公司	股份有限公司	港澳台商投资单位	外商投资单位	城镇私营企业	城镇个体	乡村私营企业	乡村个体
1952	20 729	17 317	1 531	1 881	2 486	18 243	—	—	—	—	—	—	—	—	—	883	—	—
1957	23 771	19 309	2 142	2 320	3 205	20 566	—	—	—	—	—	—	—	—	—	104	—	—
1958	26 600	15 490	7 076	4 034	5 300	21 300	—	—	—	—	—	—	—	—	—	106	—	—
1962	25 910	21 276	2 059	2 575	4 537	21 373	—	—	—	—	—	—	—	—	—	216	—	—
1965	28 670	23 396	2 408	2 866	5 136	23 534	—	—	—	—	—	—	—	—	—	171	—	—
1970	34 432	27 811	3 518	3 103	6 312	28 120	—	—	—	—	—	—	—	—	—	96	—	—
1975	38 168	29 456	5 152	3 560	8 222	29 946	6 426	1 772	—	—	—	—	—	—	—	24	—	—
1980	42 361	29 122	7 707	5 532	10 525	31 836	8 019	2 425	—	—	—	—	—	—	—	81	—	—
1985	49 873	31 130	10 384	8 359	12 808	37 065	8 990	3 324	—	—	—	—	—	—	—	450	—	—
1990	64 749	38 914	13 856	11 979	17 041	47 708	10 346	3 549	—	—	—	—	—	—	57	614	113	1 491
1995	68 065	35 530	15 655	16 880	19 040	49 025	11 261	3 147	—	—	—	—	—	—	485	1 560	471	3 054
2000	72 085	36 043	16 219	19 823	23 151	48 934	8 102	1 499	155	42	687	457	310	332	1 268	2 136	1 139	2 934
2005	74 647	33 442	17 766	23 439	28 389	46 258	6 488	810	188	45	1 750	699	557	688	3 458	2 778	2 366	2 123

续表

年份	就业人员合计	按产业分就业人员			按城乡分就业人员		按登记注册类型分城镇非私营单位就业人员								工商登记注册的私营个体就业人员			
		第一产业	第二产业	第三产业	城镇就业人员	乡村就业人员	国有单位	城镇集体单位	股份合作单位	联营单位	有限责任公司	股份有限公司	港澳台商投资单位	外商投资单位	城镇私营企业	城镇个体	乡村私营企业	乡村个体
2010	76 105	27 931	21 842	26 332	34 687	41 418	6 516	597	156	36	2 613	1 024	770	1 053	6 071	4 467	3 347	2 540
2011	76 420	26 594	22 544	27 282	35 914	40 506	6 704	603	149	37	3 269	1 183	932	1 217	6 912	5 227	3 442	2 718
2012	76 704	25 773	23 241	27 690	37 102	39 602	6 839	590	149	39	3 787	1 243	969	1 246	7 557	5 643	3 739	2 986
2013	76 977	24 171	23 170	29 636	38 240	38 737	6 365	566	108	25	6 069	1 721	1 397	1 566	8 242	6 142	4 279	3 193
2014	77 253	22 790	23 099	31 364	39 310	37 943	6 312	537	103	22	6 315	1 751	1 393	1 562	9 857	7 009	4 533	3 575
2015	77 451	21 919	22 693	32 839	40 410	37 041	6 208	481	92	20	6 389	1 798	1 344	1 446	11 180	7 800	5 215	3 882
2016	77 603	21 496	22 350	33 757	41 428	36 175	6 170	453	86	18	6 381	1 824	1 305	1 361	12 083	8 627	5 914	4 235
2017	77 640	20 944	21 824	34 872	42 462	35 178	6 064	406	77	13	6 367	1 846	1 290	1 291	13 327	9 348	6 554	4 878
2018	77 586	20 258	21 390	35 938	43 419	34 167	5 740	347	66	12	6 555	1 875	1 153	1 212	13 952	10 440	7 424	5 597

资料来源：国家统计局网站。

（三）就业质量的提升和就业公平的体现

1. 就业质量显著提升

中华人民共和国成立 70 年来，尤其是改革开放以来，在就业总量增加和结构优化的同时，就业质量也日益受到重视。中共十八大以来，中国政府更加强调要推动高质量就业。在经济发展和政策措施的带动下，就业质量显著提升。

（1）就业人员素质大幅度提高。中华人民共和国成立时，文化教育十分落后，劳动者普遍处在文盲、半文盲状态，接受过高等教育的人极少。通过发展正规学校教育，举办“扫盲班”“夜校”等多种形式，劳动者的文化素质得到快速提高。

改革开放后，教育事业的发展促使国民素质显著提升，加之市场导向就业机制的逐步形成，劳动者为了提升其在劳动力市场中的竞争力，也更加注重自身素质的提高。据初步测算，2018 年就业人员与 1982 年相比，大专及以上受教育程度人员占比由 0.9% 上升到 20.1%，高中受教育程度人员占比由 10.5% 提高到 18.0%，初中受教育程度人员占比由 26.0% 提高到 43.2%，小学及以下受教育程度人员占比由 62.6% 下降到 18.7%。

中国开展各类职业培训，包括就业前培训、在职培训、转业培训和创业培训，并实行劳动预备制和各种培训技能开发计划，建立健全职业能力评价和职业资格证书制度。技工学校是以培养技术工人为主、同时开展各类长短期培训的综合性职业培训基地，2017 年在校生达到 338 万人，面向社会培训 456 万人。企业和各类培训机构培训的人员每年达到 1 500 万人以上。2015 年，全国技能劳动者达到 1.65 亿人，其中高技能人才达 4 501 万人，占 27.3%。

（2）工资收入快速增长。改革开放前，全国平均工资增长较慢。1952—1978 年，全部职工年平均工资从 445 元增加到 615 元，增长了 38.2%，扣除物价因素，实际仅增长 10.3%。

改革开放后，经济发展不断迈上新台阶，再加上政府出台最低工资标准等一系列政策措施，城镇就业人员年平均工资快速增长。2018 年，全国城镇单位就业人员年平均工资达到 82 413 元（见表 1-3），是 1978 年的 134 倍，年均增长率达到 13.0%，扣除物价因素，实际增长了 18.3 倍，年均实际增长率为 7.7%。

表 1-3 分登记注册类型城镇单位就业人员年平均工资及指数

年份	年平均工资 / 元				指数（以上年为 100）			
	合计	国有单位	城镇集体单位	其他单位	合计	国有单位	城镇集体单位	其他单位
1981	772	812	642	—	101.3	101.1	103.0	—
1982	798	836	671	—	103.4	103.0	104.5	—
1983	826	865	698	—	103.5	103.5	104.0	—
1986	1 329	1 414	1 092	1 629	115.8	116.6	112.9	113.4
1987	1 459	1 546	1 207	1 879	109.8	109.3	110.5	115.3
1988	1 747	1 853	1 426	2 382	119.7	119.9	118.1	126.8
1989	1 935	2 055	1 557	2 707	110.8	110.9	109.2	113.6
1991	2 340	2 477	1 866	3 468	109.3	108.5	111.0	116.1
1992	2 711	2 878	2 109	3 966	115.9	116.2	113.0	114.4
1993	3 371	3 532	2 592	4 966	124.3	122.7	122.9	125.2
1994	4 538	4 797	3 245	6 302	134.6	135.8	125.2	126.9
1996	5 980	6 207	4 312	8 521	111.8	111.8	109.6	110.3
1997	6 444	6 679	4 516	9 092	107.8	107.6	104.7	106.7
1998	7 446	7 579	5 314	9 241	115.5	113.5	117.7	101.6
1999	8 319	8 443	5 758	10 142	111.7	111.4	108.4	109.8
2001	10 834	11 045	6 851	12 437	116.1	117.0	109.8	110.7
2002	12 373	12 701	7 636	13 486	114.2	115.0	111.5	108.4
2003	13 969	14 358	8 627	14 843	112.9	113.0	113.0	110.1
2004	15 920	16 445	9 723	16 519	114.0	114.5	112.7	111.3
2006	20 856	21 706	12 866	21 004	114.6	114.4	115.1	114.4

续表

年份	年平均工资 / 元				指数（以上年为 100）			
	合计	国有单位	城镇集体单位	其他单位	合计	国有单位	城镇集体单位	其他单位
2007	24 721	26 100	15 444	24 271	118.5	120.2	120.0	115.6
2008	28 898	30 287	18 103	28 552	116.9	116.0	117.2	117.6
2009	32 244	34 130	20 607	31 350	111.6	112.7	113.8	109.8
2016	67 569	72 538	50 527	65 531	108.9	111.1	108.4	107.6
2017	74 318	81 114	55 243	71 304	110.0	111.8	109.3	108.8
2018	82 413	89 474	60 664	79 453	110.9	110.3	109.8	111.4

资料来源：《中国统计年鉴》和国家统计局网站。

注：其他单位是指股份合作单位、联营单位、有限责任公司、港澳台商投资单位、外商投资单位。

（3）就业稳定性不断提高。改革开放后固定工限制的破除以及劳动合同制度的实行，促进了劳动力的流动，进而激发了劳动者的创造力。针对一些企业不签订劳动合同、随意解雇员工等现象，国家不断完善相关法律法规，加强劳动执法力度，规范劳动合同的签订，在保持劳动力市场活力的同时，不断提高就业稳定性。据人力资源社会保障部统计，2018 年全国企业劳动合同签订率达 90% 以上，全国经人力资源社会保障部门审查并在有效期内的集体合同累计为 175 万份，覆盖职工 1.55 亿人。同时，建立符合中国国情的政府、工会和企业三方协商机制，对涉及劳动关系的重大问题进行沟通和协商，并建立劳动争议调解仲裁和法律诉讼制度，将劳动争议纳入依法处理轨道。

（4）劳动保障持续加强。中华人民共和国成立 70 年来，中国的劳动保障制度经历了从无到有、从城镇到农村、从企业职工到城乡居民、从不完善到比较完善的发展过程，实现了从单位福利向统筹互济的社会保险的转变，建立起

比较健全的劳动保障制度。2019 年，全国参加基本养老保险人数由 1989 年的 5 710 万人增加到 96 748 万人，参加基本医疗保险人数由 1993 年的 290 万人增加到 135 436 万人，参加失业保险人数由 1992 年的 7 443 万人增加到 20 543 万人，参加工伤保险人数由 1993 年的 1 104 万人增加到 25 474 万人，参加生育保险人数由 1993 年的 557 万人增加到 21 432 万人。与此同时，中国政府不断完善职业安全与卫生的国家标准并全面贯彻实行，保证劳动者生产安全和健康。

（5）工作生活更加平衡。中华人民共和国刚成立时，国家实行单休工作制，全年法定休息日共计 59 天。改革开放后，为充分保障职工休假权利，经过多次完善，最终形成双休工作制，加上法定节假日和带薪年假后全年休息日可达 120 天以上。近年来，国家先后出台了一系列法律法规，对工时制度、加班费用进行明确规定，企业用工更加规范，超时用工问题得到缓解，有效减轻了劳动者工作负担。2018 年年底，全国企业就业人员周平均工作时间为 46 小时。

2. 公平就业更好的体现

（1）中国法律规定，劳动者就业，不因民族、种族、性别、宗教信仰等不同而受歧视。法律严禁用人单位招用未满 16 周岁的未成年人，为严厉查处非法使用童工和介绍童工就业的行为，中国政府通过加大执法监督力度，督促企业认真落实法律法规中有关平等就业的规定，纠正劳动力市场上的各种歧视行为，同时支持鼓励劳动者运用法律保护自身劳动就业权益。

（2）妇女就业和劳动参与率提高。中国法律对保障妇女就业权利作出专门规定，国家保护妇女享有与男子平等的劳动权利，消除就业性别歧视，实行男女同工同酬，保障女职工在经期、孕期、产期和哺乳期，以及在工作场所受到特殊劳动保护。妇女就业的领域不断拓宽，妇女就业的人数不断增长。中国城乡妇女就业人数从 1990 年的 2.91 亿人增加到 2017 年的 3.38 亿人，占全部就业人数的 43.5%；同期，城镇单位女性就业人员从 5 861 万人增加到 6 545 万人

（见表 1-4），占城镇单位从业人员总数的 37.1%。2018 年，中国女性就业人员占比继续增高，占全部就业人数的 43.7%。近些年，中国女性劳动力参与率保持在 70% 左右，在世界各国中居于前位。

表 1-4　分登记注册类型城镇单位女性就业人员年末人数

年份	就业女性 / 万人
2011	5 228
2012	5 459
2013	6 338
2014	6 546
2015	6 527
2016	6 218
2017	6 545

资料来源：《中国统计年鉴》和国家统计局网站。

（3）农村劳动者的转移和流动就业。在中国的工业化和改革开放进程中，农村劳动力的转移和城镇化发展是一个重要的标志。中国政府对农村劳动者进城实行公平对待、合理引导、完善管理、搞好服务的方针，大力加强就业服务和技能培训，保障他们的合法权益，并帮助他们解决转移到城镇的就业、社保、住房、子女教育和公共服务等问题。从 2008 年到 2018 年，从农业转移的农村劳动者从 2.25 亿人增加到 2.88 亿人，其中外出流动到城镇的就业者从 1.40 亿人增加到 1.73 亿人。

（4）困难群体的就业援助。中国法律要求各级人民政府建立健全就业援助制度，规定了就业援助的对象范围、主要措施以及就业扶持政策。中国政府采取各种有效措施，对就业困难人员实行优先扶持和重点帮助，拓宽公益性岗位范围，确保城市中有就业需求的家庭，至少有一人实现就业。从 2010 年到 2019 年，每年安置的就业困难人员都达到 160 万人以上。对农村贫困户也提出

了精准就业扶贫的要求，为他们安排能够提高技能的就业机会。到 2018 年年底，全国累计帮扶 988 万名贫困劳动力转移就业。

中国法律规定，国家保障残疾人劳动的权利，对残疾人劳动就业统筹规划，为残疾人创造就业条件。政府实行集中就业与分散就业相结合的方针，采取优惠政策和扶持保护措施，通过多渠道、多层次、多形式促进残疾人就业。同时，政府和社会组织积极开展面向残疾人的就业服务，为其免费提供职业指导、职业介绍和职业培训。到 2018 年，共对残疾人开展职业技能培训 200 万人次，全国残疾人就业达到 948 万人，就业率为 56%。

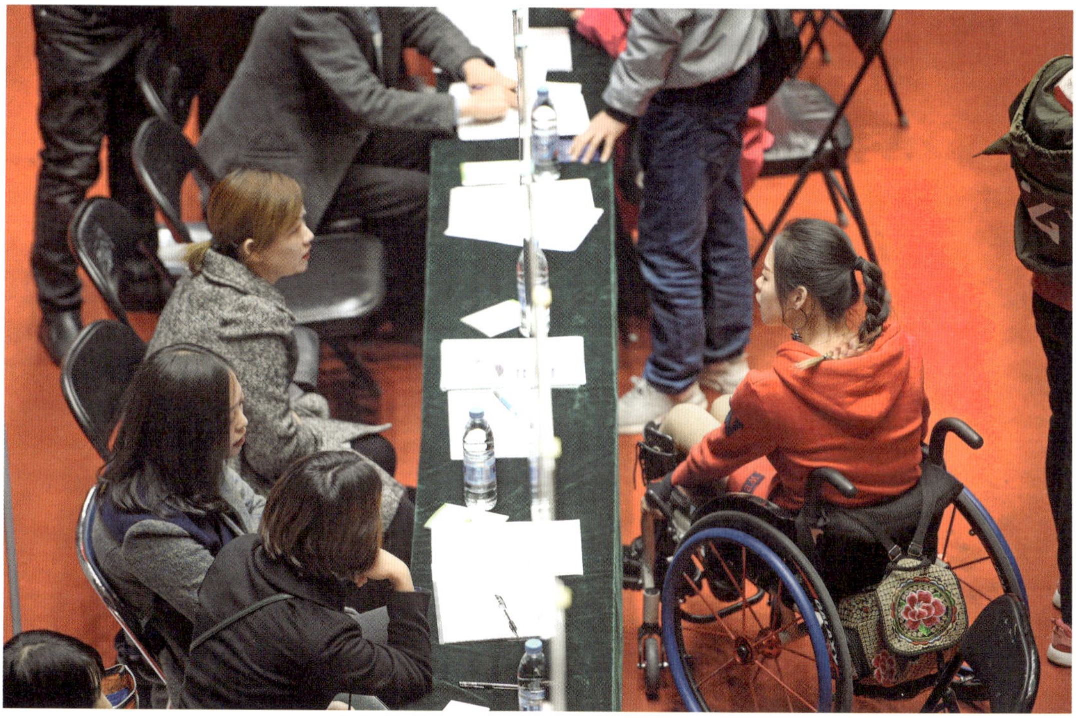

举办残疾人就业援助专场招聘会，帮助残疾人实现就业。（新华社记者冯开华摄）

二、就业政策和就业制度

（一）实现从统包统配到市场机制的跨越

计划经济时代，中国形成“统包统配”的就业管理体制，对城镇劳动者实行统一包分配就业，对企业用人实行计划指标统一管理，劳动力市场几乎完全消失，就业门路越来越窄，企业用人缺少活力，劳动者就业缺乏自主性。改革开放后，自20世纪80年代初开始实行在国家统筹规划和指导下，劳动部门介绍就业、自愿组织起来就业和自谋职业相结合的“三结合”就业方针，打开了就业的多种渠道。到了80年代中期，实行劳动制度四项改革，改变了企业固定用工制度。90年代初正式提出了培育和发展劳动力市场，而90年代末则制定实施了“劳动者自主择业、市场调节就业、政府促进就业”的新时期就业方针，市场导向的就业机制得以逐步建立和完善。城乡私营经济、外商投资企业快速发展，国有企业劳动用工自主权逐步扩大，劳动力市场迅速发展。经过几十年的培育和发展，劳动力市场逐步走向成熟，市场机制在人力资源配置方面的决定性作用不断加强。一是就业渠道多元化。通过私营企业、外资企业、自主创业和各类新就业形态实现就业的劳动者越来越多，大量农村劳动者在转移时选择进城就业。二是就业形式多样化。许多新就业形态不再有硬性的时间、地点限制，兼职就业、自由职业、灵活就业等不断出现。三是就业观念市场化。劳动者愿意为获得就业岗位或更高收入而进行流动，打破了城乡、地区、行业和所有制的界限，自主择业、自主创业、终身培训等新就业观念也越来越流行。

（二）就业法律法规体系日益健全

国家先后制定实施了一系列配套法律法规，确立了市场导向的就业机制的法律地位。1995年实施的《劳动法》，明确了劳动关系各主体的法律地位，以法律的形式规定各类企业实行全员劳动合同制，保障了企业自主用工、个人自主择业的权利，为劳动力市场的建设奠定了坚实的法律基础。2008年实施的

《就业促进法》，明确了就业工作在经济社会发展中的突出地位，将国家促进就业的方针政策制度化；明确了市场就业的决定性作用，促进用人单位自主用人和劳动者自主择业，引导劳动者合理流动；明确了政府促进就业的责任，主要通过政策引导和服务创造良好环境促进劳动者就业，并帮助困难群体实现就业；明确建立了面向全体劳动者的公共就业服务制度和体系，形成劳动者终身培训的制度和政策。2008 年实施的《中华人民共和国劳动合同法》（以下简称《劳动合同法》），完善了劳动合同制度，明确了劳动合同双方当事人的权利和义务，有利于构建并发展和谐稳定的劳动关系。

在《就业促进法》出台后，相关法律法规相继制定实施，同时随着一系列部门规章的配套出台，促进就业的法律法规体系逐步完善。

（三）就业政策和服务体系日益完善

中国政府从 2002 年开始创立积极的就业政策体系的基本框架，主要包括：有利于就业增长的经济政策、鼓励劳动者自主创业和灵活就业的政策、鼓励企业更多吸纳就业的政策、对就业困难人员的就业援助政策、加强公共就业服务的政策、强化职业技能培训的政策、加大就业资金投入的政策、做好失业调控和治理的政策、形成社会保障与促进就业联动的政策，等等。2008 年通过《就业促进法》的法律形式，将这套政策加以法制化、制度化。2008—2009 年在应对国际金融危机中，形成更加积极的就业政策。2012 年中共十八大以来，更加突出创业和就业紧密结合、支持发展新就业形态，并将政策深入为按照各类群体的特点分类指导施策。

总之，伴随着中国就业的发展变化和工作需要，积极的就业政策在解决不同阶段突出问题过程中，逐步形成了一套涉及面广、扶持力度大、项目内容丰富的较为完整的就业政策体系。这套政策不断充实完善和创新升级，指导和推进了全国就业创业工作一步一步取得新进展。

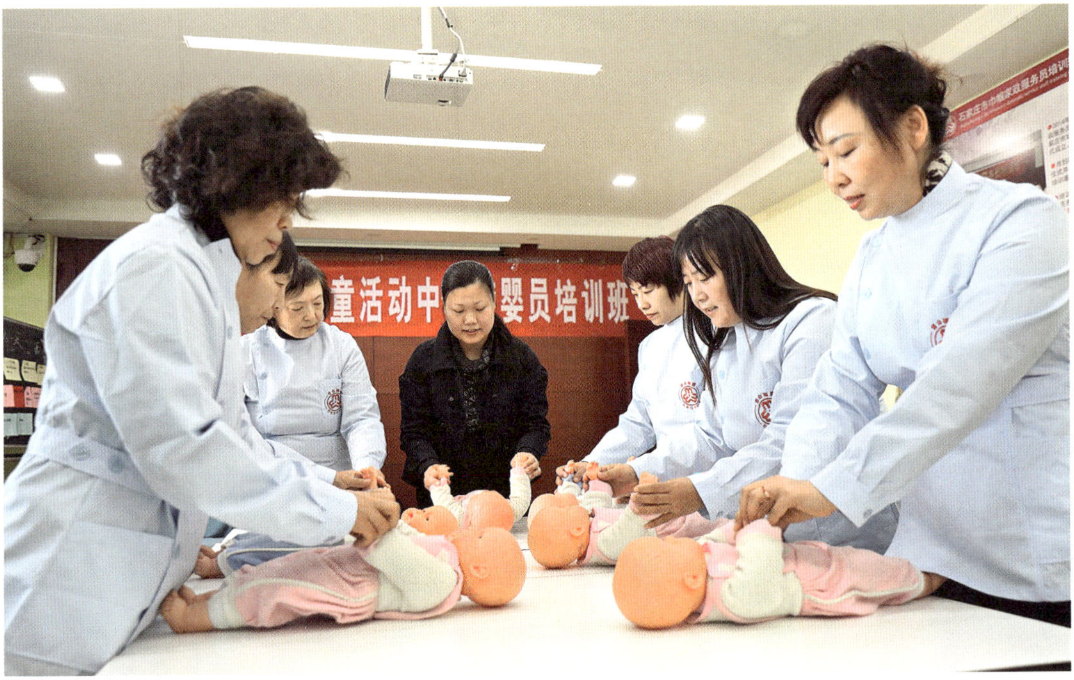

中国政府对再就业的劳动者免费开展职业培训。（新华社记者梁子栋摄）

中国政府为保障和改善民生，实施就业优先战略，为劳动者就业创业提供政策扶持和全方位服务。（新华社记者王家国摄）

在此过程中，中国逐步建立起分布在省、市、县、街道（乡镇）、社区（村）的五级公共就业服务网络，基本形成覆盖城乡、贯穿全程、功效齐全的全方位公共就业服务。加快就业服务信息化建设和街道社区服务体系建设，大力推行“一站式”和“一条龙”服务，为劳动者求职和用人单位招聘人员提供就业信息、职业指导、职业介绍、就业培训、创业指导、人力资源社会保障事务代理等多项服务。对劳动者的公共就业服务一律免费，由政府给予补贴。近些年，每年办理劳动者求职登记 4 000 多万人次，提供职业指导 1 600 多万人次。

三、促进就业的重大举措和经验启示

70 年来，中国共产党和政府始终把就业作为执政理国的头等大事，针对不同时期面临的不同就业压力，及时采取了相应的就业政策措施，不断改革就业体制和机制，使就业矛盾得到妥善化解，基本保持了就业形势的长期稳定。

（一）应对失业挑战的重大举措和成效

1. 迅速解决旧中国遗留下来的就业问题

1949 年中华人民共和国成立，由于历史遗留问题，全国城镇失业人员达到 474.2 万人，失业率高达 23.6%。党和政府采取多项稳定就业的措施，对原有失业人员采取“以工代振”“生产自救”等措施进行安置，并采取招收就业、介绍就业和自行就业相结合多种方式扩大就业。到 1952 年，城镇失业人员减少到 376.6 万人，失业率下降到 13.2%。随着第一个五年计划的顺利实施，就业状况进一步好转，到 1957 年，城镇失业率进一步下降到 5.9%。

2. 及时处理下乡知青返城就业问题

从 1962 年到 1979 年年末，全国累计下乡的城镇青年有 1 776 万人。1979 年对上山下乡政策作出调整，下乡的知青返回城市，一年内就达到数百万人。

1979 年，城镇累计待业人员达到 1 500 万人，城镇登记失业人员达到 568 万人，城镇登记失业率达到 5.4%。1980 年，中共中央提出“三结合”就业方针，采取了“劳动部门介绍就业、劳动者自愿组织起来就业和自谋职业相结合”的一系列政策措施，并开始进行就业管理体制改革。新政策的实施迅速解决了当时的城镇就业矛盾。1982 年，城镇登记失业率下降到 3.2%，全国多数地区基本解决了包括返城知青在内的城镇失业问题；1984 年，城镇登记失业率进一步下降到 1.9%。

3. 妥善化解下岗职工再就业问题

1998 年，由于经济结构调整和亚洲金融危机的影响，大量企业关闭破产，大批企业职工下岗失业。1998—2002 年间，国企下岗职工累计 2 023 万人，再加上 1998 年以前累积的下岗人员，国有企业下岗人员总量达到 2 715 万人。党和政府在保障下岗职工的基本生活的同时，制定实施了鼓励支持劳动者自主创业和企业吸纳再就业的税费减免、社会保险补贴、小额担保贷款[①]、培训补贴、就业服务等一系列政策，促进下岗失业人员再就业。1998—2005 年间，全国共有 1 975 万名国有企业下岗人员实现了再就业。到 2005 年年底，国有企业下岗人员存量已由最高峰的 650 多万人下降到 61 万人，基本消除了企业职工集中下岗对城镇就业造成的冲击。

4. 应对突发自然灾害和国际金融危机对就业的冲击

2008 年 5 月，四川省发生特大地震，灾区大批劳动者失业。中央政府制定实施对灾区的就业援助特殊政策，开发公益性岗位，结合重建项目吸纳就业，加大扶持劳动者自主创业，动员全国其他地区开展就业对口援助，从而确保了灾区就业局势的基本稳定。

2008 年年底，国际金融危机扩散蔓延，中国经济也受到严重冲击，就业工

① 2015 年 4 月 21 日召开的国务院常务会议确定将小额担保贷款调整为创业担保贷款。

作面临严峻挑战：城镇新增就业骤减，企业关闭停产、岗位流失严重，农民工失业返回乡村，大学生毕业后就业面临困局。中央政府果断决策，在保持经济增长的同时，制定并实施更加积极的就业政策，通过发展经济拉动就业、帮扶企业稳定就业、政策扶持鼓励创业、重点人群统筹就业、强化培训提升就业、加强服务促进就业，形成一整套稳定和扩大就业的组合性政策措施，使中国经济和就业在全球范围内率先走出了金融危机的影响，实施更加积极的就业政策一年后，全国城镇新增就业从 2008 年 12 月的 38 万人 / 月，上升到 2009 年 12 月的 100 万人 / 月，2009 年年末城镇登记失业率下降到 4.3%（见表 1-5），基本恢复到金融危机之前的水平。

表 1-5　　年末城镇登记失业人数及城镇登记失业率

年份	城镇登记失业人数 / 万人	城镇登记失业率 /%
1978	530.0	5.3
1980	541.5	4.9
1981	439.5	3.8
1982	379.4	3.2
1983	271.4	2.3
1984	235.7	1.9
1985	238.5	1.8
1990	383.2	2.5
1995	519.6	2.9
2000	595.0	3.1
2005	839.0	4.2
2006	847.0	4.1
2007	830.0	4.0
2008	886.0	4.2
2009	921.0	4.3

续表

年份	城镇登记失业人数 / 万人	城镇登记失业率 /%
2010	908.0	4.1
2011	922.0	4.1
2012	917.0	4.1
2013	926.0	4.1
2014	952.0	4.1
2015	966.0	4.1
2016	982.0	4.0
2017	972.0	3.9
2018	974.0	3.8
2019	945.0	3.6

资料来源：《中国统计年鉴》和国家统计局网站。

5. 积极应对经济增速放缓的就业新形势

中共十八大以来，面对就业总量压力庞大，结构性矛盾突出，经济由高速增长转向中高速增长的局面，中国政府积极培育壮大新动能，大力发展服务业，优化营商环境，鼓励创业创新，支持民营企业和小微企业发展，保持了就业形势持续稳定。2013—2019 年，高校毕业生、退役军人、农村劳动者、困难人员等重点群体的就业得到保障，就业新形态、新机会不断涌现；全国城镇新增就业每年都在 1 300 万人以上；全国城镇调查失业率稳定在 5.0% 左右的较低水平，城镇登记失业率也保持在 4.0% 左右。

（二）中国就业的经验启示

中国政府在改革发展中探索了一条独具特色的就业工作道路，取得了令世人瞩目的成就，在此过程中获得的宝贵经验，为今后继续做好就业工作提供了启示和借鉴。

1. 坚持以人民为中心促进就业，牢固树立就业是民生之本的执政理念

坚持以人民为中心是中国政府执政为民的具体体现。就业工作关系到亿万人民群众的切身利益。就劳动者来讲，就业是民生之本，是人民群众最关心、最直接、最现实的重大问题，是保障和改善民生的头等大事；就国家来讲，就业问题是否得到解决，对整个经济社会都会产生重大影响，关系到社会能否稳定、国家能否健康发展，因此促进就业是安国之策。

回顾改革开放 40 多年来的历程，可以清楚地看到，在“文化大革命”结束后，正是因为千方百计解决了上千万返城知识青年的失业问题，社会才得以稳定，从而保证全党全国一心一意谋发展。在世纪之交，国家处于面临改革调整内在压力和金融风暴外在危机的关键时刻，正是因为聚焦解决下岗职工问题，并采取一系列促进再就业的切实有效措施，才取得了改革攻坚的胜利。进入 21 世纪，从面对重大灾害及时开展就业援助，到帮助灾区群众实现就业，再到积极应对金融危机冲击，实施更加积极的就业政策，从而为实现保增长、保民生、保稳定奠定基础。总结历史经验，最根本的一条就是要坚持以人民为中心，牢固树立就业是民生之本、促进就业是安国之策的理念，并将此作为就业工作的基本指导思想，在工作实践中贯彻始终。

2. 坚持市场导向的改革，明确并强化政府促进就业的责任

坚持市场导向的就业改革，是形成自主就业格局的根本动力。改革开放后，国家改革统包统配就业制度，广开就业门路，推动了组织起来就业和自谋职业；改革固定工制度，实行劳动合同制，搞活了企业用工；加强公共就业服务，形成了双向选择和自主就业的新格局；打破城乡分割，对农村劳动者转移就业提供政策扶持和就业服务，促进了城乡统筹就业和公平。正是这样一步一步地推进，形成市场导向的就业机制，鼓励和调动了劳动者自主择业的积极性；在深化改革中构建了统一规范灵活的人力资源市场，发挥市场调节的基础作用，

不仅促进了人力资源的合理流动和优化配置，并且推动了人力资源的充分开发和有效利用。

不断强化政府促进就业的责任，充分发挥政府职能作用，是解决就业问题的重要保证。党和政府将就业作为民生之本和经济社会发展的重要战略，特别是在当时市场机制不健全、劳动者能动性不充分的情况下，政府还要承担培育市场机制、规范市场行为、弥补市场缺陷和不足、援助困难群体就业的责任，通过实施执行扩大就业的发展战略和实施积极的就业政策，加大财政投入，强化公共服务，推动就业再就业工作取得了积极进展，并有效保障了劳动者的就业权益。在推动创业的过程中，也要发挥政府主导作用，制定相应的法律法规来保护和支持劳动者创业活动，鼓励劳动者通过自主创办生产服务项目、创办企业，带动更多人实现就业。同时，政府通过加强服务和保障来帮助创业者畅通创业之路，减少其后顾之忧。总之，将强化政府责任与更好地发挥劳动者自主积极性进行了有机结合。

3. 坚持就业优先，推进发展经济与扩大就业良性互动

进入 21 世纪，中国政府学习研究国际社会，特别是发达国家的发展经验，不断更新和完善发展理念，纠正只注重经济发展和国内生产总值（GDP）指标的倾向，把保障和改善民生作为经济社会发展的重要方向，把促进就业和实现充分就业作为国民经济与社会发展的优先目标，体现了对就业与经济发展关系的认识与对客观规律的把握和战略思维。进入新时代，中共十九大（2017 年 10 月召开）进一步提出以人民为中心的发展思想，为贯彻就业优先战略注入新的动力，作出了经济社会可持续发展的理性选择。

正确处理扩大就业与经济社会发展的关系，将扩大就业与经济发展紧密结合相互促进，是解决就业问题的根本途径。中国人力资源丰富的现实国情，也决定了中国政府必须长期实行扩大就业的发展战略，必须遵循经济社会发展的

客观规律，从实际出发，通过科学确定就业发展战略和目标任务，不断完善积极的就业政策，加大资金投入，强化公共资源服务等措施，使经济持续健康发展的过程成为就业持续扩大的过程。在经济发展的总体布局、要素投入、目标导向和具体安排方面，都要将扩大就业作为一项重要内容，在实现经济快速发展的同时，要创造更多的就业机会。

4. 坚持从中国国情实际出发，推进城乡统筹就业的发展

坚持一切从实际出发，确定任务目标和方针政策，是在解决好城乡就业问题上进行正确决策的重要基础。中国是一个人口众多、劳动力资源丰富的发展中国家，解决就业问题必须充分考虑到中国国情实际。从长期来讲，就业的主要矛盾是劳动者充分就业的需求与劳动力总量过大、素质不相适应之间的矛盾。进入到现阶段，中国的就业问题更呈现出复杂性：与发达国家、其他发展中国家和转型国家不同，他们主要面临的或是结构性失业，或是总量矛盾，或是转型失业，问题较为单一；而中国面对的是劳动力供求总量矛盾与就业结构性矛盾并存、城镇就业压力加大与农村富余劳动力转移加快同时出现、新成长劳动力就业与失业人员再就业相互交织的复杂就业问题，因此就业工作任务长期、艰巨而繁重。中华人民共和国成立后一度出现“消灭失业”的提法和将城镇劳动力大规模迁移到农村的做法，由于脱离国情实际，这种没有按客观规律进行的决策带来了极为深刻的教训。

5. 坚持与时俱进确定就业方针和政策，强化执行力，务求实效

回顾中国就业改革发展的历程，从最初主要解决国有企业改制过程中大量下岗失业人员的就业问题，到统筹促进各类劳动者就业，再到促进就业与鼓励创业相结合，伴随不同时期就业形势任务的发展变化，特别是在经济形势出现波动和就业工作面临新的重大问题时，中国政府都坚持与时俱进，确定每一时期的就业战略、就业方针和目标任务。在就业战略上，从坚持扩大就业的战略

到将扩大就业摆在经济社会发展更加突出的位置，直至坚持实施就业优先战略。在就业方针上，从坚持市场导向的就业机制，同时强化政府责任，实施积极的就业政策；到劳动者自主择业、市场调节就业和政府促进就业；再到实施更加积极的就业政策，把创业和就业结合起来，以创业创新带动就业。一是与时俱进。随着形势的发展而延伸、扩展、完善、提升，始终坚持开放性和包容性，不断借鉴汲取国际经验，鼓励地方结合自身实际去创造。二是积极主动。政策制定的出发点、落脚点，政策内容的积极因素，都始终坚持了对企业和劳动者积极性的调动。三是综合施政，狠抓落实。对政策的制定不仅有原则要求，更强调可操作性；在政策实施中，不仅考虑中央层面、地方层面，而且一竿子插到基层。在解决当前治标问题的同时，提出从制度上能够长远治本的举措，搞好战略研究和政策储备，为在关键时刻出台就业新政奠定基础。

中华人民共和国成立 70 年来，中国共产党和中国政府团结带领全国人民在就业领域取得了一系列辉煌成就，就业管理体制发生了翻天覆地的变化，劳动力市场日益完善，就业人数大幅度增加，就业形势保持了长期稳定。但在当前和今后一个时期，中国经济社会发展中还存在不少困难和问题，妥善解决就业问题仍是一项长期复杂的艰巨任务。为此，要坚持以习近平新时代中国特色社会主义思想为指导，深入贯彻落实中共中央、国务院关于就业工作的重要方针政策和一系列部署，坚持市场导向的就业改革不动摇，坚持政府促进就业的责任不放松，坚持发展经济与扩大就业良性互动不偏离，坚持统筹城乡就业发展不停步，坚定信心，真抓实干，为推动实现更加充分更高质量就业而努力奋斗。

第二章 就业优先：从战略到政策

一、就业优先的提出和发展

（一）就业优先的提出

就业优先是在20世纪90年代提出来的，以后在国际社会逐步形成共识。1995年在丹麦首都哥本哈根召开的联合国社会发展问题世界首脑会议宣言提出“将促进充分就业作为经济和社会发展政策的基本优先目标”，并建议各国实行“最大限度地促进创造就业机会的经济增长模式”。中国国务院总理代表中国政府和与会各国首脑共同签署了这个宣言。国际劳工组织在2001年通过的《全球就业议程》中提出，“各国政府应把充分的、生产性的和自由选择的就业置于经济和社会政策的核心位置”；在2019年《关于劳动世界的未来百年宣言》中提出，进一步采取以人为本构建劳动世界未来的方法，将工人的权利和所有人的需求、向往和权利置于经济、社会和环境政策的核心。中国政府参与了国际劳工组织这两个宣言的讨论，不仅赞同这些主张，并且在本国实际工作中加以贯彻。

20世纪末至21世纪初，正值中国改革的攻坚阶段。亚洲金融危机的爆发，

不仅使国家经济受到严重冲击，也使全国就业面临极为严峻的形势：城镇新增劳动力处于高峰，国有企业下岗职工问题凸显，农村富余劳动力流动加快，形成“三碰头”的局面。劳动力供需矛盾十分尖锐，结构性失业问题相当突出，就业问题成为影响改革发展和社会稳定的头号难题。值此关键时刻，中国政府及时作出了大力推进就业再就业的重大决策，中共中央、国务院于2002年召开最高规格的全国再就业工作会议，对做好就业再就业工作进行部署安排，明确提出“就业是民生之本、安国之策”的理念和扩大就业的国家战略，制定并实施积极的就业政策，由此开启了中国就业的新纪元。其后，伴随就业形势的发展，特别是在经济形势出现新变化和就业工作面临重大挑战时，中国政府都坚持从实际出发，确定每一时期的就业战略、就业方针和目标任务，指导中国就业与时俱进，沿着正确的道路健康发展。

（二）就业优先：从战略到政策的发展

1. 就业战略不断提升，就业优先愈加明确

中国政府对就业工作高度重视，根据经济社会发展，不断强调就业的重要地位和突出作用。国民经济和社会发展第十个五年计划纲要（2001—2005年）提出：“把扩大就业作为经济和社会发展的重要目标，实行有利于扩大就业的经济政策和社会政策。”国民经济和社会发展第十一个五年规划纲要（2006—2010年）明确“把扩大就业摆在经济社会发展更突出的位置，实行积极的就业政策”。国民经济和社会发展第十二个五年规划纲要（2011—2015年）对实施就业优先战略和实施积极的就业政策作出部署并提出要求，“坚持把促进就业放在经济社会发展的优先位置，健全劳动者自主择业、市场调节就业、政府促进就业相结合的机制”。国民经济和社会发展第十三个五年规划纲要（2016—2020年）进一步明确“推动实现更高质量的就业，把促进充分就业作为经济社会发展优先目标，放在更加突出位置”。2018—2019年，面对全国就业的新形势、

新任务，特别是复杂多变的国际环境和多种不利因素，为保民生、稳增长，在强调稳就业的同时，进一步提出“将就业优先政策置于宏观政策层面并使之全面发力”的新要求，将就业优先政策与财政政策、货币政策并列，置于宏观政策层面，使就业优先正式从目标转化为政策，实现就业目标、工具、手段的有机统一，这是中共中央、国务院审时度势、从全局和战略高度作出的重大决策。

“就业优先”已被列为“十二五”就业规划的方针和主线，把就业作为经济社会发展的优先目标具有重大的战略意义。

2. 就业方针与时俱进，就业任务逐步扩展

1980 年在改革就业制度和促进就业中，中国政府提出在国家统筹规划和指导下，实行劳动部门介绍就业、自愿组织起来就业和自谋职业相结合的方针，从而开拓了多种渠道，使一个时期积累的下乡知青返城就业和城镇新生劳动力的失业问题得到较好解决；2000 年以后，在深入改革和推进就业工作中，又进

一步明确坚持市场导向的就业机制，同时强化政府责任，实施积极的就业政策，同时实施劳动者自主择业、市场调节就业和政府促进就业的方针，不仅实现了市场就业的改革，促进了企业下岗职工再就业，并且推进了城乡统筹就业，推动城镇就业和乡村劳动者转移就业取得重大进展；在 2015 年又结合推动大众创业、万众创新和扩大就业，进一步明确劳动者自主择业、市场调节就业、政府促进就业和鼓励创业的方针。在实现稳定和扩大就业的同时，鼓励支持各类劳动者更多地创业并带动就业。由此可以看出，中国在就业工作中针对不同时期的情况，调整和确定就业方针，推动就业事业不断取得新的进展。

（三）实行就业优先，在保障改善民生和促进经济发展中具有重大意义和积极作用

1. 就业是保障改善民生的头等大事

中国政府从中华人民共和国成立后的 70 年经历中深深体会到，就业是保障和改善民生的头等大事。进入 21 世纪以来，中国政府更是明确提出，要将民生的保障和改善作为国家发展的出发点和落脚点。在中国，保障民生的具体领域可简单归纳为三个层面：一是保障人民群众基本需求方面，包括劳动就业、工资收入和社会保障；二是满足人民群众发展需求方面，包括教育、医疗和住房；三是确保人民群众安全需求方面，包括生活生产安全、生态保护和社会治安。在此过程中，还应满足人民群众的精神文化需求。在这些以民生为重点的工作中，就业关乎劳动者的生存和发展，事关亿万劳动者及其家庭的切身利益，既是保障和改善民生的经济社会基础和重要条件，又是全面实现小康与满足人民对美好生活向往的重要标志，所以被称为“民生之本”和“最大的民生”。

历史证明，从世纪之交的国企改革到 2008 年的应对国际金融危机，从 20 世纪 90 年代的民工潮到 21 世纪的城镇化，正是由于中国政府下大决心、花大力气做好就业工作，陆续为 3 000 万名下岗职工、上千万名大学毕业生、数以

亿计的农民工等群体打开了就业之门，提供了就业机会，解除了失业之忧，使劳动群众实现了有业可就和生计保障，不仅使国家平稳渡过了改革发展的一道道难关，并且也为民生的改善、劳动者的增收和社会财富的积累奠定了坚实基础。以 2001 年以来的情况为例，城镇就业人数从 24 123 万人增加到 34 687 万人（2010 年），再增加到 43 419 万人（2018 年），17 年中增长了 80%；城镇单位在岗职工人年均工资从 10 870 元提升到 37 147 元（2010 年），再提升到 84 744 元（2018 年），同期增长了 6.8 倍；人均 GDP 从 8 717 元增加到 30 808 元（2010 年），再增加到 64 644 元（2018 年），同期增长了 6.4 倍。这些都充分说明了就业在保障和改善民生方面具有极其重要的作用。

近十几年就业援助和就业扶贫的事实也证明，对于一大批城镇就业困难人员和农村贫困劳动者，如果仅仅给予救济，是难以为继的，只有使他们实现就业和再就业，依靠其自身的努力劳动取得收入，才能使他们及其家庭走出困境。以 2018 年为例，通过就业援助实现就业的城镇困难群体人员达到 181 万人，通过就业扶贫实现脱贫的农村贫困劳动者达到 388 万人。这些都说明就业在解困扶贫中发挥了重要作用。

2. 就业对经济发展具有支撑和保障作用

回顾中华人民共和国成立 70 年，特别是改革开放 40 多年的历程，可以看到，经济发展与就业增长的互动关系是客观存在的，又是不断变化的。总体上来讲，经济发展能够拉动就业增长，而促进就业增长对保持经济的健康发展也有重要积极的作用，两者应当相辅相成，但如果处理不好两者的相互关系，也可能产生负面的影响。

改革开放以来，中国经济和就业均呈现出持续增长的态势，1978 年以后的 40 多年里，GDP 年均增长率为 9.5%，城镇就业人数年均增长率为 3.9%。一方面，经济保持高速增长，就业人数也持续增加；另一方面，就业人口的增加和

劳动投入的加大，也推动了经济的持续增长。特别是第三产业的发展和就业的增长互促互动更为明显。2018 年与 1978 年对比，第三产业产值增加 51 倍，在 GDP 中的比重从 24.6% 上升到 52.2%，上升 27.6 个百分点。同期，第三产业从业人员人数由 4 890 万人（1978 年）增加到 35 938 万人（2018 年），增长 6.3 倍；占就业总人数比例由 12.2% 上升到 46.3%，上升 34.1 个百分点。

总结世界上一些国家出现的“高增长低就业”和“经济复苏而无就业”的教训，中国也针对国内一些时期、一些地区经济发展与就业增长不匹配的问题，进行了研究分析，并采取措施加以解决。一是改变以 GDP 作为衡量经济社会发展主要指标的倾向，防止出现经济增长与社会发展畸重畸轻，甚至偏离改善民生的发展方向。中央政府要求各级人民政府在执政理念和实际工作中将改善民生作为重心，实行就业优先战略，并以此作为经济发展的出发点和落脚点。二是改变经济发展中产业结构、企业规模、经济类型的不合理格局，防止经济发展与就业分离而产生经济高增长但拉动就业较少的问题，构建经济发展和就业增长相互匹配、良性互动的新模式，优化经济布局，使之更加有利于促进和扩大就业。三是改变人力资源结构对经济升级转型的不适应状况，着力解决针对现代制造业、服务业，特别是新兴产业、高技术行业和技能型职业所需人才的短缺问题。大力推进人力资源的充分开发和高效利用，促进人力资源要素与资本、技术、土地等要素的优化组合和合理配置，更好地激发劳动者的积极性、主动性和创新创业精神，加快建设知识型、技能型、创新型劳动者大军。四是与经济高质量发展同步，推动更加充分更高质量就业，以保持国民经济与居民收入同步增长、劳动生产率与劳动报酬同步提高，实现经济健康发展与民生持续改善的良性循环。

3. 实施就业优先，要从战略总体要求具化实化到政策措施

当前和今后一个时期，中国的就业总量压力不减，结构性矛盾更为突出。

企业急需的技术技能劳动者和熟练工人紧缺，从而导致招工难已成常态；困难群体人员在观念和能力上的差距导致其就业难度加大；劳动者流动频率过高导致就业不稳定性增加。特别是新技术快速发展带来机器换人的就业“挤出”问题；新经济新业态与传统用工和就业方式产生矛盾；不少企业面临产业转型和产能紧缩压力，尤其是小微企业经营困难，扩展就业的能力下降。在这些矛盾和不确定因素影响下，经济增长受到拖累，就业的滞后效应开始显现，结构性失业、周期性失业与摩擦性失业均有加剧趋势。对此，中国政府正在设计和实施针对不同地区、重点产业、各类企业和各类群体的一整套促进就业的政策工具和措施行动；同时，通过进一步加强宏观调控来保持经济平稳运行，运用相关政策来调节市场失衡，预防大规模裁员失业，努力保持就业持续稳定增长。

与此同时，在实现更加充分更高质量就业的过程中，中国政府不断采取有效措施改进实际工作和完善政策制度，以满足广大劳动者在工作机会和职业发展、薪酬合理增长、素质能力提升、就业安全稳定和社会保险福利等多元化的诉求。努力解决好新业态与灵活就业人员的劳动关系、社会保障、就业稳定性等问题；进一步增加劳动力市场的灵活性，提升公共就业服务能力，强化对劳动者的培训教育。

二、就业优先战略和政策的内涵

（一）基本要求

（1）坚持以人民为中心。实施就业优先必须进一步树立以人民为中心的发展理念，坚持执政为民，将保障和改善民生作为根本任务。坚持将稳定和促进就业作为惠民生的基础，从解决人民群众最关心、最直接、最现实的利益问题出发，为实现更加充分更高质量就业全面发力，使就业在实现全面建成小康社会的过程中率先达标。

（2）坚持与经济高质量增长良性互动。将稳定和促进就业作为国民经济和社会发展的优先目标，在处理好经济增长与高质量发展、旧动能转换与新动能培育、传统产业升级与新兴产业发展的过程中，把握好政策取向，使政策实施的结果更多更好地促进就业。必要时，效率效益及结构转换要适度让位于扩大就业和减少失业的目标，资本利益要适度让位于劳动要素利益，从而实现就业促进与经济增长的有机结合和互促共进。

（3）坚持与经济社会政策协调衔接。在与时俱进充实提升就业创业政策的同时，在宏观调控层面使就业政策加重分量，并加强与财政、货币、产业等宏观政策的统筹协同，促进就业创业政策与有关经济、社会政策配合衔接，形成相互协调整体联动的运行机制，营造综合施策、齐抓共管、共促就业的新格局。

（二）主要导向

（1）在经济社会发展总体布局中体现就业优先。将充分就业列为宏观调控的四大目标之首，努力实现战略制定、产业规划、投资政策、项目实施与扩大就业的有机统一。在制定实施经济社会发展规划及重大计划时，优先考虑就业任务目标和核心指标；在调整经济结构优化产业布局时，将其对就业的吸纳和提升能力作为重要考量标准；在规划区域发展和实施重大工程项目前，将对就业的专项评估列为前置条件和决策的主要依据，并将人力资源开发利用作为重要内容。

（2）形成促进经济增长与扩大就业相互匹配的良性互动。在经济发展出现的新增长点中，不断发掘新的就业增长点；从产业结构、经济类型、企业规模、就业形式等多方面切入，注重支持就业容量大、岗位质量高的产业行业，注重发展吸纳就业多的民营企业，注重扶持成本低、就业多的中小微企业，注重推动灵活就业和新形态就业，组合形成有利于就业不断扩展和经济持续增长、相互匹配、良性互动的发展模式。

（3）努力减少经济结构调整对就业的冲击。在推进经济结构调整，加快产业升级和产能新旧转换的过程中，把握好相关工作的力度、节奏和社会承受度，并将对劳动者权益的保障和再就业安排做在前面，努力减少冲击，保证劳动力转移调整的总体平稳。在应对国内外不利因素对重点地区、重点行业、企业的就业产生较大冲击时，将帮助企业稳定岗位、减轻企业负担、降低税费等专项性政策作为反周期调控工具，帮助一时遇到困难的企业渡过难关，从源头控制失业。

（4）发挥积极的就业政策在宏观调控中的作用。在扩大就业需求中强化促进创业带动就业政策，出台支持与新经济并行的新形态就业发展政策，在拓展就业的同时拉动经济增长；在改善就业供给中大力组织职业培训提升劳动者素质，在缓解就业结构性矛盾的同时为经济的高质量增长提供支撑；在调节匹配劳动力供求中加强全方位公共就业服务，并以就业援助兜住困难群体就业的底线；在应对大波动大冲击中坚持实施援企稳岗类专项政策，帮助企业职工渡过难关。

（5）制定和实施有利于促进就业的社会经济综合政策。将是否有利于促进就业作为制定、实施和调整社会经济综合政策的基本目标和核心内容，通过健全完善促进就业政策与财政税收政策、货币投资政策、产业调整政策及教育培训、收入分配等政策的协同配套，激励和引导有利于扩大就业的经济投入、产业调整、项目布局和企业发展；以实现就业为目标排定政策取向的优先次序，在促进就业的决定性因素和关键领域中实施激励或扶持性政策。

在经济发展的不同时期，根据实现就业任务目标的需要，中国政府及时提供财政资金、减免税费、创业信贷、调率降准等政策支持，以增加市场与企业活力和动能，助推新的就业增长点。相关部门与就业主管部门协同发力，一方面通过降低门槛、减少环节、简化手续、提供便利服务等措施，为就业优先政策全面发力保驾护航；另一方面对损害和伤及就业的政策和做法给予及时纠正。

为求职者提供就业政策、维权咨询等服务。（新华社记者张文魁摄）

三、实施就业优先的重要举措

（一）重点政策

（1）强化就业目标优先实现。一是实施把稳就业作为下限的宏观调控。把更加充分更高质量就业作为经济社会发展的优先目标，把保就业作为经济运行合理区间的下限，把就业指标作为宏观调控取向调整的决策依据。统筹考虑人口结构调整、经济运行变化和就业形势需要，科学设定就业目标任务，将其纳入国民经济和社会发展规划与年度计划。围绕就业目标实现需要，实施有利于扩大就业的财政、货币政策，有效运用逆周期调节工具，加强预调微调。二是健全就业统计监测机制。建立全国统一的就业信息监测系统。健全就业统计监

测质量控制机制，加强就业数据与宏观经济、市场大数据等的比对分析，提高就业形势分析研判能力。三是建立就业影响评估机制。制定改革发展、产业调整、社会管理等方面重要政策时，统筹考虑政策实施可能对就业吸纳能力、就业创业环境、就业质量、公平就业等方面产生的影响，将其作为风险评估报告的重要组成部分，优先选择创造岗位能力强的项目实施。在重大政策、重点项目、专项治理实施过程中，涉及企业关停并转的，应同步做好职工安置工作。四是建立就业风险应对化解机制。当就业形势趋紧、规模性失业风险上升时，通过加大减税降费力度、扩大失业保险基金支出范围、放宽劳动关系约束、暂缓调整最低工资标准、延长就业创业政策享受期限等阶段性措施，支持企业减负稳岗，并对劳动者的合法权益进行保障。

（2）加强宏观政策优先支持。一是产业政策更加突出就业优先导向。构建更有利于扩大就业的现代化经济体系，持续优化营商环境，支持农村一二三产业融合、传统制造业转型升级、现代服务业创新发展，支持小微企业、民营企业发展，打造“双创”升级版，引导劳动密集型产业与技术密集型、资本密集型产业协同推进。坚持包容审慎原则，引导零工经济、地摊经济、夜间经济发展，扩大灵活就业、新就业形态空间。二是区域政策同步推动人力资源有效配置。加快构建区域协调发展新机制，打破地方保护和区域分割，有力有序推进产业梯度转移，同步引导劳动力有序流动。聚焦困难地区精准施策，强化项目、岗位投放，支持困难地区稳定就业形势。提高新型城镇化发展质量，加快推进户籍制度改革，推动劳动力在城乡间双向流动、平等就业。三是民生政策强化与就业政策配套衔接。深化社会保障制度改革，加快推进养老保险全国统筹，便捷社会保险关系转移接续，方便各类劳动者自由流动。优化收入分配制度，坚持多劳多得，提高劳动报酬在初次分配中的比重，建设公平效率兼顾、激发就业活力的收入分配体系。合理确定失业保险金、最低生活保障、社会救助标准，增强失业人员、困难人员的就业意愿和就业稳定性。

（3）注重激发自主创业和新形态灵活就业的活力。一是加大对创业带动就业政策支持力度。创业是发挥劳动者自主性、能动性从而实现就业的重要途径，还具有带动更多就业的倍增效应。为此，国家在资金支持、信贷融资、税费减免、场地安排等方面，要给予创业更多的支持，并加强创业培训和创业咨询指导服务，弘扬劳动者的创业精神，鼓励他们通过自主创业、自筹资金、自主经营，创造更多的就业机会。二是实行更宽松并具有保障性的政策，鼓励支持劳动者在新形态就业和灵活就业中找到更多的工作和增收机会。

（4）推动人力资源优先开发。一是优化调整教育结构。主动对接国家战略和市场需求，建立就业与招生计划、人才培养、经费拨款、院校设置、专业调整的联动机制，优化适应经济社会发展的高等教育结构。完善职业教育体系，深化产教融合、校企合作，实施产教融合发展工程，推进高职院校扩招工作。大力发展技工教育，实施技工教育质量提升工程。二是健全终身职业培训制度。强力推进职业技能提升行动，全面推行企业新型学徒制，实施面向企业职工、重点群体的专项培训计划。扩大技能人才培养培训规模，实施高技能人才培养工程，加强高技能人才培训基地、技能大师工作室建设。三是加强培训基础能力建设。加大中央预算内投资支持力度，扩大公共实训基地建设覆盖面。培育一批产教融合企业。强化培训师资队伍建设，加大教材开发力度。实施新职业开发计划和急需紧缺人才职业培训计划，推广应用“互联网 +”培训模式。

（5）突出重点群体优先安排。一是落实完善重点群体就业创业政策体系。聚焦高校毕业生、农民工、退役军人等失业率高、就业难度大的重点群体，持续完善落实支持企业吸纳就业、鼓励劳动者自主创业、强化困难人员兜底保障的就业创业政策。二是促进高校毕业生等青年群体就业。深入实施高校毕业生就业创业促进计划和基层成长计划，引导毕业生主动对接国家发展战略和产业发展方向，到战略性新兴产业、中小微企业和基层就业。搭建职业指导、实践体验、培训见习等服务平台，精准提供就业服务。实施青年见习计划、就业启

航计划，强化失业青年帮扶。三是做好农村劳动力转移就业工作。建立适应乡村振兴的就业政策体系，引导农村劳动力有序外出就业、就近就地就业、返乡创业。完善就业扶贫长效机制，夯实扶贫车间吸纳、创业带动、有组织劳务输出、公益性岗位安置四条渠道，提高劳务组织化程度，解决相对贫困问题。

（二）保障措施

（1）确保就业责任优先落实。一是加强就业工作组织领导。充分发挥国务院就业工作领导小组作用，推动各部门履职尽责，发挥各类群团组织的积极性，凝聚就业工作合力。建立健全实行就业优先的多部门协同的就业工作组织领导机制，明确目标任务和责任单位，层层压实责任。坚持全国一盘棋，建立跨层级、跨部门、跨区域的重大风险协同应对机制。二是强化就业工作绩效考评。将就业目标完成情况、就业工作开展情况纳入高质量发展综合绩效评价机制和各级人民政府绩效考核体系。对在就业创业工作中取得显著成绩的单位和个人予以表彰激励，对不履职尽责、造成恶劣社会影响的进行批评追责。三是加大就业资金投入。持续加大各级财政就业补助资金投入力度，统筹用好失业保险基金、工业企业结构调整专项奖补资金等，对实施就业政策所需资金予以保障。强化资金管理使用监督，优化支出结构，提升资金使用效益。

（2）大力加强就业服务、权益保障和困难援助。一是构建全方位公共就业服务体系。健全覆盖城乡的服务机构网络，完善全国统一的就业失业登记制度，为劳动者和企业免费提供政策咨询、职业介绍、用工指导等公共就业服务，推进服务均等化和标准化。加快应用大数据、云服务技术，建立全国统一的公共就业创业服务信息平台，健全岗位信息归集发布制度，推进智慧化服务。简化优化服务流程，全面实行“一门、一窗、一网、一次”办理的便民化服务。二是加快发展人力资源服务业。实施人力资源服务业发展行动计划，着力培育重点骨干企业，加强人力资源服务产业园的统筹规划和政策支持，推动构建公共

服务和市场化服务各有侧重、互为补充的发展格局。三是强化劳动者权益保障。健全劳动关系协调机制，全面实行劳动合同制度，完善协调劳动关系三方机制，加快构建调解仲裁服务体系。强化人力资源市场监管，严厉打击就业歧视等侵害劳动者权益的违法行为和非法职介，营造公平良好的就业环境。四是兜住困难人员就业底线。健全就业援助制度，对困难人员实行优先扶持和重点帮助。对其中难以通过市场渠道实现就业的，通过公益性岗位托底安置，确保零就业家庭动态清零。对符合条件人员落实失业保险、临时生活补助、社会救助等保障政策。

第三章
积极的就业政策

一、积极的就业政策的产生

（一）积极的就业政策产生的时代背景

从中华人民共和国成立到20世纪90年代前期，中国为解决不同时期的就业问题，制定实施了一些重点政策和针对性措施，但没有形成系统性、持续性的就业政策。20世纪90年代以来，中国政府在着力解决下岗失业人员就业再就业和探索建立市场导向就业机制的实践中，不断积累、创新、完善，逐步形成了一整套具有中国特色的积极的就业政策体系。

（1）在解决下岗失业问题过程中，将再就业工作提上日程。20世纪90年代后期，随着国有企业改革的进一步深入，作为计划经济时代主要承担安置就业任务的国有企业，其内部的冗员问题日益凸显。加之亚洲金融危机冲击和全球性经济结构调整影响，国有企业出现大面积亏损，许多企业职工下岗失业。1998年6月，中共中央、国务院及时作出决定，将保障国有企业下岗职工基本生活作为首要任务，积极推进下岗职工基本生活保障、失业保险、城市居民最低生活保障相互衔接的三条保障线制度，并要求企业建立再就业服务中心，将

下岗职工留在企业再就业服务中心，为他们发放生活保障金，准备再就业。在当时市场就业机制不健全和社会保障体系不完善的情况下，这种做法作为一种过渡性的措施，起到了保障下岗职工基本生活的作用。但是到了2001年下半年，由于大批下岗职工离开企业再就业服务中心，社会失业人数陡然增长，长期以来积累的各种矛盾集中暴露，再就业难的问题集中凸显，促进下岗失业人员再就业成为迫切需要解决的问题。针对此，中国政府决定，在切实保障下岗职工基本生活的基础上，必须着力促进再就业，并将此作为关系到改革发展稳定大局的重要举措和完善社会保险体系的内在要求。

（2）在一个时期内需要面对就业的多种矛盾，先解决最主要矛盾。随着中国人口结构的变化和农村政策的调整，城镇新增劳动力在“十五”期间每年增长近1 000万人，正处于高峰，加上历年累积的下岗失业人员，每年城镇需要安排就业的人员达到2 200万~2 300万人，而每年新增就业岗位仅有700万~800万个，劳动力年度供大于求的缺口为1 400万~1 500万人。农村还有1.5亿名富余劳动力急需转移到新的就业岗位。这样就形成了国企下岗职工转轨就业、青年就业和农村转移就业同时出现、相互交织的“三碰头”局面。面对这一复杂局面，中共中央、国务院明确提出，要从长远大局考虑，统筹兼顾，解决好就业再就业的问题，更要在一个时期内抓住主要矛盾，突出工作重点，将有限的财力、人力集中到解决主要矛盾上。为此中国政府进一步明确，在这一时期主要突出一个工作重点，着力解决下岗失业人员的再就业问题。

全力做好下岗失业人员再就业工作。（新华社记者王鹏摄）

（3）在推进市场就业的改革中，需要以就业政策作为主导。1998 年，中国政府印发《关于切实做好国有企业下岗职工基本生活保障和再就业工作的通知》，提出“争取用 5 年左右的时间，初步建立起适应社会主义市场经济体制要求的社会保障体系和就业机制”的目标。同时强调了市场就业改革的内容，即要建立和完善市场就业机制，实行在国家政策指导下，劳动者自主择业、市场调节就业和政府促进就业的方针。政府在培育调节市场和促进就业的过程中，需要建立完备的政策体系和服务体系，包括制定促进就业、调控失业的政策；建立公共就业服务体系，对困难群体实施特殊帮助，等等。同时，逐步建立起较为完善的社会保障体系。

（二）制定积极的就业政策的基础

（1）中国经济的良好发展态势为此创造了有利条件。2002 年以后，中国经济进入一个高速增长阶段。经济快速发展有利于产业结构、行业布局及经济组织形式的调整和完善，一方面为扩大就业从而解决中国就业问题提供了广阔的空间，另一方面也从财政、税收、金融等方面为支持就业提供了物质条件。

（2）各地区和有关部门的探索与实践为此奠定了坚实基础。在前期实施“再就业工程”和国有企业下岗职工基本生活保障的实践中，各地区、各有关部门按照中央的统一部署和要求，在促进再就业方面进行了积极探索，为此奠定了坚实基础。比如，通过所得税减免，发展服务业扩大就业；通过税收优惠、小额信贷，鼓励下岗失业人员自谋职业和自主创业；通过给予工资补贴，帮扶就业困难人员再就业。同时，在加强就业服务和再就业培训方面也总结出了一些成功的经验做法。

（3）发达国家的有益经验为此提供了重要借鉴。原劳动和社会保障部组织专项研究发现，不少国家的政府都把促进就业作为其施政纲领的重要内容，注重运用税收、财政、信贷、贸易以及人力资本投资等政策来促进就业，化解失

业压力，“熨平”经济周期中失业率的波动。国际上比较通行的做法是鼓励支持中小型企业发展，扶持失业者自主创业，提供找工作补助，实行岗位或工资补贴，鼓励企业吸纳困难人员就业等。这些做法都值得借鉴。结合中国国情，认真学习汲取他国有益经验。这些经验做法为中国制定积极的就业政策拓宽了思路。

（三）制定积极的就业政策的主要导向

（1）推动经济发展与扩大就业良性互动，拓展新的就业门路。积极探索有利于扩大就业的经济发展方式，推动就业总量不断增加。通过优化产业结构，加快发展服务业、个体私营等非公有制经济和中小企业，开辟新就业门路。一是大力发展第三产业，开发社区服务业。二是鼓励发展多种所有制经济，积极发展有市场需求的劳动密集型企业和中小企业，以更多地吸纳下岗失业人员。三是促进跨地区的劳务协作和对外劳务输出。四是支持有条件的国有大中型企业主辅分离和辅业改制，分流和安置企业富余人员。五是鼓励更多下岗失业人员自主创业和灵活就业。

（2）鼓励劳动者自主就业创业。解决下岗失业问题，不能只是消极地依靠失业保险、下岗职工基本生活保障，而应积极地、更多更快更好地促进就业。其中一个重要内容就是鼓励和支持劳动者自主创业，促进以创业带动就业。完善支持自主创业、自谋职业政策，包括通过小额担保贷款和财政贴息政策解决融资问题，通过税费减免政策减轻经营负担，通过提供创业培训补贴提升创业者能力，同时在经营场地上也予以支持。

（3）加强职业培训和就业服务。一是明确将培训作为促进就业再就业的重要基础和有效手段，建立健全面向全体劳动者的职业培训体系，组织开展多层次、多形式的技能培训，实行“订单”培训和定向培训，增强培训的实用性和有效性；开展创业培训和开业指导，并提供项目咨询、跟踪扶持等服务。二是建立和完善覆盖城乡的就业服务体系，推行“一站式”和“一条龙”服务，为

劳动者求职和用人单位招聘人员提供就业信息、职业指导、职业介绍、就业培训、创业指导、人力资源社会保障事务代理等服务。加快就业服务信息化建设和街道社区服务体系建设。对劳动者再就业培训和就业服务一律免费，由政府给予补贴。

二、积极的就业政策的发展阶段

中国积极的就业政策从 2002 年创立发展至今，大体经历了四个阶段（见表 3-1）。

（一）应对经济调整，创立和扩展积极的就业政策阶段（2002—2007 年）

20 世纪末至 21 世纪初，亚洲金融危机爆发，中国经济受到严重冲击，此时正值中国改革的攻坚阶段，就业形势严峻，中共中央、国务院在认真总结前期实施“再就业工程”和“两个确保”经验的基础上，作出了大力推进就业再就业的重大决策部署，于 2002 年 9 月召开全国再就业工作会议，并在同月下发了进一步做好下岗失业人员再就业工作的重要政策文件，其基本指导思想是：依靠经济发展带动就业，创造更多岗位；完善市场机制，坚持市场导向基础作用；强化政府责任，切实发挥政府促进就业再就业作用。文件提出五大支柱政策：一是提高经济增长对就业的拉动能力的宏观经济政策；二是促进下岗失业人员再就业的扶持政策；三是通过加强就业服务和职业培训促进市场供求合理匹配的劳动力市场政策；四是规范企业减员、引导大企业分流富余人员，减轻社会失业压力的失业调控政策；五是继续做好保障下岗失业人员，特别是困难群体基本生活的社会保障政策。为推动政策落实，劳动和社会保障部等十一个部门和单位协同制定出台了八个相互衔接配套具有可操作性的文件。与此同时，在国家和地方层面建立了就业工作部门联席会制度、就业工作目标责任制度和

表 3-1　　中国积极的就业政策的创立和发展

阶段 内容	创立扩展阶段 （2002—2007 年）	应对危机阶段 （2008—2011 年）	提升创新阶段 （2012—2017 年）	纳入宏观政策阶段 （2018 年至今）
战略任务	将促进再就业和扩大城乡就业作为重要目标	把稳定和扩大就业放在突出位置，实施扩大就业战略	把促进就业创业作为经济社会发展的优先目标，把稳定和扩大就业作为区间调控的下限，实施就业优先战略，推动实现更高质量就业	将就业优先政策置于宏观政策层面并使之全面发力，推动实现和更加充分更高质量就业
针对目标	应对结构调整，解决再就业问题，启动城乡统筹就业	应对自然灾害和国际金融突发危机，稳定和扩大就业	应对转型升级，把创业和就业结合起来，以创业创新带动就业	应对经济下行压力、国内外多变因素和贸易摩擦冲击，以稳就业来推动稳增长
对象内容	重点做好国有企业下岗失业人员再就业工作、农村富余劳动力转移就业和城镇新增劳动力就业工作	启动援企稳岗，重点做好企业职工稳定就业、加强高校毕业生开发就业、失业人员再就业、农民工流动就业和复转军人安置就业工作	鼓励支持各类创业者自主创业带动就业，统筹推进重点群体就业，加强对困难人员的就业援助	扩大援企稳岗支持企业稳定就业，加大鼓励支持就业创业和新形态灵活就业的力度，组织企业职工、重点群体、贫困劳动者开展大规模培训，实行援助帮扶失业人员和困难群体就业
标志性政策	《中共中央　国务院关于进一步做好下岗失业人员再就业工作的通知》 《国务院关于进一步加强就业再就业工作的通知》（国发〔2005〕36 号） 《就业促进法》（2007 年中华人民共和国主席令第 70 号）	《国务院关于做好当前经济形势下就业工作的通知》（国发〔2009〕4 号） 《国民经济和社会发展第十二个五年规划纲要》	《国务院关于批转促进就业规划（2011—2015 年）的通知》（国发〔2012〕6 号） 《国务院关于进一步做好新形势下就业创业工作的意见》（国发〔2015〕23 号） 《国务院关于做好当前和今后一段时期就业创业工作的意见》（国发〔2017〕28 号）	《国务院关于做好当前和今后一个时期促进就业工作的若干意见》（国发〔2018〕39 号） 《国务院办公厅关于印发职业技能提升行动方案（2019—2021 年）的通知》（国办发〔2019〕24 号）

就业工作监督检查机制并发挥效用。建立健全就业服务体系并开始向街道社区延伸。

到 2005 年年底，国有企业下岗失业问题已大部分得到解决，但在新的就业形势下又出现了新的问题，比如实现再就业的人员需要稳定，集体企业下岗失业问题、农民工流动就业和青年就业问题日益突出。2005 年 11 月，国务院对原有政策进行了延续、扩展、调整和充实，增强了政策的针对性和有效性。中国政府明确提出，在重点解决好体制转轨遗留的下岗失业人员再就业的同时，还要努力做好城镇新增劳动力就业和农村富余劳动力转移就业工作，有步骤地提高城乡统筹就业和劳动者素质，探索建立市场经济条件下促进就业的长效机制。

2007 年 8 月，第十届全国人民代表大会常务委员会第二十九次会议审议通过了《就业促进法》，并于 2008 年 1 月 1 日起施行。《就业促进法》确立了五项就业制度：①政府就业工作责任制度；②公共就业服务和就业援助制度；③人力资源市场管理制度；④职业能力开发制度；⑤失业保险及预防制度。同时确定了十项就业促进政策：①产业促进就业政策；②财政促进就业政策；③税收促进就业政策；④金融促进就业政策；⑤城乡统筹就业促进政策；⑥区域统筹就业促进政策；⑦群体统筹就业促进政策；⑧促进灵活就业的劳动和社会保险政策；⑨就业援助政策；⑩失业保险促进就业政策。该法将扩大就业作为经济社会发展的重要目标，明确了就业工作在经济社会发展中的重要地位，明确了政府在促进就业工作中的重要职责，并将行之有效的积极的就业政策法制化、长效化。

（二）应对危机，制定实施更加积极的就业政策阶段（2008—2011 年）

2008 年，中国发生特大地震，同时，国际金融危机扩散蔓延，中国经济受

到严重冲击，就业工作面临严峻挑战。城镇新增就业骤降，企业关闭停产岗位流失严重，上千万名农民工失业返乡，几百万名大学生毕业后就业面临困局。面对危机，中共中央、国务院果断决策，在保持经济增长的同时，实施更加积极的就业政策。从 2008 年 9 月底到 2009 年 2 月初短短不到半年的时间里，国务院制定实施关于做好当前经济形势下就业工作的重大政策，并由各有关部门配套出台相关措施，由此启动了更加积极的就业政策，主要包括：①发展经济拉动就业；②帮扶企业稳定就业；③开启创业带动就业；④实施特别职业培训计划；⑤开展公共就业服务系列活动；⑥针对高校毕业生、农村劳动者和就业困难人员等重点群体采取专项促进就业措施。与此同时，中央财政进一步加大了对就业经费的投入。在这一时期实行的 4 万亿元投资保增长拉动就业、对困难企业“五缓四减三补贴”[①]稳定就业、促进以创业带动就业等举措更是对稳定就业局势和消除突发危机对就业的不利影响起到了关键作用。

2011 年，《国民经济和社会发展第十二个五年规划纲要》中对实施就业优先战略和更加积极的就业政策作出重要部署，并将在应对重大危机挑战中形成的一系列重要措施充实到政策内容中来，由此形成了更加积极的就业政策体系。

（三）应对转型，提升创新积极的就业政策阶段（2012—2017 年）

国务院印发《关于批转促进就业规划（2011—2015 年）的通知》，这是政府履行促进就业职责的重要依据。《促进就业规划（2011—2015 年）》以“十二五”时期经济社会发展为主线、紧密结合保障和改善民生需要，把促进就业作为经济社会发展的优先目标，要求实施更加积极的就业政策和鼓励创

---

① 允许困难企业在一定期限内缓缴养老、失业、医疗、工伤、生育保险五项社会保险费；阶段性降低城镇职工基本医疗保险、失业保险、工伤保险、生育保险四项社会保险费率；使用失业保险基金向困难企业支付社会保险补贴或岗位补贴，使用就业专项资金支持困难企业开展职工在岗培训。

业，不断拓宽就业渠道，使经济结构调整、加快转变经济发展方式的进程变成对就业拉动能力不断提高的过程，并在扩大就业规模的同时注重提升就业质量。2012 年 7 月，国务院举行全国就业创业工作表彰大会，强调促进就业是保障和改善民生的头等大事，要进一步提高对就业工作极端重要性的认识，切实把促进就业创业摆在各项工作的优先位置。11 月，中共十八大报告明确提出要推动实现更高质量的就业。为促进创业带动就业，增强就业稳定性，国务院相继出台扶持小微企业发展，支持以高校毕业生为重点的青年群体和困难群体就业创业，完善城乡均等公共就业创业服务体系，构建劳动者终身职业培训体系，增强失业保险制度预防失业、促进就业功能等系列政策举措。

随着中国经济发展进入新常态，在经济下行的状况下，就业工作面临新的挑战，需要着力培育大众创业、万众创新引擎，实施更加积极的就业政策，把创业和就业结合起来，以创业创新带动就业，催生经济社会发展新动力。2015 年 4 月，国务院对进一步做好新形势下就业创业工作的提出指导意见：一是继续实施就业优先战略和积极的就业政策，使覆盖范围更广泛；二是积极推动创业带动就业，使政策措施更具体；三是统筹推进重点群体就业，在促进高校毕业生就业，帮扶困难人员就业，做好农村劳动力转移就业、复转复退军人就业和残疾人就业等方面，使扶持政策有进一步的拓展和放宽；四是加强就业服务、创业服务和职业培训、创业培训，使措施有创新、内容更丰富；五是强化组织领导和资金投入，使要求更明确、保障措施更加切实有效。2016 年，国务院相继出台文件，要求做好钢铁、煤炭行业化解过剩产能过程中的职工安置工作。2017 年 4 月，国务院对做好当前和今后一段时期就业创业工作提出指导意见：一是坚持实施就业优先战略；二是支持新就业形态发展；三是促进以创业带动就业；四是抓好重点群体就业创业；五是强化教育培训和就业创业服务。同年 10 月，中共十九大报告，进一步明确提出要坚持就业优先战略和积极的就业政策，实现更高质量和更充分就业，对就业工作提出了新的更高要求。

举办技术竞赛，鼓励大学生创新创业。（新华社记者杨世尧摄）

这一阶段积极的就业政策与前一阶段相比，政策实施的对象范围更加广泛，覆盖城乡各类劳动者，政策惠及面不断扩大。同时，国务院还相继出台了多个促进大众创业、万众创新的文件，形成了新一轮的以鼓励创业与促进就业相结合为鲜明特征的政策集成和创新，使政策的功能作用从促进各类劳动者就业提升到促进就业与鼓励创业相结合，政策导向更加积极，措施更加细化，可操作性更强，含金量越来越高，实施效果也越来越好。

（四）应对国内外经济变化的形势和多种复杂因素影响，将积极的就业政策纳入宏观政策阶段（2018 年至今）

随着中国特色社会主义进入新时代，社会主要矛盾已发生转变，在就业领域中表现为劳动者日益增长的对更加充分更高质量就业的需要和不平衡不充分的就业发展格局之间的矛盾。与此同时，在经济下行压力加大、经济转型任务

繁重、国内外经济变数和中美贸易摩擦等新的不稳定不确定因素影响下，结构性失业、周期性失业与摩擦性失业“三碰头”的局面已开始显现并有加剧趋势。2018 年 7 月，中央政府提出，要做好稳就业、稳金融、稳外贸、稳外资、稳投资、稳预期工作要求，并把稳就业作为“六稳”之首，以此来稳增长。同年 12 月，国务院印发《关于做好当前和今后一个时期促进就业工作的若干意见》，从支持企业稳定发展、鼓励支持就业创业、积极实施培训、及时开展下岗失业人员帮扶、落实各方责任五个方面，制定了十五条措施，对全面落实中央稳就业的决策部署提出明确要求。

2019 年 3 月，国务院总理李克强在第十三届全国人民代表大会上所做的政府工作报告中明确提出就业优先政策要全面发力。这是中国政府首次将就业优先政策置于宏观政策层面，旨在强化各方面重视就业、支持就业的导向。将就业优先从战略具化实化到政策，提升到宏观政策层面，这是中国政府对就业工作和宏观调控上作出的新的重大决策。同年 5 月，国家成立国务院就业工作领导小组，取代了 2003 年以来一直实行的部际联席会，并由国务院副总理任组长，为高位推动就业工作提供了组织保障。同月，国务院办公厅印发《职业技能提升行动方案（2019—2021 年）》，将大规模职业技能培训上升为国家行动，并明确提出三年开展各类补贴性职业技能培训 5 000 万人次以上，旨在推进稳定就业，积极预防失业。这一系列的部署，是将就业工作放在战略全局并上升至宏观调控层面的重要安排，是为应对国内外多变因素和中美贸易摩擦影响作出的积极反应，是保障改善民生和促进经济高质量发展的重大举措。

三、积极的就业政策的主要内容

2002 年，具有中国特色的积极的就业政策正式登上就业工作的历史舞台。伴随着中国就业的发展变化和工作需要，积极的就业政策在解决不同阶段突出

问题过程中不断调整和完善，逐步形成了一套涉及面广、扶持力度大、项目内容丰富的较为完整的就业政策体系（见表 3-2）。

表 3-2　积极的就业政策体系框架

政策要点	政策内容
（一）有利于就业增长的经济政策	1. 促进就业增长的宏观经济政策 2. 发展服务业扩大就业 3. 发展非公有制经济 4. 促进跨地区劳务协作和对外劳务输出
（二）鼓励劳动者自主创业和灵活就业的政策	1. 税收减免政策 2. 行政性收费减免政策 3. 小额担保贷款政策 4. 场地安排政策 5. 鼓励灵活就业
（三）鼓励企业吸纳就业的政策	1. 税收优惠政策 2. 社会保险补贴政策 3. 小额担保贷款政策
（四）对就业困难人员的援助政策	1. 公益性岗位社会保险补贴及岗位补贴 2. 对企业的社会保险补贴 3. 对灵活就业的社会保险补贴
（五）国有大中型企业主辅分离辅业改制政策	1. 税收减免政策 2. 冲减资本金
（六）加强公共就业服务的政策	1. 就业政策法规咨询 2. 职业供求信息、市场工资指导价位信息和职业培训信息发布 3. 职业指导和职业介绍 4. 对就业困难人员实施就业援助 5. 办理就业登记、失业登记等事务 6. 其他公共就业服务
（七）强化职业技能培训的政策	1. 对失业人员、符合条件的进城务工农村劳动者参加职业培训的，给予职业培训补贴 2. 对就业困难人员、进城务工农村劳动者通过初次职业技能鉴定（限规定工种）、取得职业资格证书的，给予一次性职业技能鉴定补贴
（八）加大就业资金投入的政策	1. 县级以上人民政府安排就业专项资金 2. 东部七省市开展适当扩大失业保险基金支出范围试点 3. 中央财政通过专项转移支付对地方给予补助

续表

政策要点	政策内容
（九）做好失业调控和治理的政策	1. 建立失业预警机制，健全失业监测体系，采取调控措施 2. 稳步推进国有企业重组改制和关闭破产工作 3. 规范企业裁员 4. 引导企业所有者和经营者树立社会责任意识
（十）形成社会保障与促进就业联动政策	1. 合理确定失业保险和城镇居民最低生活保障水平 2. 推动形成促进就业的激励约束机制 3. 扩大社会保险覆盖面

（一）积极的就业政策的基本内容

（1）有利于就业增长的经济政策。通过经济发展扩大就业是解决就业问题的根本。坚持在发展中解决就业问题，努力实现促进经济增长与扩大就业的良性互动，为此政策规定：①协调宏观经济政策，深化经济体制改革，加大结构调整力度，保持国民经济必要的增长速度，扩大就业。加强产业、财政、金融等政策与就业政策的相互协调，在制定涉及全局的经济社会政策和确定重大项目建设时，把扩大就业作为重要因素加以考虑，在注重提高竞争力、形成新的经济增长点的同时，不断形成新的就业增长点。②优化产业结构。在产业类型上，注重发展劳动密集型产业。大力发展第三产业，继续拓展传统服务业，积极开发新兴服务业，特别是社区服务业。③侧重经济形式和企业类型。在经济类型上，注重发展非公有制经济；在企业规模上，注重扶持中小企业。逐步清理对非公有制经济发展的限制，加大对私营企业和个人财产的保护，强化对企业经营与信贷的服务，加大财税金融支持，改善非公有制经济的发展环境。④开拓国际国内劳务市场。面向国际、国内两个市场，对内鼓励跨地区劳务协作，组织劳动者转移就业；对外实施“走出去”战略，努力开拓国际劳务市场。

（2）鼓励劳动者自主创业和灵活就业的政策。创业是劳动者通过自主创办生产服务项目、企业或从事个体经营实现市场就业的重要形式。劳动者通过创

业，在实现自身就业的同时，可以带动更多劳动者就业。为鼓励扶持更多的劳动者自谋职业、自主创业和灵活就业，政策规定：①税收减免。对下岗失业人员从事个体经营有关项目的，三年内按定额依次扣减营业税、城市维护建设税、教育费附加和个人所得税。②行政性收费减免。对登记失业人员从事个体经营的，三年内免收管理类、登记类和证照类等有关行政事业性收费。③小额担保贷款。符合条件人员自谋职业、自主创业或合伙经营与组织起来就业的，其自筹资金不足部分，在贷款担保机构承诺担保的前提下，可以申请小额担保贷款。对下岗失业人员合伙经营和组织起来就业的，可根据人数，适当扩大贷款规模。对其中从事微利项目的，中央财政据实全额贴息。④场地安排。各级人民政府及其国土、规划、城管等有关部门统筹安排劳动者创业所需的生产经营场地，可在土地利用总体规划确定的城镇建设用地范围内，或利用原有经批准的经济技术开发区、工业园区、高新技术园区、大学科技园区、小企业孵化园等建设创业孵化基地，为进入基地的小企业进行孵化培养，提供有效的培训指导服务和一定期限的政策扶持。⑤创业培训指导服务。根据劳动力市场变化和产业结构调整，大力加强职业教育和再就业培训。建立和完善公共就业服务制度，落实免费再就业培训和免费职业介绍政策。鼓励和支持社会力量，尤其是具有特色的民办培训机构，开展职业技能培训。对有创业愿望和具备创业条件的城乡劳动者进行创业培训，并提供开业指导、项目开发、小额担保贷款、跟踪服务等。⑥鼓励灵活就业。适应企业用工需求和就业方式的变化，鼓励和引导非全日制、非固定单位、临时性、季节性、弹性工作等灵活多样的就业方式。完善与灵活就业相适应的劳动关系、工资支付和社会保险等政策。

（3）鼓励企业吸纳就业的政策。企业吸纳就业是解决就业问题的重要渠道。为此，中国政府明确对符合条件的企业吸纳就业实行下列政策：①税收优惠。商贸企业、服务型企业（国家限制的行业除外）、劳服企业中的加工型企业和街道、社区具有加工性质的小型企业实体，新招用下岗失业人员，与其签订

一年以上期限劳动合同并缴纳社会保险费的，三年内按定额依次扣减营业税、城市维护建设税、教育费附加和企业所得税。②社会保险补贴。各类企业招用就业困难人员，并与之签订一年以上劳动合同的，可享受相应期限的社会保险补贴。③小额担保贷款。符合条件的劳动密集型小企业新招用符合条件人员达到规定比例的，可享受不超过200万元的贷款。

（4）对就业困难人员的援助政策。对就业困难人员实行以下就业援助政策：①公益性岗位社会保险补贴及岗位补贴。各地政府投资开发的公益性岗位，要优先安排符合岗位要求的就业困难人员，在相应期限内给予该岗位人员基本养老、基本医疗和失业保险补贴以及适当的岗位补贴。②对企业的社会保险补贴。各类企业招用就业困难人员，与其签订劳动合同并为其缴纳社会保险费的，在相应期限内可享受基本养老、基本医疗和失业保险补贴。③对灵活就业人员的社会保险补贴。就业困难人员灵活就业后申报就业并缴纳社会保险费的，可享受一定数额的社会保险补贴。距离法定退休年龄不足五年的就业困难人员，其社会保险补贴和岗位补贴可延长至退休。

（5）国有大中型企业主辅分离、辅业改制政策。鼓励有条件的国有大中型企业在进行结构调整、重组改制和主辅分离过程中，利用非主业资产和闲置资产安置企业富余人员，发挥企业内部潜力分流安置富余人员，而不是直接将富余人员推向社会，从而减轻社会就业压力。相关的政策包括：①税收减免。国有大中型企业通过主辅分离和辅业改制分流安置本企业富余人员兴办的经济实体（国家限制的行业除外），凡符合条件的，三年内免征企业所得税。②冲减资本金。改制企业可用国有净资产支付解除职工劳动关系的经济补偿金等，由此造成的账面国有资产减少，按规定程序报批后冲减国有资本。

（6）加强公共就业服务的政策。为加强以公共就业服务为主体的就业服务体系，规范对职业中介机构和人力资源市场的管理，提出下列要求：①各级地方政府建立健全公共就业服务体系，承担办理就业登记、失业登记等事务，向

劳动者免费提供就业政策法规咨询、职业供求、市场工资指导价位和职业培训等信息，以及职业指导、职业介绍和就业援助等公共就业服务。②向劳动者提供免费的就业服务，并将服务经费纳入同级财政预算。③积极推进街道、社区、乡镇、村的基层平台建设，开展管理服务基础工作，实施就业援助，开展政策宣传等。④鼓励各类职业中介机构开展公益性就业服务，向这些机构给予职业介绍补贴，并依法规范其服务行为。

（7）强化职业技能培训的政策。为提升劳动者参加职业培训、提高其就业能力的积极性，实行下列政策：①对失业人员、符合条件的进城务工农村劳动者参加职业培训的，向其给予职业培训补贴。②对就业困难人员、进城务工农村劳动者通过初次职业技能鉴定（限规定工种）、取得职业资格证书的，向其给予一次性职业技能鉴定补贴。③人力资源社会保障部门面向全社会各类教育培训资源，通过招投标的方式，公开认定一批定点机构，组织开展多层次、多形式的技能培训。④建立和完善政府出资购买培训成果的机制，根据培训质量和培训后的就业情况，提供相应的职业培训补贴，引导培训机构根据市场需求和就业需求，提高培训的实用性和有效性。

（8）加大就业资金投入的政策。为保障就业再就业主要政策措施的落实，对资金的筹集、使用和管理作出下列规定：①要求县级以上人民政府根据就业状况和就业工作目标，在同级财政预算中安排就业专项资金用于促进就业工作。主要用于职业介绍补贴、职业培训补贴、社会保险补贴、公益性岗位补贴、职业技能鉴定补贴、特定就业政策补助、小额担保贷款担保基金和小额担保贷款贴息，以及扶持公共就业服务等。②中央财政通过专项转移支付的方式对地方给予适当补助，并对中西部地区和老工业基地给予重点支持。③在加大财政投入的同时，根据《失业保险条例》规定，失业保险基金可以用作领取失业保险金人员接受职业培训和职业介绍的补贴。

（9）做好失业调控和治理的政策。综合运用法律的、经济的和必要的行政

手段，从源头上做好失业预防工作，并对失业进行调控，政策规定：①结合国民经济和社会发展计划中控制失业率的目标和本地区实际，建立失业预警机制，逐步健全失业监测体系，合理确定失业预警线，制定应急预案，采取调控措施，应对可能出现的就业局势不稳定问题。对因国内、国际经济形势发生重大变化直接影响就业的行业和企业，以及失业压力大的困难地区、困难行业，要对其进行指导，做好失业调控工作，保持就业局势稳定。②做好重组改制和关闭破产国有企业的职工安置工作。在工作落实过程中切实维护职工合法权益。③规范企业裁员。正常生产经营企业成规模裁减人员的，裁员方案须经企业职工代表大会讨论。凡不能依法支付解除劳动合同的经济补偿金并妥善解决企业拖欠职工债务的，不得裁减人员。企业一次性减员超过一定数量和比例的，要事前向当地政府报告。④引导企业所有者和经营者树立社会责任意识，加强集体协商制度建设。通过政府、企业和职工三方协商机制，协调好企业和职工利益，增强职工就业的稳定性。

（10）形成社会保障与促进就业联动的政策。为有效衔接社会保障与促进就业的关系，进一步完善社会保障制度，建立与促进就业联动机制，政策规定：①合理确定失业保险和城镇居民最低生活保障水平，既分清层次，又相互衔接，形成合理配套的标准体系。②推动形成促进就业的激励约束机制。严格失业保险金、城镇居民最低生活保障金的申领条件和程序，将申领条件与接受职业介绍、职业培训以及参加公益性劳动的情况相挂钩，逐步形成促进就业的政策导向。③扩大社会保险覆盖面，使更多的城乡劳动者参加社会保险，并使劳动者的社会保险关系能够在其流动就业过程中得到接续，从制度上做到“不管人在哪里干，社会保险接着算”。

（二）就业政策在新时期的创新发展

积极的就业政策自确立以来，伴随经济社会发展和就业改革的深化不断发

展完善、迭代升级、延续扩展，惠及面越来越大，政策含金量越来越高，为就业大局稳定提供了重要保障。特别是中共十八以来，中共中央、国务院主动适应和引领经济发展新常态，不断推动有中国特色的积极就业政策实现创新发展。

（1）在经济高质量发展中稳定和扩大就业。在坚持市场就业机制的同时，更好地发挥政府作用，以促进和稳定就业为重点，提出以下措施：①实施区间调控、定向调控、精准调控等宏观调控方式，明确提出把稳定和扩大就业作为区间调控的下限，保持宏观政策的连续性、稳定性，促进经济中高速增长，增强对就业的拉动能力。②加强经济政策与就业政策衔接，明确提出在制定财税、金融、产业、贸易等重大政策时，要综合评价该政策对就业岗位、就业环境、失业风险等的影响。③持续深化结构调整，大力发展现代服务业，完善多元化产业体系，支持劳动密集型产业发展，实施区域发展战略，促进产业结构、区域结构与就业协同。

（2）大力促进创业带动就业。中共十八大把“鼓励创业”写入新时期就业方针，明确要求把创业和就业结合起来，营造鼓励大众创业、万众创新的良好环境，加快培育发展新动能，在促进以创业带动就业、抓好重点群体就业创业、强化教育培训和就业创业服务等方面，制定实施一系列支持创业的政策措施。

（3）拓宽高校毕业生就业渠道。中共中央、国务院明确提出把高校毕业生就业摆在就业工作的首位，以就业促进、创业引领、基层成长为着力点，在完善促进高校毕业生就业创业政策体系、拓展高校毕业生多元化就业领域、搞好高校毕业生就业市场供需衔接的就业服务和职业指导、改善高校毕业生就业环境等多方面，制定实施具体明确的政策措施。

（4）全力推进就业扶贫。将就业扶贫纳入就业创业工作总体规划，发挥就业在精准扶贫中的重要作用，采取多种措施促进贫困劳动力实现就业和增加收入。2016 年开展发达地区与贫困地区劳务协作试点，在健全工作机制、加强对接协作、促进就地就业、提升就业技能、加强工作保障等方面探索出一套可复

制、可推广的经验做法和工作机制。2017—2018 年完善就业扶贫政策措施，提出摸清基础信息、促进就地就近就业、加强劳务协作、加强技能培训、促进稳定就业等具体措施。同时建设农村贫困家庭劳动力就业信息平台，集中发布支持贫困劳动力自主求职就业和有组织劳务输出的岗位信息，从政策上通过职业介绍补贴、职业培训补贴、社会保险补贴、交通补贴等，加强对劳务对接扶贫行动的支持。

（5）平稳有序推动去产能行业企业的职工安置。妥善做好去产能过程中的行业企业职工安置工作，将结构调整中的失业风险降到最低，为改革发展营造和谐稳定的社会环境。主要政策措施包括：鼓励企业内部多渠道分流安置职工，对促进分流职工转岗就业创业的给予扶持政策，对自主创业的分流人员落实创业扶持政策，公益性岗位优先安置就业困难人员。

贯彻落实中共中央、国务院关于去产能政策，加快推进过剩产能“关、停、并、转”，确保去产能职工安置工作平稳有序。（新华社记者徐昱摄）

（6）大力加强职业培训。为适应经济转型升级、产业结构优化和劳动者就业创业的需求，要加快人力资源供给侧结构性改革，推行终身职业技能培训制度，大规模开展在职职工、企业职工培训以及创业培训和转岗转业培训，着力提高培训的针对性、有效性，促进劳动者素质持续提升。

（7）建立全方位公共就业服务体系，推进人力资源市场建设。完善城乡统筹的公共就业服务制度，扩大服务供给，创新运行机制，建立全方位公共就业服务体系。主要政策措施包括：明确覆盖全民的公共就业服务范围，健全贯穿全程的公共就业服务功能，构建辐射全域的公共就业服务体系，完善便捷高效的公共就业服务方式，以全方位公共就业服务促进就业增长。大力促进人力资源服务业发展，努力提升人力资源服务供给水平。主要政策措施包括：实现公共服务与经营性服务分类管理、统一规范人力资源市场体系，进一步扩大人力资源市场对外资开放试点，积极推动人力资源服务业发展，完善政府购买人力资源公共服务政策，稳步推进人力资源市场对外开放。

四、实施积极的就业政策取得的成效

中国积极的就业政策的实施，在推进就业再就业工作方面发挥了重要作用，在深化体制改革、促进经济发展和维护社会稳定方面做出了重要贡献。

（一）妥善解决了再就业难题，成功化解了国有企业改革的遗留问题

积极的就业政策的制定实施，为促进再就业提供了强大的政策支撑，平稳地解决了国有企业职工下岗失业的难题，成功化解了计划体制遗留的一代人问题。2003—2007 年五年中，累计有 2 500 万名国有企业、城镇集体企业下岗失业人员实现再就业；有 700 万名困难对象获得帮助，实现再就业；年末城镇登记失业率从 2003 年的 4.3% 下降到 2007 年的 4.0%。与此同时，全国国有企业

职工人数由 1997 年年底的 7 131 万人减少到 2007 年年底的 2 846 万人。现代企业制度和新型劳动用工制度也建立起来。

（二）改善了就业格局，推动经济发展与扩大就业良性互动

贯彻实施积极的就业政策，通过优化产业结构，加快发展服务业、个体私营经济等非公有制经济和中小企业，积极探索有利于扩大就业的经济发展方式，推动就业总量不断增加，就业结构不断改善。2003—2007 年，城镇新增就业由此前五年的年均不到 800 万人提升到 1 000 万人以上（见图 3-1）。2007 年全国从业人员总量达到 78 645 万人，与 2002 年相比增加了 3 285 万人；城镇就业人口占全国就业人口的比重由 33.6% 上升到 38.1%，第一、第二、第三产业就业人员的比重分别由 50.0 ∶ 21.4 ∶ 28.6 转变为 40.8 ∶ 26.8 ∶ 32.4。这一期间，劳动者个体创业、民营企业就业和灵活就业也得到长足发展。

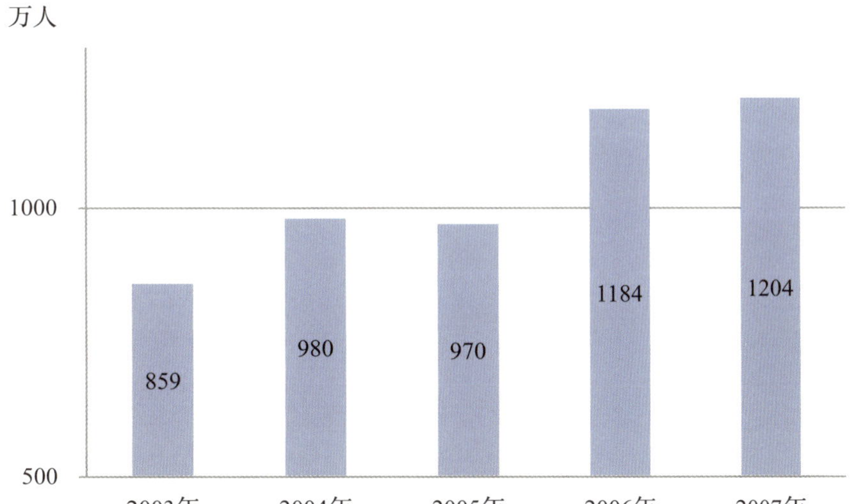

图 3-1　2003—2007 年城镇新增就业人数

资料来源：国家统计局 2003—2007 年统计公报。

（三）确立了市场导向的就业机制，促进就业制度体系日趋成熟

在制定和贯彻实施积极的就业政策过程中，始终坚持劳动者自主择业、市场调节就业、政府促进就业的就业方针，将鼓励劳动者自谋职业、自主创业作为积极的就业政策的重要内容，充分发挥了市场机制在就业中的基础作用。同时，在积极的就业政策主导下，政府促进就业和市场调节就业的机制也相应建立健全：就业工作部门联席会、就业工作目标责任和就业工作监督检查等机制逐步建立并发挥了积极作用；公共就业服务体系取得长足发展，制度化、专业化、社会化水平不断提升，初步形成了市、区县、街道（乡镇）、社区四级公共就业服务网络。

（四）有效应对金融危机的严重冲击，保持就业局势的基本稳定

2008 年，面对突如其来的国际金融危机，国务院和有关部门制定并实施了一系列稳定和扩大就业的政策措施，构成了应对金融危机的就业新政，主导着稳定和扩大就业工作。就业局势较快稳定下来，失业大潮得到控制。2009 年，全国城镇新增就业 1 102 万人（见图 3-2），为全年目标 900 万人的 122%；下

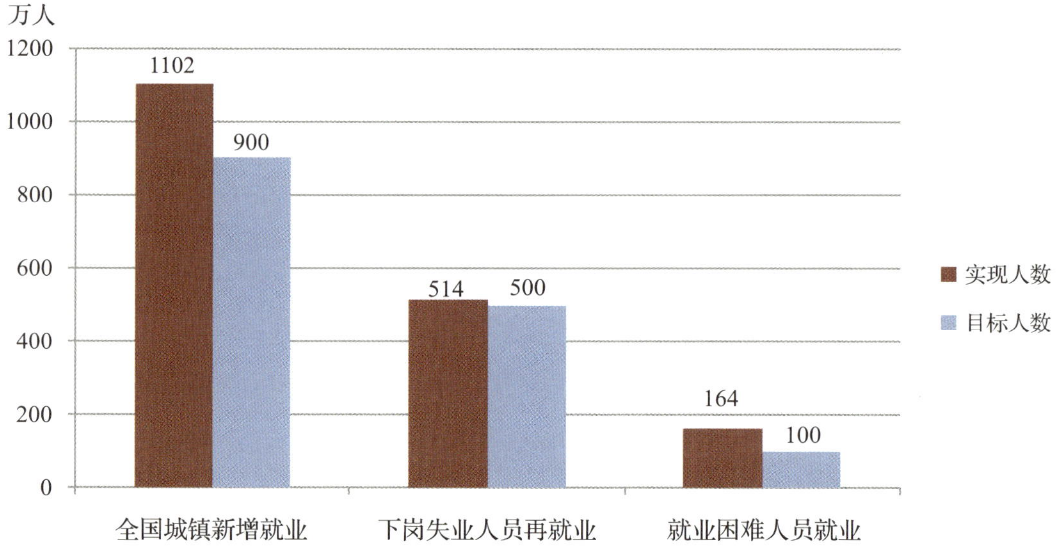

图 3-2　2009 年全国城镇新增就业、下岗失业人员再就业及就业困难人员就业情况

资料来源：2009 年度人力资源和社会保障事业发展统计公报。

岗失业人员再就业 514 万人，为全年目标 500 万人的 103%；就业困难人员就业 164 万人，为全年目标 100 万人的 164%。2009 年年底，全国实有城镇登记失业人员 921 万人，城镇登记失业率为 4.3%，基本恢复到正常水平。到 2010 年，全国城镇新增就业更达到 1 168 万人。可以说在世界各国中，中国率先走出了失业陷阱。

（五）积极的就业政策逐步扩展、充实、完善和提升，成为持续推进就业和创业的政策保障

从 2002 年确立积极的就业政策体系的初步框架，到 2005 年对积极的就业政策进一步延续、扩展，再到 2008 年正式施行《就业促进法》，促进就业的政策从产生到发展，并上升为法律制度，形成了有中国特色的积极就业政策体系。2008 年以后，中国政府积极应对国际金融危机和特大自然灾害，推动就业工作取得新的进展和成效。2012 年以后，随着中国经济发展进入新常态，针对就业工作面临的新形势，以创业创新带动就业成为新的驱动力。2015 年，国务院出台新形势下就业创业工作的重要文件，是对积极的就业政策的丰富与发展、提升和创新，推动城镇新增就业连续五年超过 1 300 万人。2017 年，国务院又出台新时期就业创业政策文件，提出坚持实施就业优先战略、支持新就业形态发展、促进以创业带动就业、抓好重点群体就业创业以及强化教育培训和就业创业服务等方面的政策措施，网商、共享经济等新的平台带动一大批新形态就业，创业实体连续五年有较大增长，从而推动全国就业创业工作迈上新台阶。

国际劳工组织专家对中国积极的就业政策给予了高度评价，指出：中国积极的就业政策是将现代就业工作理念、各国成功经验和中国国情更好地结合起来的典范，囊括了世界各国积极的就业政策的三大要素，即治理失业不仅进行救济更注重再就业，扩大就业不仅大力开发岗位同时注重开发人力资源，在促

进就业的各种形态中更鼓励劳动者自主创业。依靠积极的就业政策，中国在解决城市与乡村同时并存的严重的失业和半失业问题方面取得了成功。其他国家做不到的，中国做到了，中国的就业政策内容和实施效果值得向世界各国推荐。

第四章
就业促进法

一、《就业促进法》的制定

（一）《就业促进法》的出台

《宪法》对确保公民劳动权利和义务有明确规定：国家通过各种途径，创造劳动就业条件，加强劳动保护，改善劳动条件，并在发展生产的基础上，提高劳动报酬和福利待遇。国家对就业前的公民进行必要的劳动就业训练。《劳动法》规定：国家采取各种措施，促进劳动就业，发展职业教育，制定劳动标准，调节社会收入，完善社会保险，协调劳动关系，逐步提高劳动者的生活水平。国家通过促进经济和社会发展，创造就业条件，扩大就业机会。然而，面对长期、艰巨而复杂的就业问题，中国政府为了进一步做好就业工作，不仅需要《宪法》和《劳动法》这类综合性法律，更需要一部促进就业的专项法律。

中共中央、国务院高度重视就业工作。在2002年召开的全国再就业工作会议上，首次提出“就业是民生之本”的重要思想。中国政府明确要求把就业工作摆在经济社会发展更加突出的位置，坚持以人为本，实现社会的协调可持续发展。中国积极的就业政策也于同年制定实施。在2003—2007年期间，国务

院和各部门、各地方相继制定实施了接续和配套政策，对积极的就业政策进一步延续、扩展、调整和充实，在贯彻落实政策中取得了显著成效，为制定《就业促进法》奠定了丰富的实践基础。同时，这些改革措施在继续执行中也需要有法律进行保障，急需通过立法促进就业的政策制度化、法律化，建立促进就业的长效机制。2007 年，经多方论证，《就业促进法》应运而生。同年 8 月，经第十届全国人民代表大会常务委员会第二十九次会议审议通过《就业促进法》，由国家主席签署第 70 号主席令予以公布，自 2008 年开始施行。《就业促进法》的施行，是中国经济社会生活中的一件大事，是中国就业工作的一个重要里程碑，对建立促进就业的长效机制、推动人力资源和社会保障事业全面协调可持续发展、构建社会主义和谐社会产生了重大而深远的影响。

《中华人民共和国就业促进法》于 2008 年 1 月 1 日开始施行。（新华社记者王小川摄）

（二）《就业促进法》的指导思想

在法律拟定过程中，最重要的是要确定立法的指导思想。一是要充分体现党和国家促进就业的方针政策，并将其制度化，明确就业在经济社会发展中的中心地位和作用，以建立促进就业的长效机制。二是要明确市场就业的决定性作用与政府促进就业的责任。充分发挥人力资源市场在就业中的基础性作用，促进用人单位自主用人和劳动者自主择业，引导劳动者合理流动。同时，政府管理就业要从计划经济体制下的统包就业模式转为通过制定发展战略、实施宏观经济政策等方式，加快培育和规范管理市场就业，并通过政策引导和服务创造良好环境，促进就业发展。为弥补市场不足，政府还要通过提供就业援助等方式帮助困难群体实现就业。三是要明确建立面向全体劳动者的就业制度和政策体系。法律是保障和服务于全体劳动者和所有用人单位的，扶持政策要普惠，服务培训要均等。要构建城乡统一的公共就业服务制度和体系，形成面向所有劳动者的终身培训制度和政策。四是要明确促进就业的专项法律与相关法律的关系。在《就业促进法》出台前后，《劳动法》《劳动合同法》《中华人民共和国社会保险法》（以下简称《社会保险法》）等相关法律法规相继修订和出台，同时随着一系列部门规章的出台，促进就业的法律法规体系也在逐步完善。

（三）《就业促进法》的立法宗旨和原则

1.《就业促进法》的立法宗旨是为了促进就业，促进经济发展与扩大就业相协调，促进社会和谐稳定。

2.《就业促进法》的立法原则，一是扩大就业的原则。《就业促进法》明确提出国家要把扩大就业放在经济社会发展的突出位置。地方政府要把扩大就业作为经济社会发展和经济结构调整的重要目标，实现经济发展与扩大就业的良性互动。二是市场就业的原则。《就业促进法》要求深化劳动就业制度改革，完善市场导向的就业机制，实行市场调节就业，保证劳动者择业自主权和用人单

位用人自主权。三是平等就业的原则。《就业促进法》规定禁止就业歧视，为劳动者提供公平的就业机会。四是统筹就业的原则。《就业促进法》要求统筹社会各部门、各社会团体和组织开展促进就业工作；统筹协调产业政策和就业政策；统筹做好城镇新增劳动力就业、农村富余劳动力转移就业、下岗失业人员再就业工作，逐步形成城乡统一的劳动力市场。

二、《就业促进法》的内容和特点

《就业促进法》一共九章六十九条，涉及面广，内容丰富，涵盖了政府责任、工作方针和机制、政策支持、公平就业、就业服务和管理、职业教育和培训、就业援助、监督检查、法律责任等方面。

（一）就业方针

《就业促进法》强调要坚持“劳动者自主择业、市场调节就业、政府促进就业”的方针。2015 年，又进一步明确为“劳动者自主就业、市场调节就业、政府促进就业和鼓励创业”的方针。

（1）明确“劳动者自主就业”。倡导劳动者树立正确的就业观念，充分调动自身的主动性和能动性，发挥就业潜能和提高职业技能，依靠自身努力，求职应聘、自谋职业和自主创业，尽快实现就业。

（2）明确“市场调节就业”。充分发挥人力资源市场在促进就业中的基础性作用。通过市场职业供求信息，引导劳动者合理流动和就业；通过用人单位自主用人和劳动者自主就业，实现供求双方相互选择；通过市场工资价位信息，调节劳动力的供求。

（3）明确“政府促进就业和鼓励创业”。充分发挥政府在促进就业中的重要职责，即承担创造就业条件、扩大就业机会、改善就业环境、提供就业扶助等重要职责。同时，在当前市场机制不健全、劳动者能动性不充分的情况下，

政府要承担更多的培育完善市场机制、规范市场行为、弥补市场不足的责任；加大鼓励支持劳动者自主择业、自主创业和企业增加就业岗位的力度。

（二）公平就业

实行公平就业，反对就业歧视，保障劳动者的平等就业权利，既是促进就业工作的一项重要原则，也是社会关注的一个重要问题。《就业促进法》高举公平就业的旗帜，创造公平的就业环境，它明确规定：“劳动者依法享有平等就业和自主择业的权利。劳动者就业，不因民族、种族、性别、宗教信仰等不同而受歧视。”法律设立“公平就业”专章，强调残疾人、传染病病原携带者和进城就业的农村劳动者等群体享有与其他劳动者平等的劳动权利；用人单位招用人员、职业中介机构从事职业中介活动，应当向劳动者提供平等的就业机会和公平的就业条件，不得实施就业歧视。《就业促进法》为解决就业歧视问题，提供了有力的法律保障。

（三）政府职责

促进就业和治理失业是各国政府的重要职责，也是世界各国政府执政的重要目标，在中国这更是各级人民政府执政为民的重要体现。《就业促进法》对政府在促进就业中的职责作出了明确规定，包括六个方面：

（1）发展经济和调整产业结构增加就业岗位。处理好经济发展、结构调整与扩大就业、减少失业之间的关系，并将其作为政府促进就业的首要责任。《就业促进法》规定，县级以上人民政府把扩大就业作为经济和社会发展的重要目标和重要职责，通过发展经济和调整产业结构，实行有利于促进就业的产业政策、财政政策、税收政策等各项经济和社会政策，多渠道扩大就业、增加就业岗位。

（2）制定实施积极的就业政策。制定符合国情的、系统的、积极的政策并付诸实施，是政府履行职责的具体体现。《就业促进法》专设“政策支持”一

章，确立了国家实行有利于促进就业的产业、财政、税收、金融、投资、贸易等各方面政策，要求实行统筹城乡、区域和不同就业群体的就业政策，要求对失业进行预防、调节和控制。

（3）规范人力资源市场。人力资源市场是对现有的劳动力市场、人才市场、毕业生就业市场等各类市场的总概括。《就业促进法》明确规定县级以上人民政府要培育和完善统一开放、竞争有序的人力资源市场，加强人力资源市场信息网络及相关设施建设，建立健全市场信息服务体系，完善市场信息发布制度，为劳动者就业提供服务。

（4）完善就业服务。《就业促进法》在“就业服务和管理”一章中对完善就业服务，特别是加强公共就业服务做了明确规定，要求县级以上人民政府鼓励社会各方面依法开展就业服务活动，加强对公共就业服务和职业中介服务的指导和监督，逐步完善覆盖城乡的就业服务体系，提高服务的质量和效率，促进劳动力供给与需求的有效匹配；履行为劳动者提供免费公共就业服务的职责。

（5）加强职业教育和培训。《就业促进法》专设“职业教育和培训”一章，提出要依法发展职业教育，鼓励开展职业培训，促进劳动者提高职业技能，增强就业能力和创业能力。要求各级人民政府根据经济社会发展和市场需求，制订并实施职业能力开发计划；鼓励和支持培训机构和用人单位开展就业前培训、在职培训、再就业培训、职业技能培训和创业培训。建立健全劳动预备制度，实行职业资格证书制度等。

（6）实施就业援助。《就业促进法》规定，各级人民政府要建立健全就业援助制度，采取各种有效措施，对就业困难人员和就业困难地区实行优先扶持和重点帮助，拓宽公益性岗位范围，确保城市有就业需求的家庭至少有一人实现就业。同时，规定了就业援助的对象范围、主要措施以及对就业压力大的特定地区实施就业扶持等内容。对困难群体实施就业援助，是保障公民实现劳动就业权、维护和改善劳动者生存状况、促进社会公平与和谐的基本要求。同时，

《就业促进法》还明确就业困难人员的范围由省级人民政府根据本行政区域的实际情况来规定，从而使各地能够从实际出发解决就业困难人员问题，更有利于充分发挥援助政策效应。

（四）就业制度

《就业促进法》通过法律形式将就业工作制度化，从而使就业工作纳入法制化轨道，主要包括五个方面：

（1）加强对就业工作组织领导的政府责任制度。政府责任制度包括目标责任制度、促进就业工作协调机制等。《就业促进法》明确规定，县级以上人民政府把扩大就业作为经济和社会发展的重要目标，纳入国民经济和社会发展规划，并制定促进就业的中长期规划和年度工作计划。各级人民政府和有关部门应当建立促进就业的目标责任制度。县级以上人民政府按照促进就业的目标责任制的要求，对所属的有关部门和下一级人民政府进行考核和监督。它不仅将政府和有关部门建立促进就业的目标责任制度通过法律形式固定下来，而且还进一步确定了就业工作部际联席会议[①]制度的重要作用，并对进一步完善这一制度提出了明确要求，确保对就业工作的各部门齐抓共管持续有效。与此同时，建立劳动力调查统计制度和就业登记、失业登记制度，开展劳动力资源和就业、失业状况调查统计，并公布调查统计结果。

（2）加强对劳动者帮扶的公共就业服务和就业援助制度。这项制度是政府履行公共服务职能的重要体现。《就业促进法》明确规定，县级以上人民政府要设立公共就业服务机构，向劳动者提供免费服务，经费纳入同级财政预算；通过对援助对象、途径、政策措施和资金的制度性安排使就业援助工作常规化和制度化。

---

① 部际联席会议在国务院直接领导下开展工作，定期交流工作进展情况，协调解决政策落实中的难点问题，督促检查各部门政策落实情况，统一协调各部门行动，指导推动全国就业工作，对就业工作中的重大问题，及时向国务院报告。

（3）加强对市场行为规范的人力资源市场管理制度。《就业促进法》不仅规范了公共就业服务的服务内容，还对设立职业中介机构的条件、职业中介机构的行为和管理作出了明确规定。

（4）加强对人力资源素质提升的职业能力开发制度。《就业促进法》进一步明确对初高中毕业生、失业人员和进城就业的农村劳动者等各类群体开展职业培训的制度安排，明确用人单位和培训机构的责任和权利，用制度保证人力资源开发和促进就业的有机结合；鼓励和支持各类职业院校、职业技能培训机构和用人单位开展各种职业培训。先培训后就业、先培训后上岗的制度基本确立。

（5）失业保险和失业调控制度。《就业促进法》规定，国家建立健全失业保险制度，在充分发挥失业保险保障失业人员基本生活的基础上，发挥其预防失业和促进就业功能；同时建立失业预警制度，对可能出现的较大规模的失业，实施预防、调节和控制。

（五）就业政策

政策是政府履行责任的具体体现。《就业促进法》将经过实践检验的积极的就业政策上升为法律规范。这些政策主要包括：

（1）有利于促进就业的经济发展政策。《就业促进法》规定，县级以上人民政府统筹协调产业政策与就业政策，通过鼓励发展劳动密集型产业、服务业，扶持中小企业，鼓励、支持、引导非公有制经济发展，增加就业岗位。发展国内外贸易和国际经济合作，发挥投资和重大建设项目带动就业的作用，拓宽就业渠道。

（2）有利于促进就业的财政保障政策。《就业促进法》规定，国家实行有利于促进就业的财政政策，加大资金投入，县级以上人民政府在财政预算中安排就业专项资金用于促进就业工作，并规定就业专项资金的具体用途。同

时，审计机关、财政部门应当依法对就业专项资金的管理和使用情况进行监督检查。

（3）有利于促进就业的税收优惠政策。《就业促进法》规定，国家鼓励企业增加就业岗位，扶持失业人员和残疾人就业，对符合国家规定条件的企业和人员依法给予税收优惠，并对从事个体经营的符合国家规定的失业人员和残疾人免除行政事业性收费。

（4）有利于促进就业的金融支持政策。《就业促进法》规定，增加中小企业的融资渠道；鼓励金融机构改进金融服务，加大对中小企业的信贷支持，并对自主创业人员在一定期限内给予小额信贷等扶持。

（5）城乡统筹的就业政策。《就业促进法》规定，国家建立健全城乡劳动者平等就业的制度，引导农业富余劳动力有序转移就业。

（6）区域统筹的就业政策。《就业促进法》规定，国家支持区域经济发展，鼓励区域协作，统筹协调不同地区就业的均衡增长；支持民族地区发展经济，扩大就业，实现中国不同区域就业均衡增长和区域经济协调发展。

（7）群体统筹的就业政策。《就业促进法》规定，各级人民政府统筹做好城镇新增劳动力就业、农业富余劳动力转移就业和失业人员就业工作。

（8）有利于灵活就业的劳动和社会保险政策。《就业促进法》规定，各级人民政府采取措施，逐步完善和实施与非全日制用工等灵活就业相适应的劳动和社会保险政策，为灵活就业人员提供帮助和服务，有利于促进灵活就业的规范健康发展。

（9）援助困难群体的就业政策。《就业促进法》规定，各级人民政府建立健全就业援助制度，对就业困难人员给予扶持和帮助。

（10）实行失业保险促进就业政策。《就业促进法》规定了失业保险制度保障失业人员基本生活和促进就业的功能，并要求加强对大规模失业的预防、调节和控制。

三、《就业促进法》的实施和成效

（一）《就业促进法》的实施

（1）加快配套法规和文件研究，完善对积极的就业政策的传承。《就业促进法》的出台为就业工作法制化提供了良好契机，但是法律的有些规定还比较原则化。因此，各职能部门抓紧研究制定相关配套法规，使《就业促进法》的主要内容具体化，更具操作性。同时，指导推动地方根据实际情况制定相应的地方规章，制定地方《就业促进条例》或相关办法。积极的就业政策的实践为贯彻实施《就业促进法》奠定了坚实的基础，为更好地实现政策与法律的衔接，《就业促进法》在保留现行积极的就业政策体系核心内容的基础上，还要着重解决好三个问题：一是保持政策的连续性，使职业培训、职业介绍、鼓励自主创业和就业援助等有关政策长效化、普惠化、规范化。二是在总结现行政策操作实践的基础上，进一步充实和调整相关政策，使法律规定的政策支持对象和项目能够得到落实。三是增强政策的操作性，使法律规定能够取得实效。2008 年 2 月，《国务院关于做好促进就业工作的通知》（国发〔2008〕5 号）对现行就业政策与法律衔接及做好法律的贯彻落实提出明确要求。围绕贯彻这一文件，人力资源社会保障部、发展改革委、财政部、人民银行等部门加强协调配合，制定了资金管理、小额信贷、收费减免等配套政策。各地也根据新形势和新任务，对现行就业政策进行了调整和完善，制定地方性实施意见。

（2）加强学习培训和宣传。《就业促进法》的颁布实施，既使促进就业工作及各项扶持政策有法可依，更对各级人民政府和各有关部门的依法行政能力提出了新的更高要求。为此，各有关部门针对加强各级干部的培训进行专门安排。一方面，组织开展对各级人力资源社会保障部门及其就业服务机构人员的培训，培养一批知法、懂法、善于执法的骨干队伍；另一方面，组织就业工作部际联席会议各部门成员单位的工作人员进行学习培训，使其深入了解贯彻

《就业促进法》与本部门本职工作相关的内容和要求。同时，采取多种有效形式，广泛深入地开展普法宣传工作，使各级人民政府和各有关部门、用人单位和社会各界，特别是广大劳动者，全面了解这部法律的重大意义和主要内容。为增强普法宣传和政策讲解的实际效果，各级人民政府和各有关部门组织开展了灵活多样和贴近实际、贴近生活、贴近群众的法律宣传，特别是宣传一些地方和单位近年来促进就业再就业的好做法，宣传一批自谋职业和自主创业典型的经验，动员全社会力量共同做好就业再就业工作。

2007 年 9—12 月，劳动保障部、司法部、中华全国总工会、中华全国工商业联合会、中国企业联合会和中央电视台联合主办全国《就业促进法》《劳动合同法》知识电视大赛。

（二）就业立法的成效

《就业促进法》完善了中国劳动保障法律体系，为实施积极的就业政策和推动就业改革发展提供了法律保障，对推动经济发展与扩大就业良性互动，促

进实现社会和谐稳定具有积极作用。

（1）奠定了就业工作在国家经济社会发展中的重要地位，明确了政府在促进就业工作中的重要职责。就业是老百姓安身立命之本。实现社会就业更加充分是构建社会主义和谐社会的一项重要任务。《就业促进法》不仅明确规定，国家把扩大就业放在经济社会发展的突出位置，并且规定了政府扩大就业的重要职责，以及建立促进就业的目标责任制度并进行考核和监督，用法制手段强化了政府促进就业的重要职责。

（2）推进了就业工作法制化进程。通过法制化手段进一步加大就业工作力度，建立起促进就业的长效机制。《就业促进法》明确规定，实施积极的就业政策，坚持劳动者自主择业、市场调节就业、政府促进就业的方针。《就业促进法》不仅将经过实践检验行之有效的积极的就业政策上升为法律规范，并且进一步明确了要使促进就业的大政方针法定化，使促进就业的工作机制和工作体系法制化，使促进就业的各项政策措施和资金投入制度化，为解决好国家长期的就业问题提供了坚实的制度支持和法律保障。

（3）为加强就业服务和管理提供了强有力的保障。针对就业工作中基础薄弱、制度建设不足的问题，《就业促进法》从加强制度和基础建设着手，对政策支持、公平就业、就业服务和管理、职业教育和培训、就业援助、监督检查以及法律责任等做了具体的、明确的规定，使对市场的培育发展与对市场行为的规范有机结合，使强化公共就业服务和职业培训发展与相关制度的建设紧密结合，使运用政策促进就业与严格执行政策规定相互结合，为解决政策不落实以及基础建设和推进环节不到位、不规范、无保障等问题提供了保证，进一步促进就业管理服务组织体系更加健全，保障措施更为有力。

（4）进一步完善了劳动保障法律体系。《就业促进法》不仅填补了《劳动法》通过后国家法律层面在就业领域的缺位，并且标志着中国以《宪法》为根本依据，以《劳动法》为基础，以《就业促进法》《劳动合同法》《中华人民共

和国劳动争议调解仲裁法》《社会保险法》为主干，以相关法律法规为配套的劳动保障法律体系建设的进一步完善。

随着经济社会不断发展，就业及相关领域立法工作也面临许多新的挑战：一是现有法律法规滞后于改革实践，立法修法工作要与时俱进。如统筹城乡就业提出的建立统一开放、公平有序的人力资源市场等发展要求，又如人口发展带来的社会老龄化问题对就业的影响，再如应对突发性危机和重大灾害冲击时的相关政策还存在空白，以及有关创业促就业的内容在法律层面体现不足，等等。同时，实现高质量的充分就业，需要以法律的执行来保驾护航。中共中央、国务院将就业作为最大的民生，提出实现更加充分更高质量就业的目标，实现这一目标不仅需要以深入贯彻《就业促进法》来推进，并且也要在法律修订中得到更明确的体现。

第五章 创业促进就业

一、创业促进就业的发展历程

（一）创业促进就业的提出

1. 自主创业的启动和重大突破

20 世纪 80 年代初，面对 1 700 万名知青回城导致的城镇就业压力骤增，原来管束和限制的统包统配政策得到松动，实行劳动部门介绍就业、自愿组织起来就业和自谋职业相结合的“三结合”就业方针，打开了就业的多种渠道，特别是推动了自谋职业和个体经济的发展，劳动者创业由此开始启动。90 年代实行打破城乡就业界限的改革，农业劳动力的转移带来了小城镇个体经济和乡镇企业的发展，从而突破了原来控制农村劳动者流动的体制，为他们到城镇就业打开了大门，农村劳动者的创业空间得到了拓展。进入 21 世纪后，面对 3 000 万名下岗失业人员的突出矛盾，在为促进再就业所制定的政策中，将鼓励和扶持自主创业作为重要支柱，帮助许多下岗职工走上了再就业之路。2008 年以后，突发的国际金融危机对中国企业和就业产生了重大冲击。在应对危机所实施的政策措施中，将鼓励支持农民工返乡创业和大学生自主创业作为重大举

措，从而打开了新的局面，实现了创业带动就业，在短时间内使中国就业走出困境。2015 年，中共中央确立了劳动者自主就业、市场调节就业、政府促进就业和鼓励创业的新就业方针，进一步推动中国创业带动就业取得新的进展。

2. 被列为积极的就业政策的重要内容

2002 年以来实施的积极的就业政策，其中一个重要内容就是鼓励和支持劳动者自主创业，通过小额担保贷款和财政贴息政策解决融资问题，通过税费减免政策降低经营负担，通过提供创业培训提升创业者能力，通过帮助解决经营场地问题予以支持。近十几年，劳动者自主创业、自主择业和自由流动成为市场就业的主流，特别是自主创业，不仅打开就业新天地，而且对中国就业格局的变化产生了深刻影响。中国积极的就业政策包括三个层次的含义：第一个层次是解决失业问题，不能只是消极地提供失业保险和生活保障，而是积极地、更多更快更好地促进就业。第二个层次，促进就业不仅要千方百计地开发就业岗位，而且要更加注重开发人力资源，提高劳动者的职业能力和就业能力。第三个层次，在促进就业的过程中，特别要鼓励和支持创业，推动创业促就业。因此，2007 年中共十七大明确提出，实施扩大就业的发展战略，促进以创业带动就业，完善支持自主创业、自谋职业政策，加强就业观念教育，使更多的劳动者成为创业者。在 2008 年开始实施的《就业促进法》也明确提出：倡导劳动者树立正确的择业观念，提高就业能力和创业能力；鼓励劳动者自主创业、自谋职业。

（二）创业促进就业的发展

1. 应对金融危机冲击的重要举措

2008 年 9 月，国务院对创业促进就业工作提出指导意见，并对此进行专项部署和具体安排。特别是在应对国际金融危机的冲击时，将其作为主动出击的第一个重大举措，目的就是将金融危机的压力转变为动力，促使越来越多的劳

动者不等不靠，通过自主创业寻找新的门路，从而破解金融危机带来的就业困局，在保增长、保民生中创造更多就业岗位。同时，鼓励以创业带动就业，积极主动调整就业结构，进一步扶持中小企业、第三产业发展。

2. 新时期促进创业新政

2010 年后，中国政府确定促进就业创业的政策和计划，提出新形势下推进就业工作的总体要求和指导思想，对实施就业优先战略和实施积极的就业政策提出明确要求，特别是将鼓励支持创业的政策措施作为一项重要内容。

2012 年以后，随着中国经济发展进入新常态，针对就业工作面临的新形势，以创业创新带动就业成为新的驱动力。2015 年 4 月，国务院出台《关于进一步做好新形势下就业创业工作的意见》。这一文件最大的亮点就是落实了中共十八大提出的政府促进就业和鼓励创业相结合的新方针和新要求，并做到与时俱进，对积极的就业政策进行了扩展、充实、提升和创新。文件提出支持新就业形态发展，将鼓励创业创新发展的优惠政策面向新兴业态企业开放；对高校毕业生就业实施创业促进计划、基层成长计划，引导鼓励高校毕业生到城乡基层、中小微企业、社会组织等就业；扩大见习补贴、求职创业补贴政策的适用范围；强调简政放权，注重服务便民；营造创业环境，深化“放管服”改革，推进个体工商户登记管理的便利便捷；简化留学人员学历认证等手续，鼓励留学人员回国就业；细化服务标准和流程，建立“互联网 +”公共就业创业服务平台。不断加大政策支持力度和服务保障，营造良好的创业环境，调动劳动者创业的积极性和主动性，从而大力推动大众创业，以创业促进就业。

2017 年 4 月，国务院又出台《关于做好当前和今后一段时期就业创业工作的意见》，提出坚持实施就业优先战略、支持新就业形态发展、促进以创业带动就业、抓好重点群体就业创业，以及强化教育培训和就业创业服务五个方面的政策措施。网络经济、共享经济等新的平台带动了一大批新形态就业，创业实

体连续五年有较大增长，从而推动全国就业创业工作迈上新台阶。

2018 年 9 月，国务院印发《关于推动创新创业高质量发展打造“双创”升级版的意见》（国发〔2018〕32 号），深入实施创新驱动发展战略，进一步激发市场活力和社会创造力，推动创新创业高质量发展。一是抓政策升级。聚焦降成本，落实好阶段性降低社会保险费率；聚焦简政放权，进一步深化人力资源和社会保障领域的资质资格和行政审批改革；聚焦融资难题，落实好创业担保贷款扩大覆盖。二是抓培训升级。针对创业不同群体、不同阶段、不同领域，开展更具针对性的创业培训。同时，加强创业带头人的培养，培育一批创业引领者。三是抓服务升级。普遍设立创业服务窗口，增强公共就业服务机构在创业服务指导方面的功能。健全政府购买社会服务机制，建设创业孵化基地和园区，提供综合配套服务。在此过程中，加大政策支持力度，着力促进高校毕业生、返乡农民工、留学回国人员等重点群体自主创业。2019 年 4 月，中共中央、国务院印发《关于促进中小企业健康发展的指导意见》，进一步激发中小企业活力和发展动力，认真实施中小企业促进法，纾解中小企业困难，稳定和增强企业信心及预期，加大创新支持力度，提升中小企业专业化发展能力和大中小企业融通发展水平，促进中小企业健康发展。一是营造良好发展环境，进一步放宽市场准入，主动服务中小企业，实行公平统一的市场监管制度。二是破解融资难、融资贵问题，完善中小企业融资政策，积极拓宽融资渠道，支持利用资本市场直接融资，减轻企业融资负担，建立分类监管考核机制。三是完善财税支持政策，改进财税对小微企业融资的支持，减轻中小企业税费负担，完善政府采购支持中小企业的政策，充分发挥各类基金的引导带动作用。四是提升创新发展能力，完善创新创业环境，切实保护知识产权，引导中小企业专精特新发展，为中小企业提供信息化服务。五是改进服务保障工作，完善公共服务体系，推动信用信息共享，重视培育企业家队伍，支持对外合作与交流。六是强化组织领导和统筹协调，加强支持和统筹指导，加强工作督导评估，营造良好

舆论氛围，形成有利于中小企业健康发展的良好环境。

多措并举，助力中小企业发展。（新华社记者白禹摄）

2019年12月，人力资源社会保障部、财政部、农业农村部印发《关于进一步推动返乡入乡创业工作的意见》（人社部发〔2019〕129号），支持农民工、高校毕业生和退役军人等人员返乡入乡创业，以创新带动创业，以创业带动就业，促进农村一二三产业融合发展，实现更加充分更高质量就业。一是加大政策支持，落实创业扶持政策和创业担保贷款政策。二是提升创业培训，扩大培训规模，落实培训补贴。三是优化创业服务，提升服务能力，强化载体服务，健全社会保险和社会救助机制。四是加强人才支撑，做好用工服务，建立本地外出人员联络机制。五是强化组织实施，加强组织领导和引导扶持，强化示范带动，加大宣传力度。结合各地实际，积极探索、大胆创新，加强对返乡入乡创业人员的政策支持和服务保障，优化返乡入乡创业环境，推动返乡入乡创业工作不断开创新局面。

二、创业促进就业的政策措施

（一）创业促进就业政策的内容

1. 鼓励支持自主创业的政策

积极的就业政策主要从四个方面鼓励扶持更多的劳动者自谋职业、自主创业。一是实行税收减免政策，同时实行行政性收费减免政策，以鼓励支持更多劳动者自主创业，减轻他们的负担。随着形势发展，这项政策的扶持对象从最初的下岗失业人员逐步扩大，目前已扩展到城乡创业各类群体，包括失业人员、大学生、返乡农民工、复转军人、科技人员等；实施的期限也有所延长。二是实行小额担保贷款政策，解决劳动者自主创业需要启动资金和流动资金的问题。符合条件人员自谋职业、自主创业或合伙经营的，其自筹资金不足部分，在贷款担保机构承诺担保的前提下，该人员可向商业银行或其分支机构申请小额担保贷款。对下岗失业人员合伙经营和组织起来就业的，可根据人数适当扩大其贷款规模。对其中从事微利项目的，中央财政据实对其进行全额贴息。随着形势发展，这项政策扶持的对象也逐步扩大了，目前扩展到城乡几类创业重点群体，贷款额度也几次提高。三是在经营场地和工商管理方面作出安排，以解决劳动者创业场地难、办事难的问题。统筹安排劳动者创业所需的生产经营场地，并利用经济技术开发区、工业园区、高新技术园区、大学科技园区、小企业孵化园等建设创业孵化基地。简化开业手续，实行“一条龙”服务、“一个窗口”受理，放宽市场准入，营造宽松的环境，为劳动者创业创造更好的条件。四是加强创业培训指导服务，探索形成创业培训模式和构建创业服务平台。

2. 多部门合作，多方面推动创业的措施

2008 年 9 月，国务院办公厅印发了《转发人力资源社会保障部等部门关于

促进以创业带动就业工作指导意见的通知》（国办发〔2008〕111 号）。作为专门推动创业的第一个文件，《关于促进以创业带动就业工作的指导意见》由十一个部门联合制定，针对创业中遇到的问题，逐一梳理，提出解决办法，形成多部门配套政策措施的合力。其主要内容是：

（1）完善扶持政策，改善创业环境。一是放宽市场准入。加快清理和消除阻碍创业的各种行业性、地区性、经营性壁垒。各地区、各有关部门可根据实际情况，适当放宽高校毕业生、失业人员以及返乡农民工创业的市场准入条件。二是改善行政管理。全面实行收费公示制度和企业交费登记卡制度；进一步清理和规范涉及创业的行政审批事项，简化立项、审批和办证手续，开辟创业“绿色通道”。三是强化政策扶持。全面落实有利于劳动者创业的税收优惠、小额担保贷款、资金补贴、场地安排等扶持政策，促进中小企业和个体私营等非公有制经济发展，扶持劳动者创业。四是拓宽融资渠道。积极推动金融产品和金融服务创新，支持推动以创业带动就业。

（2）强化创业培训，提高创业能力。一是加大培训力度。建立满足城乡各类劳动者创业的创业培训体系，扩大创业培训范围，逐步将所有有创业愿望和培训需求的劳动者纳入创业培训。加强普通高校和职业学校的创业课程设置和师资配备，开展创业培训和创业实训。对参加创业培训的创业者，按有关政策规定，给予职业培训补贴。对领取失业保险金人员参加创业培训的，其职业培训补贴由失业保险基金开支。二是提高培训质量。从规范培训标准、提高师资水平、完善培训模式等方面入手，不断提高创业培训的质量。三是建立孵化基地。地方各级人民政府统筹安排劳动者创业所需的生产经营场地，搞好基础设施及配套建设，优先保障创业场地。

（3）健全服务体系，提供优质服务。一是健全服务组织。依托公共就业服务体系，健全创业指导服务组织，开发创业指导技术，完善创业服务功能，提高创业服务效率，承担创业带动就业工作的组织、服务和实施责任。二是完善

服务内容。组织开展项目开发、方案设计、风险评估、开业指导、融资服务、跟踪扶持等“一条龙”创业服务，建立创业信息、政策发布平台，搭建创业者交流互助的有效渠道。建立政府支持并监管、企业与个人开发、市场运作的创业项目评估和推介制度，建立创业项目资源库，形成有效采集和定期发布制度。三是提供用工服务。为创业者、新创办企业及其吸纳的员工提供公共就业服务。组织各类培训机构按照用工需求开展定向、订单培训，为创业企业提供合适人才。对参加职业技能培训的符合条件人员，按规定给予相应的职业培训补贴和职业技能鉴定补贴。

为创业者提供创业指导服务。（新华社记者许畅摄）

（4）加强组织领导，推动工作开展。一是强化政府责任。地方各级人民政府要将促进创业作为一项重要任务，摆上就业工作的重要议事日程，积极推动创业带动就业工作的全面开展。二是完善工作机制。建立人力资源社会保障、发展改革、中小企业管理、教育、建设、国土资源、财政、商务、银行、税务、工商等部门共同参与、分工负责、协调配合的工作小组，共同研究制定和实施促进以创业带动就业的政策措施和工作计划。将优化创业环境、完善落实创业政策以及提高创业培训效果、创业服务质量、创业初始成功率、创业稳定率、创业带动就业率等作为衡量促进以创业带动就业的主要工作指标，列入当地就业工作考核的重要内容。三是营造良好氛围。加强创业教育，发挥社会各方面

支持和推动创业工作的积极作用，加强舆论引导，树立创业典型。对在创业带动就业工作中取得显著成绩的单位和个人给予表彰。

（二）SIYB 项目的实施及成效

2004 年，中国劳动和社会保障部与国际劳工组织（ILO）正式合作开展“创办和改善你的企业”（SIYB）创业培训项目。经过十几年的发展，SIYB 创业培训项目在中国已经成为创业培训领域规模最大、知名度最高、普及率最高、效果最显著、最具可持续性的创业培训品牌，在推进创业促进就业工作中发挥了重要作用。

1. SIYB 项目的发展阶段

（1）摸索开发阶段（1997—2003 年）。中国劳动和社会保障部通过与国际劳工组织合作，实施“国际劳工组织 / 中国 / 日本国家间农村就业促进战略项目”，在甘肃省、河北省、江西省的国家级贫困县富余劳动力中开展创业培训。由于该项目取得了一定成效，在国际劳工组织的支持下，劳动和社会保障部继续实施“国际劳工组织 / 中国 / 日本国家间城市就业促进战略项目”，在内蒙古自治区包头市、吉林省吉林市和河北省张家口市三个项目城市对国有企业下岗失业人员开展创业培训。这一阶段最主要的成果就是通过国际合作，引进了国际先进的培训技术，并本土化改版了“创办你的企业”（SYB）培训课程及教材。同时，为了更好地适应中国国情需要，国家推出积极的就业政策，探索政府补贴创业培训与小额担保贷款政策相结合的工作模式，使下岗失业人员掌握了创业方法，解决了资金困难问题，降低了创业风险。

（2）巩固提高阶段（2004—2007 年）。劳动和社会保障部与国际劳工组织再次合作，在全国范围引进并实施“创办和改善你的企业中国项目”，引进了 SIYB 全套培训技术和项目管理方法，培养了上百万名具有较强创业能力的小企业创办者。培训对象也从当初的下岗失业人员扩展到返乡农民工、大学毕业生、

复转军人、残疾人等。通过实践，SIYB 培训已经成为各地推动创业促就业工作的一个品牌。同时，为了更好地扩大国际项目成果，通过落实积极的就业政策，实施“能力促创业计划”。各地依托就业训练中心、职业介绍中心等服务机构增设创业服务窗口，开展以小额担保贷款为基础，以开业指导、项目展示、创业孵化、跟踪扶持为主体的“一条龙”创业服务，逐步探索出了符合中国国情的政策扶持、创业培训与创业服务“三位一体”的工作模式，使创业带动就业的倍增效应越来越大、民众的创业精神意识越来越强。

（3）持续发展阶段（2008—2013 年）。国家把鼓励创业摆在就业工作更加突出的位置。在积极的就业政策的驱动下，全社会掀起了又一轮创业促就业新高潮。人力资源社会保障部总结经验和成果，探索出创业型城市以点带面推进工作的新格局。通过开展创业型城市创建工作，激发主要城市的社会活力，树立全民创业品牌。同时，通过开展创业主题论坛、创业训练营、创业专项大赛等系列活动，助推创业促就业工作；通过新项目合作，完善创业培训技术体系；学习“欧洲模拟公司”技术，研究开发适用于中国的创业实训技术；与国际劳工组织合作，实施了针对汶川灾后重建的“紧急创办和改善你的企业”（E-SIYB）项目、针对女性创业的“提高女性创业能力”（GET Ahead）项目和针对绿色环保创业的“绿色商业选择”（GBO）项目。此外，通过借鉴国外先进经验，发布“创业咨询师”国家职业资格，开发创业服务功能标准，指导各地成立创业指导中心，建立符合中国国情的公共创业服务体系。在这个阶段，创业环境显著改善，创业氛围显著提升，创业培训模式和技术方法更加成熟。

（4）推进创新阶段（2014 年至今）。国家将大众创业、万众创新提到战略高度，明确提出以创业创新带动就业。一方面，通过落实新的就业政策，放宽政策、放开市场、放活主体，形成创业创新的良好局面。另一方面，优化创业服务，打造“1+X”创业培训品牌。在以 SIYB 课程为核心的企业创办管理通用能力培训的基础上，根据创业的不同群体、不同阶段、不同行业，增加与职

业技能（如美容美发等）、专业技术（如 3D 打印等）、产业发展（如互联网产业等）和区域经济（如电商村等）相结合的“X”课程。同时，在公共创业服务体系建设成果的基础上，加强网络化信息资源共享，优化融资新模式，做大做强众创空间，使其成为承载创业服务的重要载体。

2. SIYB 项目的成效

（1）创业促就业方面的成果。在 SIYB 项目实施期间，培养了 6 万名创业培训师，建立了 3 000 余家创业培训机构。随着培训对象范围不断扩大，SIYB 项目最终帮助近千万名创业者获得培训并最终实现创业梦想。SIYB 项目的引进和实施适应了中国就业再就业工作发展的需要。由政府组织开发和整体推动的创业培训体系初步建立，该体系与小额担保贷款等一系列积极的就业政策相结合，为中国以创业促进就业工作奠定了坚实的基础。

（2）全国创业培训体系建设方面的成果。人力资源社会保障部在巩固 SIYB 项目成果的基础上，进一步结合中国国情，寻求创业培训的持续创新发展。通过完善技术标准、丰富课程资源、提升师资能力、组织讲师大赛、搭建信息化平台、创新服务手段，人力资源社会保障部已基本建立了培训主体多元、培训模式多样、覆盖创业活动不同阶段的创业培训体系，并打造出“马兰花中国创业培训”品牌示范项目。目前，该项目每年培训学员 70 万人次，累计培训创业讲师 6 万余人。

三、创业促进就业的成果

按照中共中央、国务院关于促进以创业带动就业的战略部署，各地以创建创业型城市工作为抓手，通过建立高效的组织推动机制，因地制宜，完善政策体系，实施有效的创业培训，开展有针对性的创业服务，营造有利于创业的舆论氛围，有效促进了创业带动就业工作。

（一）创业型城市的示范带动

2008 年 9 月，国务院对促进以创业带动就业工作进行专项部署和具体安排，提出要重点指导推动工作基础较好、条件相对成熟的城市，实施以创业带动就业相关扶持政策，在组织领导、创业培训、创业服务和社会参与等方面积极探索，建立以创业带动就业的创业型城市。2009 年年初，人力资源社会保障部作为牵头部门成立了促进以创业带动就业工作领导小组，统筹规划大学毕业生、下岗失业人员、返乡农民工、复转军人和归国留学人员的创业工作，并积极协调有关部门，直接指导各省及城市的创业促进就业工作。经全国各省评选推荐，人力资源社会保障部公布了首批 82 个国家级创建创业型城市名单。2009 年 3 月，召开全国创建创业型城市工作座谈会，部署推进创业型城市创建工作。同年 11 月，在上海市举办首届国家级创建创业型城市市长培训班，强化领导认识和责任，使一批市长成为抓好创业工作的带头人。2011 年 11 月，召开全国创业带动就业工作推进会，总结交流工作经验，部署实施推进工作新举措。

1. 充分发挥创建创业型城市的先导作用

总结成功经验，以城市为新的重要抓手，率先实现突破。在研究总结过去各项工作以抓试点城市为先导，迅速打开工作局面的成功经验后，人力资源社会保障部决定在全国推动以创业带动就业的工作首先从城市抓起。对那些一时在全国解决不了、全省解决不了的制度问题、政策问题，通过一批城市率先实现突破。

抓住城市创业机会较多，又是促进以创业带动就业的主战场的特点，开展创业型城市的创建工作。这既有利于城市创业者队伍扩大，带动就业增加，又有利于拓展城市新的经济增长点，还有利于改善城市发展环境。首批 82 个国家级创建创业型城市共同的特点是，经济发展环境比较好，公共就业服务体系比较健全，创业培训工作比较扎实，落实积极的就业政策取得了较好的工作成绩，

特别是小额担保贷款政策和税费减免政策落实有成效。

创业型城市先行一步，率先建树，率先突破，率先取得成效，就能开辟促进以创业带动就业工作的新局面。同时，通过以典型带路，以点带面，使全国层面的工作切切实实迈上一个新台阶。

2. 指导创业型城市建立健全五大体系

（1）建立组织领导体系。工作内容和考查重点包括四个方面：一是政府领导靠前指挥，工作摆到重要位置；二是部门形成合力，协调推动机制有效；三是社会积极参与，充分发挥工商联、工会、共青团、妇联、残联以及行业协会、企业家协会的作用，探索建立创业带动就业的社会化运作机制；四是职责任务明确，目标责任层层落实。

（2）完善政策支持体系。工作内容和考查重点包括四个方面：一是真正放宽市场准入、注册条件和场所安排，实现未禁即放；二是切实改善行政管理和办证手续，构建绿色通道；三是大力强化政策扶持，健全和落实税费减免、小额担保贷款、场地安排等扶持政策；四是拓宽融资渠道，建立创业专项扶持资金和小额担保贷款长效机制。

（3）健全创业培训体系。工作内容和考查重点包括三个方面：一是扩大创业培训范围，将新一轮创业者全部纳入创业培训轮训，并大力提高创业培训质量；二是充分利用现有条件和闲置资源建立健全创业孵化基地，推进创业实训；三是落实培训补贴政策，并将创业培训与项目开发、小额贷款、开业指导等有机结合起来。

（4）构建创业服务体系。工作内容和考查重点包括两个方面：一是根据创建工作的需要，依托公共就业服务体系，建立健全创业指导服务组织，加强创业服务队伍建设，新建或改建创业指导服务中心；二是积极研究创业服务的形式和内容，建立创业服务公共平台，改善服务手段，建立创业信息服务网络和

信息发布机制。

（5）健全工作业绩考核体系。考核体系主要包括四个指标：一是通过政府行为来考查五大体系建设是否健全完善；二是通过问卷调查来客观了解和反映对城市创业环境的满意度是否提升；三是通过创业活动指标来看城市就业者中创业含量是否真的加大，小企业、微型企业是否比以前生长发展得更好；四是通过创业贡献指标来看创业带动就业倍增效应是否真正提升。

3. 创建创业型城市取得的突破和成效

为检验工作效果，进一步推进工作，2012 年，受人力资源社会保障部委托，中国就业促进会成立专家评估组，会同社会专业调查机构和权威研究机构，对首批创业型城市创建工作进行评估。结果表明，各个创业型城市在促进创业带动就业方面取得了明显成效。由此看出，在全国推动创业带动就业工作，首先抓一批城市，率先建立体系，率先突破难点，率先取得成效，然后在此基础上逐步推开，这是落实促进创业带动就业战略部署的最实际、最有效的途径。

（1）推进五大体系建设。①在组织领导体系建设方面，各个创业型城市成立了创业工作领导小组，并积极开展工作，实现了市委、市政府的直接领导和靠前指挥，各有关部门和社会组织齐抓共管，共同促创业的新局面。②在政策支持体系建设方面，实现了由就业单项政策扩展到经济社会综合性政策，形成了多项政策支持的联动效应。各个创业型城市在放宽市场准入、改善行政管理、解决融资瓶颈、落实税收优惠、增加创业场地、鼓励带动就业等方面，出台了一系列更加优惠的扶持政策，不仅推进了创业工作，并且实现了制度性突破和创新。③在创业培训体系建设方面，初步建立了面向城乡各类有创业愿望的劳动者的培训体系，开展了多种形式的创业培训，为创业者的创业能力和素质的提升奠定了良好基础。④在创业服务体系建设方面，普遍建立了创业服务公共平台和社会中介组织，针对不同人群开展了“一条龙”的全方位服务，大大改

善了创业环境，方便了创业者，实现了由消极被动服务转变为积极主动服务。⑤在工作考核体系建设方面，建立了科学客观的绩效考评机制和相应的统计指标体系，开展了对创业带动就业工作的评估、检查和督促。

（2）突破性地解决创业门槛高、融资难等难点问题。针对创业门槛高、办事难的问题，各个创业型城市积极清理各种壁垒，进一步降低准入门槛，实行“非禁即入”原则，简化登记注册程序，降低创业服务成本。针对融资难和场地难的问题，不少省市把小额担保贷款工作作为重要突破口，大胆创新，建立起“贷得出、用得好、收得回”的良好机制，使小额担保贷款政策和资金充分发挥作用，为劳动者创业提供了有力支持，破解了融资难的瓶颈问题。许多城市通过依托各种园区、利用闲置厂房和建设孵化基地等方式，为创业者提供了创业场所，逐步缓解了场地难问题。针对大学生创业成功率低的问题，各个创业型城市大力推进大学生创业引领计划，积极开拓智力型创业领域，加大孵化服务和政策支持力度，大学生创业成功率已大幅提高。

（3）创业者和创业实体数量大幅增加。各个创业型城市积极消除市场壁垒，制止乱收费、乱摊派，严禁干预创业企业正常经营，对创业立项、核准、备案、审批和办证等实行联合审批、限时办结和“一站式”承诺服务。2011 年，创业型城市当年新创办的私营企业和个体户数量比 2008 年分别增长了 109% 和 66%。2011 年与 2008 年相比，创业型城市每万名经济活动人口中的个体私营经济实体户数增加了 33%，超过同期全国平均水平 3 个百分点；创业型城市个体私营经济实体数量增加了 42%，超过同期全国平均水平 10 个百分点；创业型城市个体私营经济实体从业人数增加了 52%，超过同期全国平均水平 18 个百分点。

（4）创业培训逐步推开。80% 以上的创业型城市初步建立起多方力量积极参与、面向城乡各类创业者的创业培训体系和创业服务体系。2011 年，全国参加创业培训的劳动者达到 145.5 万人，比 2008 年的培训人数增加 80%，培训质量水平也有相应提升。在创业型城市这种效果更为明显，普遍以高校毕业生、

失业人员和返乡农民工为重点，制订创业培训计划，出台经费补贴政策，整合社会教育培训资源，推动创业培训进校园、进社区、进农村，加强师资队伍和实训基地建设，采用先进课程和培训技术，努力提高培训水平。2009—2011 年，将近 76% 的创业型城市的“创业培训合格率”和“创业培训后半年开业率”两项指标有较大提高或保持在较高水平。

（二）“双创”逐步形成带动就业的新高潮

1.“双创”成为新常态下经济发展“双引擎”

“大众创业、万众创新”是适应经济社会发展需要而作出的一项重大决策。中共十八大召开以来，中国经济发展进入了新常态，在经济步入中高速发展阶段的同时，产业发展也进入了一个新的阶段。“大众创业、万众创新”是党和国家根据中国当前乃至今后一个时期经济发展提出的战略号召，成为新时期中国改革发展的强劲动力。

2015 年 6 月，国务院印发《关于大力推进大众创业万众创新若干政策措施的意见》(国发〔2015〕32 号)，提出大力推进大众创业、万众创新。“大众创业、万众创新”的提出，有其重要意义。一是培育和催生经济社会发展新动力的必然选择。经济发展进入新常态，需要从要素驱动、投资驱动转向创新驱动。推进大众创业、万众创新，就是要通过结构性改革、体制机制创新，消除不利于创业创新发展的各种制度束缚和桎梏，支持各类市场主体不断开办新企业、开发新产品、开拓新市场，从而培育新兴产业。二是扩大就业、实现富民之道的根本举措。当前中国就业总量压力较大，结构性矛盾凸显。推进大众创业、万众创新，就是要营造公平竞争的创业环境，使有梦想、有意愿、有能力的各类市场创业主体“如鱼得水”，通过创业增加收入，实现创业带动就业的良性互动发展。三是激发全社会创新潜能和创业活力的有效途径。目前，中国创业创新理念还没有深入人心，创业教育培训体系还不健全，善于创造、勇于创业的

能力不足，鼓励创新、宽容失败的良好环境尚未形成。推进大众创业、万众创新，就是要通过加强全社会以创新为核心的创业教育，弘扬“敢为人先、追求创新、百折不挠”的创业精神，不断增强创业创新意识，使创业创新成为全社会共同的价值追求和行为习惯。

深入实施创新驱动发展战略，推进“双创”不断向纵深发展，促进更加充分更高质量就业。（新华社记者罗晓光摄）

2.“双创”新政为创新创业者提供更好的服务

自提出推进大众创业、万众创新以来，国家和地方陆续出台了一系列支持“双创”的政策措施，创业带动就业倍增效应进一步释放，创业带动就业能力不断增强，重点群体就业工作扎实推进。

（1）畅通创业通道，扩大创业带动就业效应。坚持深化“放管服”改革，不断优化创业环境，通过深化行政审批制度、商事制度改革，降低市场准入门

槛，破除制约劳动者创业的体制机制障碍。落实促进高校毕业生、退役军人、残疾人、登记失业人员等群体创业的税费优惠政策。加大对初创企业的场地支持、设施提供、房租减免、住房优惠等政策扶持力度，降低创业成本，加快形成有利于劳动者参与创业的政策环境。

（2）调动劳动者的创业积极性。实施创新创业人才引进计划，创业培训计划，开展支持农民工等人员返乡创业试点等，支持鼓励大中专毕业生及专业人才转变观念，发挥知识和技术优势，成为创业的引领者。进一步放宽外国人才申请签证、工作许可、居留许可和永久居留证的条件，简化审批流程，加大创业启动资金支持力度，吸引更多境外高端人才来华创业创新。在全社会大力弘扬创业风尚，培育创业意识，营造鼓励创业、宽容失败的社会氛围。

（3）强化创业服务，提高创业成功率。建设有特色、高水平的区域、高校和科研院所以及企业的“双创”示范基地，提升创业服务能力。推广新型孵化模式，发展众创空间、孵化基地、创业园区等，提供项目开发、开业指导、融资等“一条龙”服务，支持劳动者成功创业。建设小微企业创业创新基地，形成线上与线下、孵化与投资相结合的开放式综合服务载体，根据创业主体的不同阶段、不同需求，向其提供有针对性的专业化、差别化、定制化指导服务，为企业创业兴业提供低成本、便利化服务，促进创业企业快速发展。同时，构建面向人人的创业服务平台，深入推进创业型城市创建活动，积极培育创业生态系统。

3. 小微企业就业主渠道作用得到进一步发挥

大众创业、万众创新的推进催生了小微企业“遍地开花”，支持小微企业发展成为“双创”背景下的重要议题之一。促进“双创”、优化“双创”政策环境，就是促进和优化小微企业健康发展的政策环境。推进大众创业、万众创新，需要更多地发挥社会力量，让小微企业真正活下来、发展好，这样才能更好地

激发市场活力和社会创造力，从而在更广阔的领域实现就业供需对接。通过扩大市场准入范围，落实小微企业降税减负等一系列扶持政策和清理规范涉企收费有关政策，优化创业环境，着力推进小微企业创新发展，推动小微企业创业创新示范基地建设，鼓励小微企业利用电商平台等多种方式开拓市场，增强其吸纳就业的能力，使小微企业成为吸纳就业的主力军，成为中国经济发展的新引擎。

4. 新形态就业发展迅速

据估算，在全部新增的就业中，新动能的贡献率达到 70% 左右。研究显示，以新产业、新业态、新模式为代表的新动能对促进以创业带动就业产生了积极作用，形成一种最活跃、最具能动性的机制。围绕适应新就业形态特点，国家提出了支持发展的政策：一是支持新兴业态发展。加快调整政策取向，通过完善税收、社会保障等方面政策法规，促进社会资源通过共享实现高效充分利用，推动共享经济等新经济形态加快发展，创造更多就业机会。二是完善适应新就业形态特点的用工和社会保障制度。支持劳动者通过新兴业态实现多元化就业，从业者与新兴业态企业签订劳动合同的，企业要依法为其参加城镇职工社会保险，符合条件的企业可按规定享受企业吸纳就业扶持政策。探索适应灵活就业人员的失业、工伤保险保障方式，符合条件的可享受灵活就业、自主创业扶持政策。

（三）创业促进就业的主要成果

1. 激发市场活力和创新动力，拓展就业新空间

近年来，国家大力推进简政放权、“放管服”改革，改革红利不断释放，各类市场主体的活力竞相迸发。自 2014 年推行商事制度改革以来，截至 2018 年年底，日均新设企业由 2013 年的 0.69 万户提高到 1.84 万户，每千人企业数从 2013 年的 11.4 户提高到 23.9 户，增加了 1 倍多。全国实有市场主体在 2018

年达到 1.06 亿户，其中 2014—2018 年这五年新设立的市场主体占比达到 73%。

实践证明，大众创业、万众创新是培育新动能、发展新兴产业、增加新就业的重要举措。市场活力和创新动力被全面激活，新经济、新就业不断涌现，成为就业增长的重要源泉。截至 2018 年年底，全国经工商登记注册的私营企业达 3 143.3 万户、个体户 7 328.6 万户，分别比 2009 年的 657.4 万户和 2 917.3 万户增加了 2 485.9 万户和 4 411.3 万户；全国私营企业就业人数达 21 375.4 万人，个体就业人数为 16 037.6 万人，分别比 2009 年的 7 904 万人和 5 776.4 万人增加了 13 471.4 万人和 10 261.2 万人。

2. 重点群体创业持续增长，网络创业成为新增长点

近年来，中国城镇新增就业已连续七年超过 1 300 万人，31 个大城市的城镇调查失业率也保持低位运行。积极的就业政策不断得到完善，重点人群就业成效明显。2013 年以来，高校毕业生连续四年实现就业创业人数“双增长”，累计有数百万名大学生登记注册市场主体。2013—2016 年，在工商部门登记注册的高校毕业生创业人数分别为 35.9 万人、47.8 万人、55.9 万人、61.5 万人（见图 5-1）。支持鼓励农民工返乡创业政策力度的不断加大，也使农民工返乡创业成为新趋势。据统计，截至 2018 年年底，全国返乡下乡创业人数达 780 万人。

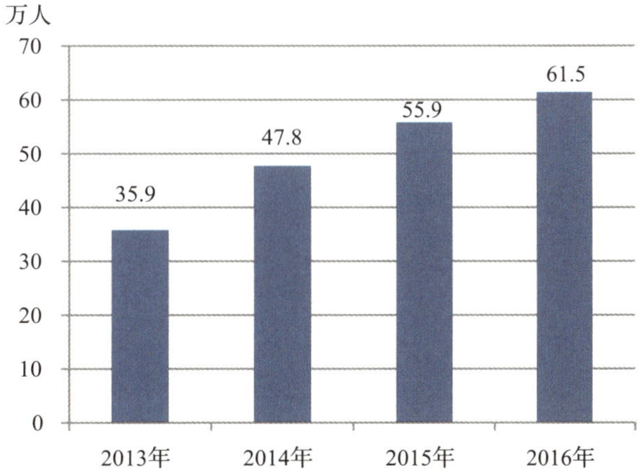

图 5-1　2013—2016 年登记注册的高校毕业生创业人数

随着网络经济和电子商务的快速发展，大量新职业涌现出来。截至2018年年底，平台经济拉动直接就业598万人，参与提供服务的人数约为7 500万人，电商平台为许多草根创业就业者拓展了工作与发展空间。一是扩大就业规模，拓宽就业领域。网上创业进入门槛低、开业成本低、发展迅速、业态灵活，带动的链条长，上升空间大，在带动相关产业扩大直接就业的同时，也有力地拉动了物流、支付、客服等行业、产业链的就业。同时，网络创业会催生许多“新鲜”职业发展，为就业提供扩容空间。二是优化就业结构，创新就业模式。劳动者不断提高自己的认知水平和掌握最新知识的能力，逐步成为知识经济时代所需要的具有随时掌握新技术、新知识的能力和素质的劳动者，从而大大增加了智能型就业，同时促进了智能密集型产业的兴起和就业结构的优化。三是提高就业质量，促进公平就业。网络创业为就业提供了更多的选择，既可以进一步拓展就业形式、丰富就业内容、提高就业率，又可以提高就业弹性、满足多种就业需求，这大大提高了劳动者的自由度。

3. 创业观念转变提升，创业环境得到改善

创业带来了就业观念的根本转变。特别是经历过金融危机之后，更多的劳动者转变了就业观念，认识到就业要靠自己，他们由过去向政府要工作、给别人打工“找饭碗”转变为自主创业、自负盈亏、自担风险“造饭碗”。中国的创业劳动者树立起五种精神：一是敢于冲破世俗观念的束缚、勇于创新的开拓精神；二是自强自立、艰苦奋斗、苦干实干的务实精神；三是能经受挫折和磨难、不折不挠的进取精神；四是讲究职业道德和信用、重诺守信的诚信精神；五是创业成功后不忘初心、回报社会的奉献精神。这五种精神成为劳动者创业的动力源泉，对带动新一代劳动者就业观念的转变产生了积极作用。培养和鼓励更多的创业劳动者具备这种精神，并使这种精神在全社会发扬光大，对劳动者就业观念的提升具有更加重要的意义。

创业型城市创建活动探索了建立组织领导、政策支持、创业培训、创业服务和工作考核五大体系，为创业者提供了更好的创业环境。扩大创业场地，建立孵化基地，同时允许创业者将家庭住所、租借房、临时商业用房等作为创业经营场所。很多城市利用现有的闲置厂房和各种园区建设创业孵化基地，并为创业者提供创业指导服务和一定期限的政策扶持。通过拓宽融资渠道，把小额担保贷款作为重要的融资来源，贷款数量大大增加，贷款服务效率也大大提升。全国大、中、小城市都已建立起创业指导机构和公共服务平台。根据世界银行营商环境评估报告，中国 2018 年营商环境总体评价在全球 190 个经济体中已经跃居第 46 位，比 2013 年累计上升 50 位，其中开办企业的便利度大幅度跃升至第 28 位，五年累计上升 130 位。

第六章 就业服务

一、就业服务概述

就业服务是指由特定的机构提供一系列服务措施，以满足劳动者求职就业或用人单位招用人员的需求的活动。就业服务的主要内容包括提供就业信息、职业指导、职业介绍、就业培训、创业指导、人力资源社会保障事务代理，以及随之产生的其他相关服务。就业服务的核心是为劳动者与用人单位提供进行相互对接匹配的中介服务。

就业服务机构是指专门从事就业服务活动的机构。就业服务机构从基本性质来看，可分为两类：一是公共就业服务机构。按照相关法律法规和政策要求，这类就业服务机构承担着向劳动者提供免费的公益性就业服务的职责，由县级以上人民政府设立举办。二是职业中介机构。按照人力资源市场运行管理规则，这类就业服务机构通过经营性运作，向劳动者、用人单位提供有偿性的相关职业中介服务，由社会组织或个人按照《中华人民共和国公司法》和《就业促进法》中有关职业中介机构管理的规定设立。

就业服务体系是各类从事就业服务的机构、中介组织等的总称。中国的就业服务体系目前主要由隶属于人力资源社会保障部门的公共就业服务机构、其

他部门和社会办的职业中介机构等共同组成。

中国政府高度重视就业工作，不断加大政策支持，强化就业服务，积极为劳动者就业搭建广阔平台。（新华社记者刘潇摄）

（一）公共就业服务发展历程

《就业促进法》规定，县级以上人民政府设立公共就业服务机构。随着经济社会的不断发展，公共就业服务机构逐步形成网络，公共就业服务制度逐步建立和完善，初步形成了具有中国特色的公共就业服务体系。公共就业服务的发展主要经历了五个阶段：

（1）公共就业服务初创阶段（20 世纪 80 年代）。改革开放之初，对计划经济体制下由政府指标控制、统包统配的城镇就业制度进行改革，实行了劳动部

门介绍就业、自愿组织起来就业和自谋职业相结合的“三结合”就业方针，市场机制逐渐在劳动力资源配置中发挥作用，出现了以劳动服务公司为代表的就业服务机构雏形。劳动服务公司是由政府劳动部门倡导的、集安置就业和培训于一体的社会组织形式，它逐步承担起组织管理社会劳动力、促进就业的多种职能。到20世纪80年代末，劳动服务公司已在全国基本普及。同时，随着人事制度改革，从80年代初开始，一些地区人事部门开始设立人才交流中心，为本地招聘人才提供交流服务和人才管理服务。

（2）就业服务体系逐步成型阶段（20世纪90年代）。20世纪80年代中期以后，市场对于劳动力资源的配置作用日趋明显。进入90年代后，随着劳动力市场的发展，各类职业介绍机构应运而生。劳动部门举办的就业服务机构逐步发展成为主要开展职业介绍、就业训练、失业保险、生产自救四项重要服务活动并使相关工作相互配合的就业服务体系。各省、市和主要区、县劳动部门相应成立了专门管理就业服务的机构，兴办了职业介绍中心、就业训练中心、失业保险所和劳动就业服务企业管理中心等服务实体，初步建立了针对登记失业人员的生活保障、介绍就业、组织培训、促进就业的一整套制度。公共就业服务网络体系初具规模。同时，各级人民政府鼓励社会团体和公民个人依法举办职业介绍机构。各类职业介绍机构发展迅速，成为就业服务体系的重要补充。这一期间，全国各地的省、市、县各级也普遍建立了人才交流服务机构，主要承担档案管理、毕业生就业手续办理、市场信息发布、组织人才招聘会等工作。

（3）公共就业服务制度建立健全阶段（20世纪90年代后期）。1998年，中共中央、国务院下发通知，要求各地切实做好国有企业下岗职工基本生活保障和再就业工作，将建立市场就业机制作为其中的工作目标之一，大力加强劳动力市场建设；公共职业介绍机构要开设专门服务窗口，加强对下岗职工的职业指导，并为其提供免费服务。为此，劳动和社会保障部自1999年开始，组织全国100个大中城市开展科学化、规范化、现代化“三化”建设试点，着力完

善公共就业服务的功能。2000 年年底，劳动和社会保障部在其颁布的《劳动力市场管理规定》（劳动和社会保障部令第 10 号）中明确规定了公共就业服务的性质、内容、免费服务对象，以及政府组织开展公共就业服务的职责。

（4）公共就业服务体系和制度的快步发展阶段（21 世纪初）。进入 21 世纪以来，随着积极的就业政策的实施，中国公共就业服务体系和制度建设进入了快车道。2002 年，中国开始实施积极的就业政策，其中明确要求各级人民政府建立公共就业服务制度，对全部城镇登记失业人员和国有企业下岗职工提供免费职业介绍，对城镇就业转失业人员和国有企业下岗职工提供免费再就业培训，所需经费主要由地方财政承担，中央财政对困难地方给予适当补助。2003 年，在总结劳动力市场“三化”建设的基础上，中共中央、国务院进一步提出就业服务要实行制度化、专业化和社会化（简称“新三化”）的要求。2005 年，按照国务院要求，公共就业服务机构向所有求职者免费开放，职业培训补贴范围也覆盖到进城务工的农村劳动者。2007 年，劳动和社会保障部下发《关于完善公共就业服务功能有关工作的通知》（劳社部函〔2007〕63 号），对公共就业服务的六项服务职能（综合服务、信息发布、职业介绍、职业指导、培训与创业服务、就业和失业管理）做了具体规定，并大力推行“一站式”服务。通过“新三化”的实施，在制度化建设方面，失业人员登记制度、就业困难人员就业援助制度以及就业登记、失业登记与就业服务有机衔接的流程得到进一步加强；在专业化建设方面，服务功能多元化建设、服务理念人性化建设、工作队伍专业化建设和服务手段信息化建设得到进一步强化；在社会化程度方面，农村进城务工人员、高技能人才和高校毕业生等各类求职者和用人单位已被全部纳入服务范围，社会各类职业中介、劳务派遣、职业咨询、职业培训等民营服务机构参与公益性就业服务受到鼓励，以服务对象满意度为衡量标准的服务评价体系开始建立起来。

（5）公共就业服务的充实完善阶段（2008 年以后）。自 2008 年起实施的

《就业促进法》进一步明确，县级以上人民政府要把公共就业服务经费纳入同级财政预算，要建立健全公共就业服务体系和制度，设立公共就业服务机构，为劳动者提供免费的就业政策法规咨询、职业供求信息、市场工资指导价位和职业培训信息、职业介绍和职业指导、就业和失业登记，以及就业援助等服务。劳动和社会保障部颁布的《就业服务与就业管理规定》（劳动和社会保障部令第28号）同样自2008年1月1日起施行。2009年为应对国际金融危机对就业的冲击所出台的六大举措中，多部门联合开展了就业服务系列活动，实施特别职业培训计划，并对困难群体提供就业援助等，这些举措在化解危机的同时，丰富充实了公共就业服务功能，促进了公共就业服务体系的进一步完善。例如，人力资源社会保障部会同教育部、全国总工会、共青团中央、全国妇联和全国残联等社会团体联合组织开展了系列就业服务活动，主要包括以促进零就业家庭就业为重点的再就业援助活动、以促进高校毕业生就业为重点的民营企业招聘周和高校毕业生就业服务月活动，以及为方便满足农村劳动者每年春节后集中进城务工需求开展的“春风行动”等；又如，针对困难群体实行的就业援助制度，主要是依托街道、社区等公共就业服务机构，为就业困难群体开设专门服务窗口，提供政策咨询、职业介绍、技能培训、事务代理等专项援助服务，对特困就业人员提供“一对一”的跟踪服务和指导。特别是中国面向城乡劳动者均等化服务的公共就业服务也在逐步形成和不断完善。自2005年起，中国政府在全国范围内实行城乡劳动者平等的就业服务，使农村劳动者进城就业的环境得到了改善。

公共就业服务机构为高校毕业生提供就业服务。（新华社记者刘颖摄）

大中城市市、区两级及部分有条件的小城市都建立了以公共职业介绍机构为窗口的综合性服务场所，在基层街道和社区设立了劳动保障工作平台。中央、省、市、区（县）、街道（乡镇）、社区五级管理、六级服务的公共就业服务网络逐步构建起来，形成了集就业政策信息、职业介绍、职业指导以及劳动保障事务代理服务于一体，并同职业培训、失业人员管理、就业岗位开发、创业培训、开业指导等职能相衔接的“一站式”便捷服务体系。2018 年，全国区（县）及以上公共就业和人才交流服务机构共计 5 618 个，绝大多数街道和乡镇设立了基层工作平台，大部分社区和行政村配备了劳动保障工作人员。各级公共就业和人才服务机构累计办理登记招聘 5 518 万人次、登记求职 3 774 万人次，提供职业指导 1 719 万人次、职业介绍 1 859 万人次、创业指导 436 万人次、创业培训 201 万人次。

（二）民办职业中介机构的地位

民办职业中介机构是指由非政府部门的法人、社会组织和公民个人开办的，为用人单位招用人员和劳动者求职提供中介服务以及其他相关服务的经营性组织。

2002 年以来，中国政府出台了一系列积极的就业政策，一方面，将民办职业中介机构作为促进就业的重要力量，鼓励其发展，使其参与对下岗失业人员和农民工的就业服务工作，并向其给予政策支持；另一方面，加强对职业中介机构规范管理，严厉打击非法职业中介行为和中介活动中侵犯求职者权益的行为。

《就业促进法》规定，各级人民政府要鼓励职业中介机构依法开展就业服务活动，并对其提供的公益性就业服务活动给予补贴。该法还对职业中介机构设立的条件、审批程序以及禁止从事的活动和对违法行为的惩处作出了明确规定。《劳动合同法》和《劳务派遣暂行规定》则对相关机构开展劳务派遣业务的相关权利、责任、义务和对被派遣劳动者的权益保护作出了相应规定。《中华人

民共和国政府采购法》（以下简称《政府采购法》）对政府的采购活动做了明确界定。《政府购买服务管理办法》则对购买主体和承接主体、购买服务内容和购买服务指导性目录、采购方式和程序、预算和财务管理、绩效评价和监督管理等做了详细规定，从而优化社会资源配置，降低成本，促进公平竞争，提高服务质量和效率，以满足人民群众对公共服务的需求。

截至 2017 年年底，全国设立各类人力资源服务机构 3.02 万家，同比增加 13%，其中民营性质服务企业 21 990 家，占 72.9%（见表 6–1）；行业从业人员为 58.4 万人，同比增长 5.6%，其中民营性质服务企业为 39.6 万人，占 67.8%（见表 6–2）。

表 6–1　2016—2017 年各类人力资源服务机构变化情况

	机构数量 / 家		占比 /%	
	2016 年	2017 年	2016 年	2017 年
公共就业和人才服务机构	5 262	5 259	19.7	17.4
国有性质服务企业	1 493	1 793	5.6	6.0
民营性质服务企业	18 859	21 990	70.6	72.9
港、澳、台及外资性质服务企业	227	235	0.9	0.8
其他性质人力资源服务机构	854	885	3.2	2.9

资料来源：孙建立 . 中国人力资源服务业发展报告（2018）[M] . 北京：中国人事出版社，2018.

表 6–2　2016—2017 年人力资源服务业从业人员情况（按机构性质分）

	人员总数 / 万人		占行业总人数比例 /%	
	2016 年	2017 年	2016 年	2017 年
政府所属人力资源服务机构	9.1	8.8	16.5	15.1
国有性质服务企业	6.0	6.6	10.8	11.3
民营性质服务企业	37.0	39.6	66.9	67.8
港、澳、台及外资性质服务企业	1.9	2.1	3.4	3.6
其他性质人力资源服务机构	1.3	1.3	2.4	2.2

资料来源：孙建立 . 中国人力资源服务业发展报告（2018）[M] . 北京：中国人事出版社，2018.

（三）公共就业服务机构与民办职业中介机构的合作

在国际上，许多国家在实施有关劳动力市场的政策时，已形成一种鼓励公共就业服务机构与民办职业中介机构开展合作的趋势。中国在面对新时期就业工作的新挑战时，需要对现行公共就业服务体制机制、运行模式等进行改革，同时大力探索推进公共就业服务机构与民办职业中介机构的合作，逐步建立公共就业服务机构、社会伙伴就业服务机构、民办职业中介机构“三位一体”的就业服务新格局。

1. 推进公共就业服务机构与民办职业中介机构开展合作的积极意义

一是有利于政府转变职能，扩大和延伸公共就业服务的范围和领域，形成多元化、多层次的就业服务供给体系；二是有利于弥补现行公共就业服务体系和力量的不足，提高公共就业服务的整体质量和效率；三是有利于降低公共就业服务运行成本，提高公共资金使用效率，实现政府投入资金效益最大化；四是有利于公共就业服务机构与民办职业中介机构优势互补，形成合力，高效便捷地为求职者和雇主提供全方位、高质量的就业和培训服务。

2. 公共就业服务机构与民办职业中介机构在合作中的责权利

目前，中国一些地区公共就业服务机构与民办职业中介机构之间的合作，主要是按照《政府采购法》和《政府购买服务管理办法》的规定，依据合作的具体内容签订合同进行的。合同规定了双方的责权利。

（1）公共就业服务机构及其主管部门的责任和义务。一是制定购买服务的规划并实施。根据法律、法规的要求，同时满足公众多元化就业服务的需求，明确合作制度框架，制定政府购买就业服务的整体规划、具体计划 / 项目及实施细则。二是确立购买服务的原则和目标任务。在符合国家相关法律、法规和政策的条件下，选择有资质和能力的民办职业中介机构等社会力量开展公共就业服务。三是确定合作伙伴的基本条件与标准。合作服务机构须具备独立法人

资格，经营业务范围包括创业就业服务；须具备专职人员、相应设施设备和一定的财力；同时具备举办各种就业创业服务活动的能力和实践经验，以及与外界开展良好合作的基础，且取得过开展高效服务的业绩。四是确立购买服务的程序与方法。依法制定并实行公开、公平、公正的招投标程序，遴选合作服务机构，并与其签订购买就业服务合同，规定双方的责任、权利与义务。五是负责政府购买服务经费的测算、拨付，并对经费的使用进行检查监督。六是负责合作项目的评估、监督和奖惩。按照法规规定和服务合同确定的服务内容、范围、数量和质量标准对合作项目实施事前、事中和事后评估和监管，并依据项目绩效评估结果实行奖惩。

（2）民办职业中介机构的责权利。一是运营管理合同约定的公共就业创业服务项目。遵照国家法规和政策的要求，在政府主管部门的指导和监督下，按合同管理和使用好公共就业创业服务资源，包括人员、资金、信息、设施和设备等资源。二是建立并开展网络服务。提供劳动力供求双方沟通、交流、联结、配置服务相结合的交流配置服务平台，同时改进传统服务模式，提供线上线下一体化的就业创业服务。三是组织专家队伍提供就业创业服务。指导咨询服务，并动员和吸纳其他社会力量参与到合作项目中来。四是举办大型就业创业活动，为求职者和创业者搭建服务平台，如举办招聘会、创业项目推介会、创业沙龙、技能培训等活动。五是主动做好合作项目的总结，定期自行检查并进行客户回访，及时将相关信息呈报公共就业服务机构及主管政府部门，配合后者做好绩效评估与考核。

3. 公共就业服务机构与民办职业中介机构的合作形式

（1）整合就业信息资源，建立就业信息平台。充分运用公共就业服务机构成熟的公共就业人才服务信息系统，将民办职业中介机构相对分散的就业岗位信息，纳入信息系统进行集中管理与发布应用，实现招聘信息与求职信息的共

享与服务。

（2）联动开展就业服务专项活动，扩大就业服务效果。联合开展“春风行动”、高校毕业生就业服务月等活动，为外来务工人员和高校毕业生等求职人员提供就业岗位信息对接服务，扩大就业服务的覆盖面，提高职业介绍的服务效率。

（3）加强交流与合作，共同提升专业水平。依托公共就业服务资源，发挥民办职业中介机构的主动性，开展业务研讨和互动交流，共同促进就业服务工作的发展。

二、公共就业服务体系

（一）公共就业服务的布局和机构

1. 公共就业服务机构

公共就业服务机构是具体承担公共就业服务活动的载体，是政府按照有关法律法规的要求设立的为劳动者和用人单位提供就业服务的专门机构。中国的公共就业服务机构主要包括三类：一是公共就业服务管理机构，承担本地区公共就业服务规划、公共就业服务机构管理和人力资源市场管理工作。二是公共就业服务工作机构，以职业介绍服务为主，按照统一服务窗口的要求，设立专门服务场所，作为直接面向求职者和用人单位提供服务的综合性服务窗口，承担政策咨询、信息发布、职业介绍、职业指导、职业培训、创业服务和劳动保障事务代理等多项就业服务功能。三是以街道（乡镇）社区劳动保障工作平台为主的基层公共就业服务机构，承担面向基层群众提供公共就业服务、向就业困难群体提供就业援助等基础性工作。

公共就业服务机构具有三个特点：一是公共就业服务机构代表政府履行公共就业服务职能，具有公益性质。二是公共就业服务机构是负责为劳动者提供

公共就业服务机构为创业者介绍相关优惠政策。（新华社记者杨扬摄）

就业服务的专门机构，具备相应的专业服务能力，包括基本服务功能、服务场所、服务人员和服务技术与设备等。三是公共就业服务机构的公益性服务是通过向劳动者提供免费服务和就业援助来实现的。

2. 公共就业服务体系

公共就业服务体系是国家根据促进就业的总体政策制度要求建立的为劳动者提供就业服务的工作体系，由各级各类公共就业服务机构组成。公共就业服务体系按照服务内容划分，包括综合性服务机构、专业性服务机构和基层服务窗口。综合性服务机构负责为各类劳动者提供各种就业服务。专业性服务机构负责提供某些专项或某些领域的专门服务，如高校毕业生就业服务、残疾人就业服务、创业服务等。基层服务窗口负责基础性人力资源社会保障服务、就业援助和人力资源调查统计等。

县级以上各级公共就业服务机构根据政府确定的就业工作目标任务，制定年度就业服务工作规划和公共就业服务机构年度目标任务；承担贯彻落实国家促进就业的法律、行政法规和相关政策的有关工作，参与制定和组织落实各项就业政策；直接承担统筹做好城镇失业人员和新成长劳动力、高校毕业生和农村富余劳动力等各类群体就业服务工作的职责。

（二）公共就业服务项目内容和功能作用

《就业促进法》规定，公共就业服务机构应当免费为劳动者提供六项基本服务，即就业政策法规咨询，职业供求信息、市场工资指导价位信息和职业培训信息发布，职业指导和职业介绍，对就业困难人员实施就业援助，办理就业登记、失业登记等事务，其他公共就业服务。市场条件下的公共就业服务职能示意图见图 6-1。

1. 就业政策法规咨询

公共就业服务机构为用人单位、求职者等服务对象提供常见劳动保障法律、法规、政策等方面问题的咨询指导服务，主要涉及就业扶持政策、社会保障政策、劳动权益保护等内容。

2. 信息收集和发布

公共就业服务机构通过多种形式收集和发布与就业服务对象求职就业、招聘人员有关的人力资源市场信息。收集和发布的信息主要包括职业供求信息、人力资源市场工资指导价位信息、职业培训信息。此外，公共就业服务机构还应当提供职业供求分析预测信息、就业服务项目信息、劳动保障和就业政策法规等其他就业服务相关信息。

3. 职业指导

公共就业服务机构为求职者选择职业、准备就业并为用人单位招聘用人提

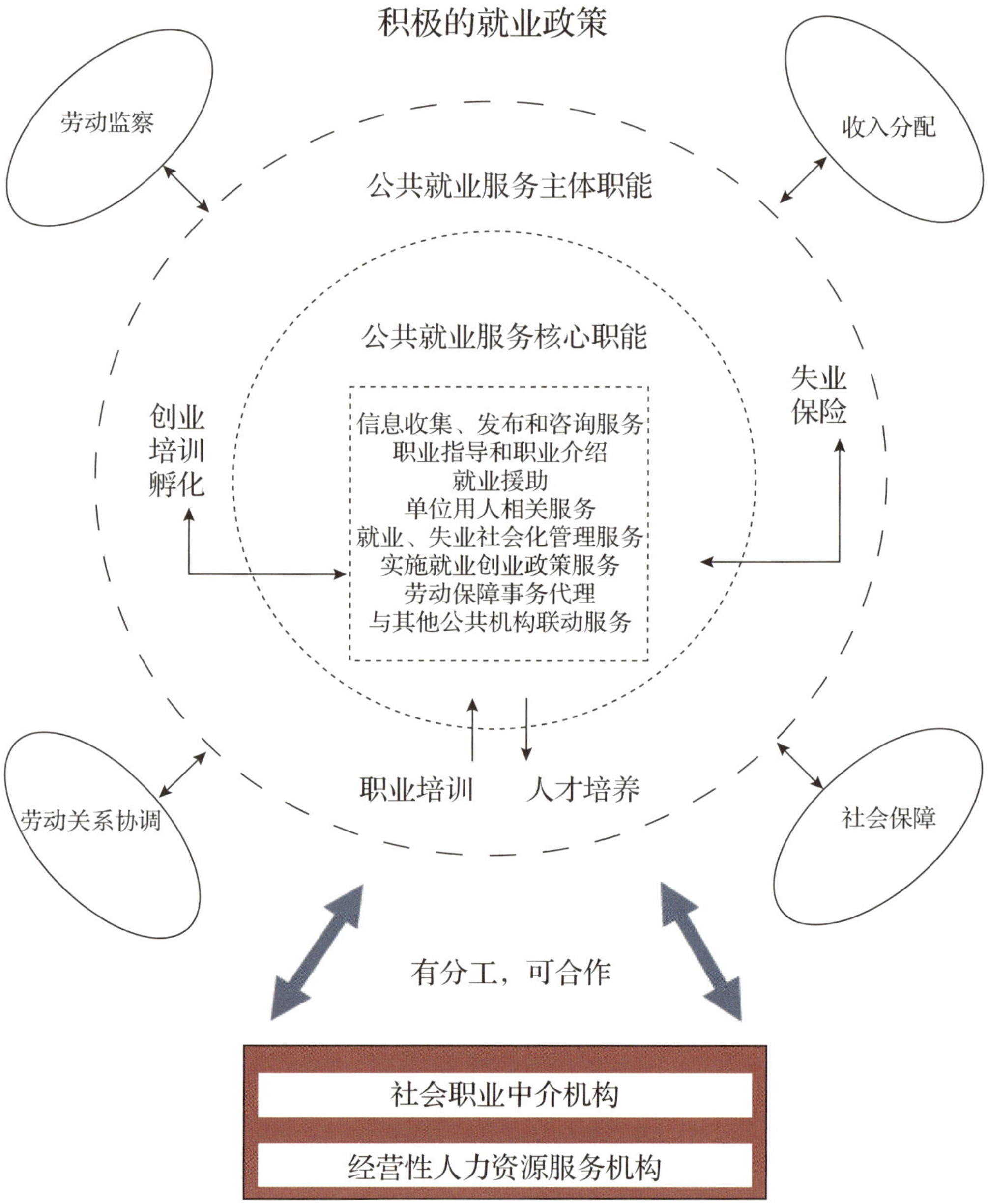

图 6-1　市场条件下的公共就业服务职能示意图

供专业指导。职业指导按指导对象的不同，可以分为对个人求职者的指导和对用人单位的指导；按指导方式的不同，可以分为“一对一”的个体指导和专项小组的群体指导；按就业阶段的不同，可以分为就业前指导、就业中（在岗）指导和就业后指导。职业指导服务主要包括以下内容：调查分析社会职业变动

趋势和人力资源市场供求状况；开展对劳动者职业素质和就业能力测评；帮助劳动者了解职业状况，掌握求职方法，确定择业方向，规划职业生涯；向劳动者提出职业培训建议，并推介职业培训项目；为妇女、残疾人、退役军人、高校毕业生及就业困难人员等群体提供专门的职业指导服务；指导用人单位选择招聘方法，确定用人条件和标准；向从事个体经营、自主创业的劳动者提供开业和生产经营方面的咨询服务。

4. 职业介绍

职业介绍是通过为人力资源供求双方提供中介服务以促进就业的活动，包括收集、发布职业供求信息，对用人单位招聘人员和劳动者求职就业提供中介服务等。公共就业服务机构职业介绍方面的主要任务是提供求职登记、企业用工调查与登记、市场供求信息的收集和传播、就业与用工的指导与咨询。

公共就业服务机构提供职业介绍服务的具体步骤为：一是对到公共就业服务机构求职或招聘的求职者或用人单位进行登记。二是公共就业服务机构按照服务对象求职或招聘的需求和条件，为其推荐提供符合条件的职业供求信息；同时，根据已登记的求职、招聘信息中的需求和条件，主动匹配条件相互符合的职业供求信息。三是根据公共就业服务对象选择的职业供求信息或公共就业服务机构匹配出的职业供求信息，主动与求职者和用人单位双方联系，并为求职者和用人单位面对面的双向选择提供现场招聘等。依托互联网等现代化技术手段，建立人力资源市场信息库，开展人力资源供求分析、预测，搜集、整理和定期发布人力资源市场信息。

5. 就业援助

公共就业服务机构采取专门措施，提供专门就业政策，对就业困难人员实施优先扶持和重点帮助，使其实现就业和稳定就业。

公共就业服务机构开展就业援助服务的具体步骤为：一是针对就业困难人

员开展专门性的指导，提供“一对一”服务。二是对推荐就业的就业困难人员实行跟踪服务和指导，持续了解就业困难人员的就业情况。三是积极与当地用人单位进行联系，有针对性地开发适合就业困难人员的公益性岗位。四是建立就业援助制度，定期开展针对就业困难群体的专项服务活动，将日常援助与集中援助结合起来。

6. 办理就业登记、失业登记等事务

公共就业服务机构承担政府行政部门委托的就业和失业管理事务。为单位录用人员以及自谋职业、灵活就业的人员办理就业登记手续，并建立相应台账；为法定年龄内有劳动能力及就业要求的失业人员办理登记手续，并提供有关就业政策和就业服务方面的咨询服务；为失业人员提供核定失业保险待遇、失业人员档案管理、就业失业登记证（后更名为就业创业证）管理、核定各项补贴等服务，并提供创业担保贷款的配套服务。公共就业服务机构还要指导用人单位做好解聘备案、录用备案等工作。

（三）构建全方位公共就业服务体系

中共十九大提出了实现更高质量和更充分就业的新目标。加快构建全方位公共就业服务体系的建设，是实现就业任务目标的重大举措。

1. 全方位公共就业服务体系的主要内涵和基本要素

全方位公共就业服务是以促进就业创业为宗旨，以落实就业创业政策为主导，以满足劳动者实现就业和自主创业的多元需求与单位用人基本需求、实现劳动力供求相互匹配为主线的全面、便捷、高效的服务。

（1）全方位公共就业服务体系的主要内涵。包括：①服务覆盖全体对象，表现为服务对象的全方位。一是面向有就业创业意愿的城乡劳动者的就业创业服务，二是面向有招聘需求的社会各类单位的用人服务，三是面向有服务需求的各类社会培训、中介等机构的支持服务。②服务贯穿就业全程，表现为服务

过程的全方位。一是对就业政策落实各环节的全程服务，二是对劳动者职业生涯各阶段的全程服务，三是对单位用人相关方面的全程服务。③服务配备齐全功能，表现为服务项目的全方位。一是提供职业指导服务和职业介绍服务，二是提供就业技能培训服务，三是提供专项援助服务，四是提供就业扶贫和劳务输出服务，五是提供创业全程服务，六是提供失业保障服务，七是提供就业合作服务，八是提供信息和数据分析服务。④服务运用多种方式，表现为服务手段的全方位。一是场所窗口服务，二是线上网络服务，三是线上线下结合的综合服务，四是宣传咨询服务。⑤服务实现便捷高效，表现为能效提升的全方位。一是实现就地就近办理和网上快捷办理，二是简化服务流程，三是实施精准化服务。

（2）构建全方位公共就业服务体系包含六项基本要素。包括：①制度标准要素，包括基本服务均等制度体系和公共服务标准体系建设。②硬件建设要素，包括服务机构规划建设和服务网点合理布局。③智能建设要素，包括服务功能设置和信息服务平台建设。④机构合成要素，包括公共就业服务组织体系和合作机构网络建设。⑤能力建设要素，包括专业化工作队伍建设和岗位定责、绩效管理。⑥体制保障要素，包括落实就业工作法律地位和提供经费保障。

2. 重点工作

（1）推进均等化，实现普惠化。包括推进城乡全体劳动者服务的均等化，推进各类用人单位服务的均等化，推进不同地域服务的均等化。

（2）推进标准化，实现规范化。包括加快建立健全国家和地方标准体系，贯彻执行标准促进规范化服务管理。

（3）推进专业化，实现服务精细化。包括打造“智能匹配、精准高效”的职业介绍服务，探索“精准识别判断、精细服务”的职业指导服务，提供与“提升能力、培育引导和扶持”的创业培训指导相连接的服务，提供与“紧贴

市场、按需定向、注重实效”的职业技能培训相衔接的服务，提供与失业保险“保障生活、促进就业、预防失业”的“三位一体”功能紧密衔接的服务，实施“按人分级分类、精准施策帮扶”的就业援助服务。

（4）全力提升信息化，实现服务智能化。包括建立全国统一的公共就业服务信息平台，大力推进信息互联互通和数据共享，进一步强化就业信息大数据的开发利用。

（5）充分运用市场化机制，实现服务社会化。包括运用市场机制整合市场资源，探索建立购买服务机制，加强与社会机构合作从而形成就业服务合力，加强部门间协调从而形成服务工作联动。

3. 保障措施

（1）加强组织领导。制定城乡一体化的就业创业服务总体规划，完善制度、机制和体制建设；确定年度目标任务，明确责任，组织开展对各地推动全方位公共就业服务工作的进度和质量的考核评估。

（2）加强队伍建设。构建公共就业服务人员职业稳定发展的平台，加速完善人员队伍构建机制，促进人员队伍发展和稳定；制订实施公共就业服务人员能力提升计划，加快建立各层次、专职领域服务人才培养机制，全面提升公共就业服务人员的专业水平和服务能力。

（3）加强资金保障。各级人民政府根据完成新时代就业目标任务和提供全方位就业服务的需要，不断加大同级财政预算投入力度；整合现有资源，统筹就业等各项资金，提高资金使用效益，加强对就业专项资金的监管和使用的指导。

（4）加强绩效评价。与推进服务标准化、规范化建设有机结合，加强服务评价和效能考核；引导激励工作人员改进服务行为和提高工作业绩；及时发现和解决问题，提升服务效能和质量。

（四）公共就业服务信息化建设

按照人力资源社会保障信息化建设工作的总体部署，完善公共就业服务信息系统建设。

1. 信息系统建设内容

（1）就业服务的信息化。包括服务对象信息和服务资源（如岗位）信息的数据库、供求信息检索与匹配子系统、服务对象自助型信息子系统等。

将“互联网 +”的创新成果与就业服务深度融合，不断拓展服务内容，创新服务方式。（新华社记者李少鹏摄）

（2）就业服务管理信息系统。包括各类就业服务机构的业务经办信息管理子系统、服务成效信息等方面的存储与分析统计子系统等。

（3）人力资源市场信息发布系统。包括人力资源市场供求信息分析与预测子系统、专用信息发布子系统、公众信息发布子系统等。

2. 公共就业服务信息化的作用

（1）信息网络是就业服务的有效工具。通过信息网络建设，为服务对象提供更多的、更及时的信息；通过信息网络向街道、社区和乡镇、村延伸，更贴近服务对象；通过信息网络的分析和自动匹配，为服务对象提供个性化或打包式服务。

（2）信息网络是业务管理的有力手段。通过信息网络建设，实现信息管理和信息共享，从而有效地提高各项业务自身和业务间协调的管理水平，提供及时、准确的资源信息和管理信息，以保证就业服务领域中各项业务管理到位。

（3）信息网络是宏观决策的有益支持。信息网络是各级人民政府和有关部门进行相关决策的重要信息来源。通过信息化，汇总提炼大量人力资源市场具有完整性和统一性的信息，在统计分析的基础上，为相关部门的政策制定和管理决策服务。

3. 建立健全就业信息服务体系

建立健全就业信息服务体系是指建立健全为社会提供人力资源市场供求状况和相关信息等方面服务的工作体系。一是通过信息服务，有效引导和调节市场资源的流动和配置。一方面，可以帮助劳动者实现自主择业，帮助用人单位实现成功招聘；另一方面，可以有效地引导人力资源的流动，提高人力资源配置的效率和质量。同时，市场信息对职业培训机构选择培训方向、对劳动者为进入市场做好准备、对用人单位合理确定招聘人员范围和劳动报酬，都有引导作用。二是政府通过发布市场供求信息，有效地提升了在市场中处于弱势地位的劳动者对市场状况信息的了解掌握程度，可以较为显著地减少劳动者因信息了解不及时或不正确而出现的问题。三是就业信息服务体系不仅服务于社会公众，同时也是各级人民政府和有关部门了解人力资源市场现状和发展趋势信息的重要渠道，以及进行有关就业方面宏观决策的重要信息来源。

三、民办职业中介机构的发展

民办职业中介机构是中国就业服务体系的组成部分。《就业促进法》规定，各级人民政府要鼓励社会各方面依法开展就业服务活动，加强对公共就业服务和职业中介服务的指导和监督，逐步完善覆盖城乡的就业服务体系。这不仅为民办职业中介机构的设立提供了法律依据，也为其发展指明了方向。

（一）民办职业中介机构的特点

民办职业中介机构作为随市场经济的发育完善而出现的新生事物，具有以下特点：一是组织形式的公司化和经营方式的企业化。大多数民办职业中介机构都要到工商行政管理部门办理登记手续，以公司名义开展业务，自主经营，自负盈亏。二是服务方式的多样化和服务内容的广泛化。民办职业中介机构的服务方式以满足用人单位和求职者的要求为宗旨，由其充当人才经纪人。其服务内容包括：组织各种人才交流活动，为企业招聘人才，为人才介绍职业，进行人才素质测评，举办专业技术培训，进行人才咨询服务等。三是服务对象的差别化。有的民办职业中介机构面对所有劳动者和用人单位，有的则是为高端专业人才服务，有的为国内人才走出国门搭桥铺路，有的则为企业在人力资源管理方面出谋划策。四是服务手段的现代化。许多民办职业中介机构以高科技为手段，利用互联网建立人才库和信息网络，通过各种媒体发布人才供求信息。

（二）民办职业中介服务的主要内容

1. 服务内容

（1）信息服务。信息服务包括人力资源市场信息收集、信息交流与信息发布等。

（2）人力资源管理咨询服务。人力资源管理咨询服务是运用人力资源开发与管理的理论和方法，对企业的人力资源开发与管理进行分析，找出其中的薄弱环节，帮助其加以改善，以促进企业正确、有效地开发人力资源和合理、科学地管理人力资源，从而为企业创造永续的竞争力。

（3）人才测评服务。人才测评是指通过一系列科学的手段和方法对劳动者的基本素质及其绩效进行测量和评定的活动，包括职业能力测试评估、职业分析与评价等。

（4）招聘服务。招聘服务是民办职业中介机构运用人力资源市场机制，依

法为劳动者求职和用人单位招聘用人提供中介服务的活动，包括求职和用人面谈、介绍就业和推荐用人、举办招聘洽谈会等。

（5）人事外包服务。人事外包服务是指企业根据自身需要将某一项或某几项人力资源管理工作或职能外包出去，交由其他企业或组织进行管理，以降低其人力成本，从而实现企业的效率最大化。人事外包服务包括受用人单位委托组织招聘，受求职人员委托存放档案，以及受劳动行政部门委托办理劳动和社会保险等事务。

（6）猎头服务。猎头服务是帮助优秀企业找到其所需要的人才的服务，也叫作高级人才寻访。猎头也可称为猎夺人才，即发现、追踪、评价、甄选和提供高级人才的行为。猎头服务已成为企业获取高级人才的一种重要选择，并形成了一种产业。

2. 服务标准

（1）文明服务。场所整洁，设施便利；工作人员挂牌服务，语言文明；尊重隐私，保守秘密，诚实守信。

（2）公平服务。对各类求职人员和用人单位一律平等对待，公平服务，不歧视。

（3）高效服务。尽最大努力提供全面、快捷、准确的服务，使求职人员和用人单位满意。注重增强求职人员竞争就业能力，培养其自主就业意识。

（4）灵活服务。服务方式多样化，能满足不同求职人员和用人单位的服务需求；服务内容和服务约定建立在与求职人员和用人单位共同协商的基础上。

（三）民办职业中介服务的作用

（1）为求职人员提供个性化服务。公共职业介绍机构提供的是基本就业服务，针对所有劳动者，尤其是人力资源市场中的弱势群体。民办职业中介机构提供的是差别化、个性化的就业服务，能够满足求职人员的特定需求，提高其

职场竞争能力。

（2）弥补公共职业介绍机构的不足。多年实践证明，放开人力资源市场，允许甚至鼓励民办职业中介机构在法律框架下开展职业介绍工作，发挥民办职业中介机构在就业服务中机制灵活、市场开发能力强、运用新技术快、为服务对象提供专业化和个性化服务等优势，能够有效地弥补公共职业介绍机构的不足。国际劳工组织在1997年通过了《私营就业机构公约》（第181号）和《私营就业机构建议书》（第188号），废止了职业介绍工作的政府垄断，盘活了劳动力市场，实现了劳动力资源的合理配置，也是顺应了这一发展趋势。

（3）促进充分就业的实现。实现充分就业需要多方主体共同努力。民办职业中介机构的规范运作和高效服务将有助于目标的实现。在现代市场经济体制下，民办职业中介机构在日常经营活动过程中，不仅掌握了诸多岗位空缺和劳动者求职信息，而且其服务方式更加多样，工作机制更加灵活，讲求网络技术运用和效率提升，能够促进劳动者和用人单位之间的快速匹配和对接，从而为实现充分就业做出了贡献。

第七章 职业培训

一、职业培训与促进就业

（一）中国职业培训发展历程

（1）国民经济恢复时期（1950—1952 年），以失业工人转业训练为主阶段。在中华人民共和国刚刚成立之后，全国城市有（旧中国遗留下来的）失业工人和其他失业人员 400 多万人。政府在采取以工代赈、生产自救、回乡生产和发放救济金等多种办法对失业人员进行安置的同时，还大量举办各种转业训练班，按照当地生产建设的实际需要设置专业，对失业工人进行转业训练。训练期限一般为 3~6 个月或 1 年不等，长短结合，以短期为主。训练内容以操作技能为主，加上必要的政治、文化学习。这种转业训练不仅在解决当时就业问题的过程中起到了良好作用，而且为中华人民共和国的职业培训工作积累了一定经验。

（2）大规模经济建设时期（1953—1966 年），以培养后备技术工人为主阶段。1953 年，中国开始实施第一个五年计划，进入大规模经济建设时期。这期间，各产业部门都提出了大量招用新技术工人的要求，有计划地培养后备技术

工人就成为这一时期职业培训的主要任务。这一时期的后备技术工人培训主要采取技工学校教育和学徒培训两种形式。一些条件较好的转业培训班，经过整顿、巩固、提高、充实，办成了技工学校。技工学校以培养技术比较复杂的工种（专业）的人才为主，学制一般为 2~3 年，要求学生毕业时在操作技术上达到中级技术工人的水平。学徒培训则主要招收 16 周岁以上的城镇社会青年，按照国家规定的学徒期限、培养目标和要求，以师傅带徒弟的形式在生产现场进行培训，以培养初级技术工人为主。学徒培训曾一度成为中国培训后备技术工人的主要形式。这一时期，国家还建立了八级工资制度和与此相适应的八级技能等级制度。通过学徒工转正考核和工人升级考核等形式，中国的工人考核制度开始建立。

（3）改革开放以后（1979—2000 年），职业培训蓬勃发展阶段。20 世纪 70 年代末期，中国开始改革开放，由此进入了现代化建设新的历史时期。这一时期，职业培训得到前所未有的全面发展。技工学校迅速恢复和发展，学徒培训继续发挥着其应有的作用，就业训练中心异军突起，在职工人技术培训日益正规化，工人考核制度得到恢复和完善。经过 20 多年的改革历程，社会主义市场经济体制初步建立，劳动力市场机制开始对劳动力资源配置发挥基础性作用，以市场为导向的就业机制逐步形成。根据劳动力市场需求开发劳动者职业技能的机制开始建立，一个包括职业分类、职业需求预测、职业技能标准制定、职业培训、职业技能鉴定、职业指导、职业技能竞赛等内容的职业培训工作体系初步形成。

（4）2001—2010 年期间的职业培训调整改革发展阶段。20 世纪末，受经济结构调整和职工大规模下岗失业影响，职业培训工作受到一定冲击。要想使经济和社会发展对技能人才的需求得到满足，就必须加强职业教育和职业培训工作。国务院于 2002 年和 2005 年两次召开全国职业教育工作会议，分析职业教育工作面临的形势和问题，进一步明确加强职业学校教育和职业培训工作的目

标任务和方针政策。2010 年，国务院印发《关于加强职业培训促进就业的意见》（国发〔2010〕36 号）。这是中华人民共和国成立以来，国务院第一次就加强职业培训工作印发专门文件。随后，国务院召开全国职业培训工作会议。国务院文件和全国职业培训工作会议提出：深入贯彻落实科学发展观，以服务就业和经济发展为宗旨，坚持城乡统筹、就业导向、技能为本、终身培训的原则，建立覆盖对象广泛、培训形式多样、管理运作规范、保障措施健全的职业培训工作新机制，健全面向全体劳动者的职业培训制度，加快培养数以亿计的高素质技能劳动者。职业培训工作的主要任务是：适应扩大就业规模、提高就业质量和增强企业竞争力的需要，完善制度、创新机制、加大投入，大规模开展就业技能培训、岗位技能提升培训和创业培训，切实提高职业培训的针对性和有效性，努力实现“培训一人、就业一人”和“就业一人、培训一人”的目标，为促进就业和经济社会发展提供强有力的技能人才支持。力争使新进入人力资源市场的劳动者都有机会接受相应的职业培训，使企业技能岗位的职工得到至少一次技能提升培训，使每个有培训愿望的创业者都参加一次创业培训，使高技能人才培训满足产业结构优化升级和企业发展需求。

（5）“十二五”规划（2011—2015 年）开启职业培训的进一步发展完善阶段。国家促进就业“十二五”规划对职业培训作出专门部署安排。2014 年，针对技工院校招生难、资金缺、待遇差等突出问题，人力资源社会保障部出台《关于推进技工院校改革创新的若干意见》（人社部发〔2014〕96 号），明确当前和今后一个时期，技工院校的改革发展要以适应市场需求为目标，坚持“高端引领、校企合作、多元办学、内涵发展”的办学理念，坚持学制教育与职业培训并举，深化办学体制机制改革，创新技能人才培养模式，全面提升技能人才培养能力，探索构建国家技能人才培养标准体系框架。2015 年，人力资源社会保障部办公厅、财政部办公厅印发《关于开展企业新型学徒制试点工作的通知》（人社厅发〔2015〕127 号），通过在企业推行以“招工即招生、入企即入

校、企校双师联合培养”为主要内容的企业新型学徒制，组织企业新招用人员和新转岗人员参加新型学徒制培训，加快企业青年技能人才的培养。同时，人力资源社会保障部还针对离校未就业高校毕业生、农村劳动者和残疾人群体提升职业技能先后印发了一系列文件，初步建立起面向城乡全体劳动者的普惠性职业培训制度。通过推进职业技能实训基地建设，开展企业新型学徒制试点，加大岗位技能提升培训力度，基本形成了以企业行业为主体、以技工院校为基础、学校教育与企业培养紧密联系、政府推动与社会支持相互结合的技能人才培养体系，建立了覆盖城乡全体劳动者、贯穿劳动者学习工作终身、适应劳动者需求的职业培训制度。

（二）职业培训与促进就业

职业培训必须坚持以就业为导向，扩大就业必须以提高劳动者素质为根本，二者要以市场需求为核心，紧密结合起来。实践证明，职业培训对促进就业发挥了至关重要的作用。

1. 开展职业培训是促进就业的重要途径

（1）职业培训增强了劳动者的就业能力，能够促进劳动者就业。一方面，接受过职业培训的劳动者，由于其技能和市场意识都得到了提高，具有一定的市场竞争力，从而具备相应的就业能力。另一方面，企业要求劳动者具有岗位所必备的素质，那些接受过专业培训的劳动者由于具备了相应技能，因此他们被企业录用的机会就增大了。

（2）职业培训对促进就业和提高劳动生产率产生了积极作用。在劳动密集型和技术密集型产业中，劳动者技能水平的高低决定了生产效率和产品质量。同时，接受过职业培训的高素质劳动者提高了社会劳动生产率，增加了产出和国民收入，从而提高了社会总体消费水平，这有利于刺激投资增长，扩大社会就业规模。

（3）职业培训起到了预防失业的作用。随着产业升级和技术进步，新兴的行业和职业大量涌现，传统行业和职业逐渐被淘汰，失业与岗位空缺并存。而经过职业培训的劳动者，尤其是掌握了多种技能的劳动者，在面对市场和产业结构变化时，能够适应不同岗位的需要，其失业风险大大降低。

2. 扩大就业要以提高劳动者素质为基础

一是提高劳动者素质，使其具有更高的从业能力和更好的技术水平。这是扩大就业的重要途径，也是改善就业质量的有效方式。

二是大力加强就业技能培训，提高新生劳动力的就业能力。参加必要的岗前培训和上岗培训，有利于劳动者尽快找到工作，并更好地适应就业岗位的要求。

三是大力加强在岗职工培训工作，培养和造就一支高素质的产业工人队伍。经济结构调整和企业技术发展对劳动者的技术技能提出了更高要求。要应对这些挑战，就必须按照终身培训的要求，不断加强对职工的岗位技能培训，持续提高职工队伍的工作能力，促进他们在职业岗位上稳定发展，进而不断提高其就业质量。

四是加强再就业培训，努力提高失业人员的转岗转业能力，为下岗失业人员实现再就业创造有利条件。组织开展创业培训，加强培养劳动者的创业意识和创业能力，实现以培训促创业，以创业促就业。

（三）近三十年职业培训重要行动计划

（1）大力开展就业训练。20 世纪 70 年代末，伴随大批知青返城，就业压力空前巨大。国家劳动总局按照中央要求，创立劳动服务公司，针对待业人员开展就业训练，为延缓就业压力、增强就业能力、解决待业问题做出了重大贡献。1994 年，劳动部发布《就业训练规定》，对就业训练进行规范。1990 年，国务院提出建立劳动预备制度，就业训练这一特定的培训形式在新的条件下得

到了新的发展。2008 年实施的《就业促进法》明确要求，国家采取措施建立健全劳动预备制度，对有就业要求的初高中毕业生实行一定期限的职业培训，使其掌握一定的职业技能；地方各级人民政府鼓励和支持开展就业培训，帮助失业人员提高职业技能；采取有效措施，组织和引导进城就业的农村劳动者参加技能培训，增强其就业能力和创业能力。

（2）实施再就业培训计划。1998—2000 年、2001—2003 年，劳动和社会保障部相继组织实施了两期"'三年千万'再就业培训计划"；2004—2005 年，继续深入实施再就业培训计划。广泛利用社会资源，加强职业指导和技能培训。实施政府购买培训成果，在对培训合格率和就业率进行综合考核与评估的基础上，由政府公共财政支付培训经费补贴。这一机制的形成和完善使社会机构的培训供给与劳动者自身的需要相结合，培训项目与市场就业需求相适应，经费补贴与培训效果相挂钩。

（3）积极探索创业培训模式。1999 年，劳动和社会保障部在总结北京市、上海市、苏州市三地试点经验的基础上，大力推动创业培训工作。到 2003 年，创业培训扩展到全国 100 多个城市。2005—2007 年，劳动和社会保障部与国际劳工组织、英国政府合作，广泛组织创业培训中国项目，为失业人员提供创业帮扶。创业培训在立足本土实践、吸收国际经验的基础上逐步发展，建立了培训与开业指导、项目开发、小额贷款、税费减免、创业孵化"一条龙"的创业政策和服务体系，帮助失业人员及其他就业人员实现技能创业，为国家制定创业促就业政策奠定了基础。

（4）加强职业培训提高就业能力计划。2002 年，劳动和社会保障部发布《加强职业培训提高就业能力计划》，强调通过大力加强下岗失业人员、青年劳动者、企业在职职工和农村富余劳动力的职业培训工作，提高他们的就业能力、工作能力和职业转换能力。这一计划的目标任务是：强化再就业培训，力争使培训合格率达到 90%，培训后就业率达到 50% 以上；推行创业培训，力争使成

功创业率达到40%；加快培养技术技能劳动者，使技术工人特别是高级技工、技师和高级技师的数量和比重有明显提高；全面推行职业资格证书制度，大力推行就业准入制度。

（5）职业培训“5+1”计划行动。2005年，劳动和社会保障部配合国家“十一五”规划的制定，全面启动职业培训的“5+1”计划行动，加快培养技能人才和数以千万计的高素质技能劳动者。这一行动包括新技师培养带动计划、城镇技能再就业计划、能力促创业计划、农村劳动力技能就业计划、国家技能资格导航计划5项计划以及技能岗位对接行动。这是一项培训促就业的系统工程，瞄准处于不同就业状态的各类群体，通过有针对性的职业培训和就业服务，全面提高其就业能力、创业能力、工作能力和职业转换能力。

（6）特别职业培训计划。2008年年底爆发的全球性金融危机，对就业形势产生了重大影响。为保持就业局势稳定，充分发挥职业培训对于促进全方位就业和服务经济稳定发展的重要基础作用，按照中共中央、国务院的总体部署，2009年和2010年期间，人力资源社会保障部、发展改革委和财政部联合启动实施了特别职业培训计划。依托技工院校和各类职业培训机构，通过政府购买培训成果的方式，完成好既定的职业培训任务。总的思路是扩大培训规模、延长培训期限、增加培训投入、提升培训能力、保持就业稳定。

（7）国家高技能人才振兴计划。以习近平同志为核心的党中央高度重视人才工作，强调把人才作为支撑发展的第一资源。2011年，人力资源社会保障部会同财政部出台了《关于印发〈国家高技能人才振兴计划实施方案〉的通知》（人社部发〔2011〕109号），明确从2011年到2020年，实施高技能人才培训基地建设项目、技能大师工作室建设项目和技师培训项目。2011年，人力资源社会保障部与财政部开展了首批20个高技能人才培训基地和50个技能大师工作室建设工作。2016年以来，中国政府在经济新常态下进行供给侧结构性改革，这对高技能人才队伍建设提出了新要求。2016年，人力资源社会保障部、财政

部印发《关于深入推进国家高技能人才振兴计划的通知》（人社部发〔2016〕74号），提出“十三五”期间（2016—2020年），要紧密结合先进制造业、战略性新兴产业、现代服务业发展需要，重点培养造就一大批具有高超技艺、精湛技能和工匠精神的高技能人才，稳步提升中国产业工人队伍的整体素质。

（8）国家大规模职业技能提升行动。当前和今后一个时期，结构性就业矛盾凸显，国内外经济环境将对就业产生深刻影响，也会对推进产业升级和劳动者素质提出新的要求。中共中央、国务院高度重视职业技能培训工作，2019年政府工作报告提出，实施职业技能提升行动，从失业保险基金结余中拿出1 000亿元，用于1 500万人次以上的职工技能提升和转岗转业培训。同年，国务院办公厅印发《职业技能提升行动方案（2019—2021年）》（国办发〔2019〕24号，以下简称《方案》），这是当前和今后一个时期大规模开展职业技能培训工作的指导性文件。《方案》确定了企业职工、就业重点群体、贫困劳动力三个方面的培训重点，通过企业、职业院校（含技工院校）、社会培训和评价机构三类培训主体大力开展培训，有效增加了培训供给，调动起各类培训主体的积极性。职业技能提升行动重点在于通过政策引导激励，发动劳动者和培训主体大规模参与职业技能培训活动。

二、职业培训体系的健全完善

（一）概述

中国职业培训体系包括：职业分类与职业标准、职业培训与办学机构、技能人才评价制度、职业技能竞赛与技能人才表彰制度。

（1）职业分类与职业标准。1988年，劳动部会同国务院45个行业主管部门进行第三次全国工人技术等级标准的修订工作，1992年，完成了第一部《中华人民共和国工种分类目录》。1999年，劳动和社会保障部、国家质量技术监

督局、国家统计局联合颁布第一部对中国职业进行科学分类的权威性文献——《中华人民共和国职业分类大典》。2010 年年底，人力资源社会保障部会同相关部门启动修订《中华人民共和国职业分类大典》，并于 2015 年正式发布新版本。职业标准和职业技能鉴定规范也在分批制定和颁布，初步建立起了动态的国家职业分类和职业标准体系，同时建立了由初级工、中级工、高级工、技师和高级技师五个等级构成的国家职业资格体系。职业分类和职业标准制定工作的开展，为劳动力管理和职业培训工作提供了科学的依据。

（2）职业培训与办学机构。职业培训包括就业技能培训（含劳动预备制培训、再就业培训和农村劳动力转移培训）、岗位技能提升培训和创业培训。依据职业技能标准，培训的层次又分为初级、中级、高级职业培训和其他适应性培训，以培养技术技能型人才为主。培训工作主要由技工院校和各类职业培训机构承担。

（3）技能人才评价制度。技能人才评价是对技能劳动者从事某项职业所具备的学识、技术、能力的认可。与学历教育不同，技能人才评价与职业劳动的具体要求密切结合，更多地反映了特定职业的实际工作标准和规范，以及劳动者从事这种职业所达到的实际能力水平。

（4）职业技能竞赛与技能人才表彰制度。职业技能竞赛分为国家、省（包括自治区、直辖市）和地市三级。国家级职业技能竞赛一般每两年举办一次。同时，建立了技能人才表彰制度。职业技能竞赛和技能人才表彰制度的建立，提高了技能人才的社会地位，调动了广大职工参加职业培训的积极性，营造了有利于技能人才成长的社会环境。

（二）技工院校和职业培训机构

1. 技工院校

技工教育是国民教育体系和人力资源开发的重要组成部分，承担着为经济

社会发展培养高素质技能人才的重要任务。技工院校是承担技工教育、职业培训、技能鉴定、竞赛集训、公共实训、就业服务等工作的综合性技工教育培训基地，是构建劳动者终身职业培训体系的重要载体和培养技能人才的重要平台。技工院校分为以下三种类型：

（1）普通技工学校。普通技工学校学制教育以培养中级技术工人为主。普通技工学校招收初中毕业生，学制一般为三年；招收高中毕业生，学制一般为两年。

（2）高级技工学校。高级技工学校学制教育以培养高级技术工人为主。高级技工学校招收普通技工学校及其他中等职业学校同专业或相近专业毕业生，学制一般为两年；招收高中毕业生，学制一般为三年。

（3）技师学院。技师学院通过学制教育培养预备技师，承担企业在职职工晋升技师的培训研修和技师考核评审，以及技工院校师资培训任务。技师学院学制教育一般以培养高级工和预备技师为主。培养预备技师的，技师学院招收初中毕业生，学制一般为七年；招收高中毕业生，学制一般为五年；招收高级技工学校毕业生和其他取得高级工职业资格的职业院校毕业生，学制一般为两年。

全国技工院校具备“校企双制、工学一体”的办学特色，已经成为中国技术工人培养主阵地、高技能人才培养基地、与企业融合发展的办学实体，形成了鲜明的办学特色和独特的技能人才培养优势（综合情况见表 7-1）。

表 7-1　历年技工院校综合情况

年份	技工院校个数 / 个	招生数 / 万人	在校学生数 / 万人	毕业生数 / 万人	教职工数 / 万人	培训社会人员人次数 / 万人次	培训社会人员结业人数 / 万人
1999	4 098	51.5	156.0	66.2	26.9	149.1	144.6
2000	3 792	50.4	140.1	64.6	24.0	158.5	156.7

续表

年份	技工院校个数/个	招生数/万人	在校学生数/万人	毕业生数/万人	教职工数/万人	培训社会人员人次数/万人次	培训社会人员结业人数/万人
2001	3 470	55.1	134.7	47.7	22.0	151.7	163.9
2002	3 075	73.3	153.0	45.4	20.3	208.6	196.9
2003	2 970	91.6	193.1	45.3	20.2	226.9	226.7
2004	2 884	109.7	234.4	53.5	20.4	265.6	257.5
2005	2 855	118.4	275.3	69.0	20.4	273.3	270.1
2006	2 880	134.8	320.8	86.4	21.5	337.7	330.2
2007	2 995	158.5	367.1	99.7	24.0	380.7	369.8
2008	3 075	161.4	397.5	109.0	24.7	400.0	389.8
2009	3 064	156.4	414.3	115.2	25.8	484.1	382.9
2010	2 998	158.6	421.0	121.3	26.5	468.4	371.3
2011	2 914	163.5	429.4	118.9	26.5	527.5	416.1
2012	2 892	156.8	422.8	120.2	26.7	551.3	441.6
2013	2 882	133.5	386.6	116.9	26.9	525.3	397.1
2014	2 818	124.4	339.0	106.8	26.5	508.5	372.3
2015	2 545	121.4	321.5	94.6	26.0	476.6	378.9
2016	2 526	127.2	323.2	93.1	26.5	451.6	349.9
2017	2 490	130.9	338.2	90.5	26.9	456.4	326.1
2018	2 379	128.5	341.6	90.3	26.7	420.6	301.6

资料来源：国家统计局。

2. 职业培训机构

职业培训机构主要承担各类职业培训任务，为社会培养具有职业技能的劳动者。中国职业培训机构主要包括就业训练中心、民办职业培训机构、中外合作办职业培训机构、企业培训机构等。

（1）就业训练中心。就业训练中心是主要为新生劳动力和失业人员提供就业技能培训的职业培训基地。随着就业形势的发展，就业训练中心还承担了为城乡创业者提供创业培训的任务。就业训练中心的特点是培训以短期为主，以单项技能为主，以就业上岗为主；培训内容以操作技能为主，辅以相关的理论知识学习，属于非学制教育；培训经费主要依靠生产经营创收和学费。经过多年的发展，有些就业训练中心已经成为具有相当实力和规模的培训实体。

（2）民办职业培训机构。民办职业培训机构是指国家机构以外的社会组织或者个人，利用非国家财政性经费，面向社会举办的学校或其他培训机构。国家对民办职业培训机构实行积极鼓励、大力支持、正确引导、依法管理的方针。民办职业培训机构在开展再就业培训、农村劳动力转移培训方面发挥了重要作用。

（3）中外合作办职业培训机构。中外合作办职业培训机构是外国教育培训机构同中国教育培训机构在中国境内合作举办的以中国公民为主要招生对象的职业培训机构。国家对中外合作办职业培训机构实行扩大开放、规范办学、依法管理、促进发展的方针，鼓励引进外国优质教育培训资源开展职业培训工作。

（4）企业培训机构。企业职工培训是职业培训的重要环节。中国政府历来重视企业在职职工培训和加强技能劳动者培养。在建立学习型企业和学习型社会中，要充分依靠企业，发挥行业作用，逐步形成政府统筹、行业指导、市场调节、企业自主开展培训的运行机制。

（三）职业资格证书制度和职业技能等级制度

1. 职业技能鉴定

职业技能鉴定是一项对职业技能水平的考核活动，属于标准参照型考试。它是由考核机构对劳动者从事某种职业所应掌握的技术理论知识和实际操作能力作出客观的测量和评价。中国的职业技能鉴定是按照国家规定的职业标准或

任职资格条件，通过政府人力资源社会保障行政部门认定的考核鉴定机构，对劳动者的技能水平或职业资格进行客观公正、科学规范的评价与认证活动，主要包括初级、中级、高级技能等级考核和技师、高级技师的资格考评。职业技能鉴定是国家职业资格证书制度的重要组成部分，劳动者在通过鉴定合格后所取得的职业资格证书是表明其职业技能水平的凭证。

2. 职业资格证书制度

职业资格证书是国家对劳动者从事某项职业所具备的学识、技术、能力的认可，是劳动者求职、任职、独立开业和单位录用的主要依据。职业资格证书与职业劳动的具体要求密切结合，更多地反映了特定职业的实际工作标准和规范，以及劳动者从事这种职业所达到的实际能力水平。职业技能等级一般分为初级工、中级工、高级工、技师和高级技师五级，分别对应为国家职业资格五级、四级、三级、二级和一级。职业资格证书制度是国际上通行的一种对技术技能人才的资格认证制度。

3. 职业技能等级制度

职业技能等级认定是依据国家职业技能标准或行业企业评价规范，由用人单位和社会培训评价组织开展的人才评价制度。符合条件的用人单位可结合实际面向本单位职工自主开展职业技能等级认定，或面向本单位以外人员提供职业技能等级认定服务；符合条件的社会培训评价组织可根据市场和就业需要，面向全体劳动者开展职业技能等级认定。职业技能等级证书由用人单位和社会培训评价组织颁发，由人力资源社会保障部制定编码规则，规范证书（或电子证书）样式。职业技能等级制度是实行多元化人才评价的重要组成部分。

（四）职业能力建设基础工作

职业能力建设工作包括相关人员队伍建设、教材建设和教学研究等工作。

1. 相关人员队伍建设

（1）技工院校师资队伍建设。师资队伍建设是加强技工教育和职业培训工作的重要基础。随着校企合作制度的逐步深入，为进一步提高技工教育和职业培训质量，越来越多的技工院校开始注重培养造就既能讲授专业理论、又能指导生产实习的“一体化”教师队伍，不断加强技工院校教师培训、进修力度，提升职业培训师资队伍能力，以不断适应改革发展的新需要。

（2）创业培训师资队伍建设。创业培训是提高劳动者创业能力的重要手段，是推进创业促就业工作的重要内容。为推动创业培训工作的开展，人力资源社会保障部成立了创业培训工作指导委员会，负责全国创业培训服务工作的总体规划和协调推动。创业培训师资分为培训师和讲师，具有以下特点：①覆盖较广。全国大部分省份都有了自己的培训师，能够基本满足各地的培训需求。②层次丰富。除人力资源社会保障系统外，来自工青妇、高校、民办机构、咨询公司等单位的人越来越多地加入培训师队伍，他们当中不乏企业管理经验丰富的专业人士。③在队伍管理上，在选拔、培养、派遣和选评各环节都严格执行相应的技术标准。

（3）职业技能鉴定考评人员队伍建设。职业技能鉴定考评人员是指在规定职业（工种）、等级和类别范围内，按照统一的考核方法和评审标准及考核要求，对职业（工种）技能鉴定对象进行考核、评审的人员。具体包括考评员和高级考评员两类。

（4）职业技能鉴定督导员队伍建设。职业技能鉴定质量督导是指对职业技能鉴定机构贯彻国家职业技能鉴定有关法规、规章和政策，执行国家职业标准、考务管理及证书管理等工作进行监督、检查的行为。职业技能鉴定督导员受人力资源社会保障部门或国务院有关部门相关工作机构委托，执行本地区、本行业的职业技能鉴定质量督导工作。

2. 教材建设和教学研究

教材建设是职业培训工作的重要组成部分。教材是集中反映教育思想、教育观念和教学内容的载体，也是劳动者自学成才、岗位成才的必备工具。教学研究是完善教学、提高教育质量的必要手段。2000 年，劳动和社会保障部成立了职业培训教材工作委员会，负责研究制定职业培训教材建设的总体思路和发展规划，统筹协调各地区、各部门职业培训教材建设工作。

三、终身职业技能培训制度的发展

根据培训对象和培训内容的不同，职业培训分成就业技能培训（含劳动预备制培训、再就业培训、农村劳动力转移培训）、岗位技能提升培训和创业培训三类，基本涵盖了劳动者职业生涯的各个阶段，也可以满足劳动者提高职业素质和就业能力的要求，从总体上构成了中国劳动者终身职业技能培训体系。

（一）就业技能培训

1. 就业技能培训的功能和作用

就业技能培训一般是指为城乡各类有就业要求和培训愿望的劳动者提高就业能力而开展的必备的职业道德、专业理论、职业技能等方面的培训和训练活动，主要由各级各类职业学校、就业训练中心和民办职业培训机构实施。

就业技能培训的对象主要包括城乡新成长劳动力、向非农产业或城镇转移就业的农村劳动力等初次就业人员、就业转失业人员、其他在就业和上岗前需要学习和提高职业技能的劳动者。

就业技能培训的作用，一是通过大力发展就业技能培训，落实科教兴国战略，使经济建设转移到依靠科技进步和劳动者素质提高的轨道上来；二是提高劳动者就业能力促进就业，为他们参与市场竞争和就业上岗创造条件；三是提高企业后备技术工人素质，以适应产业结构调整步伐加快和企业改革不断深化

对劳动者素质提出的更高要求。

2. 劳动预备制培训

劳动预备制度是对青年劳动者就业前必须经过培训的制度规定。其基本内涵是组织城镇新生劳动力和其他求职人员，使其在就业前接受一定期限的职业培训和职业教育，并取得相应的职业资格或掌握一定的职业技能后，在国家政策的指导和帮助下，通过劳动力市场实现就业。通过延长这部分劳动者进入劳动力市场的时间，减少劳动力供给，调节劳动力供求关系，从而缓解就业压力。

20 世纪 90 年代，中国进入新一轮就业高峰。劳动者素质与生产发展不相适应的结构性失业问题日益突出，加上大量的初、高中毕业生没有经过必要的职业培训就进入劳动力市场或就业岗位，既形成了巨大的就业压力，也影响了企业劳动生产率和经济效益的提高，培训与就业在一定程度上存在脱节和错位。

为缓解就业压力，提高劳动者素质，1996 年，劳动部提出了“对新生劳动力追加 1~2 年职业培训，以缓解就业压力，提高劳动者素质”的建议，得到中央领导的高度重视。1997 年，在全国 36 个城市中组织实施了劳动预备制度试点工作，取得了较好的效果。1998 年，在推进全国就业再就业的工作部署中，中共中央、国务院要求各地“普遍实行劳动预备制度，对城镇未能继续升学的初、高中毕业生，进行 1~3 年的职业技术培训”。1999 年，中共中央、国务院在《关于深化教育改革，全面推进素质教育的决定》中，再次重申“积极推行劳动预备制度，坚持实行‘先培训、后上岗’的就业制度”。自 1999 年起，在全国城镇普遍推行劳动预备制度。通过组织推动和大力宣传，一大批初、高中毕业生受到动员，参加到劳动预备制培训中来。

3. 再就业培训

再就业培训是指在有过一次以上工作经历的职工失业后，对其进行的从事职业所必需的职业指导、职业技能、职业道德和职业纪律的培训。再就业培训

的对象主要是下岗失业人员。

20 世纪 80 年代末期，随着全员劳动合同制、优化组合的推行，企业开始出现富余职工。为帮助需要转换职业的企业富余职工尽快实现再就业，劳动部制定了国有企业富余职工要参加转业培训，培训人员可享受减免培训费用和优先就业的优惠政策。到 90 年代中期，在失业职工数量逐年增加的背景下，为减少失业，促进就业，中国开始实施再就业工程，其中一项重要内容就是要求失业职工在失业期间应参加转业转岗培训，并针对参加此类培训的人员制定了免费培训政策。1998 年以来，国有企业职工下岗问题日益突出。中共中央、国务院非常重视和关心职工的生活和再就业问题，要求在做好国有企业职工基本生活保障的同时，强化再就业培训力度，并明确了再就业培训的对象、目标和任务。劳动保障部门制定了一系列推动再就业培训工作的政策措施，使得再就业培训工作逐渐规范化，这些政策措施在再就业工作中发挥了积极的作用。再就业培训的组织实施具体包括以下七个环节：

（1）搞好摸底调查，制订再就业培训计划。开展再就业培训，首先是深入开展调查研究，了解和掌握本地下岗失业人员基本情况、社会生产发展的态势、劳动力市场对劳动者技能的需求状况和各类职业培训机构的培训条件，并以此为依据，制订再就业培训计划，统筹安排好有关工作。

（2）面向社会，确立定点培训机构。再就业培训要充分动员全社会的力量，利用各级各类教育培训机构的资源优势开展培训。要从具有资质的教育培训机构中选择一批培训设施好、培训能力强、培训质量高的机构，作为再就业培训定点机构。指导它们与企业再就业服务中心、职业介绍机构和用人单位建立联系，为下岗失业人员提供符合市场需求的培训和指导。

（3）立足市场需求，组织灵活多样的技能培训。再就业培训定点机构要根据劳动力市场的需求和下岗失业人员的特点，确定培训项目，制订培训计划，开展针对性强的培训活动。在培训形式上，结合下岗失业人员的实际情况，应

灵活多样，可以实行全日制集中培训与半日制、夜校分散培训相结合；也可以采取在培训机构集中办班或企业与培训机构联合办班等，组织下岗失业人员就地、就近接受培训；还要充分发挥远程职业培训量大、面广、成本低的优势，广泛利用广播电视、电化教育以及计算机互联网，形成远程职业培训网络，把培训课程送到教室、送到企业、送到劳动者家里。

（4）针对下岗失业人员特点，开展个性化职业指导。在再就业培训中要开设专门的职业指导课，帮助失业人员认清就业形势，更新就业观念，树立自主就业的意识，并为他们提供职业需求信息并介绍求职方法，指导他们制订个人再就业计划和措施，积极引导他们实现再就业。

（5）加强创业能力培训，培养一批小老板。对下岗失业人员中具有较强创业意识和一定创业条件的人员，开展创业能力培训，指导他们在市场调查的基础上，制订切实可行的创业方案，并通过向他们提供持续的咨询、指导和服务，帮助这些创业者解决在开业和经营过程中遇到的问题，培养和造就一批成功创业的小老板。

（6）落实培训经费，实施政府购买培训成果。开展再就业培训，落实经费是关键。再就业培训经费采取多渠道筹措、合理使用的原则。再就业培训的经费来源包括：①中央和地方各级财政的投入，主要由地方财政承担，中央财政对困难地方给予适当补助；②失业保险金可用于对享受失业保险期间失业人员的职业培训进行补贴；③行业、企业组织培训，所需经费从职工教育经费中支付；④社会捐赠。再就业培训实行经费补贴与培训促进就业效果相挂钩的原则，对符合条件的下岗失业人员，实行免费培训；对承担免费培训任务的培训机构，根据培训的数量、培训的期限、培训的合格率、培训后再就业率等指标，由政府有关部门核拨经费补贴。政府购买培训成果的机制有效地引导了培训机构紧密结合市场需求开展培训，使其努力提高培训质量，并积极主动地与用人单位取得联系，拓宽下岗失业人员培训后的就业渠道，从而提高经费的使用效率。

（7）搞好就业服务，密切培训与就业的衔接。建立职业需求预测、失业登记、职业培训、职业介绍、职业指导“一条龙”服务机制，促使培训与就业有机结合。对于有自谋职业、自主创业意向的劳动者，就业服务机构要联合有关部门，帮助落实工商登记、税费减免、场地安排、资金信贷等方面的优惠政策。

4. 农村劳动力转移培训

农村劳动力转移培训是指对农村劳动者从农业转移到非农产业时，有针对性地对他们进行的职业技能、职业道德、职业纪律、相关法律法规、维权知识以及城市生活常识的培训。开展这类培训有效地促进了农村劳动者转移就业技能水平的提升，是增强他们就业竞争力和工作能力的重要手段。按照中共中央、国务院提出的持续扩大农村劳动力转移培训规模、提高培训质量、统筹使用培训资金的要求，从 2006 年起，劳动保障部门积极采取措施，大规模开展农村劳动力转移培训工作，提高农民工的职业技能水平和整体素质，引导其在非农产业就业。

（1）实施农村劳动力转移培训专项工作计划。从 2006 年开始，劳动保障部门在全国范围内组织实施了“农村劳动力技能就业计划”，利用 5 年时间，对 4 000 万名农村劳动者进行非农技能培训，每年培训 800 万人。根据农村劳动者的特点，将培训分为三类进行：组织农村初、高中毕业未升学人员和农村退役士兵以及其他农村新生劳动力参加劳动预备制培训，组织有意愿外出务工的农村富余劳动力参加劳务输出培训，组织在城镇务工的农村劳动者参加技能提升培训。2009—2010 年间，实施特别职业培训计划，将农村新成长劳动力、返乡农民工、企业新录用农民工等群体的职业技能培训作为重点。据统计，2006—2009 年，全国共有 3 700 多万名农村劳动者参加培训。

（2）面向社会，择优确定定点培训机构。各级人力资源社会保障部门面向社会各类有资质的教育培训机构，通过招标认定等方式，确定了一批培训质量

好、社会信誉佳的机构作为定点培训机构，指导其按照人力资源市场需求，采取灵活多样的方式，开展劳动预备制培训和各种短期实用技术培训或职业资格培训，帮助农村劳动者在掌握一技之长或取得相应职业资格证书后再进入人力资源市场竞争就业。

（3）落实培训经费，完善经费补贴机制。根据国务院要求，农村劳动力转移培训实行政府、用人单位和个人共同负担的培训投入机制。为提升经费使用效果，各地还建立了经费补贴与培训质量和就业效果挂钩的机制，完善补贴办法。由培训机构组织培训的，培训机构可在培训结束后，持培训合格人员名单、培训证书或职业资格证书以及就业情况等资料到人力资源社会保障部门申请相应补贴。由用人单位组织培训的，用人单位可到当地人力资源社会保障部门申领培训补贴。此外，一些地区还探索了发放培训券、设立培训账户等方式，用以调动农村劳动者参加培训和培训机构组织培训的积极性。

（二）岗位技能提升培训

岗位技能提升培训是指企业按照其生产经营需要，对职工进行的思想政治、职业道德、管理知识、技术业务、操作技能等方面的教育和训练活动。企业职工岗位技能提升培训任务可采取三种方式实施：一是由企业设立的职工培训机构实施，二是由企业联合企业外各类教育培训机构实施，三是由企业有偿委托企业外职业培训机构实施。

加强技工教育和职业培训，促进高素质技能人才队伍建设。（新华社记者柏志勇摄）

开展企业职工岗位技能提升培训，就是要通过建立制度、完善机制、创新

模式，打造企业发展的三支人才队伍：培养一支熟悉国内外企业经营管理，有较强管理能力、专业能力和社会活动能力的现代化管理人才队伍；培养一支具有较高的理论水平和科技造诣，熟练掌握相关专业技术的科研开发人才队伍；培养一支技艺精湛、作风优良、具有敬业精神的技术技能劳动者队伍。为实现这些目标，企业主要在以下八个方面开展工作：

（1）建立与现代企业制度相适应的培训管理体制。按照建立现代企业制度的要求，从适应最大限度发挥职工岗位成才积极性的需要出发，建立与之相匹配的企业职工培训管理体制，实现“培训、考核、使用、待遇”四结合的运行机制，为推动企业人力资源的深度开发提供组织保证。

（2）根据培训需求制订培训计划。立足企业实际需要，结合企业发展战略和生产经营的总体布局对各级各类职工的需求，制订科学合理的培训计划，明确近期和中长期职工培训的目标任务，形成培训制度，采取有效措施，推动培训工作的开展。

（3）建立企业职工培训基地。依托企业职工培训基地、社会公共实训基地以及高级技工学校、技师学院等职业院校作为开展企业职工培训的基地，开展各级各类职业培训和继续教育，采用多种手段和渠道对企业职工进行实用、高效的培训。

（4）通过高端带动实现技能人才队伍梯次发展。企业在全面开展职工培训工作的基础上，重点做好高技能人才培养工作，通过建立技师研修制度、名师带徒制度、企业培训师和技能带头人制度，加快高技能人才培养。广泛开展岗位练兵和各种职业技能竞赛活动，选拔和表彰一批技艺精湛、贡献突出的技术尖子，发挥他们的示范和带动作用，以此推动技能人才队伍整体建设。

（5）加强基础工作。选拔具有较高水平专业知识和技能特长的人员担任培训师，结合企业的生产实际和技术的最新发展编写教学课程，有条件的企业要

大力开发和使用多媒体教材和仿真模拟教学设备及软件，更好地开展培训工作。

（6）加大培训投入，落实培训经费。按照《就业促进法》和《中华人民共和国职业教育法》的规定，企业应当承担实施职业教育和职工培训的经费。要保证经费专项用于职工，特别是一线职工的教育和培训。

（7）坚持持证上岗制度。将职业资格证书的推行与开展职工培训和改革企业用人制度紧密结合。企业在招聘职工时，应从取得相应的职业学校学历证书、职业培训合格证书的人员中优先录用；在招用从事国家规定实行就业准入控制的人员时，录用人员必须取得相应的职业资格证书。

（8）推行“使用与培训考核相结合，待遇与业绩贡献相联系”的做法。制定与技能水平挂钩的企业工资制度和岗位津贴制度，在薪酬、福利、培训等方面向关键技术岗位高技能人才倾斜。

（三）创业培训

创业培训是对具有创业愿望和相应条件的人员进行的开办小企业或自谋职业所必备的基础知识和能力的培训。创业培训有以下三种模式：

（1）SIYB 培训模式。SIYB 培训是国际劳工组织针对培养微（小）型企业创办者的需要而专门开发的一个培训项目，在世界 80 多个国家推广。2001 年，劳动和社会保障部与国际劳工组织共同实施了试点项目，将 SIYB 培训技术引入中国。SIYB 培训现已在中国大多数城市实施。培训采取小班制教学，采用知识培训、案例分析、角色扮演、自由讨论等多种形式，培训效果明显。

（2）三段式培训模式。三段式培训将整个创业培训过程分为理论学习阶段、咨询辅导阶段和后续扶持阶段。在理论学习阶段，主要对学员进行创业意识、创业基础知识和有关经济法规的教育。在咨询辅导阶段，则由咨询委员会专家或培训机构教师针对学员编制的创业计划书进行分类指导和咨询，帮助学

员确定有发展前景、符合市场需求的创业项目，修改和完善其创业计划书。在后续扶持阶段，主要针对学员在实际创业过程中遇到的问题，由有关专家向学员提供咨询和服务。

（3）各地自创模式。各地结合自身的实际需要，开发教学计划，组织实施创业培训。如上海市针对参加培训学员的不同需要，将培训分为创业入门班、创业实训班和创业提高班三种类型，采取模块式的培训方式组织培训，并加强对学员的开业指导、个性化辅导和跟踪服务。云南省则针对失业人员的创业心理、技能等方面问题，推出模拟创业训练模式，帮助学员在最短时间内掌握别人要通过长期实践才能总结出的经验，并向他们提供必要的政策扶持，帮助他们成功开业。

上述三种创业培训模式，尽管在培训内容和方式上各有特点和侧重，但是它们有一个共性，即它们都是将创业培训与开业指导、小额贷款等有关活动有机结合，为创业者提供全方位的服务。

四、高技能人才队伍建设

（一）概述

高技能人才是指具有高超技艺和精湛技能，能够进行创造性劳动并对社会做出贡献的人才，具体是指技能劳动者中取得高级工、技师和高级技师职业资格及相应职级的人员。高技能人才主要包括以下三种类型：

（1）技术技能型人才。技术技能型人才是指在企业生产加工一线中从事技术操作，具有较高技能水平，能够解决操作性难题的人员。技术技能型人才主要分布在加工、制造、服务等职业领域。

（2）复合技能型人才。复合技能型人才是指在企业生产加工一线中掌握一门以上操作技能，能够在生产中从事多工种、多岗位的复杂劳动，并能解决生

产操作难题的人员，如数控加工中心技术师、机电一体化人才、综合服务一体化人才，以及新兴的创意和操作一体化人才等。

（3）知识技能型人才。知识技能型人才是指既具备较高的专业理论知识水平，又具备较高的操作技能水平的人员。他们能够将所掌握的理论知识用于指导生产实践，创造性地开展工作。知识技能型人才主要分布在高新技术产业和新兴职业领域。

（二）政策措施

（1）进一步加强组织领导，完善相关法律法规。根据经济社会发展需要制定高技能人才队伍建设规划，并将其纳入经济社会发展总体规划和人才队伍建设规划。中国政府建立了由多个部门以及工会、共青团、妇联等人民团体参加的高技能人才工作协调机制，负责高技能人才工作的宏观指导、政策协调和组织推动。加快推进职业技能培训有关立法，从法律上对政府、企业、院校在职业技能培训和技能人才培养中的职责作出更加明确、具体的规定，将技能人才工作纳入法制化轨道。

（2）完善培养培训体系，加快高技能人才培养。结合区域经济发展、产业结构调整和技术升级对高技能人才的需要，进一步发挥企业和职业院校两个主体的作用，加快培养高技能人才。重点依托规模较大、水平较高、特色鲜明的高级技工学校、技师学院、高等职业院校和大型骨干企业（集团），建设高技能人才培养培训示范基地，进一步改善教学设施和实习实训条件，提升培养能力。同时，鼓励职业院校与企业以互利双赢为基础，开展多种形式的合作，不断增强技能人才培养的针对性。鼓励有条件的地方结合当地产业布局和支柱产业发展需要，通过财政投入和多种筹资方式，建设公共实训基地，面向社会各类企业职工、院校学生和其他劳动者提供公益性、高水平的技能实训和技能鉴定等服务。

以“校企结合”“工学结合”等订单式职业培训加快高技能人才培养。（新华社记者沈伯韩摄）

（3）健全评价激励体系，畅通技能人才成长通道。进一步突破年龄、资历、身份和比例限制，积极探索和完善符合高技能人才成长规律的多元化评价体系。依托具备条件的国有大中型企业，继续推进高技能人才评价工作，完善贴近企业生产实际、以职业能力和工作业绩为重点、注重职业道德和职业知识水平的高技能人才评价模式。根据国家职业技能标准和职业院校教学实际，开发职业技能教育培训标准，指导职业院校调整课程设置和教学内容，规范职业技能鉴定活动，使毕业生在取得学历证书的同时获得相应的职业资格证书。

（4）完善使用机制，充分发挥高技能人才作用。鼓励企业根据自身发展需要，建立高技能人才带头人制度，发挥高技能人才在解决技术难题、进行技术创新和带徒传技等方面的重要作用。鼓励各级人民政府、行业、企业选拔在生产和服务岗位一线的中华技能大奖获得者、全国技术能手及其他有绝技绝活的

高技能人才，依托其所在单位建立技能大师工作室，为技能大师开展技能研修、技术攻关、技术技能创新等活动创造条件，同时也为青年职工向名师学习、提升技能、参与创新活动提供机会和环境，推动技能大师绝技绝活及技术技能创新成果得以加速传承和推广。

（5）广泛开展技能竞赛，促使更多高技能人才脱颖而出。进一步发挥职业技能竞赛（见图 7–1）在发现和选拔优秀高技能人才中的作用，以企业岗位练兵为基础，以国内职业技能竞赛为主体，以世界技能大赛为龙头，全面推动国内、国际职业技能竞赛协调发展，引导和带动广大企业职工和院校学生积极参加岗位练兵和技能竞赛活动，不断提高其技能水平，为更多优秀的高技能人才脱颖而出搭建平台。

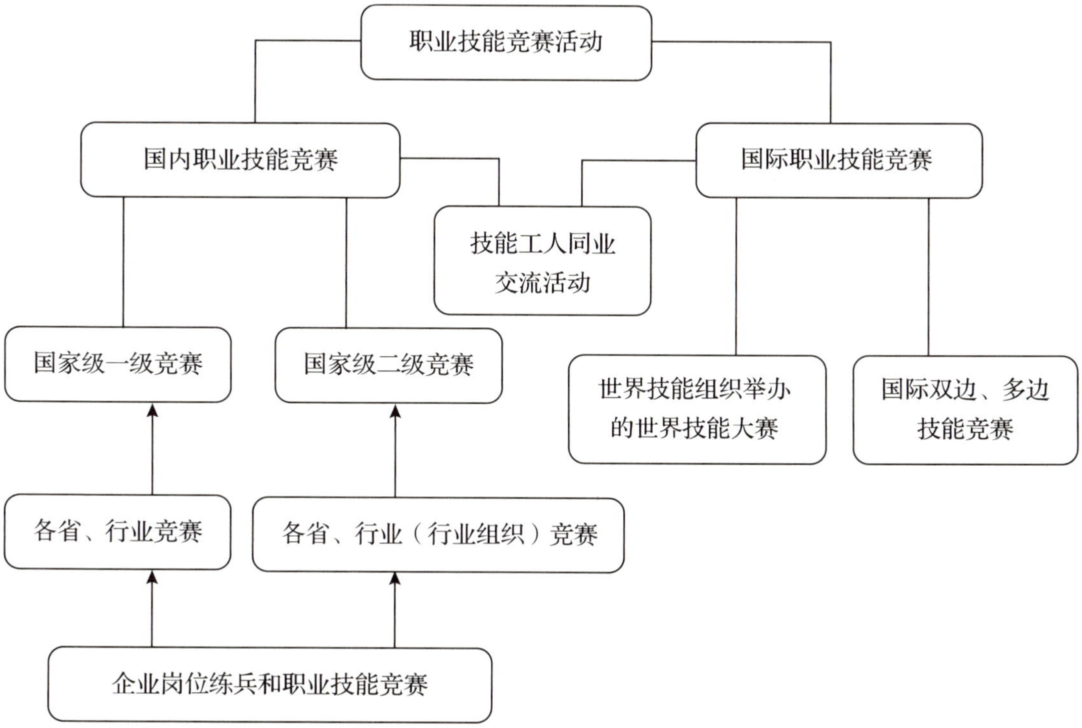

图 7–1　职业技能竞赛活动类别和运行图

（6）加大表彰奖励力度，提高高技能人才的经济待遇和社会地位。完善以政府表彰奖励为导向、用人单位和社会力量奖励为主体的表彰奖励体系。健全高技能人才激励制度和机制，对做出突出贡献的高技能人才给予表彰和奖励，形成以政府奖励为导向、企业奖励为主体，辅以必要的社会奖励的高技能人才奖励体系，不断提升高技能人才的经济待遇和社会地位。

（7）加强技术支持，夯实工作基础。根据经济社会发展需要，对职业进行科学分类，为开展高技能人才培养、评价等工作提供依据。进一步加大高技能人才师资培养力度，优化师资结构。同时，要加强对高技能人才培养规律的研究，深化职业院校教学改革，加强适用于高技能人才的现代培训技术的开发，做好高技能人才培养特色教材的建设工作，加快技师、高级技师国家职业技能标准的编制、修订和职业技能鉴定题库的开发，满足高技能人才培养的需要。

（8）加大资金投入，提供资金保障。要建立政府、企业、社会多渠道筹资的高技能人才资金投入机制。各级人民政府要对高技能人才培养给予支持，使用国家安排的职业教育基础建设专项经费，择优支持高技能人才培养成效显著的职业院校。将高技能人才实训基地建设纳入国家支持职业教育发展的规划。引导企业履行技能人才培养的责任和义务，保障企业对于技能人才培养的资金投入。努力构建社会力量广泛参与高技能人才培养和职业教育培训的政策环境，鼓励社会各界和海外人士对技能人才培养提供捐赠和其他培训服务，鼓励金融机构为公共实训基地建设和以校企合作方式培养技能人才的职业院校提供融资服务。

（三）主要成就

中共中央、国务院高度重视高技能人才队伍建设工作。2003 年召开的全国人才工作会议将高技能人才队伍建设纳入国家人才队伍建设总体规划，作出了

一系列具有战略意义的安排部署。在此后多年中，中央及各地有关部门采取有效措施，优化政策环境，建立工作机制，改善舆论氛围，紧扣高技能人才队伍建设的各个环节，推动高技能人才工作步入快车道，高技能人才培养规模不断扩大。主要成就表现在以下四个方面：

（1）高技能人才的素质和供给数量明显提升。大国工匠不断涌现。截至 2016 年年底，全国高技能人才达 4 791 万人，国家层面建设 476 个高技能人才培训基地、594 个技能大师工作室，实施技师培训项目，中央财政累计投入资金 20.5 亿元。

（2）培养体系逐步形成。基本建立了以企业行业为主体、职业院校为基础、学校教育与企业培养紧密联系、政府推动与社会支持相互结合的高技能人才培养体系。截至目前，全国有技工院校 2 500 余所，在校生 300 多万人。作为培养后备中、高级技能人才的重要阵地，许多城市还建设了一批公共实训中心。在政府部门的引导下，一些大中型企业逐步建立健全职工培训制度，积极开展企业技能人才培养培训，在技能人才培养中发挥了重要作用。

（3）技能竞赛为祖国和人民赢得荣誉。2010 年，中国加入世界技能组织后，更加注重世界技能大赛的引领带动作用，进而推动了国内竞赛和职业教育培训水平的提高。2011 年、2013 年、2015 年、2017 年、2019 年中国先后参加了第 41 届至第 45 届世界技能大赛，累计取得 36 金、29 银、20 铜和 58 个优胜奖（见图 7-2）。2017 年，中国在阿联酋阿布扎比第 44 届世界技能大赛中，取得 15 金、7 银、8 铜和 12 个优胜奖，金牌数、奖牌数和团体总分均居榜首。2019 年，中国在俄罗斯喀山第 45 届世界技能大赛上，取得 16 金、14 银、5 铜和 17 个优胜奖，再次位居金牌榜、奖牌榜和团体总分榜首，创造了中国参加世界技能大赛以来的最好成绩。第 46 届世界技能大赛已确定在中国上海举办。

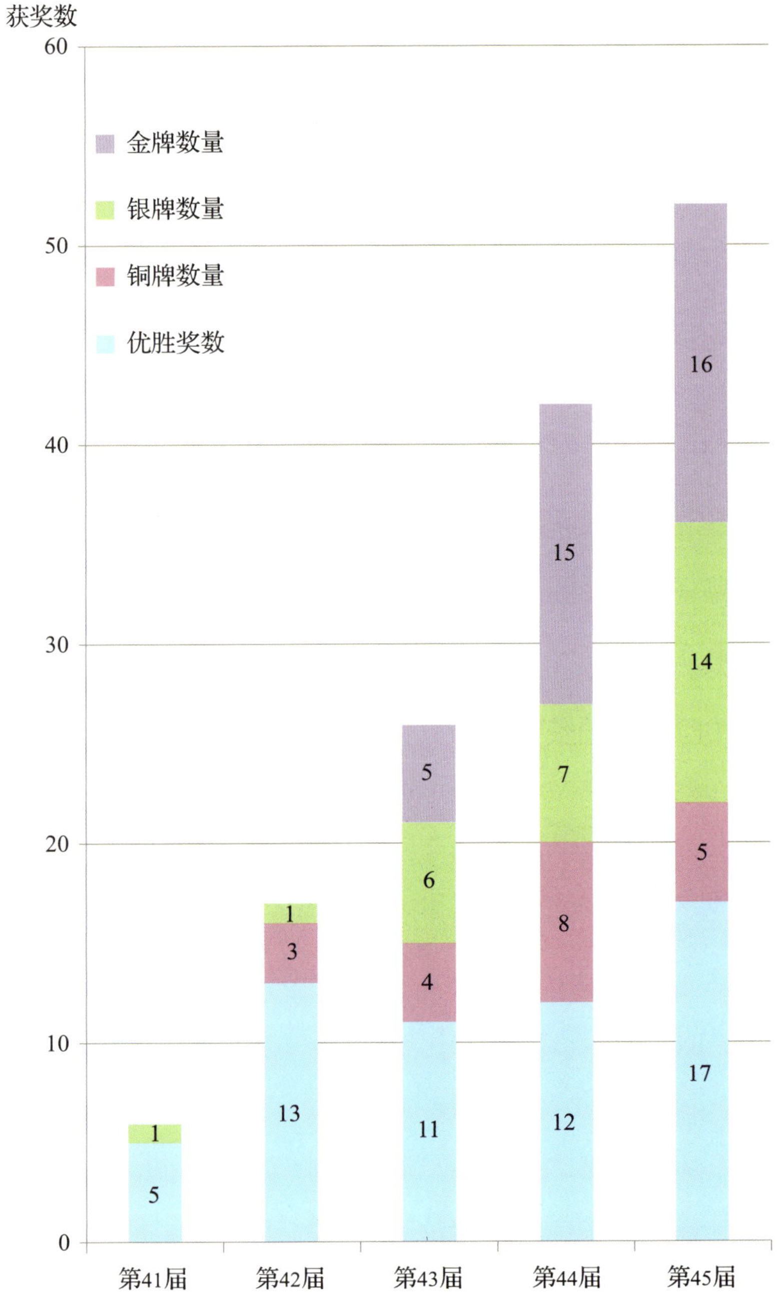

图 7-2 中国代表团在第 41 届至第 45 届世界技能大赛上获奖数量统计图

资料来源：人力资源社会保障部。

中国代表团在第 45 届世界技能大赛中表现十分出色，共获得了 16 枚金牌、14 枚银牌、5 枚铜牌和 17 个优胜奖，再次位居金牌榜、奖牌榜、团体总分榜首。

（4）以评价激励畅通职业发展通道。每两年开展一次高技能人才评选表彰活动，每次表彰 30 名中华技能大奖获得者和 300 名全国技术能手，并给予他们一定的物质奖励。1995 年以来，累计评选表彰中华技能大奖获得者 260 人，有 3 028 人获得全国技术能手称号（另外，通过竞赛获得全国技术能手称号的达到 5 349 人）。持续推进高技能人才享受国务院政府特殊津贴工作。从 2008 年起，每两年选拔 400 名高技能人才享受国务院政府特殊津贴（从 2012 年开始，每次选拔 500 名），向其颁发荣誉证书并给予一次性特殊津贴。截至 2018 年年底，共有 2 729 名高技能人才享受国务院政府特殊津贴。

第八章
群体就业

一、青年就业

（一）青年就业概况

青年就业是世界性的难题。据2007年中国人口变动情况抽样调查结果显示，中国15~34岁人口占全国总人口数的28.7%。2008年年底，中国青年（16~34岁）就业人数占全国总就业人数的32.5%。

随着中国教育的发展，接受过高等教育的人员已经成为青年劳动者的主流。高校毕业生逐年增加，2018年达到820万人（见表8-1），比2008年的559万人增加了261万人，增长了近46.7%。据国家统计局初步测算，2018年就业人员与1982年相比，大专及以上受教育程度人员占比由0.9%上升到20.1%，高中受教育程度人员占比由10.5%提高到18.0%，初中受教育程度人员占比由26.0%提高到43.2%。[①] 为更好地适应人力资源市场的变化，中国还采取各种措施大力发展职业教育和培训事业，将职业教育和技能培训作为预防失业、稳定就业和促进再就业的重要举措。

① 数据来自国家统计局发布的《新中国成立70周年经济社会发展成就系列报告》。

表 8-1　　2008—2018 年全国普通高校毕业生人数　单位：万人

年份	本科毕业生
2008	559
2009	611
2010	631
2011	660
2012	680
2013	699
2014	727
2015	749
2016	756
2017	795
2018	820

资料来源：教育部。

在中国，部分高校毕业生等青年群体还存在就业难题。一方面，就业总量压力大。每年需要在城镇就业的新成长劳动力超过 1 500 万人，其中高校毕业生占半数以上，还有不少农村青年劳动力需要转移就业。另一方面，就业结构性矛盾突出。中国目前仍处于工业化中期和产业链的中低端，市场中的岗位大部分是制造业一线普工和服务业的普通服务员，优质岗位相对不足，而新一代年轻求职者更注重职业发展、薪酬待遇、工作条件，岗位供需对接存在错位。部分青年的能力素质与企业岗位需求不适应，创新型、技术技能型人才尚难以满足经济转型升级的需要。

（二）促进青年就业的主要政策措施

1. 促进青年就业的主要措施

促进青年就业关系着众多家庭的福祉，关系着国家发展的未来。中国政府

坚持把以高校毕业生为重点的青年就业作为就业工作的重中之重，采取一系列措施促进青年就业创业。

（1）采取综合性措施促进青年就业创业。中国政府从以下四个方面采取了有针对性的措施。一是发展经济，扩大就业空间。实施就业优先政策，坚持把稳定和扩大就业作为经济运行合理区间的下限，加强就业政策与宏观经济、产业、财政、金融等政策的衔接，实现促进经济发展与扩大就业的良性互动。培育壮大新动能，促进新产业、新业态、新模式快速发展，拓展适合青年的多元化就业空间。二是鼓励创业创新带动就业。持续推进简政放权，降低创业门槛，加大创业政策扶持力度，通过减免税费、提供贷款、加强创业孵化载体建设等方式鼓励青年创业。三是加强职业技能培训。实施职业技能提升行动，加快建设知识型、技能型、创新型劳动者大军。四是加快建设覆盖全民、贯穿全程、辐射全城、便捷高效的公共就业服务体系，为包括青年在内的所有劳动者免费提供政策咨询、职业介绍、就业创业指导、困难帮扶等服务，特别是根据青年的特点，更多地运用微博、微信、手机应用软件等提供更加灵活便捷的就业服务。

（2）制定专项规划。近年来，中国政府制定实施了《中长期青年发展规划（2016—2025 年）》，提出促进青年就业创业的目标任务和重点举措。该规划提出的青年就业创业的发展目标是：青年就业比较充分，高校毕业生就业保持在较高水平；青年就业权利保障更加完善，青年的薪资待遇、劳动保护、社会保险等合法权益得到充分保护；青年创业服务体系更加完善，创业活力明显提升。青年就业创业的发展措施包括：推动完善促进青年就业创业政策体系，加强青年就业服务，推动青年投身创业实践，加强青年就业权益保障等。

（3）有针对性地实施具体计划。近年来，人力资源社会保障部发布了一系列文件，有针对性地实施了多项促进青年就业的具体计划，如面向未就业毕业生和失业青年实施三年百万青年见习计划，面向长期失业青年实施青年就业启

航计划，对农村新生代青年劳动者实施新生代农民工职业技能提升计划，对城乡未继续升学的初高中毕业生开展劳动预备制培训，对有培训愿望的青年创业者开展创业培训，对企业新招用和新转岗人员开展新型学徒制培训等。

在三年百万青年见习计划中提出了五项工作内容。一是明确见习对象。对象为离校两年内未就业高校毕业生和16~24岁失业青年。二是开发见习岗位。要根据优势产业发展和青年见习需求，确定一批企事业单位、社会组织作为青年就业见习单位，充分挖掘见习岗位。三是搭建对接平台。组织见习岗位推荐、双向选择洽谈活动，多渠道助力见习供需双方对接。四是加强见习管理。要确保见习活动规范有序。五是加大跟踪扶持。见习期满，鼓励见习单位留用见习人员；对未被留用的人员，要根据其求职意向持续提供服务，促进其尽快实现就业创业。

在青年就业启航计划中提出了五项主要措施。一是摸清基本情况。要了解掌握失业青年的家庭情况、失业原因、求职意向、技能水平等基本信息。二是开展实践指导。鼓励失业青年走出家门，为其创造更多与社会接触交往的机会。三是提升就业能力。根据失业青年的能力水平和就业意向，有针对性地提供培训项目，使之至少掌握一种专项技能。四是扶持自主创业。组织有创业意愿的失业青年参观创业园区，感受创业氛围，激发其创业原动力。五是实施托底帮扶。将建档立卡贫困家庭、城乡低保家庭、零就业家庭和残疾失业青年作为重点援助对象，提供专门的职业指导和心理咨询服务，组织其参加专场招聘活动，优先向企业推荐。

2. 促进高校毕业生就业创业的政策措施

中国政府高度重视高校毕业生就业工作，2009年以来，制定出台了一系列促进高校毕业生就业的政策措施。2011年、2013年、2014年，国务院办公厅连续印发促进高校毕业生就业创业工作的文件；2016年，中共中央办公厅、国

务院办公厅出台进一步引导和鼓励高校毕业生到基层工作的意见；2016年，人力资源社会保障部、教育部启动实施高校毕业生就业创业促进计划；2019年，人力资源社会保障部、教育部、公安部、财政部、人民银行五部门联合印发做好高校毕业生就业创业工作的新文件，全方位促进高校毕业生就业创业。

（1）积极拓宽高校毕业生就业领域。结合发展战略性新兴产业、转变经济发展方式和调整经济结构，着力发展既具有较高科技含量又具有较强吸纳就业能力的智力密集型、技术密集型产业，大力发展具有增长潜力的生产性服务业和生活性服务业，促进“互联网+”新技术、新业态、新模式发展，继续开发社会管理和公共教育、卫生、文化等领域服务岗位，不断拓宽高校毕业生就业渠道，努力扩大经济发展吸纳高校毕业生就业的规模。

在中国经济从劳动密集型向智力密集型升级的过程中，以中国青年为主的产业大军发展势头迅猛。（新华社记者唐奕摄）

（2）加大政策支持，引导多渠道就业。中国政府不断完善促进高校毕业生就业的政策体系，充分运用财税、金融、资金补贴等各类政策，引导高校毕业生到城乡基层、中小微企业就业，支持就业新形态和多种形式的灵活就业。对到基层就业，特别是到中西部地区和艰苦边远地区基层就业的高校毕业生，落实学费补偿和助学贷款代偿、高定工资、资金补贴、放宽职称评定条件等政策。实施“三支一扶”计划、农村教师特岗计划等基层服务项目，引导高校毕业生到城乡基层教育、医疗、卫生等领域从事志愿服务，期满后给予考研加分、定向招录等优惠政策。对中小企业吸纳高校毕业生就业的，落实税收减免、社会保险补贴、职业培训补贴等政策。对高校毕业生到民营企业就业的，在专业技术职称评定等方面享受国有企事业单位同类人员的同等待遇；对灵活就业的，落实社会保险补贴等政策。

（3）鼓励高校毕业生自主创业。一是优化创业政策环境。对符合条件的高校毕业生自主创业的，落实 3 年内每户每年 12 000 元限额税收减免，提供最高 15 万元的创业担保贷款贴息，发放一次性创业补贴等优惠政策。支持有条件的地方设立高校毕业生就业创业基金，助力高校毕业生创业创新。二是加强创新创业教育。将创新创业教育纳入高校人才培养全过程，指导高校开发、开设创新创业教育课程，制定学分转换、弹性学制、保留学籍休学创业等措施，开展各类创业实践活动，增强大学生创新精神、创业意识和创新创业能力。三是强化能力素质培养。组织有创业意愿的高校毕业生参加创业培训，并按规定给予培训补贴。依托各类培训机构、企业培训中心等，创新开发质量高、特色鲜明、针对性强的培训实训课程，以满足高校毕业生在创业不同阶段、不同领域、不同业态的需求。四是做优创业服务。将高校毕业生纳入各地创业服务体系，根据高校毕业生的特点和需求，提供政策咨询、项目开发、风险评估、开业指导、融资服务、跟踪扶持、创业孵化等“一条龙”创业服务。积极搭建众创空间、大学生创业园等创业孵化载体，举办“中国创翼”创业创新大赛等各类活动，

全方位助力高校毕业生创业。

（4）支持高校毕业生参加就业见习和职业技能培训。结合各地优势产业的发展情况和青年的就业见习需求，组织信誉良好、管理规范的企事业单位和社会组织作为就业见习单位，落实见习补贴政策，帮助失业青年增加实践经验，提升其就业竞争力。积极组织有培训需求的高校毕业生参加职业技能培训和职业技能鉴定，帮助其提高就业能力，并给予培训补贴和职业技能鉴定补贴。对企业新招用毕业年度高校毕业生，在一年内对其开展岗位技能培训的，按规定给予职业培训补贴。

（5）强化对高校毕业生的就业指导和就业服务。建立贯穿于整个大学教育期间的职业发展和就业指导课程体系；举办专场招聘会、供求洽谈会，开展组织企业进校园招聘等常态化就业服务活动；适应高校毕业生求职需求和特点，积极运用网络开展就业服务。把离校未就业高校毕业生纳入就业帮扶对象，针对其需求提供岗位信息、职业指导、职业培训等服务。将就业困难的高校毕业生纳入就业援助体系，提供“一对一”就业援助。加强人力资源市场监管，维护高校毕业生就业权益。

（三）促进青年就业取得的成就

近年来，中国政府实施了一系列政策措施，青年就业形势总体保持稳定，高校毕业生就业率保持在较高水平，自主创业规模不断扩大。参加培训人员更加踊跃，2018 年参加职业培训的高校毕业生人数达到 33 万人，其中培训后当期成功创业的人数为 2.2 万人；在城乡未继续升学的高中毕业生中也有 37 万人参加职业培训，培训后当期成功创业者达到 2.1 万人。

二、妇女就业

（一）妇女就业概况

截至2017年年底，中国人口中妇女占49%，她们是劳动力资源的重要组成部分。广大妇女积极投身国家建设，为经济发展和社会进步做出了巨大的贡献，妇女的经济地位和社会地位也有了明显提高。改革开放以来，随着国民经济持续、稳定发展，国家制定并实施了一系列促进就业再就业的扶持政策，妇女就业人数不断提高，从1978年的1.7亿人上升至2018年的3.4亿人，全国就业人口中妇女占43.7%。

中华人民共和国成立以来，制定了一系列法律法规，用以保障妇女的劳动就业权益。1949年制定的临时宪章《中国人民政治协商会议共同纲领》就明确规定，废除束缚妇女的封建制度，妇女在政治的、经济的、文化教育的、社会生活的各方面，均有与男子平等的权利。目前，中国已基本形成了以《宪法》为依据，以《中华人民共和国妇女权益保障法》《劳动法》和《就业促进法》为主线，以《女职工劳动保护特别规定》《女职工禁忌劳动范围的规定》《女职工保健工作规定》《企业职工生育保险试行办法》等法规规章为实体的一整套保障妇女劳动权益和促进妇女就业的法规体系，有效地维护了妇女的劳动就业权益。

（二）促进妇女就业的政策措施

中华人民共和国成立以来，中国政府始终重视妇女就业问题，制定实施了多项法律法规来保障妇女的就业权利，采取多种措施促进妇女就业。中共十八大以来，中国实行就业优先战略，积极推动男女平等就业。2019年，人力资源社会保障部等九部门印发《关于进一步规范招聘行为促进妇女就业的通知》（人社部发〔2019〕17号），明确了不得实施的六种就业性别歧视行为，建立健全

多部门联合约谈、人力资源市场监管、司法救济三种机制，为保障妇女平等享有就业权提供有力支持。

（1）积极开发就业岗位，完善就业政策，促进妇女就业。近年来，中国大力发展适合妇女就业的第三产业，特别是社区服务业，不断提高劳动密集型企业、中小企业和非公有制企业吸纳妇女就业的能力，拓宽妇女就业领域。截至2017年年底，全国城镇单位女性就业人员达到6 545.3万人。

（2）加大政策扶持，鼓励妇女自主创业。面向有创业意愿的妇女，积极开展创业培训，提供政策咨询、项目推荐、开业指导、后续支持等“一条龙”创业服务，对符合条件的落实小额担保贷款、贴息等优惠政策。近年来，人力资源社会保障部门联合有关部门开展女性就业创业典型宣传，引导和激励更多的女性劳动者成为创业者。

（3）加强教育培训，提高妇女素质。中华人民共和国成立以来，中国政府通过法律赋予妇女同男子平等受教育的权利，改变了妇女文盲率大大高于男性的情况。改革开放以来，中国大力普及高中阶段教育。随着对中西部地区和家庭经济困难学生资助政策扶持力度日益加大，女性接受高中阶段教育的机会显著增多。截至2017年，高中阶段教育在校女生占在校生总数的47.7%；2017年，普通高等学校本专科在校女生占在校生总数的52.5%，比1978年提高了28.4个百分点；研究生在校女生占比达48.4%，比1985年提高了29.8个百分点。

（4）积极为女性求职者提供有针对性的就业服务。全国省、市、县、乡四级公共就业服务机构免费向女性求职者开放，不少城市公共就业服务机构还专门设立窗口，举办专场招聘洽谈会，为女性求职者提供就业信息、政策咨询、职业指导、职业介绍等就业服务。人力资源社会保障部门和妇联联合组织开展专门面向女性农村劳动者的“春风送岗位”活动，向进城务工的农村妇女免费提供有针对性的就业服务。

（5）完善生育保险制度，改善妇女就业环境。为了避免用人单位因考虑妇女生育负担而不愿招用女性劳动者，近年来，中国一直在大力推进生育保险制度建设。与2009年年底相比，全国生育保险参保人数从10 876万人增长到2018年年底的20 434万人，当年享受保险待遇人次从174万人次增长到1 089万人次。

（6）加大执法监察力度，保障女职工合法权益。劳动保障监察机构加大对使用女职工较多的行业或企业的监督检查力度，积极开展规范人力资源市场秩序和女职工特殊劳动保护专项检查活动，集中查处侵害女职工权益的违法行为；规范用人单位招聘用工行为，指导企业认真落实法律法规中有关平等就业的规定，并积极受理女职工的投诉举报，纠正各种歧视行为。

（三）促进妇女就业取得的成就

随着国家经济社会快速发展，妇女就业选择更加多元，创业之路更加宽广，就业和创业人数大幅增加。2017年，全国妇女就业人数达3.4亿人，比1978年翻了一番。2017年，公有经济企事业单位女性专业技术人员达1 529.7万人，占比48.6%，比1982年提高了9.5个百分点。2009—2018年全国累计发放3 837.7亿元支持妇女就业创业的小额担保贷款，获贷妇女达656.9万人次，使妇女就业创业得到大力支持。2017年，全国妇联举办中国妇女创业创新大赛，吸引了56万名妇女参与。妇联组织培养巾帼电商带头人10万人带动1 500多万名妇女增收致富，初步形成“互联网＋女性创业”的服务体系，互联网领域创业者中女性达到55%。2017年落实女职工劳动保护的企业占比达到71.2%，比2002年提高了35.2个百分点。建立女职工休息哺乳室的基层企事业工会达到近30万个，覆盖女职工1 849.4万人。

广大妇女积极投身国家建设，为经济发展和社会进步做出了巨大的贡献。（新华社记者牟宇摄）

三、农村劳动者就业

中国农村人口为数众多，劳动力资源丰富。中华人民共和国成立初期，农村劳动者主要以从事农业生产为主。20 世纪 50 年代至 70 年代，通过积极发展农村经济，农村就业状况逐步改善，1978 年农村就业人员[①] 达 30 638 万人。改革开放以来，国家实行家庭联产承包责任制，鼓励发展农业多种经营和乡镇企业，相关政策的实施调动了农村劳动者生产经营的积极性，劳动效率大大提高，农村出现大量富余劳动力。随着乡镇企业快速发展，劳动力市场逐步建立和完善，农村富余劳动力开始向非农产业转移，并向城市流动就业。截至 1997 年，

① 农村就业人员是指农村人口中 16 岁以上实际参加生产经营活动并取得实物或货币收入的人员，既包括劳动年龄内实际参加劳动的人员，也包括超过劳动年龄但实际参加劳动的人员，但不包括户口在家的在外学生、现役军人和丧失劳动能力的人，也不包括待业人员和家务劳动者。

农村就业人员达到 49 039 万人。进入 21 世纪后，中国政府大力促进农村劳动者就业创业，非农产业就业的农村劳动者数量持续增大，流动到城市就业并成为新市民的人数不断增多。他们投身到制造业和服务业，参与城市建设发展，在中国经济社会发展中发挥了重要作用。

随着乡镇企业快速发展，劳动力市场逐步建立和完善，农村富余劳动力开始向非农产业转移。

（一）农村劳动者就业的基本情况

1. 中国农村劳动力就业结构

就业结构与产业结构是紧密相关的。中华人民共和国成立以来，农村劳动力就业结构呈现出以下变化：第一产业劳动力就业比例呈下降趋势，第二、第三产业就业人员比重呈上升趋势。截至 2018 年，农村就业人员达 34 167 万人，

其中非农产业就业的农村劳动者达 28 836 万人（含外出从事非农产业工作的农村劳动者 17 266 万人）。第二产业就业的农村劳动者为 14 158 万人，占 49.1%；第三产业就业的农村劳动者为 14 562 万人，占 50.5%；从事第一产业工作的仅占 0.4%。

2. 农村劳动者就业途径

从改革开放以来的实践来看，农村劳动者就业主要有三条途径：一是农业就业，主要从事种植业、养殖业劳动；二是就地就近转移就业，即在当地从事非农生产工作；三是跨地区流动就业，包括进入城市务工和经商。

（1）农业就业。自 20 世纪 80 年代以来，中国农业就业呈现快速增长态势。农村实行联产承包责任制生产经营模式以后，农村劳动者生产的自主性和积极性受到激发，农村生产力得到极大解放，农业内部就业机会大大增加。近年来，各地积极拓展农村就业空间，通过大力发展高产、优质、高效农业，加快发展林业、水产养殖业、畜牧业等产业；发展农业产业化经营，延长农业产业链；加快农业生产的深度和广度开发，特别是探索开发荒山、荒沟、荒丘、荒滩等非耕地资源的途径，深度挖掘农业内部就业潜力。

（2）就地就近转移就业。在农村发展非农产业，促进农村劳动者就地就近转移就业，是解决农村富余劳动力就业的一个重要方向。改革开放以来，东部沿海发达地区依托乡镇企业、民营经济、县域经济的蓬勃发展，创造了大量就业岗位，率先实现了大量农村劳动者的就地就近转移就业。近年来，随着中西部大开发和区域经济协调发展战略的深入推进，农村劳动者就地就近转移就业的规模也随之扩大。这对加快县域经济和欠发达地区经济社会的全面发展，促进社会主义新农村建设产生了积极作用。

（3）跨地区流动就业。20 世纪 70 年代末，一大批农村劳动者开始从事家庭工商业，早期的流动就业主要是外出运销和搞建筑工程。截至 1984 年，外出

乡镇企业成为吸纳农村劳动者就业的主要渠道，这不仅使农村劳动者实现收入增长，而且促进了农村劳动者的转移就业。

务工的农村劳动者还不到 200 万人。在随后的几年里，随着乡镇企业的快速发展，农村劳动者跨地区流动就业人数迅速增加。截至 1988 年，外出就业的农村劳动者达 1 000 万人左右。此后，随着国家经济，特别是东部沿海经济的快速发展，农村劳动者跨地区，特别是向城市流动的就业人数迅猛增长，1994 年达到 4 000 万人，2018 年则达到 28 836 万人。

3. 农村劳动者在非农产业就业的基本情况

（1）就业的总体规模和就业的地域分布。依据国家统计局对全国农村地域开展的入户访问调查统计，2018 年全国非农产业就业的农村劳动者总量为 28 836 万人（见图 8-1）。其中，外出从事非农产业工作的农村劳动者为 17 266 万人（含进入城镇的农村劳动者 13 506 万人）；在本地就地就近就业的为 11 570 万人。

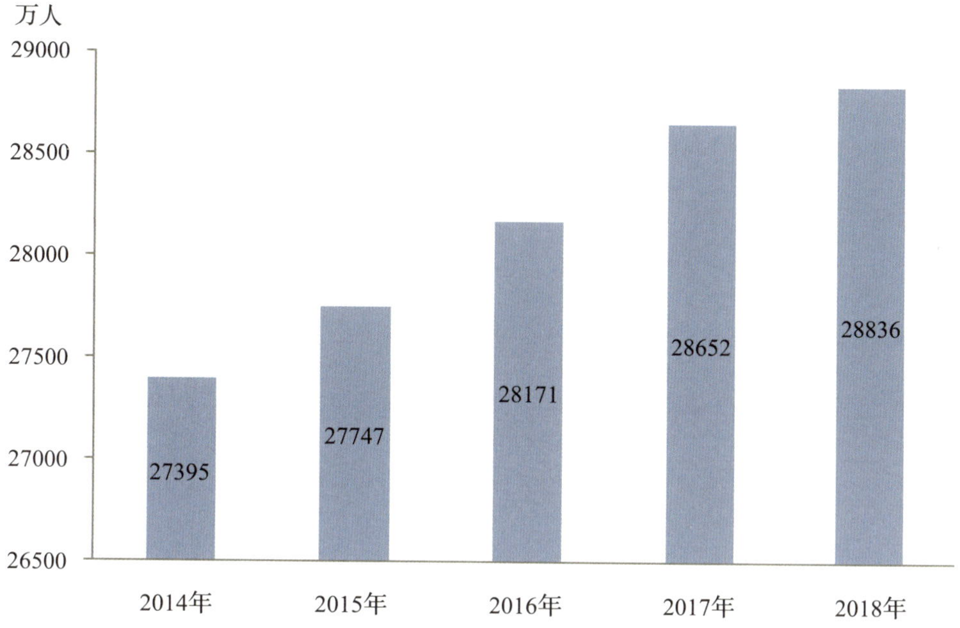

图 8-1 2014—2018 年非农产业就业的农村劳动者总量

资料来源：国家统计局网站。

（2）主要特征。一是在全部非农产业就业的农村劳动者中，男性占 65.2%，女性占 34.8%。其中，在外出从事非农产业工作的农村劳动者中，女性占 30.8%；在本地从事非农产业工作的农村劳动者中，女性占 38.6%。二是非农产业就业的农村劳动者平均年龄为 40.2 岁。从年龄结构来看，40 岁及以下从事非农产业工作的农村劳动者占 52.1%，50 岁以上从事非农产业工作的农村劳动者占 22.4%。三是在全部非农产业就业的农村劳动者中，小学文化程度的占 15.5%，初中文化程度的占 55.8%，高中文化程度的占 16.6%，大专及以上文化程度的占 10.9%。

（3）工资收入情况。国家统计局专项调查结果显示，2006 年非农产业就业的农村劳动者月平均工资为 966 元。中共十八大以来，非农产业就业的农村劳动者的收入实现了较快增长。据国家统计局调查，2018 年非农产业就业的农村劳动者月平均收入为 3 721 元，比 2006 年增加 2 755 元，增长 285.2%。

（4）农村教育情况。中华人民共和国成立初期，中国农村教育十分落后。改革开放以来，农村义务教育被纳入公共财政的保障范围，从而取得了全面发展。中共十八大以来，国家大力支持农村教育，实施农村寄宿制学校建设、教育脱贫攻坚等重大工程。据教育部统计，截至 2018 年，全国超过 90% 的县实现义务教育均衡发展，更多农村青少年享受到更好、更公平的教育。全国农业普查结果显示，初中文化程度的农村居民占 42.5%，高中或中专文化程度的农村居民占 11.0%，大专及以上文化程度的农村居民占 3.9%。农村居民文化素质的提升带动了农村劳动者整体素质的提升，从而为经济发展提供了高质量的劳动力。

（二）促进农村劳动者转移就业的政策措施

1. 农村劳动力流动就业政策演变

国家对农村劳动力流动就业的政策经历了三个阶段的演变：20 世纪 70 年代末至 80 年代末，从控制流动到允许流动；20 世纪 80 年代末至 90 年代末，从无序流动到有序流动；20 世纪 90 年代末至今，从城乡有别到统筹城乡就业。

2. 出台政策促进统筹城乡就业

一是为给予非农产业就业的农村劳动者平等待遇，原劳动和社会保障部出台规定，清理取消限制流动就业的政策和不合理收费，改善农村劳动者进城务工环境。

二是加强就业服务，促进农村劳动者转移就业。①建立面向包括农村劳动者在内的公共就业服务制度。国家明确提出，在就业服务方面，对进城登记求职的农村劳动者，公共就业服务机构要提供免费的职业介绍服务；在城镇常住并处于无业状态的农村劳动者，可在其常住地进行失业登记，享受均等化公共就业服务和普惠性就业政策。②实施“春风行动”，强化对进城求职农村劳动

者的就业服务。在春节后、农村劳动者外出务工高峰时期，在全国范围内开展“春风行动”。其间，各地的公共就业服务机构集中免费为农村劳动者提供服务，同时推荐一批诚信的民办职业中介机构，打击非法职业中介组织，改善就业环境。③创建劳务输出工作示范县和转移就业工作示范县，推动农村就业工作深入开展。为进一步做好劳务输出工作，人力资源社会保障部门提出大力推行职业培训、就业服务、劳动维权“三位一体”的工作模式，切实加强输出、输入双向对接。之后，在全国确定 190 多个劳务输出示范县，着重总结推广示范县的经验，在面上推动全国农村劳动者转移就业工作，促进了县乡的就业服务工作。④建立健全县乡公共就业服务体系。2002 年，国家就业政策明确提出，在街道和工作任务重的乡镇，可设立或确定负责劳动保障事务的机构。随后，原劳动和社会保障部对街道（乡镇）和社区工作平台的建设提出要求，明确实现机构、人员、经费、场地、制度、工作“六到位”。截至 2009 年年底，全国 89% 的乡镇都建立了相应的工作机构，41% 的行政村聘用了专职或兼职的工作人员，主要开展劳动力资源统计、职业介绍、劳务输出以及引导性培训等工作。截至 2018 年，全国大多数基层街道、乡镇都建立了工作平台，设立专门服务场所或服务窗口，承担就业工作的基本职责；社区、行政村设立专门服务窗口，并开展上门入户服务。⑤组织实施农村劳动力技能就业计划，提高农村劳动者的职业技能水平。从 2006 年开始，在全国范围内组织实施农村劳动力技能就业计划，并为进城务工的农村劳动者提供一次性职业培训补贴。此后实施的多项全国职业技能培训计划，也都覆盖了农村劳动者。

三是开展统筹城乡就业试点，健全城乡一体化劳动力市场。为进一步促进农村劳动者转移就业，2006 年，劳动和社会保障部、发展改革委、财政部、农业部联合部署决定选择一些就业工作基础较好、管理服务能力较强、改革创新积极性高的地区开展统筹城乡就业的试点工作，建立城乡一体化的劳动力市场，形成保障城乡劳动者平等就业的制度，促进城乡劳动者实现比较充分的就业。

在试点地区建立健全管理城乡就业的组织体系，建立覆盖城乡的职业培训体系和公共就业服务体系，健全劳动用工管理制度，妥善解决农村劳动者的社会保障问题，并在取得成果和经验后向全国推广。

四是扶持流动出外就业的农村劳动者返乡创业。2008 年，为贯彻中共十七大提出的“实施扩大就业的发展战略，促进以创业带动就业”，国务院办公厅转发了人力资源社会保障部等部门《关于促进以创业带动就业工作的指导意见》（国办发〔2008〕111 号），从完善扶持政策、改善创业环境，强化创业培训、提高创业能力，健全服务体系、提供优质服务等方面促进创业。政策明确适用于包括农村劳动者在内的各类群体。上述指导意见还专门提出，对流动出外就业的农村劳动者返乡创业的，劳务输出地区要提供相关政策扶持；积极做好他们返乡创业的金融服务及创业服务。

（三）促进农村劳动者转移就业对经济社会发展的贡献

中华人民共和国成立以来，党和国家结合国情农情，推进农村改革发展。从 20 世纪 50 年代开展土地改革到实行农业合作化，从 80 年代建立家庭联产承包责任制到推进农村承包地“三权”分置，从 21 世纪以来打好脱贫攻坚战到实施乡村振兴战略，一系列改革建设的创举推动了农村体制机制不断创新，促进了农业和农村第二、第三产业生产力的解放发展。中共十八大以来，以习近平同志为核心的党中央，坚持把解决好“三农”问题[①]作为全党工作的重中之重，持续加大强农惠农富农政策力度，建立健全城乡融合发展体制机制和政策体系，全面深化农村改革，稳步实施乡村振兴战略，精准扶贫成效举世瞩目，农业农村发展取得了历史性成就。

一是农村劳动者的转移和流动就业是继农村实行家庭承包经营制度和乡镇企业崛起之后，中国农村劳动者的又一伟大创造，是解放农村生产力的又一伟

① “三农”问题是指农业问题、农村问题、农民问题。

大创举。农村劳动者一头连着城市和发达地区，一头连着农村和落后地区。促进农村劳动者转移就业工作带动了城乡之间劳动力资源和生产力布局的优化配置，把解决“三农”问题和工业化、城镇化、现代化发展有机地联系在一起，闯出了一条城乡融合发展的新路子。二是农村劳动者外出务工已经成为扩大就业、增加农村劳动者收入的主要途径，也成为工业带动农业、城市带动农村、发达地区带动落后地区的有效形式。通过在城市和发达地区就业，农村劳动者每年为农村带回了数以千亿计的资金，这些资金成为其购买农业生产资料和改善生活条件的重要来源，同时也为农业和农村发展提供了资金积累，这些劳动者掌握了技术，提高了素质，开阔了视野，积累了经验，丰富了社会关系网络，提升了农村人力资本。一批带着资金、技术和市场经济观念返乡创业的农村劳动者，已经成为农村经济发展的一支新生力量，推动了欠发达地区县域经济的发展，直接助推了社会主义新农村建设。三是转移就业的农村劳动者已成为中国城镇化建设和城市发展的重要力量，为城市第二、第三产业发展提供了源源不断的劳动力，进而成为有生产力和消费力的新市民，推动了市场经济的全面发展，为国家经济建设做出了重要贡献。

四、就业困难人员就业

《就业促进法》规定，就业困难人员是指因身体状况、技能水平、家庭因素、失去土地等原因难以实现就业，以及连续失业一定时间仍未能实现就业的人员。就业困难人员的具体范围，由省、自治区、直辖市人民政府根据本行政区域的实际情况规定。各级人民政府建立健全就业援助制度，采取税费减免、贷款贴息、社会保险补贴、岗位补贴等办法，通过公益性岗位安置等途径，对就业困难人员实行优先扶持和重点帮助。

（一）促进城镇困难人员就业的政策措施与取得的成效

就业援助制度是指政府建立的以就业困难人员为主要对象，制定各类特殊扶持政策，多渠道开发公益性就业岗位，提供有针对性的援助措施，帮扶就业困难人员尽快再就业的专项制度。目前，中国已经基本建立了比较完整的就业援助制度，作为政府向就业困难人员和零就业家庭提供优先扶持和重点帮助的制度性安排，在促进就业和稳定就业、保持就业局势总体稳定方面发挥了重要作用。

1. 就业援助政策

（1）鼓励就业困难人员自谋职业、自主创业。一是税费减免政策。对符合条件的劳动者从事个体经营的，在规定限额内依次减免营业税、城市维护建设税、教育费附加和个人所得税，并免收属于管理类、登记类和证照类的各项行政事业性收费。二是贷款贴息政策。对符合条件的劳动者自谋职业、自主创业或合伙经营与组织起来就业的，其自筹资金不足部分由政府建立担保基金，提供贷款担保，银行发放小额担保贷款，财政提供一定额度或者全额的贷款贴息。三是社会保险补贴政策。对符合条件的劳动者通过灵活就业等方式实现再就业的，给予一定比例的社会保险补贴，增强其就业的稳定性。四是各地采取多种措施，落实经营场地问题，方便就业困难人员接续社会保险。通过各项政策降低就业困难人员自谋职业、自主创业的生产经营成本，解决其融资难题，解除其后顾之忧，增强其就业的发展能力和可持续性。

（2）鼓励企业吸纳就业困难人员就业。一是税收优惠政策。对符合条件的企业，在新增岗位中新招用就业困难人员，与其签订一年以上期限劳动合同并为其缴纳社会保险费的，按实际招用人数，在相应期限内定额依次减免营业税、城市维护建设税、教育费附加和企业所得税。二是社会保险补贴政策。对符合条件的企业，在新增岗位中新招用就业困难人员，与其签订一年以上期限劳动

合同并为其缴纳社会保险费的，在相应期限内给予社会保险补贴。三是创业担保贷款政策。对符合贷款条件的劳动密集型小企业，在新增岗位中新招用就业困难人员达到企业现有在职职工总数一定比例以上，并与其签订一年以上期限劳动合同的，根据实际招用人数，提供最高不超过 100 万元的贷款。

（3）政府投资开发的公益性岗位，优先安排就业困难人员。一是开发更多公益性岗位，特别是由政府作为出资主体扶持或通过社会筹集资金开发的、以安置就业困难人员为主的、符合社会公共利益需要的服务性岗位和协助管理岗位。二是实行优先安排的援助。各级公共就业服务机构要在同等条件下，优先为就业困难人员提供岗位信息、职业介绍、职业指导等就业服务，优先录用和安排就业困难人员。三是落实相关扶持政策。按照公益性岗位安置就业困难人员的人数，在相应期限内给予就业困难人员社会保险补贴，同时提供适当的岗位补贴。

2. 实施专项就业服务措施

（1）求职登记和职业指导。为急需就业的就业困难人员量身订制服务方案，针对其在求职就业、享受再就业扶持政策和其他劳动保障政策方面的不同需求，确定具体服务内容，综合运用职业介绍、职业指导、就业培训、公益性岗位和其他劳动保障相关服务措施，向其提供有针对性的服务。

（2）岗位援助开发。掌握一批适合就业困难人员的就业岗位，通过组织就业困难人员参加招聘活动或个别介绍、送岗位到家等形式，使有就业愿望的就业困难人员了解岗位信息，及时落实就业岗位。同时，对在公益性岗位实现就业的就业困难人员，落实社会保险补贴和岗位补贴政策。对已灵活就业的就业困难人员，组织其申报就业、参加社会保险，并帮助其落实社会保险补贴。

（3）职业技能培训。根据就业岗位的需求，结合就业困难人员的特点，介绍并指导就业困难人员选择职业技能培训课程，组织并推荐其参加职业技能培

训。一些地方不仅向就业困难人员给予培训补贴，还为参加培训的就业困难人员提供生活补贴、交通补贴等，鼓励和支持他们积极参加培训。

（4）跟踪各项服务措施的落实。及时了解推荐人员的上岗情况，以及办理招聘备案手续情况、缴纳社会保险和发放工资情况等。将定期援助与不定期援助相结合，在健全完善就业援助服务的同时，积极开展形式多样的其他援助活动。

中国政府依托基层公共就业服务机构，将日常援助与集中援助相结合，通过多种渠道帮扶就业困难人员就业。2018 年，全国共帮助 181 万名就业困难人员实现就业，其中 5 万户零就业家庭中有 5.5 万人实现了就业，实现了零就业家庭动态清零。

（二）促进农村贫困者就业的政策措施与取得的成效

一人就业、全家脱贫，实现就业是最有效、最直接的脱贫方式。中国政府高度重视就业扶贫工作，在 2017 年提出对有劳动能力的，要鼓励劳动、鼓励就业，通过生产奖补、以工代赈，引导广大群众通过自己的辛勤劳动实现脱贫。为贯彻落实中央脱贫攻坚总体部署，人力资源社会保障部制定了《打赢人力资源社会保障扶贫攻坚战三年行动方案》（人社部发〔2018〕54 号），作出加大力度、精准施策的具体安排，明确相关要求和工作措施。

1. 做好就业扶贫的七项基本要求

（1）多渠道开发就地就近就业岗位。加强就业扶贫车间、社区工厂、卫星工厂等就业扶贫载体建设，因地制宜探索运行机制，加大政策扶持力度，促进可持续发展，引导就业扶贫载体吸纳更多贫困人口就业。培育贫困村创业致富带头人，支持农村电商发展，支持贫困县建设创业园区。挖掘农业就业潜力，鼓励各种农业经营主体更多吸纳贫困劳动力就业。结合当地传统文化、自然生态、产业基础等情况，鼓励居家灵活就业。统筹开发公益性岗位，鼓励引导贫

困县乡积极开发养路、护林、护草、生态管护等用于扶贫的就业岗位。

（2）深入开展劳务协作。统筹东部发达地区和西部欠发达地区的劳务协作，要求发达地区根据劳务协作进展情况及时调整补充协议内容，完善协作措施，提高协作有效性。广泛搜集适合贫困劳动力的岗位信息，为贫困劳动力和用人单位搭建对接平台，引导更多贫困劳动力参与劳务协作实现转移就业。

（3）大力加强就业服务。注重与扶志扶智相结合，提供全方位、精准化、精细化就业服务；积极开展职业指导，引导贫困劳动力树立正确的就业观念，提升就业意愿，激发劳动致富内生动力，调动贫困劳动力就业积极性，提高贫困劳动力劳动参与率。同时，结合地方特色产业和人力资源优势，打造和推广一批劳务品牌，以劳务品牌带动转移就业。

（4）开展技能扶贫行动。确保有培训意愿的贫困劳动力都能得到职业技能培训机会；广泛发动各级各类职业院校、职业培训机构和企业面向贫困劳动力开展职业技能培训，落实培训补贴政策，推行项目制培训，向政府认定的培训机构整建制购买就业技能培训项目，从而实现“教育培训一人，就业创业一人，脱贫致富一户”的目标。

（5）切实做好深度贫困地区就业扶贫工作。把深度贫困地区就业扶贫作为重中之重，制订专门的就业扶贫工作方案，明确目标任务，确定每年促进贫困劳动力就业人数和渠道，建立工作责任制。积极协调发改、财政等部门在资金分配、项目安排上向深度贫困地区倾斜，帮助解决实际问题。

（6）加强就业扶贫作风建设。进一步落实政策，完善操作办法，降低政策门槛，增强可操作性，确保符合条件的贫困劳动力、用人单位都能享受到政策扶持。深入实地走访调查，指导解决工作中存在的突出问题。

（7）营造良好社会氛围。加强就业扶贫工作宣传，大力宣传就业扶贫的政策措施、工作中好的经验做法，以及通过就业创业脱贫致富的先进人物和典型事例，营造支持贫困劳动力就业创业、劳动致富光荣的良好社会氛围。

2. 推进就业扶贫的五项措施

（1）强化就业服务。各地制订切实可行的就业扶贫计划，准确掌握贫困劳动力基本信息，加强就业服务，开展“一对一”精准帮扶，充分调动贫困劳动力就业积极性。各地公共就业服务机构要深入摸查贫困劳动力的情况，针对其贫困特点，积极开展职业指导，加强职业介绍，推动就业意愿、就业技能与就业岗位精准对接，提高就业脱贫覆盖面。发挥人力资源服务机构作用，加强人力资源市场供求信息监测，开展专场招聘、就业创业指导、技能培训等活动。

（2）扶持发展扶贫车间等载体吸纳就业。在贫困乡镇、村建设一批扶贫车间、社区工厂、卫星工厂等就业扶贫载体。配合扶贫部门将扶贫车间等载体建设纳入扶贫项目建设规划，不断规范建设标准。鼓励企业、农民专业合作社、扶贫车间等各类用人单位吸纳贫困劳动力就业，对开展以工代训的，给予职业培训补贴；对企业按规定给予一定数额的社会保险费补贴；对吸纳就业成效好的就业扶贫基地，给予一次性资金奖补。

（3）鼓励返乡下乡创业带动就业。积极推进贫困县返乡创业园建设，加大创业扶持政策、创业服务支持力度，引导各类人员到贫困县创业，带动贫困劳动力就业。通过承接产业转移、发展农村电商、创意农业、乡村旅游等措施，在贫困地区培育一批创业项目。其中办理工商登记注册的，按规定落实小微企业扶持政策；对吸纳贫困劳动力多的创业企业，优先落实扶持政策；对贫困劳动力、农民工等返乡下乡创业人员首次创办小微企业或从事个体经营并且正常运营6个月以上的，给予一次性创业补贴；对入驻实体数量多、孵化效果好的贫困县创业孵化载体，提高创业孵化基地奖补标准。

（4）深化扶贫劳务协作。加强输出地与输入地的劳务协作，完善落实劳务协议，努力扩大劳务输出规模，提高劳务组织化程度。鼓励支持输出地政府在贫困劳动力务工较集中的城市或地区建立劳务站，为外出务工人员提供持续帮

扶。输入地政府要搞好与输出地政府的劳务对接，着力开发和提供就业岗位，为贫困劳动力转移就业提供职业培训、就业服务、劳动维权“三位一体”的服务，增强贫困劳动力的就业稳定性。对接受外地贫困劳动力就业的企业，参照当地就业困难人员落实社会保险补贴、创业担保贷款及贴息等政策。

（5）开发公益性岗位托底安置。统筹考虑乡村建设实际需要，开发农村保洁、治安、护路、管水、扶残助残、养老护理等公益性岗位，帮扶贫困劳动力就业。贫困地区新增和腾退的公益性岗位应优先安置贫困劳动力，可由就业补助资金给予一定期限的岗位补贴。积极协调林业草原、交通、扶贫等部门，开发各类公益性岗位安置贫困劳动力。鼓励各地通过以工代赈、以奖代补、劳务补助等方式，动员更多贫困劳动力参与小型基础设施、农村人居环境整治等项目建设。

3. 就业扶贫的工作成效

经过艰苦努力，就业扶贫工作取得了积极的成效。一是建立了有效的就业扶贫工作机制，并依此建立了精准帮扶和资金保障等机制。二是形成了就业扶贫政策体系。人力资源社会保障部、财政部、国务院扶贫办等部门出台了一系列促进贫困劳动力就业创业的支持政策，各地也因地制宜制定了许多政策，形成了覆盖广大贫困劳动力、用人单位、就业服务机构的政策体系。三是构建了就业扶贫工作格局。各地方从实际出发，不断创新工作思路和方法，确定了就业扶贫工作以就近就地就业与外出务工并重为工作总思路，一些地方还建立了重大项目与贫困地区结对帮扶的劳务协作渠道。通过这些努力，截至 2019 年年底，全国已累计帮扶 1 213 万名贫困劳动力实现就业，全国农村贫困人口从 2012 年的 9 899 万人减少到 551 万人，贫困发生率从 2012 年的 10.2% 下降至 0.6%。①

① 数据来源于国家统计局、人力资源社会保障部。

实施精准就业扶贫措施，把岗位送到村民家门口。（新华社记者万象摄）

（三）促进残疾人就业的政策措施与取得的成效

中国有 8 500 万名残疾人。保障残疾人的劳动就业权益，帮助他们实现就业和创业，是改善残疾人自身状况和提高其社会地位的基础，是其实现“平等、参与、共享”的基础条件和主要路径。

1. 法律法规保障

中国政府一直高度重视残疾人就业问题，制定了一系列法律、法规，保障残疾人就业的合法权益。《宪法》明确规定，国家和社会帮助安排盲、聋、哑和其他有残疾的公民的劳动、生活和教育。《中华人民共和国残疾人保障法》规定，国家保障残疾人劳动的权利。残疾人劳动就业，实行集中与分散相结合的方针，采取优惠政策和扶持保护措施，通过多渠道、多层次、多种形式，使残疾人劳动就业逐步普及、稳定、合理。同时，国家对安置残疾人达到一定比例

的福利企业，在资金支持、税收减免等方面制定了相应的扶持政策。《就业促进法》规定，各级人民政府应当对残疾人就业统筹规划，为残疾人创造就业条件。用人单位招用人员，不得歧视残疾人。《残疾人就业条例》对用人单位按照一定比例安排残疾人就业的责任、各级人民政府保障残疾人就业的政策措施、政府为残疾人提供免费就业服务等作出了更加具体的规定。

2. 政策措施促进

（1）拓展就业形态，开发适合残疾人就业的岗位。一方面，举办福利企业及机构安置残疾人就业，规定用人单位按比例安排残疾人就业，支持残疾人自主创业和自谋职业；另一方面，积极发展社区服务事业，优先考虑安排残疾人就业。大力开发公益性岗位，保障残疾人、下岗失业人员等就业困难人员就业。在农村，组织并扶持残疾人从事种植、养殖、手工业和其他生产劳动，为残疾人提供生产服务、技术指导、农用物资供应、农副产品收购、信贷等支持。同时，国家制定并实施了一系列扶贫和惠农政策，这些政策对残疾人就业也起到了积极的推动作用。

（2）完善公共就业服务体系，为残疾人提供就业服务。在就业服务方面，各级人民政府举办的公共就业服务机构免费向残疾人开放，提供职业指导、职业介绍等就业服务；将残疾人纳入就业困难人员中，通过街道、社区、乡镇公共就业服务机构建立台账，实施一对一的就业援助，并落实社会保险补贴、岗位补贴等政策，帮助他们实现就业。各地残疾人联合会建立残疾人就业服务机构，负责收集残疾求职者的信息、向用人单位推荐残疾人、组织残疾人开展培训，并接受人力资源社会保障部门的委托，为残疾人进行失业登记。

（3）实施劳动保护，提高残疾人就业质量。用人单位招用残疾人职工，应当依法签订劳动合同或服务协议。用人单位应当为残疾人职工提供适合其自身状况的劳动条件和劳动保护，不得在晋职、晋级、评定职称、报酬、社会保险、

社会福利等方面歧视残疾人职工。残疾人职工与用人单位发生争议的，当地法律援助机构依法为其提供法律援助，并由各级残疾人联合会给予支持和帮助。

（4）加强执法监察力度，保障残疾人就业的合法权益。各级劳动保障监察机构及时发现和纠正用人单位违反人力资源和社会保障法律法规侵害残疾人合法权益的行为，重点查处不与残疾人签订劳动合同、克扣或无故拖欠工资及不给残疾人缴纳社会保险费等行为。

（5）完善社会保障制度，提高残疾人社会保障水平。近年来，中国政府不断完善残疾人社会保险政策，提高社会保险覆盖面，推动城镇残疾人职工按照规定参加基本养老、医疗、失业、工伤和生育保险。积极落实城镇贫困残疾人个体户参加基本养老保险补贴政策，鼓励并组织个体就业残疾人参加社会保险。自 2009 年起，在全国推行新型农村社会养老保险的过程中，积极帮助农村残疾人参加新型农村社会养老保险。

3. 取得的成效

2011 年以来，中国扶持近 1 300 万名残疾人发展生产，其中 676 万名贫困残疾人摆脱贫困。截至 2018 年，全国持证残疾人就业人数达 948.4 万人。2018 年当年，城乡新增残疾人实名制培训 49.4 万人；城乡持证残疾人新增就业 36.7 万人，其中，城镇新增就业 11.8 万人，农村新增就业 24.9 万人。同时，各地还建立残疾人就业服务机构 2 811 家，共有工作人员 3.4 万人；建立残疾人扶贫基地 5 490 个，安置 88.1 万名残疾人就业，扶持带动 176.9 万户残疾人家庭增加收入。

第九章
失业保险与失业预防

中国现行的失业保险制度，是在1986年推行劳动制度改革的背景下建立的，最初的目的是解决企业职工失业后的基本生活问题，并为他们实现再就业提供帮助。以后，失业保险制度不断完善，进一步发挥保生活、防失业、促就业“三位一体”的功能，相关部门突出抓好参保扩面、提高待遇、降低费率、援企稳岗、技能提升等惠企利民政策的制定实施，工作取得显著成果。

一、失业统计和失业动态监测

（一）失业统计

失业统计是就业统计的一部分，一般分为统计设计、调查登记、资料搜集整理、统计分析四个阶段。失业统计指标主要包括失业人员数量和失业率。

（1）失业人员。失业人员数据按登记和调查两种途径获得。登记失业人员是指在劳动年龄内，有劳动能力，无业而要求就业，并到当地公共就业服务机构进行求职登记的人员。调查失业人员是指16周岁以上（无年龄上限），有劳动能力，在调查周期内未从事有收入的劳动，当前有就业可能并以某种方式正

在寻找工作的人员。

（2）城镇登记失业率。这是指报告期末城镇登记失业人员数量占同期城镇从业人员总数与实有城镇登记失业人员数量之和的比重。其中，城镇登记失业人员主要是指已在公共就业服务机构进行登记的失业人员。

劳动者可在常住地的公共就业服务机构进行失业登记。（新华社记者何江华摄）

中国自20世纪80年代初建立失业登记制度以来，一直将城镇登记失业率作为宏观调控的重要指标，为国家制定政策、进行决策提供了重要依据。由于不是所有失业人员都去公共就业服务机构进行登记，并且城镇登记失业人员没有包括进城务工的农村劳动者，因此城镇登记失业率在反映国家或地区总体失业状况时不够灵敏。

（3）城镇调查失业率。这是反映城镇常住经济活动人口中（包括在城镇常住半年以上的农村劳动者）符合失业条件的人数（即城镇调查失业人员数量）占同期城镇从业人员总数与城镇调查失业人员数量之和的比重。失业率调查由

国家统计局组织实施。

2016 年，国家统计局正式发布月度调查失业率数据。在经过科学抽样并保证一定规模样本量的情况下，调查失业率的统计数据可以比较灵敏地反映国家和地区的就业和失业状况，同时还能将在城镇常住半年以上的农村劳动者的就业和失业状况一并反映出来。

（二）失业动态监测

1. 概念与沿革

2008 年 6 月，人力资源社会保障部建立了失业动态监测制度。通过对部分城市企业因破产关闭或停业整顿、外迁、生产经营发生严重困难、转产、发生重大技术革新或者经营方式调整等造成就业人员变化的状况进行监测，及时掌握经济波动期内被监测企业岗位增减情况，为采取预防和调控失业措施提供依据，并以此作为建立失业预警制度的基础。

监测结果定期形成三级失业动态监测报告。一是形成全国失业动态监测报告。人力资源社会保障部在对全国失业动态监测数据进行汇总分析的基础上，形成全国失业动态监测报告。二是形成省级失业动态监测报告。省级人力资源社会保障部门对本地区失业动态监测数据进行汇总分析，并结合省（自治区、直辖市）城镇登记失业率、企业劳动用工备案、人力资源市场供求比例等情况，形成省级失业动态监测报告，向人力资源社会保障部报送，同时向省级人民政府报告。三是形成城市失业动态监测报告。由城市的人力资源社会保障部门对采集的数据进行对比分析，重点分析从业人员增减原因，在此基础上形成失业动态监测报告，向省级人力资源社会保障部门报送，同时向当地人民政府报告。

2. 建立失业动态监测报告制度的目的与意义

（1）失业动态监测报告制度是全面把握就业和失业状况的有效途径。失业动态监测报告制度会对企业就业岗位变化信息进行直接调查收集，分析岗位流

失原因，从而实现了对一些重点行业、重点企业岗位流失情况的监测。失业动态监测报告制度作为全面把握失业状况的一项有效手段，有助于更加准确、及时地反映就业和失业状况。

（2）失业动态监测报告制度为制定政策提供了重要的信息支持。实行失业动态监测报告制度，可以使相关部门在全面把握部分重点企业就业和失业状况的基础上，对当地整体的就业形势也作出研判。这不仅为制定稳定就业政策提供了支持，而且提高了就业政策的针对性和有效性。同时，实施就业政策措施的效果也能通过相关监测数据得到印证。

（3）失业动态监测报告制度为建立失业预警制度奠定了基础。实施失业动态监测报告制度，进一步健全了就业和失业信息调查系统。通过采集失业预警所需数据并进行分析，相关部门能够在复杂多变的经济形势下，及时掌握经济波动期内重点行业、重点企业的岗位流失情况，从而增强失业调控政策的预见性、针对性和有效性，有利于其及时、准确地判断和把握失业状况，为其及时采取更加有效的措施，防范和化解较大规模失业风险提供依据。

3. 失业动态监测报告制度取得的成效

2009 年 11 月，人力资源社会保障部在六省部分城市开展的失业动态监测报告制度试点工作取得效果的基础上，决定在全国建立失业动态监测制度。截至 2019 年年底，纳入监测的企业达到 5.2 万户。

二、失业保险制度

（一）失业保险制度的建立和发展

1. 中华人民共和国成立初期的失业救济

1949 年中华人民共和国成立前夕，全国的失业状况十分严重，城镇失业人

员就有 472 万人，失业率高达 23.6%。中华人民共和国成立后，中国政府采取了一系列政策措施解决城市失业问题，其中一项重要举措就是建立失业救济制度来保障失业人员的基本生活。这是中华人民共和国失业保险制度最早的雏形。

2. 建立符合中国国情的失业保险制度的基本原则

（1）广覆盖。保障每一位劳动者的基本权益是社会保障制度的宗旨。失业保险制度应覆盖到城镇各类单位及其职工。

（2）保障待遇适度。保障失业人员基本生活的待遇标准不能过低或过高，应当与经济社会发展水平相适应。根据不同经济社会发展阶段人民群众生活水平的改善程度，适时调整失业保险待遇水平，以切实保障失业人员的基本生活。

（3）保障基本生活、预防失业和促进就业并重。失业保险不同于社会救济，在保障失业人员基本生活的同时，还要通过对失业人员开展就业服务，提供资金补贴，从而帮助失业人员实现重新就业。同时，通过向不裁员或少裁员的参保企业发放稳岗返还，向取得相应职业资格证书或职业技能等级证书的参保职工发放技能提升补贴等措施，来稳定职工队伍，防止出现大规模的集中失业。

（4）用人单位、劳动者和国家共同承担费用。失业保险费应由用人单位和劳动者个人共同缴纳，由国家财政给予补贴。这种由三方负担费用的机制，有利于增强劳动者参加社会保险的意识，也可以分散资金筹集压力，增加资金来源渠道，以保证失业保险基金正常使用。

（5）权利与义务对等。只有用人单位及其职工依法参加失业保险，并履行缴费义务，该职工在失业后才能享受失业保险待遇。

3. 中国现行失业保险制度的建立、发展及意义

中国现行的失业保险制度自 1986 年建立至今，大体可划分为三个阶段。

第一阶段（1986—1993 年）。1986 年 7 月，国务院颁布《国营企业职工待

业保险暂行规定》（国发〔1986〕77 号），标志着中国现行的失业保险制度开始正式建立，确立了失业保险制度的基本框架，失业保险制度初步发挥作用。

第二阶段（1993—1999 年）。1993 年 4 月，国务院颁布《国有企业职工待业保险规定》（中华人民共和国国务院令第 110 号），将“暂行”法规变为正式法规，对 1986 年的《国营企业职工待业保险暂行规定》进行了调整完善。

第三阶段（1999 年至今）。1999 年 1 月，国务院颁布《失业保险条例》（中华人民共和国国务院令第 258 号）和《社会保险费征缴暂行条例》（中华人民共和国国务院令第 259 号），标志着中国失业保险制度的改革进入了一个新的阶段，失业保险制度得到进一步完善。自 2011 年 7 月 1 日起施行的《社会保险法》进一步明确了失业保险覆盖范围、失业保险金申领条件和期限、待遇标准、关系转移等，从法律层面确立了失业保险制度。

失业保险制度的建立和逐步完善，是中国就业制度的一项重大变革。失业保险制度作为市场导向就业机制的一个重要环节，在就业制度的改革中发挥了积极作用。同时，这一制度的建立和实施，填补了中国社会保障体系的一项空白，成为中国社会保障体系的一个重要组成部分，为劳动制度从计划经济体制向市场经济体制过渡创造了有利条件，为建立独立于企业之外的社会保障体系开了一个好头，为促进发展和稳定大局做出了贡献。

（二）失业保险基金的筹集、使用和管理

1. 失业保险基金的筹集

失业保险基金是通过征缴失业保险费的方式筹集，费用由用人单位、劳动者和国家共同承担。

（1）基金收入的构成。失业保险基金筹集遵循以支定收、适度性、公平性等原则。根据《失业保险条例》规定，失业保险基金由失业保险费、失业保险基金的利息、财政补贴、依法应纳入失业保险基金的其他资金构成。

（2）失业保险费的征缴。失业保险费的缴费主体是城镇企业事业单位及其职工，由二者按照规定缴纳失业保险费，个人缴费由单位代为扣缴。城镇企业事业单位和其他参保单位以本单位工资总额作为缴费基数，城镇企事业单位和其他参保单位的职工以本人工资作为缴费基数；参保单位和个人分别按其缴费基数的2%和1%缴纳失业保险费。参保单位必须按月向失业保险经办机构申报应缴纳的失业保险费数额，经核定后，在规定的期限内缴纳失业保险费。参保个人应当缴纳的失业保险费，由所在单位代扣代缴。失业保险费必须以货币形式缴纳，不得以实物抵顶。社会保险费（包括失业保险费）的征收机构由省、自治区、直辖市人民政府规定。2015年以来，为减轻企业负担，促进就业稳定，相关部门出台了一系列失业保险费率调整政策（见表9-1）。

表9-1　　2015年以来失业保险费率调整政策情况

发布时间	文件名称	内容
2015年2月	《人力资源社会保障部　财政部关于调整失业保险费率有关问题的通知》（人社部发〔2015〕24号）	明确失业保险费率整体下调1个百分点。将失业保险费率暂由现行条例规定的3%降至2%，单位和个人缴费的具体比例由各省、自治区、直辖市人民政府确定
2016年4月	《人力资源社会保障部　财政部关于阶段性降低社会保险费率的通知》（人社部发〔2016〕36号）	失业保险总费率阶段性降至1%~1.5%（其中个人缴费率不超过0.5%）
2017年2月	《人力资源社会保障部　财政部关于阶段性降低失业保险费率有关问题的通知》（人社部发〔2017〕14号）	失业保险总费率为1.5%的省（区、市），可以将总费率降至1%
2018年4月	《人力资源社会保障部　财政部关于继续阶段性降低社会保险费率的通知》（人社部发〔2018〕25号）	实施失业保险总费率为1%的省（区、市），延长阶段性降低费率的期限至2019年4月30日
2019年4月	《国务院办公厅关于印发降低社会保险费率综合方案的通知》（国办发〔2019〕13号）	实施失业保险总费率1%的省，延长阶段性降低失业保险费率的期限至2020年4月30日
2019年12月	《国务院关于进一步做好稳就业工作的意见》（国发〔2019〕28号）	阶段性降低失业保险费率的政策，实施期限延长至2021年4月30日

（3）财政对失业保险基金的补贴。为应对可能发生的支付困难，《失业保险条例》规定，可以在省一级建立失业保险调剂金。如有城市的失业保险基金不敷使用时，由省级失业保险调剂金给予补充；仍然不能满足支付需要时，由当地财政给予补贴，必要时可以按照规定的条件和程序调整失业保险费的费率。其中，财政对失业保险基金的补贴是政府在特定情况下对失业保险直接给予的支持，包括经常性补贴和临时性补贴，从而在制度安排上保证了失业保险制度正常、稳定地运行。

2. 失业保险基金的使用

失业保险基金支出包括基本生活保障支出、促进再就业支出、基金往来支出以及其他支出等不同项目。失业保险基金按规定的项目拨付使用，不得随意增减开支项目和变更开支标准，也不得擅自挪作他用。

（1）基本生活保障支出。基本生活保障支出是指直接用于保障失业人员和其他相关人员的基本生活，包括失业保险金支出、医疗补助金支出（2011 年《社会保险法》施行后调整为代缴基本医疗保险费）、丧葬抚恤补助支出、农民合同制工人的一次性生活补助支出和国有企业下岗职工的基本生活保障支出（1998 年实施，2006 年取消）。

（2）促进再就业支出。这项支出是为了帮助失业人员尽快实现再就业，按规定从失业保险基金中列支的费用，包括对失业人员开展职业技能培训的职业培训补贴和向他们提供职业介绍服务的职业介绍补贴。这两项补贴可以支付给有关机构，也可以直接支付给参加培训或接受职业介绍服务的失业人员个人。

随着失业保险制度促进再就业、预防失业功能的进一步完善，用于促进再就业的支出项目进一步增加，范围进一步扩展。失业保险基金在用于支付失业人员的职业培训补贴和职业介绍补贴的同时，为稳定就业，支付项目还增加了

对参保企业职工的社会保险补贴支出、岗位补贴支出和对创业者的小额担保贷款贴息支出。

（3）其他支出。失业保险基金的其他支出项目是指除上述支出项目外，国务院规定或者批准的与失业保险有关的其他支出项目。

3. 失业保险基金的管理

（1）失业保险基金预、决算管理。失业保险基金预算是根据就业、失业状况和基金需求编制，并按规定报经政府批准的年度失业保险基金收支计划，主要包括预算编制、审批、执行和调整。失业保险基金决算是按规定程序编制并报经政府批准，总结、反映当年度基金实际运行情况的财务报告，主要包括资产负债表、基金收支表及有关附表和财务情况说明书等内容。失业保险基金预、决算管理是基金管理的重要手段，有利于加强对基金收支的预测和监管，强化预算约束，实现基金收支平衡，保证基金安全。

（2）失业保险基金财务管理。这是对基金总体运行全过程进行的监督。其任务是依法筹集和使用失业保险基金。主要工作是建立健全基金财务制度，做好基金的计划、控制、核算、分析和考核工作，包括基金收支管理、基金投资管理、基金资产和负债管理、财务报表管理。

（3）失业保险基金会计核算。这是对基金收入、支出和管理进行序时反映和监督。为了加强对失业保险业务活动的管理，准确、全面地反映和监督失业保险基金的筹集、支出、结余和投资等活动，保证基金安全，失业保险基金实行单独建账、独立核算。同时，按相关制度要求对失业保险基金会计核算进行规范。失业保险基金会计核算具有以下特点：一是以收付实现制作为核算基础；二是会计要素包括资产、负债、基金结余和收入、支出等内容。为了有效地开展失业保险基金会计核算，失业保险经办机构在加强对会计工作的组织和管理同时，要加强会计监督和约束，并建立内部稽核制度和会计档案。

（三）失业保险待遇

1. 失业保险待遇构成

失业保险待遇是指参加失业保险的劳动者因失业而暂时中断生活来源时，由失业保险基金提供的、以现金为基本形式的各种帮助。失业保险待遇对于保障失业人员的基本生活并促进其尽快实现再就业具有重要作用。

失业保险待遇包括：①用于保障基本生活的失业保险金；②领取失业保险金期间的医疗补助金（2011 年《社会保险法》施行后调整为代缴基本医疗保险费）；③领取失业保险金期间死亡的失业人员的丧葬补助金和其供养的配偶、直系亲属的抚恤金；④领取失业保险金期间接受职业培训、职业介绍的补贴。

2. 失业保险金的申领条件

具备下列条件的失业人员，可以申请领取失业保险金：①按照规定参加失业保险，所在单位和本人已按照规定履行缴费义务满 1 年的；②非因本人意愿中断就业的；③已办理失业登记，并有求职要求的。失业人员在领取失业保险金期间，按照规定同时享受其他失业保险待遇。

3. 失业保险待遇给付标准

失业保险金的标准，不得低于城市居民最低生活保障标准，具体标准由省、自治区、直辖市人民政府确定。

（1）参加职工基本医疗保险及其相关待遇。为提高失业人员医疗保险待遇，《社会保险法》规定，失业人员参加职工基本医疗保险。2011 年，人力资源社会保障部针对失业人员参加职工基本医疗保险制定了具体政策。政策规定，失业人员参加职工基本医疗保险，所需费用从失业保险基金中支付，个人不缴纳基本医疗保险费。领取失业保险金人员自参加职工基本医疗保险当月起，按规定享受相应的住院和门诊医疗保险待遇，享受待遇期限与领取失业保险金期限相一致。领取失业保险金人员参加职工基本医疗保险的缴费年限与其失业前参

加职工基本医疗保险的缴费年限累计计算。

（2）丧葬补助金和抚恤金及其给付标准。失业人员在领取失业保险金期间死亡的，参照当地对在职职工死亡的规定，向其遗属发给一次性丧葬补助金和抚恤金。

（3）职业培训补贴和职业介绍补贴及其给付标准。失业人员在领取失业保险金期间接受职业培训、职业介绍的，由失业保险基金支付职业培训和职业介绍的补贴。补贴的办法和标准由省、自治区、直辖市人民政府规定。

（4）农民合同制工人一次性生活补助标准。单位招用的农民合同制工人连续工作满 1 年，解除或终止劳动合同后，由社会保险经办机构根据其工作时间的长短，向其支付一次性生活补助。补助的办法和标准由省、自治区、直辖市人民政府规定。

4. 失业保险待遇给付期限

《社会保险法》和《失业保险条例》规定，失业人员领取失业保险金的期限，根据失业人员失业前所在单位和其本人累计缴费时间长短的不同，划分为三个档次：①累计缴费时间满 1 年不足 5 年的，最长能够领取 12 个月的失业保险金；②累计缴费时间满 5 年不足 10 年的，最长能够领取 18 个月的失业保险金；③累计缴费时间 10 年以上的，最长能够领取 24 个月的失业保险金。

5. 失业保险待遇的终止

失业人员在领取失业保险金期间有下列情形之一的，停止领取失业保险金，并同时停止享受其他失业保险待遇：①重新就业的；②应征服兵役的；③移居境外的；④享受基本养老保险待遇的；⑤无正当理由，拒不接受当地人民政府指定部门或者机构介绍的适当工作或者提供的培训的。

2018 年年底，全国参加失业保险人数为 19 643.5 万人，年末领取失业保险金人数为 223.1 万人，失业保险金月人均水平 1 266 元。全年失业保险基金收入

1 171.1 亿元，基金支出 915.3 亿元（见表 9-2）。

表 9-2　2014—2018 年失业保险发展状况

年份	年末参保人数 / 万人	年末领取失业保险金人数 / 万人	当年基金收入 / 亿元	当年基金支出 / 亿元	基金累计结余 / 亿元
2014	17 042.6	207.2	1 379.8	614.7	4 451.5
2015	17 326.0	226.8	1 367.8	736.4	5 083.0
2016	18 088.8	230.4	1 228.9	976.1	5 333.3
2017	18 784.2	220.2	1 112.6	893.8	5 552.4
2018	19 643.5	223.1	1 171.1	915.3	5 817.0

资料来源：国家统计局。

三、失业预防

失业预防的主要措施是进行失业调控，实施援企稳岗。

（一）失业调控的提出和工作重点

1. 失业调控的提出

失业调控是指通过法律手段、经济手段和必要的行政手段等，控制失业人员数量增长，并通过落实国家制定的促进失业人员再就业的各项政策措施，开展就业服务工作，促进失业人员尽快再就业。

失业调控的核心目标是控制失业率上升。其具体目标包括控制失业人员数量不能超过经济活动人口的一定比例，失业群体出现的时间和地区不能过于集中，失业人员个人失业时间不能过长。同时，对于那些暂时不能就业的失业人员，要在保障其基本生活的基础上，把他们组织到各项就业准备活动中来。努力防范失业增加带来的风险，为经济社会持续健康发展创造有利的社会环境。

2. 失业调控的主要政策措施

（1）从源头上调控就业转失业人员规模。通过发挥政府职能作用，在经济结构调整中将就业转失业人员规模控制在社会可承受的程度。特别是要规范企业裁员行为，做好关闭破产企业职工安置工作。

（2）搞好帮扶，减少失业增加带来的负面影响。通过加强和改善就业服务，对失业人员个人、家庭搞好帮扶，特别是对就业特困人员进行重点帮助，通过实施社会保险补贴和工资补贴等扶持政策，帮助失业时间较长的长期失业人员从事公益性岗位工作实现再就业；通过组织实施劳动者见习计划，鼓励和引导失业人员通过非全日制、临时性、季节性、弹性工作等多种灵活形式实现就业；完善社会保障体系，减少失业增加带来的负面影响。

（3）充分发挥失业保险的作用，促进失业人员再就业。对符合条件的失业人员按时足额发放失业保险金，加大失业保险基金在促进失业人员实现再就业方面的投入。

（二）援企稳岗的实行及其成效

1. 援企稳岗的提出和发展

援企稳岗是指在特定时期，通过扩大失业保险基金使用范围，使用失业保险基金向困难企业支付社会保险补贴和岗位补贴，鼓励企业不裁员、少裁员，保企业稳就业。稳定就业岗位，从源头上控制失业，是保持就业局势稳定的重要手段，也是维护职工合法权益的重要举措。

（1）援企稳岗预防失业是应对国际金融危机时期倒逼出的新举措。2008年年底，国际金融危机对中国企业的影响愈加明显，保企业稳就业的工作日益紧迫。为了稳定就业，通过“五缓四减三补贴”政策来援企稳岗，稳定企业职工队伍；此外，通过社会保险补贴来稳定灵活就业人员的就业。在实施上述政策的同时，中国政府还鼓励企业承担社会责任，稳定劳动关系，在特殊时期努力

不减员、不裁员。实行社会保险费延期征缴，以及使用失业保险基金帮助企业减负稳岗的措施，不仅稳定了企业职工的就业，还带动了其他经济政策对企业的保护和支持，这极大地增强了企业应对金融危机的信心，不仅使一批企业度过了最困难的阶段，并且保住了一批就业岗位和职工的“饭碗”，达到了失业预防的效果。同时，这也为相关部门解决突发的大规模失业问题提供了很好的经验，为建立长效失业应急预案奠定了很好的基础。可以说运用失业保险实施援企稳岗，是中国更加积极的就业政策的一项重大创新。

（2）援企稳岗预防失业在化解产能过剩过程中再次发挥了积极作用。为化解钢铁、煤炭等行业产能过剩重点地区存在的规模性失业和集体劳动争议的潜在风险，妥善安置职工，促进再就业，2014 年 11 月，国家采取措施，支持兼并重组企业、化解过剩产能企业、淘汰落后产能企业，做好稳定职工队伍工作，由失业保险基金给予稳岗补贴，补贴标准为不超过本企业及其职工上年度实际缴纳失业保险费总额的 50%。2015 年 4 月，国务院印发《关于进一步做好新形势下就业创业工作的意见》，要求将失业保险基金支持企业稳岗政策实施范围由上述三类企业扩大到所有符合条件的企业。

发挥失业保险稳定和促进就业的作用，对经营困难的企业进行重点扶持。（新华社记者杨世尧摄）

（3）援企稳岗预防失业在稳就业中持续发力。2017 年 4 月，根据国务院对不裁员或少裁员的钢铁、煤炭、煤电行业企业降低稳岗补贴门槛，提高稳岗补贴标

准的政策要求，人力资源社会保障部决定从 2018 年至 2020 年在全国实施失业保险援企稳岗“护航行动”。推动各地全面、规范实施失业保险支持企业稳定岗位政策，实现失业保险基金统筹地区政策全覆盖和符合申领条件企业的主体全覆盖，为企业脱困发展、减少失业、稳定就业护航。

2018 年 11 月出台的《国务院关于做好当前和今后一个时期促进就业工作的若干意见》(国发〔2018〕39 号)明确规定，对不裁员或少裁员的参保企业，可返还其上年度实际缴纳失业保险费的 50%。2019 年 1 月 1 日至 12 月 31 日，对面临暂时性生产经营困难且恢复有望、坚持不裁员或少裁员的参保企业，返还 6 个月失业保险金或 3 个月社会保险费。2019 年 3 月，人力资源社会保障部会同财政部、发展改革委、工业和信息化部印发《关于失业保险支持企业稳定就业岗位的通知》(人社部发〔2019〕23 号)，对实施企业稳岗返还等稳就业政策提出细化要求。2019 年 12 月出台的《国务院关于进一步做好稳就业工作的意见》规定，将困难企业稳岗返还政策的实施期限延长至 2020 年 12 月 31 日。从而进一步支持企业稳定岗位，维护就业局势总体稳定。

2. 实施援企稳岗政策的成效

实践证明，援企稳岗政策的实施为帮助困难企业渡过难关、稳定就业、保持就业局势基本稳定发挥了不可或缺的作用。从 2015 年至 2019 年，使用失业保险基金向近 283 万户企业发放稳岗返还 1 311 亿元，惠及职工 2.5 亿人次，援企稳岗政策取得了积极的成效。

3. 失业保险新举措

为更加充分地发挥失业保险制度的作用，近些年来，中国政府还在实施上述政策措施的基础上制定了一些新的政策举措。

(1) 失业保险基金支持参保职工技能提升。技能提升补贴政策是失业保险制度“防失业、促就业”功能作用的具体体现，目的就是激励参保职工提升职

业技能和就业竞争力，降低失业风险，增强就业稳定性，从源头上减少失业。2017 年，中国政府决定从失业保险基金中列支参保企业职工技能提升补贴，明确了申领条件、审核程序、补贴标准等。2018 年，又进一步在全国实施失业保险支持技能提升“展翅行动”，推动各地积极主动、全面规范地落实失业保险技能提升补贴政策，使符合条件的参保职工都能享受到技能提升补贴。为进一步发挥政策效应，2019 年经国务院同意，自 2019 年 1 月 1 日至 2020 年 12 月 31 日，放宽补贴申领条件，由企业在职职工参加失业保险 3 年及以上放宽至参保 1 年及以上。截至 2019 年年底，全年累计发放补贴 32.6 亿元，惠及参保职工近 200 万人次。

（2）减轻企业负担，下调失业保险费率。为落实中央减税降费决策部署，自 2015 年起，相关部门连续三次阶段性降低失业保险费率，三次延长降费率政策执行期限，总费率已由 3% 普降至 1%，政策执行期限至 2021 年 4 月 30 日。自降费率政策实施以来，累计为企业减负近 4 000 亿元，切实降低了企业成本，为实体经济发展和供给侧结构性改革做出了积极贡献。

（3）发放价格临时补贴，保障基本生活。2016 年，国家规定为领取失业保险金人员发放价格临时补贴，所需资金在失业保险基金中列支。建立保障标准与物价上涨挂钩联动机制，通过使用失业保险基金发放价格临时补贴，这对缓解物价上涨影响和保障失业人员基本生活发挥了积极的作用。

（4）支持脱贫攻坚，加大扶持深度贫困地区力度。为贯彻落实国家关于打赢脱贫攻坚战的决策部署，2018 年 6 月，人力资源社会保障部、财政部联合印发《关于使用失业保险基金支持脱贫攻坚的通知》（人社部发〔2018〕35 号），充分发挥失业保险功能作用，支持精准扶贫、精准脱贫。一是将深度贫困地区失业保险金标准上调至最低工资标准的 90%。二是对深度贫困地区的失业保险参保企业，可以将稳岗补贴标准提高到该企业及其职工上年度实际缴纳失业保险费总额的 60%。三是将技能提升补贴申领条件由累计参保缴费满 3 年放宽到

累计参保缴费满 1 年，激励深度贫困地区参保职工提升职业技能，增强脱贫内生动力，实现就业和收入稳定。此外，对吸纳建档立卡贫困人员就业并签订劳动合同的事业单位，允许其享受稳岗补贴政策和技能提升补贴政策，从而激发深度贫困地区所有用人主体吸纳贫困劳动力的积极性。

（5）加强高龄参保职工失业保障。针对高龄参保职工失业后再就业难度大的实际情况，2019 年 12 月，国务院印发《关于进一步做好稳就业工作的意见》，明确规定对领取失业保险金期满仍未就业且距离法定退休年龄不足 1 年的人员，可继续发放失业保险金直至法定退休年龄。对高龄参保失业人员实现失业保障与养老保障的无缝对接，创新了针对就业困难人群的保障机制，填补了一项社会保障政策覆盖空白。

第十章 就业发展规划目标：更加充分更高质量就业

一、中国就业发展规划目标[1]

就业是最大的民生，是民生之本、财富之源、稳定之基。中国政府始终高度重视就业问题，将就业工作摆在经济社会发展的突出位置，并为此制定了促进就业、减少失业的发展规划和工作目标。

（一）国民经济和社会发展规划对就业工作的部署

国民经济和社会发展规划是中国政府根据不同时期的情况按五年一个周期制定的全国经济、社会发展的总体纲要，是对全国社会、经济、民生和文化建设工作具有战略指导作用的重要文件，也是政府履行经济调节、市场监管、社会管理和公共服务职责的重要依据。

1. 将扩大就业摆在经济和社会发展的突出位置

中国有 14 亿人口，就业问题比世界上任何一个国家的情况都复杂，扩大就业的任务十分繁重。中国政府对此高度重视，坚持就业是民生之本的施政理念，在研究制定国民经济和社会发展规划时，把扩大就业作为重要内容予以考虑。

---

① 本部分所列规划主要是 21 世纪以来在市场经济体制下开始实施的有关就业的发展规划。

2001 年 3 月颁布的《中华人民共和国国民经济和社会发展第十个五年计划纲要》（以下简称“十五”计划）是中国进入 21 世纪在市场经济体制下实施的第一个五年计划。与以往计划更加偏重于经济增长速度的内容不同，“十五”计划的主要目标涵盖了经济增长、改革开放和社会进步等多个领域，是一个更加强调均衡发展的五年计划。“十五”计划首次明确将扩大就业作为经济和社会发展的重要目标，实行有利于扩大就业的经济政策和社会政策。同时在宏观调控主要预期中明确了经济与就业并重的目标，即经济增长速度预期为年均 7% 左右；五年城镇新增就业和转移农业劳动力各达到 4 000 万人，城镇登记失业率控制在 5% 左右等。“十五”计划还提出保持较快的经济增长速度，创造更多的就业岗位。2006 年 3 月颁布的《中华人民共和国国民经济和社会发展第十一个五年规划纲要》（以下简称“十一五”规划），更加注重经济社会协调发展，明确提出了“千方百计扩大就业”的总目标，并将经济社会发展的主要目标确定为国内生产总值年均增长 7.5%，城镇新增就业和转移农业劳动力各 4 500 万人，城镇登记失业率控制在 5% 等。“十一五”规划还提出把扩大就业摆在经济社会发展更突出的位置，实行积极的就业政策。2011 年 3 月颁布的《中华人民共和国国民经济和社会发展第十二个五年规划纲要》（以下简称“十二五”规划）将保障和改善民生作为加快转变经济发展方式的根本出发点和落脚点，同时明确提出把促进就业放在经济社会发展的优先位置。“十二五”规划将经济社会发展的主要目标确定为经济平稳较快发展，国内生产总值年均增长 7%，城镇新增就业 4 500 万人，城镇登记失业率控制在 5% 以内等；并对实施就业优先战略进行部署，要求提高就业质量，努力实现充分就业。2016 年 3 月颁布的《中华人民共和国国民经济和社会发展第十三个五年规划纲要》（以下简称“十三五”规划）提出要坚持以人民为中心的发展思想，把增进人民福祉、促进人的全面发展作为发展的出发点和落脚点；要坚持科学发展，加快转变经济发展方式，实现更高质量、更有效率、更加公平、更可持续的发展。“十三五”规划将经济社会发展的

主要目标确定为经济保持中高速增长；主要经济指标平衡协调，发展质量和效益明显提高；人民生活水平和质量普遍提高，就业比较充分等。“十三五”规划明确提出实施就业优先战略；实施更加积极的就业政策，创造更多就业岗位，着力解决结构性就业矛盾，鼓励以创业带就业，实现比较充分和高质量就业。

2. 将促进就业作为加强宏观调控的重要目标

作为宏观调控的四大指标，经济增长率、通货膨胀率、失业率和国际收支平衡彼此相互联系，相互影响，相互制约。历史经验也表明，治理通胀不易，解决失业更难。因此，把失业率作为观察经济运行和社会动向的“晴雨表”，在密切关注经济增长率、通货膨胀率、国际收支平衡以及固定资产投资、货币发行量的同时，必须高度关注就业率、失业率的变化，及时采取有效措施扩大就业、减少失业。为此，2002 年中共中央、国务院印发《关于进一步做好下岗失业人员再就业工作的通知》提出，要把控制失业率和增加就业岗位作为宏观调控的重要指标，纳入国民经济和社会发展计划（见表 10-1）。从 2003 年起，中国政府开始付诸实施，将实现“城镇新增就业人数”、控制“城镇登记失业率”指标，作为经济社会发展的重要内容，正式纳入国民经济和社会发展年度计划，以加大宏观调控力度，确保经济与就业协调增长。自 2008 年开始施行的《就业促进法》也对此作出专项规定，要求县级以上人民政府把扩大就业作为经济和社会发展的重要目标，纳入国民经济和社会发展规划，并制定促进就业的中长期规划和年度工作计划。

表 10-1　国民经济和社会发展规划纲要对就业工作的部署和要求

	“十五”计划	“十一五”规划	“十二五”规划	“十三五”规划
目标	把扩大就业作为经济和社会发展的重要目标，实行有利于扩大就业的经济政策和社会政策	把扩大就业摆在经济社会发展更突出的位置，千方百计扩大就业	把促进就业放在经济社会发展的优先位置	人民生活水平和质量普遍提高，就业比较充分

续表

	“十五”计划	“十一五”规划	“十二五”规划	“十三五”规划
任务	五年城镇新增就业和转移农业劳动力各达到 4 000 万人，城镇登记失业率控制在 5% 左右；2005 年第一、第二、第三产业从业人员占全社会从业人员的比重分别为 44%、23% 和 33%；城镇化水平有所提高	五年城镇新增就业和转移农业劳动力各 4 500 万人，城镇登记失业率控制在 5%；服务业就业人员占全社会就业人员比重提高 4 个百分点	五年城镇新增就业 4 500 万人，城镇登记失业率控制在 5% 以内。城镇化率提高 4 个百分点；城镇居民人均可支配收入和农村居民人均纯收入分别年均增长 7% 以上	主要经济指标平衡协调，发展质量和效益明显提高；就业、教育、文化体育、社保、医疗、住房等公共服务体系更加健全，基本公共服务均等化水平稳步提高；就业比较充分；中国现行标准下农村贫困人口实现脱贫，贫困县全部摘帽，解决区域性整体贫困
部署安排	保持较快的经济增长速度，创造更多的就业岗位；制定和落实优惠政策，发展具有比较优势的劳动密集型产业，发展就业容量大的服务企业、中小企业和非公有制企业；引导劳动者采取灵活多样的就业形式，提倡自主就业；加大在职和再就业培训力度，完善就业服务体系	实行积极的就业政策，统筹城乡就业，努力控制失业规模；继续实施和完善鼓励企业增加就业岗位、加强就业培训的优惠政策；鼓励劳动者自主创业和自谋职业，促进多种形式就业；健全就业服务体系，加快建立政府扶助、社会参与的职业技能培训机制，完善就业援助制度	实施就业优先战略；健全劳动者自主择业、市场调节就业、政府促进就业相结合的机制，创造平等就业机会，提高就业质量，努力实现充分就业；对实施更加积极的就业政策、加强公共就业服务和职业培训、构建和谐劳动关系提出具体要求	实施更加积极的就业政策，创造更多就业岗位，着力解决结构性就业矛盾，鼓励以创业带就业，实现比较充分和高质量就业；对稳定并扩大城镇就业规模，加强对灵活就业、新就业形态的扶持，提高公共就业创业服务能力，完善就业创业服务体系，推行终身职业技能培训制度，完善就业失业统计指标体系，健全失业监测预警机制提出具体要求

资料来源：有关内容摘自中国政府网。

（二）促进就业规划及年度就业计划有关就业工作部署

1. 促进就业规划对就业工作的部署

促进就业规划是人力资源社会保障部（2008 年国务院机构改革前为劳动和社会保障部）按照国民经济和社会发展规划纲要总体要求制定的本部门的工作规划和部署安排。促进就业规划自 2012 年起以国务院名义印发，此前主要是在

部门的劳动和社会保障发展计划中明确就业工作的目标和部署安排。

2001年4月，劳动和社会保障部印发《劳动和社会保障事业发展第十个五年计划纲要》（劳社部发〔2001〕5号，以下简称劳动和社会保障“十五”计划），确定了“十五”期间就业的主要目标是形成市场导向的就业机制，扩大就业规模，改善就业结构，提高劳动者素质。劳动和社会保障“十五”计划还明确了这一时期的主要任务，并对做好就业和再就业工作作出明确部署（具体见表10-2）。2006年10月，国务院批转《劳动和社会保障事业发展“十一五”规划纲要（2006年—2010年）》（国发〔2006〕35号，以下简称劳动和社会保障“十一五”规划），确定了“十一五”期间就业的主要目标是实现就业持续增长；同时要求在重点解决体制转轨遗留的下岗失业人员再就业问题的同时，努力做好城镇新增劳动力就业和农村富余劳动力转移就业工作，广开就业门路，增加就业岗位，改善就业结构，提高就业质量，加强失业调控，保持就业形势稳定。劳动和社会保障“十一五”规划进一步明确了这一时期的主要任务（见表10-2）并对实施促进就业的长期战略和政策，千方百计扩大就业作出明确部署。2012年1月，国务院印发《关于批转促进就业规划（2011—2015年）的通知》（国发〔2012〕6号，以下简称促进就业规划）。这是中国首个以国务院名义出台的专项就业规划，明确了“十二五”期间促进就业的发展目标是要实现就业规模持续扩大，就业结构更加合理（见表10-2）。促进就业规划从提高经济发展对就业的拉动能力、实施更加积极的就业政策、统筹做好城乡及重点群体就业工作等八个方面提出了未来五年促进就业的主要任务和政策措施。2017年1月，国务院印发《“十三五”促进就业规划》（国发〔2017〕10号），明确提出到2020年要实现就业规模稳步扩大，就业质量进一步提升，就业结构持续优化，城乡均等的公共就业创业服务体系更加健全，劳动者权益保护制度不断完善等（见表10-2）。《“十三五”促进就业规划》从增强经济发展创造就业岗位能力、提升创业带动就业能力、加强重点群体就业保障能力等五个方面提出

了未来五年促进就业的重点任务。

表 10-2　　促进就业规划对就业工作的部署和安排

	劳动和社会保障“十五”计划	劳动和社会保障“十一五”规划	促进就业规划	“十三五”促进就业规划
目标	形成市场导向的就业机制，扩大就业规模，改善就业结构，提高劳动者素质	就业持续增长；增加就业岗位，改善就业结构，提高就业质量，加强失业调控	就业规模持续扩大，就业结构更加合理；有效控制失业；人力资源开发水平明显提高；就业质量进一步提升；统一规范灵活的人力资源市场基本形成；劳动者权益保障机制更加完善	就业规模稳步扩大，就业质量进一步提升；创业环境显著改善，带动就业能力持续增强；人力资源结构不断优化，劳动者就业创业能力明显提高
任务	全国城镇新增就业 4 000 万人，转移农业劳动力 4 000 万人，城镇登记失业率控制在 5% 左右；到“十五”期末，三次产业就业人数比重调整为 44∶23∶33	全国城镇实现新增就业 4 500 万人，城镇登记失业率控制在 5% 以内，转移农业劳动力 4 500 万人	城镇新增就业 4 500 万人，转移农业劳动力 4 000 万人，城镇就业比重逐步提高，三次产业就业结构更加优化；有效控制失业，城镇登记失业率控制在 5% 以内	城镇新增就业 5 000 万人以上，全国城镇登记失业率控制在 5% 以内，带动 1 000 万人脱贫
部署安排	从继续实行积极的就业政策，广开就业门路，拓宽就业渠道；进一步培育和发展劳动力市场，完善就业服务体系；适应农村经济结构调整和城镇化进程加快，做好农村劳动力开发就业工作，多渠道解决农业剩余劳动力就业问题；以及做好下岗职工基本生活保障和促进再就业等方面作出具体安排	从实施发展经济与促进就业并举的战略，确立有利于扩大就业的经济增长方式；继续实施积极的就业政策，促进下岗失业人员再就业；不断完善市场就业机制，促进城乡统筹就业；建立制度化、专业化、社会化的公共就业服务体系；加强失业调控；完善境外就业管理体制等方面作出具体安排	从提高经济发展对就业的拉动能力、实施更加积极的就业政策、统筹做好城乡及重点群体就业工作、大力开发人力资源、加强人力资源市场建设、加强失业预防和调控等八个方面作出具体安排	从增强经济发展创造就业岗位能力、提升创业带动就业能力、加强重点群体就业保障能力、提高人力资源市场供求匹配能力、强化劳动者素质提升能力五个方面作出具体安排

资料来源：有关内容摘自人力资源社会保障部网站。

2. 年度就业工作目标任务的确定和完成

根据国民经济和社会发展规划纲要总体要求和部署，每年年底由人力资源社会保障部会同发展改革委、财政部、国家统计局，在综合考虑国民经济增长预测速度、城镇劳动力资源供给数量、近几年就业增长规律等因素的基础上，预测判断下一年度就业和再就业工作面临的形势和任务，在与各省协商后，向国务院提出下一年度城镇新增就业、失业率目标任务的建议。年度就业工作目标任务经国务院确定后，在第二年全国人民代表大会会议上以政府工作报告的形式向社会公开承诺。

年度就业工作目标任务确定后，再由人力资源社会保障部细化分解到各省、自治区、直辖市。各地区按照统一确定的目标任务，在认真分析本地区就业工作形势的基础上，研究确定本地区的就业工作目标任务和具体措施，层层分解，明确责任，并将就业工作作为考核各级人民政府和各部门政绩与工作情况的重要指标，进行考核评估，确保落实。2007 年颁布的《就业促进法》对此也作出了专门规定：各级人民政府和有关部门应当建立促进就业的目标责任制度。县级以上人民政府按照促进就业目标责任制的要求，对所属的有关部门和下一级人民政府进行考核和监督。

在目标任务中，城镇新增就业人数[①]是 2003 年以后，政府部门为及时掌握全国各地区就业目标完成情况而开始采用的指标（见表 10–3）。城镇调查失业率于 2018 年首次使用，与以前一直使用的城镇登记失业率并行，作为宏观经济预期目标。城镇调查失业率涵盖了农村劳动者流动到城镇的常住人口。采用调查失业率，是为了便于与国际对标，也能更加全面地掌握社会失业状况及其变化。

---

① 年度城镇新增就业人数 = 年度城镇累计新就业人数 − 年度城镇累计自然减员人数。

表 10-3 历年全国就业主要目标任务完成情况

年份	城镇新增就业人数 / 万人		年末城镇登记失业率 /%		年末城镇调查失业率 /%	
	目标	完成	目标	完成	目标	完成
2003	800	850	4.5	4.3	—	—
2004	900	980	4.7	4.2	—	—
2005	900	970	4.6	4.2	—	—
2006	900	1 184	4.6	4.1	—	—
2007	900	1 204	4.5	4.0	—	—
2008	1 000	1 113	4.5	4.2	—	—
2009	900	1 102	4.6	4.3	—	—
2010	900	1 168	4.6	4.1	—	—
2011	900	1 221	4.6	4.1	—	—
2012	900	1 266	4.6	4.1	—	—
2013	900	1 310	4.6	4.1	—	—
2014	1 000	1 322	4.6	4.1	—	—
2015	1 000	1 312	4.5	4.1	—	—
2016	1 000	1 314	4.5	4.0	—	—
2017	1 100	1 351	4.5	3.9	—	5.0
2018	1 100	1 361	4.5	3.8	5.5	4.9
2019	1 100	1 352	4.5	3.6	5.5	5.2

资料来源：中国政府网上的历年政府工作报告和人力资源社会保障部网站上的统计公报。

自 2003 年实施积极的就业政策以来，中国平均每年城镇新增就业 1 189.3 万人。特别是 2013 年以来，每年城镇新增就业人数均超过 1 300 万人。就业人员总量于 2019 年年底达到 77 471 万人，城镇登记失业率为 3.6%，31 个大城市的城镇调查失业率基本稳定在 5% 左右，就业局势总体稳定。

二、更加充分更高质量就业的目标

（一）更加充分更高质量就业目标的提出

1. 目标提出的背景

推动实现更加充分更高质量就业是中国经济发展由高速增长转向高质量发展的内在要求，也是贯彻以人民为中心的发展思想、满足人民群众在就业方面美好展望的体现。

（1）顺应经济转型的要求。改革开放以来，中国经济实现了长达 40 年的高速增长，但也出现了结构优化和质量提高的步伐较慢、可持续发展动力不足、就业质量不高、劳动收入份额偏低等问题。“十二五”规划要求，要以加快转变经济发展方式为主线。中共十八大报告提出，把推动经济发展的立足点转到提高质量和效益上来，更多依靠科技进步、劳动者素质提高、管理创新驱动。“十三五”规划进一步提出，要加快转变经济发展方式，实现更高质量、更有效率、更加公平、更可持续的发展。随着经济从粗放扩张型向质量效益型转变，就业也需要从原来的数量扩张型转变到在保证相应数量的同时更加注重质量的提升。

（2）顺应就业转型的要求。新时代背景下就业呈现出许多新的特征，特别是伴随经济转型和城市化、工业化、市场化、国际化步伐加快，中国就业面临许多新的挑战：从宏观上来看，中国劳动力供大于求的总量性矛盾仍然存在，就业结构性矛盾更加突出；高校毕业生就业形势依然严峻，几亿农村劳动者转移就业后的城镇化、市民化提上日程；增长引擎更新，创业带动就业成为新的增长点；新旧动能转换，新产业、新业态不断涌现。从微观上来看，一些深层次的矛盾和问题逐渐显露，如企业职工工资增长缓慢，超长加班时有发生，社会保障仍不充分，劳动者素质有待提升，企业岗位流失与劳动者就业不稳定相互交织等，就业矛盾更多地聚焦在就业质量上，因此需要在保证就业增长的同

时，下大力气推进就业质量的提高。

（3）适应国内外形势的需要。当前，为应对新技术发展产生的“机器换人”对就业的挤出效应、新业态涌现与传统用工和就业的矛盾、国内外不确定因素的影响等问题，中国政府提出了以稳就业来稳增长、保民生的战略要求。做好稳就业工作不仅要保障就业的数量，还要逐步提高就业的质量。因为只有提高就业质量，才能更充分、更有效地发挥人力资源效能，才能真正保证就业的持续和稳定。同时，面对全球贸易摩擦和就业竞争，中国的就业必须提高档次、提升质量。

（4）顺应劳动者的期待。实现更加充分更高质量就业是人民群众的美好愿望，使自己和子女获得一份更好的、更稳定的工作是每一个劳动者的最大期盼。从长远来看，这是在就业转型过程中坚持贯彻以人为本的体现；从当前来看，解决好就业质量不高的主要问题，也是进一步推进就业深化改革与创新发展的任务。因此，必须坚持贯彻以人为本，以满足劳动者更高质量就业的要求为出发点和落脚点，这样才能使就业工作的整体水平有一个新的提高。

2. 目标提出的过程

从中共十六大（2002 年）到中共十九大（2017 年），中共中央对中国就业目标的设定是在一步一步提高的。中共十六大将“社会就业比较充分”作为到 2020 年全面建设小康社会的重要目标，中共十七大作出全面建设小康社会重要决策并提出“社会就业更加充分”目标，中共十八大提出“就业更加充分”目标并明确要求推动实现更高质量的就业，直到中共十九大提出“实现更高质量和更充分就业”目标。可以看出，每一个时期提出的目标（见表 10-4）都与当时的就业形势、经济环境和社会发展紧密相关。2002 年，中国还有大量下岗职工，中国政府提出充分就业的目标，体现了中国政府解决好下岗职工再就业问题的决心，使全国人民对光明前景充满信心。但考虑到当时条件的局限，中

国政府先提出实现社会就业比较充分。到 2007 年，中国城乡就业进入新阶段，《就业促进法》成功出台，中国政府提出了实现社会就业更加充分。到 2012 年，中国已连续多年保持新增就业在 1 100 万人以上，劳动力供大于求的总量性矛盾有所缓解，劳动者对就业质量提出了更高诉求，对国家而言这就意味着需要创造更多好的就业岗位。到 2017 年，随着中国特色社会主义进入了新时代，中国经济发展的基本特征由高速增长转向高质量发展，这一时期需要解决的社会主要矛盾是发展的不平衡不充分问题，需要通过提升就业质量来进一步增强人民的获得感，为此中共十九大提出“实现更高质量和更充分就业”的新目标。

十几年来，就业目标任务的变化与中国经济社会发展的进程和社会主要矛盾的转化是相适应的，也充分体现了中国人民对美好生活、对更好工作的向往与追求。为了解决新时代社会主要矛盾，增加广大劳动者的获得感、幸福感、安全感，促进社会公平正义，必须把实现更加充分更高质量就业作为促进就业工作不断追求的首要目标，竭尽全力努力实现。

表 10-4　中共十六大至中共十九大有关就业的目标要求和方针政策

	中共十六大（2002 年）	中共十七大（2007 年）	中共十八大（2012 年）	中共十九大（2017 年）
目标	社会就业比较充分	社会就业更加充分	就业更加充分	实现更高质量和更充分就业
总要求	千方百计扩大就业，不断改善人民生活	实施扩大就业的发展战略，促进以创业带动就业	推动实现更高质量的就业	提高就业质量
理念方针政策	就业是民生之本。实行促进就业的长期战略和政策。鼓励自谋职业和自主创业	就业是民生之本。坚持实施积极的就业政策，加强政府引导，完善市场就业机制，完善支持自主创业、自谋职业政策	就业是民生之本。贯彻劳动者自主就业、市场调节就业、政府促进就业和鼓励创业的方针，实施就业优先战略和更加积极的就业政策	就业是最大的民生。坚持就业优先战略和积极就业政策，实现更高质量和更充分就业

资料来源：有关内容摘自中国政府网。

（二）充分就业和就业质量的基本内涵

1. 充分就业

充分就业是指在某一工资水平之下，所有愿意接受工作的劳动者都有机会获得就业。充分就业并不是人人都有就业岗位，在充分就业状态下仍然存在一定数量的结构性失业和摩擦性失业，即因技术进步、产业结构、劳动年龄和需求偏好变化而引起的职业转换过程中的暂时性失业。

2. 就业质量

就业质量是指在劳动者从事社会劳动的过程中相关要素的优劣程度及其与劳动者个人的适合度。就业质量主要涉及劳动报酬、社会保障、工作条件、就业的稳定性、劳动者权益保护，以及劳动者个人的感受、职业发展空间和社会评价等要素。

3. 更加充分更高质量就业

更加充分更高质量就业是指通过发展经济创造更多就业机会，改善就业结构，提高劳动者素质，消除劳动者流动障碍，优化就业创业服务，使劳动者能够获得更加充分和公平的就业机会和职业发展机会，使人力资源和其他资源不断得到优化配置。与此同时，随着经济社会发展、劳动生产率提高以及科技进步，劳动者的劳动报酬水平、社会保障水平不断提高，职业安全等工作条件不断改善，就业的稳定性得以保持，劳动者的权益得到保护，劳动关系更加和谐稳定，进而使劳动者及其家庭的获得感、幸福感、安全感更加充实、更有保障、更可持续。更加充分更高质量就业目标是一个有机的整体，两者相辅相成，是促进就业工作的总要求和首要目标。

（三）更加充分更高质量就业的衡量标准

1. 充分就业的衡量标准

在中国，实现充分就业的目标是与和谐社会发展相适应的一种状态，主要是对国家和地区，即宏观和中观层面讲的，具体体现在四个方面：一是劳动力资源得到更加充分的开发和利用，这是实现充分就业的出发点。社会有更多的就业机会，就业总量持续增长，就业结构进一步优化，城乡统筹就业较好实现。城乡劳动者应普遍得到教育培训和就业机会，面向全体劳动者的职业技能培训制度健全。二是市场就业机制健全，就业渠道通畅，这是实现充分就业的条件。劳动者自主择业、自由流动、自主创业的环境良好，依法调整政府、用人主体、劳动者和社会中介组织的行为，统一开放的人力资源市场机制发挥基础性作用，公共就业人才服务体系覆盖城乡。三是社会失业率和平均失业周期控制在社会能承受的水平，这是实现充分就业的标志。失业人员能获得失业保险金并通过就业服务组织参与到相应的就业准备活动中，困难群体人员能得到有效的就业援助；失业保险发挥保障生活、促进就业和预防失业的重要作用。四是就业的稳定性进一步提高，劳动者的就业权益得到有效保障，这是实现充分就业的结果。劳动关系更加和谐，劳动收入水平有稳定提升的机制，社会保障覆盖所有劳动者。

2. 就业质量的衡量标准

就业质量主要从宏观、中观和微观三个层面来考量。从宏观层面考量，即是从国家、地区层面来看，就业规模扩大是否与劳动力供给平衡，就业素质提升是否与产业发展相匹配，就业结构优化是否与就业扩展相适应，就业环境改善是否满足自主公平创业就业，劳动关系和谐是否构建劳资协调共赢，等等。从中观层面考量，即是从市场主体企业层面来看①，工作环境与企业文化是否得

① 中观企业层面有关标准来源于2018年中国就业促进会与麦当劳（中国）有限公司合作开展的企业提升就业质量调查研究。

到认同；劳动报酬是否保持持续增长，保险福利是否满足需求；能力培训系统是否具备，职业发展通道是否畅通；工作稳定性能否持续，劳动用工是否规范，等等。从微观层面考量，即是从广大劳动者个人角度来看，主要由五个核心要素构成。一是更多的就业选择和职业发展通道。具体包括就业环境的改善和优化，劳动者是否得到较好的就业创业机会。二是不断提高的劳动报酬和福利待遇。具体包括劳动报酬是否得到提高，就业公平是否得到保证并有效防止就业歧视。三是就业稳定性和可靠的社会保障。具体包括就业的稳定性是否得到加强，就业者是否享有社会保障。四是更高的职业素质和工作能力。具体包括劳动者素质是否提高，教育和培训是否取得实效，人才队伍是否增长。五是良好的劳动条件及和谐的劳动关系。具体包括和谐劳动关系以及劳动者与用人单位双方权益保护是否有所保证，劳动安全卫生条件和劳动者的安全健康状况是否有所改善。

三、努力实现更加充分更高质量就业的政策措施

（一）推进工作的关键环节

当前和今后一个时期，在推动实现更加充分更高质量就业的过程中，应把握好以下三个关键环节。

（1）坚持与经济社会发展的进程相一致。就业目标作为整个经济社会发展目标的重要组成部分，它的实现与经济社会其他发展目标的实现相辅相成。因此，要实现更加充分更高质量就业，就需要经济健康稳定和更高质量地发展，需要企业不断提高效益和社会责任感，需要坚持在经济增长的同时实现居民收入同步增长、在劳动生产率提高的同时实现劳动报酬同步提高。实现更加充分更高质量就业，既要尽力而为，又要量力而行，进而满足广大劳动者通过劳动过上美好生活的需要。

（2）坚持从实际出发，分类分别施策。在对就业质量进行衡量时，也应充

分考虑不同区域的发展不平衡性，如东、中、西部地区的差异，经济发达城市与资源枯竭城市的差异；不同行业企业的属性，如受结构转型影响的煤炭和钢铁行业、受互联网技术影响的零售和服务行业，还有受智能新技术影响的制造业的不同；不同的就业形式，如传统经济中的工薪劳动者与个体劳动者，以及前者与共享经济下的新形态就业者的不同；不同群体，如青年与大龄人员、男性与女性劳动者的差异性。选取具有针对性的、代表性的和可衡量的指标，开展就业质量和充分就业评估调查，为实施精准化服务和开展分级分类帮扶保障提供依据。

（3）坚持动员全社会之力共同推进。首先，政府部门要在进一步完善政策、加强服务、做好管理、提供保障上下功夫；企业和用人单位也要大力提高人力资源管理水平，在构建和谐劳动关系、促进职工职业生涯发展上下功夫；劳动者也要努力提高自己的素质能力，来适应高质量就业的要求。应将国家推进更加充分更高质量就业的战略目标和方针政策同解决与劳动者切身利益相关的问题紧密结合，使提高就业质量成为全社会共同奋斗的目标。

（二）推进工作的政策措施及其成效

为实现更加充分更高质量就业，中国政府不仅在不同阶段提出了明确的目标要求，而且采取了一系列政策措施来促进和推动目标的实现。经过长期努力，推进工作取得了明显效果。具体来说，结合实现更加充分更高质量就业的基本要求，在以下六个方面制定政策措施，并推动落实见效。

（1）改善就业结构和就业环境，打造就业新增长点。合理的就业结构和良好的就业环境是扩大就业和推动创业发展的重要条件，也是增加就业机会和提高就业质量的重要基础。中国政府通过政策支持和引领，逐步改善了就业结构，并使就业环境不断得到优化。在改善就业结构方面，通过鼓励发展第三产业和现代农业、引导农村富余劳动力转移就业和融入城镇化进程等多项措施，稳定

和改善了第二产业的就业，扩大了第三产业的就业规模，减少了第一产业的就业人数，使三大产业的就业结构趋于合理。通过推动转变经济发展方式、调整经济结构、促进新兴产业发展，打造了就业的新增长点，创造了更多就业机会。在改善就业环境方面，通过实施财政、货币政策，落实金融贷款、小额贷款贴息、税费减免等优惠措施，扶持民营企业、小微企业发展，鼓励劳动者个人自主创业；相关政府部门在促进劳动者就业和创业时，简化程序、提供便利、做好服务；公共就业服务机构通过不断加强和完善人力资源市场信息系统的建设，为求职者、创业者及时提供劳动力供求信息，帮助他们尽快实现就业和创业。实行这些有力的扶持政策和全面的公共服务，有助于营造良好的就业环境，推进充分就业和提高就业质量工作取得明显成效，城镇新增就业连续 6 年保持在 1 300 万人以上，更多的创业企业和小微企业获得长足发展，中国就业实现倍增。

新技术对传统业态的改造提升——现代化仓储车间既提高了劳动效率，同时也降低了人工成本。

（2）控制失业率增长，保持就业局势稳定。控制失业率增长的内在要求是，将失业率维持在社会可承受的范围之内，并将失业人员数量控制为不超过经济活动人口的一定比例；失业群体出现的时间和地区不能过于集中，个人失业时间不能过长。为此，中国政府坚持就业优先战略，通过制定和实施积极的就业政策，在促进经济增长的同时，创造就业岗位，扩大就业需求，使更多的劳动者实现了就业，这是控制失业率增长的最主要因素。同时，从预防失业、稳定就业入手，实行援企稳岗政策，帮助企业克服暂时困难，稳定了员工队伍，减少了失业。特别是在国际金融危机时期，没有出现规模性的集中失业，并对下岗失业人员作出保障生活和鼓励支持再就业的安排，保持了就业局势的总体稳定。长期以来，将失业率维持在5%左右，实现了比较充分的就业。

（3）改革收入分配制度，促进实现就业公平。劳动报酬是衡量就业质量高低的重要因素，公平就业是提高就业质量的基本保证，这两者直接关系到劳动者的切身利益。因此，实现就业公平、收入公平和同工同酬十分重要。自改革开放以来，中国政府采取了一系列政策措施改革收入分配制度，具体包括：根据国民经济发展状况，由各地政府适时确定和提高最低工资标准；实行国有企业职工工资水平与经济效益挂钩；民营企业职工工资由企业自主决定；对公益性就业岗位，政府给予工资补贴和社会保险补贴，以保证就业人员得到合理的劳动报酬；对从事同一岗位工作的不同人员实行同工同酬，等等。通过这些措施，建立了收入分配的新机制，使劳动者得到的劳动报酬更加合理并实现逐年增加，从而促进了就业质量的提升。在推动公平就业方面，通过制定相关法律法规、加强监督检查等措施，防止了就业歧视，做到了对劳动者不分城乡来源、性别差异、民族区别，在就业权益上一律平等，企业按需招用。中国政府实施的积极的就业政策和开展的公共就业服务，覆盖了城乡劳动者和各类群体，实现了在政策扶持上一视同仁，在就业服务上同等对待。这些措施保证了就业公平的实现。

电商平台降低了就业门槛，有助于促进实现公平就业。在阿里全球十佳网商大会上，一位残疾人网商在接受颁奖。

（4）加强教育培训，提升就业能力。提升就业能力和职业素质可以为劳动者实现就业和良好的职业发展创造有利条件，为此，加强教育培训是提升就业质量的关键所在。中国政府通过深化教育体制改革，特别是强化职业技能培训，大力提升劳动者的就业能力和职业素质。具体措施包括：在改善培训供给方面，根据人力资源市场需求，调整和创新高校专业设置，使大学生能够接受有利于就业的专业教育，打通大学生毕业后的职业发展通道；引导和推动企业、职业院校、社会培训机构相互融合，面向城乡劳动者大规模开展各类职业培训。在创新培训内容和方式方面，增强培训的针对性、有效性、实用性和可持续性，构建面向城乡全体劳动者的终身职业培训制度；同时采取订单定向、线上线下等手段，创新培训的方式和方法。在加强政策引导和支持方面，政府通过实行

职业培训补贴，为推动职业技能培训提供资金保障。在提高培训质量方面，通过实行职业技能鉴定制度，激励劳动者积极参加职业培训并获取从业资质，进而提高培训质量。通过实施以上措施，中国政府加强职业培训，为提升劳动者的就业能力和职业素质创造了条件，为实现高质量就业打下了良好的基础。

（5）稳定就业，完善社会保障制度。保持就业稳定是中国经济社会发展转型时期劳动者的最大期望，而社会保障是稳定就业和提高就业质量的重要保证条件。改革开放以来，中国政府着力加强社会保障制度建设，逐步建立了覆盖城乡劳动者和各类企业，包含养老、医疗、失业、工伤和生育保险的项目齐备的社会保险制度。劳动者无论是处于就业还是失业状况，无论流动到城镇或乡村就业还是跨地区就业，都可以按规定享受相应的保险待遇，其合法权益得到了保障。消除了后顾之忧，劳动者能够更加安心地工作，谋求职业发展。中国社会保障制度的不断完善，对提升就业质量产生了重要的保障作用。与此同时，中国政府在稳定就业方面采取了若干政策措施，努力保持了员工队伍的稳定。虽然在遇到严重自然灾害和受到金融危机冲击时，出现过失业和岗位流失增多的现象，但中国政府均采取措施在短期内使上述问题得以缓解。从整体上来看，劳动者就业基本保持稳定状态，这也体现了就业质量的提升。

（6）保持和谐劳动关系，创造良好劳动条件。劳动关系和劳动条件关系到用人单位和劳动者的合法权益，关系到劳动者的职业安全与身心健康。保持和谐劳动关系，创造良好劳动条件，是提升就业质量的重要内容。中国政府高度关注劳动关系处理问题，通过制定政策法规和建立相应制度来引导企业和劳动者建立和谐的劳动关系，在发生劳动争议时依法妥善处理。具体措施包括：规定企业招用职工时，双方要签订劳动合同，明确各自的权利和义务并严格履行；规定企业和创业者要参加社会保险，按时定额缴纳社会保险费；要求企业参照工资指导线来确定工资水平，不得降低劳动报酬；规范企业裁员行为，要求企业不得随意裁员；劳动关系双方发生劳动争议时，按照规定程序向劳动争议仲

裁机构申请调解仲裁；同时，对用人单位依法自主招用人员和进行人力资源管理给予保障。这些措施对建立和谐劳动关系，保障劳动关系双方的合法权益产生了良好作用，也有利于提升就业质量。在创造良好劳动条件方面，中国政府采取的主要措施包括：通过制定和实施政策规定来推动企业增强职业安全意识，加强安全设施建设；引导企业根据自身条件，尽力改善工作条件，为职工安心就业创造良好环境。同时，有关部门通过监督检查，促进相关政策的落实，发现问题，依法处理。这些措施有力地督促企业在职业安全保护上加强管理，加大投入，逐步改善了工作条件，在稳定职工就业和保证劳动者健康安全生产上取得了良好效果。

参考文献

［1］张小建．中国就业的改革发展［M］．北京：中国劳动社会保障出版社，2008.

［2］张小建．中国就业改革发展40年［M］．北京：中国劳动社会保障出版社，2019.

［3］莫荣，陈云，熊颖．中国就业发展报告（2019）［M］．北京：社会科学文献出版社，2019.

［4］赖德胜，李长安，张琪．中国就业70年（1949—2019）［M］．北京：中国劳动社会保障出版社，2019.

［5］刘燕斌．更高质量和更充分就业的内涵及其衡量指标——学习党的十九大报告体会［J］．中国就业，2017（12）.

［6］人力资源和社会保障部．增进人民福祉　促进人的全面发展——党的十八大以来人力资源社会保障事业改革与发展［M］．北京：中国劳动社会保障出版社，中国人事出版社，2017.

［7］中国就业促进会．中国积极就业政策创立与发展［M］．北京：中国劳动社会保障出版社，2016.

[8] 中国就业促进会 . 就业课题研究 [M] . 北京：中国劳动社会保障出版社，2015.

[9] 中国就业促进会 . 中国就业最新理论研究成果（2003—2012）[M] . 北京：中国劳动社会保障出版社，2012.

[10] 中国就业促进会 . 中国就业走向世界之路（研究篇）[M] . 北京：中国劳动社会保障出版社，2016.

[11] 中国就业促进会 . 中国就业走向世界之路（实践篇）[M] . 北京：中国劳动社会保障出版社，2016.

[12] 中国就业促进会 . 聚焦 2010 中国就业 [M] . 北京：中国劳动社会保障出版社，2011.

[13] 中国就业促进会 . 聚焦 2011 中国就业 [M] . 北京：中国劳动社会保障出版社，2012.

[14] 中国就业促进会 . 聚焦 2012 中国就业 [M] . 北京：中国劳动社会保障出版社，2013.

[15] 中国就业促进会 . 聚焦中国就业（2013—2014）[M] . 北京：中国劳动社会保障出版社，2014.

[16] 中国就业促进会 . 聚焦中国就业（2014—2015）[M] . 北京：中国劳动社会保障出版社，2015.

[17] 中国就业促进会 . 聚焦中国就业（2015—2016）[M] . 北京：中国劳动社会保障出版社，2016.

[18] 中国就业促进会 . 聚焦中国就业（2016—2017）[M] . 北京：中国劳动社会保障出版社，2017.

[19] 信长星 . 失业保险 [M] . 北京：中国劳动社会保障出版社，2011.

[20] 全国人力资源社会保障系统普法领导小组 . 人力资源和社会保障法律制度读本 [M] . 北京：中国劳动社会保障出版社，2013.

［21］王晓初，信长星．就业促进与职业能力建设［M］．北京：中国劳动社会保障出版社，2012.

［22］中国就业促进会．失业保险文集［M］．北京：中国劳动社会保障出版社，2015.

［23］中国就业促进会课题组．关于我国就业统计的研究报告［R］．2017.

［24］中国就业促进会课题组．加快构建全方位公共就业服务体系研究报告［R］．2018.

［25］马永堂，田光哲．关于我国公共与民营就业服务机构合作状况研究报告（上）［J］．中国就业，2018（1）．

［26］马永堂，田光哲．关于我国公共与民营就业服务机构合作状况研究报告（下）［J］．中国就业，2018（2）．

［27］章辉．论民营职业中介机构的作用与完善路径［J］．江西社会科学，2010（8）．

［28］人力资源和社会保障部．中国人力资源和社会保障年鉴（2009）［M］．北京：中国劳动社会保障出版社，中国人事出版社，2009.

［29］人力资源和社会保障部．中国人力资源和社会保障年鉴（2010）［M］．北京：中国劳动社会保障出版社，中国人事出版社，2011.

［30］人力资源和社会保障部．中国人力资源和社会保障年鉴（2011）［M］．北京：中国劳动社会保障出版社，中国人事出版社，2011.

［31］人力资源和社会保障部．中国人力资源和社会保障年鉴（2012）［M］．北京：中国劳动社会保障出版社，中国人事出版社，2012.

［32］人力资源和社会保障部．中国人力资源和社会保障年鉴（2013）［M］．北京：中国劳动社会保障出版社，中国人事出版社，2013.

［33］人力资源和社会保障部．中国人力资源和社会保障年鉴（2014）［M］．北京：中国劳动社会保障出版社，中国人事出版社，2014.

［34］人力资源和社会保障部 . 中国人力资源和社会保障年鉴（2015）［M］. 北京：中国劳动社会保障出版社，中国人事出版社，2016.

［35］人力资源和社会保障部 . 中国人力资源和社会保障年鉴（2016）［M］. 北京：中国劳动社会保障出版社，中国人事出版社，2017.

［36］人力资源和社会保障部 . 中国人力资源和社会保障年鉴（2017）［M］. 北京：中国劳动社会保障出版社，中国人事出版社，2017.

［37］人力资源和社会保障部 . 中国人力资源和社会保障年鉴（2018）［M］. 北京：中国劳动社会保障出版社，中国人事出版社，2019.

［38］国家统计局 . 中国统计年鉴 2019［M］. 北京：中国统计出版社，2019.

［39］国家统计局人口和就业统计司，人力资源和社会保障部规划财务司 . 中国劳动统计年鉴（2018）［M］. 北京：中国统计出版社，2019.

［40］国家统计局 . 新中国成立 70 周年经济社会发展成就系列报告［R］. 2019.

［41］中华人民共和国国务院新闻办公室 . 平等　发展　共享：新中国 70 年妇女事业的发展与进步［M］. 北京：人民出版社，2019.

［42］中华人民共和国国务院新闻办公室 . 平等、参与、共享：新中国残疾人权益保障 70 年［M］. 北京：人民出版社，2019.